CROSSING BOUNDARIES FOR INTERGOVERNMENTAL MANAGEMENT

CROSSING BOUNDARIES FOR INTERGOVERNMENTAL MANAGEMENT

ROBERT AGRANOFF

Georgetown University Press / Washington, DC

The publisher is not responsible for third-party websites or their content. URL links were active at time of publication.

Library of Congress Cataloging-in-Publication Data

Names: Agranoff, Robert, author.
Title: Crossing boundaries for intergovernmental management / Robert Agranoff.
Description: Washington, DC : Georgetown University Press, 2017. | Series: Public
   management and change series | Includes bibliographical references and index. |
   Description based on print version record and CIP data provided by publisher;
   resource not viewed.
Identifiers: LCCN 2017007578 (print) | LCCN 2017015462 (ebook) |
   ISBN 9781626164819 (ebook) | ISBN 9781626164796 (hc : alk. paper) |
   ISBN 9781626164802 (pb : alk. paper)
Subjects: LCSH: Federal government—United States—Management. | Central-
   local government relations—United States—Management. | Intergovernmental
   cooperation—United States—Management. | Decentralization in government—
   United States—Management. | Public administration—United States.
Classification: LCC JK421 (ebook) | LCC JK421 .A558 2017 (print) |
   DDC 352.10973—dc23
LC record available at https://lccn.loc.gov/2017007578

♾ This book is printed on acid-free paper meeting the requirements of the American National Standard for Permanence in Paper for Printed Library Materials.

18 17   9 8 7 6 5 4 3 2 First printing

Printed in the United States of America

Cover design by Debra Naylor. Cover image by shutterstock.com.

CONTENTS

ILLUSTRATIONS

PREFACE

When people inquire regarding my specialty as an academic, I relate that it involves intergovernmental management (IGM). Clearly they are not immediately familiar with it or they even think it is not related to what is happening in the real world. Only the latter is not the case, as four current examples indicate. First, the media repeatedly reports that nearly half of the states have elected not to take full advantage of 100 percent federal funding of Medicaid expansion to a broadened eligible group under the Patient Protection and Affordable Care Act of 2010. State participation in this extension was made voluntary under a 2012 US Supreme Court decision that upheld the health care law but ruled that states could not be compelled to expand Medicaid. Many states that chose to opt out did so based on political decisions. Second, every state participates in the Supplemental Nutrition Assistance Program, formerly known as the Food Stamp Program, that provides federal money through state government–operated programs and gives states considerable operating flexibility. Third, Medicaid's Home and Community-Based Services 1915 Waiver program for lower-income elderly and disabled persons also goes through the states, which then design their own programs. The program even permits some states to include payments to in-home caregivers, sometimes including family members. For seniors the Medicaid Waiver program is initiated by substate (local government or nonprofit) Area Agencies on Aging that directly oversee service delivery by nonprofit or for-profit organizations under contract with the agencies. Fourth, a myriad of intergovernmental networks now try to solve cross-agency, cross-jurisdiction, and cross-sector problems. Such networks range from the voluntary Eastern Tall Grass Prairie and Big Rivers Landscape Conservation Cooperative—comprising conservation officers from federal, state, local, and nongovernmental organizations and covering parts of ten states—to transportation metropolitan planning organizations that under the federal statute Transportation Equity Act for the 21st Century (or TEA-21) are statutorily composed of local elected officials, local planning and engineering staff, and various advisory bodies. These examples all represent various aspects of intergovernmental relations (IGR) at their administrative stages of intergovernmental management. They demonstrate the four thematic foci of the book: law and politics, jurisdiction interdependency, government and nongovernmental organization partnerships, and intergovernmental networking and networks.

IGM "found" me as much as I found it some thirty-five years ago. In a "job talk" presentation at Indiana University in 1980, I discussed the multilevel management dimensions of a monograph on human services integration that I had recently coauthored with Alex Pattakos. We were charged with going through a huge government research library on this topic and synthesizing a mini-mountain of Department of Health, Education, and Welfare (now Health and Human Services [HHS]) project reports into a single monograph. During my talk two colleagues kept whispering to one another. After the talk I asked, was it really boring stuff or what? Charles Wise answered, "No, not at all. It's that we just got curricular approval for a graduate class in intergovernmental management, and since no one here knows what that is, we decided that you would be the perfect person to teach it." I was hired, and the rest is history, as they say.

A few years later I published an article in *Public Administration Review* with Valerie Lindsay (now Rinkle) based on a large HHS-funded study of local problem-solving. We concluded from numerous cases that IGM almost always involves focusing on joint intergovernmental tasks while recognizing the importance of and operating within the structural-legal, political, and technical contexts of intergovernmental relations. This finding led to a very kind and supportive two-page, single-spaced letter from the late Deil Wright, the guru of IGR, suggesting that I clarify whether IGM is a distinct public activity or a spin-off of IGR. This prompt helped me understand that, of course, IGR and IGM are to a great degree two sides of the same coin, demonstrating not only the complexity of government operations but also the influence of Wright's overlapping (as opposed to hierarchical or exclusive) governmental authority model. Again, the rest is history, with my subsequent work focusing on federal and state projects with Beryl Radin, on IGM in local economic development and other networks with Michael McGuire, and on local government IGR in Spain, as well as more recent work on collaborative management.

Charles Wise later said after one of my research presentations, "Agranoff has to have an extremely high level of tolerance for ambiguity to do what he does." What I have tried to do here in *Crossing Boundaries for Intergovernmental Management* is to sort out at least some of the ambiguities, recognizing that "to network" is unlikely to be the final chapter in IGM. Nor does this analysis provide all the answers.

A few words about what this volume is not. It does not focus on administration trends and patterns in IGR, as the US Advisory Commission on Intergovernmental Relations was known for. Also, it is not an operations manual about how to manage. Nor does it provide a guide on how to obtain grants or how to operate in a regime that is highly regulated. It is also not a blueprint on how to manage contracts or how to form and maintain networks. Rather, it is designed to understand the political and managerial challenges of navigating within the protracted multi-entity system that involves layers and sets of legal-political, interdependent operations, or partnerships that require degrees of interoperation and networked connections. It takes on more of a manager-to-manager perspective.

Some of the material that appears in the book is based on my previous work—for example, the work on the Medicaid Waiver (2013, 2014)—whereas others are refinements of my study of fourteen networks (2007c) and my analysis of collaborative management (2012). I make no apologies for this. The great composer Johann Sebastian Bach (1685–1750) built some of his larger works—for example, the Mass in B Minor, BWV332—on earlier works. To Bach such revision may involve anything from literal repeating to extensive editing and recomposing. The chance to rework and refine earlier work "allowed Bach to graft new ideas into old ones; it became an art of 'super-variation' stretching from work to work across the years" (Sousa 2013, 2). I make no pretensions that my work is anything like that of the great composer Bach; I only want to alert readers that I am hardly the first to engage in super variated revision.

This volume would never have seen the light of day without the generous help of many colleagues. First, thanks to Michael McGuire, who read through one of the early drafts and allowed me to rely extensively on our joint 237-city study, and to Beryl Radin, who encouraged me to step into these waters and take the next steps in analysis. Thanks are also to the manuscript readers and to Lua Aline and Charlie Lynn Abbott, who prepared the manuscript. Finally, I am forever indebted to the late Charles Backstrom, who replaced William Anderson at the University of Minnesota. Charles was never my formal teacher, but over the years as a colleague, he encouraged me to "get in and dig" into the field of public affairs. I miss his guidance.

Finally, the book is dedicated to my wife Susan Klein and my grandchildren: Ayala, Lily, Zada, Zevan, and Zeke. The future is in their hands.

INTRODUCTION

Politics, Government, Management across Boundaries

Intergovernmental management (IGM) has become a pervasive yet less visible administrative activity. On the same day in April 2016 that the US Supreme Court in effect upheld state apportionment of congressional legislative seats in Texas based on population as opposed to voter registration numbers, officials in Indiana disputed which agencies should have access to the keys to a locked gate that allows for emergency crossing of an interstate under construction. Such questioning of an agreement among federal, state, and county agencies regarding who shall have how many keys to the emergency access for improved emergency response times is also part of IGM. The case was remanded to the Indiana Department of Transportation for resettlement. Indeed, intergovernmental process involves a broad scope of activities to manage in a system when there are many hoops and connections.

In June 2015 the Supreme Court issued another important ruling that directly affects relations between the states and the federal government, between the states and the private power industry, and between the industry and consumers. In *Michigan v. the Environmental Protection Agency* (EPA), the court ruled that the EPA needs to consider the costs associated with limiting the mercury emissions of power plants as related to its Mercury and Air Toxics Standards. In effect, the court requires states, and through states' power plants, to assess costs along with health risks before they order substantial emissions reductions. The decision neither pleased the power industry, because of the time and costs involved, nor the environmental groups, which saw continuing uncertainty regarding mercury controls. Within the states a great deal of political rhetoric has been traded back and forth regarding costs and health impacts, and it will continue over time regarding state-generated industry-related costs. The *Michigan v. EPA* case was remanded to the US Court of Appeals for the District of Columbia Circuit, but it will not end there, because the EPA is unlikely to end its attempts to regulate mercury emissions after incorporating court-ordered cost analyses.

Michigan v. EPA is symbolic of the complex boundary-spanning activities now involved in affairs between the federal government and the states, the states and local governments, and nongovernmental organizations (NGOs) and citizen organizations. It demonstrates contemporary complex inter-actions among core actors in the intergovernmental system that constantly define the federal system in its working dynamics. The case brings out the four theoretical and practical themes of this volume as intergovernmental man-agement is analyzed. First is the centrality of law and the political forces that define and redefine issues like air quality and, in this case, mercury emissions. Second is the accelerated interdependencies brought on by an expanded wel-fare state that has grown far beyond income support to broadly include social protection and support for a variety of public concerns like clean air. Third, governments at all levels have externalized their policy-making and service delivery to include a variety of NGO actors that partner with governments. In this case, the mercury cost-benefit assessment will likely be conducted for the government but not necessarily by the government and probably on a contract basis. And, fourth, the myriad of state and local governments, plus NGOs and interest groups, in numerous policy and administrative arenas of government programs, including that of mercury emissions, will operate by networking or in networks representing parts of organizations that cross many public and nonpublic lines to accomplish tasks. Thus, ongoing issues such as federal, state, and private mercury controls now include the active mixtures of law and politics, the protective aims of an interdependent state, and the complex of multilevel governments and NGOs all working in some networked fashion.

These four dimensions represent the thematic thrust of this volume. While the subject of intergovernmental management is well below the media screen of most people, when the issue makes the Supreme Court, it hits the headlines. IGM operates behind these headlines, as did all the actions pre-ceding *Michigan v. EPA*, with literally thousands of transactions regarding law and politics, government and NGO interdependencies, and networks and networking. These processes are at the heart of IGM as the federal sys-tem has been made to work among all the entities now involved in "govern-ing" through government.

Governance and Government

It has indeed become almost a truism in government these days to refer to its metamorphosis into a system of "governance," as more and more actors enter the public stage to carry out government functions and programs. What is less understood is the continuing "central" role that government plays. It remains as a viable and authoritative entity as it interacts with other govern-ments and nongovernmental actors in emergent systems of governance, in many respects through IGM. Literally thousands of governments exist in the United States, making policies and seeing that such policies are transformed into public programs at the delivery level. Governance largely comes in with the latter functions, "a mix of all kinds of governing efforts by all manner of socio-political actors, public as well as private; occurring between them at different levels, in different governance modes and orders" (Kooiman 2003, 3). Governance has indeed expanded the traditional concept of intergovernmental relations (IGR), once thought to involve "the various combinations of interdependencies and influences among public officials—elected and administrative—in all types and levels of governmental units with particular emphasis on financial policy and political issues" (Krane and Wright 1998, 1163–64). Contemporary IGR, as this volume documents, involves real-world management as people interact. Today it entails more than officials representing governments; it includes NGOs and other groups that interact with governments as advocates or in contractual, legal, collaborative, and working partner connections. These forces constitute the heart of IGM.

Theory and practice in IGR and subsequent IGM must account for the cumulative development of government policy and administration—the changing terrain—yet maintain traditional institutional processes. IGR has been a deep and long-standing tradition in the study of administration and, more important, is "not so much focused on the reconstruction of past events in itself as it is on reconstructing the facts of government in development in the context of deeply grounded political theories about governance" (Raadschelders 2000, 513; see also John 1997; Robertson 1993). As this work journeys through evolving relationships that involve law and state building, working interdependencies among governments, partnerships with NGOS, and complex multi-sector networks, certain verities of political science remain as part of the story—in particular, how government institutions and later NGOs interact to shape politics, government, and transactional management across sectors.

It reveals that while some things change—for example, the range of actors that are involved in how programs are organized, administered, and evaluated—others remain the same. For instance, reviewing the work of those involved in the processes of government has led to the art of administration, as first identified by Leonard White in his four volumes of administrative history (1948, 1951, 1954, 1958). These studies reviewed service delivery under intergovernmental programs within the basic parameters regarding the type of services to be financed, to whom they may be delivered, and with whom programs are fixed in law and regulations. Those factors do not change. As the practice of IGR expands administratively, it becomes apparent that the old is seldom replaced by the new. Rather, the new builds on the old. Thus, any theory of IGM follows suit.

Studying IGR as a Framework for IGM

Although conceptually coined some eight decades ago, IGR is hardly new to politics and government. Problems of central-local relations, particularly questions of centralization and the rights and obligations of constituent units, are quite long-standing. For example, for about three hundred years (between 200 BCE and 100 CE), the Roman Empire maintained a careful balance between matters of imperial control and those left to provinces and municipalities. Indeed, the Romans deferred to the concept of states' rights, respecting certain traditions of conquered nations (Bendix 1978). Rulers of most empires were aware that they confronted a differentiated entity, normally finding that "the confederal structure has functioned most effectively when limiting its ambitions to administration and regulation" (Burbank and Cooper 2010, 456). In the period before the American Revolution, the colonies used official agents in London to serve as emissaries, who were employed to articulate colonial sentiments at the hub of decisions and to exert more informal political influence. During the postrevolutionary period in the United States, the founding fathers wrestled with the proper relationship between the states and the general government. The debates over the Constitution were to a great degree over the respective powers of the two levels. Local governments, meanwhile, were being incorporated under the legal powers of the colonies and later those of the states.

Further, IGR is not unique to federal systems of government, however more numerous or difficult these relationships may be when power is constitutionally divided. The United Kingdom, for example, has always had issues and concerns with the level and concentration or de-concentration of power as well as concern for the supervision of local governments. Long-standing regional and national governing problems have also involved Scotland, Wales, Ireland, and later Northern Ireland.

Indeed, constants across both unitary and federal systems include problems of centralization and decentralization, as local functions are often passed on to counties, village issues to metropolitan areas, county concerns to states or provinces, and state or provincial matters to the central government level. Increased central intervention can be seen as a working adaptation of the principle of governing to modern conditions, in some cases even on a global scale (Graves 1964, 17).

What makes IGR and its management component most distinctive is its involvement in the boundary-spanning activities of distinctive units that possess territory, identity, and ascribed powers. With regard to the United States, in the words of William Anderson (1960, 3),

> Underlying the concept of intergovernmental relations is the fact that the nation as a whole, each one of the States, and every county, town,

city, village, school district, and other special district or local unit is a
territorial and corporate or quasi-corporate entity that has a legal existence, rights, functions, powers, and duties within its territory, distinct from those of every other such unit. This is true even though the
smaller units are generally embraced geographically within the larger
ones. Being all separate legal entities, they are all capable of legal and
other relations with each other.

Governments are not, as Anderson observes, organized in some hierarchical fashion as military, industrial, or internal bureaucratic entities are. While
there may be legal, economic, and fiscal controls, mayors, governors, or their
legislators are not under the direct authority of national officials. Over time
this has implied that a different kind of management is in order.

The relative independence of US jurisdictions has led to increasing interdependence as programs expand, decentralize, and externalize. Every institution of government—legislative, executive, and judicial—is involved in
IGM. For example, the largest intergovernmental program in terms of dollars (if not clients) is Medicaid, which provides medical assistance for low-
income persons, including the elderly, disabled, and others under a federal,
state, and NGO program that requires constant legislative review and oversight regarding allowable benefits, eligibility parameters, general standards,
and the like. The federal Centers for Medicaid and Medicare Services and the
fifty-six state units transact with the federal agency and their delivery agents
over program plans, guidelines, regulations, audits, and contractor relationships. Meanwhile, the courts adjudicate a range of broad program parameters
from eligibility to such details as what constitutes a basic change in a person's
medication regime. While all this work goes on, virtual armies of local eligibility and benefits workers turn over services to thousands of medical vendors and practitioners, who are in turn audited and reviewed by other private
firms, and so on. With regard to the federal government, the result, observes
Paul Light (2008, 4) is "a vast, growing, and mostly hidden workforce of contractors, grantees, and state and local government employees who work for
the federal government under mandates. . . . This hidden workforce would
include the networks of public, private, and nonprofit employees that must
work together to execute many of the laws."

As subsequent analysis in this volume indicates, with the expansion of
federal programming in the 1960s and the resultant administrative complexity, the term *intergovernmental management* entered the public management
lexicon somewhat ambiguously as a way to describe the activities, ranging
from program design concerns to clerical and auditing actions, of administrators working across the lines and across governments and as a means for
"insiders" to capture the essence of the processes and routines that program
administrators must follow. IGM has been characterized as a term of "recent

BOX I.1

- The US federal system developed over interacting powers and responsibilities between the general (federal) government and the states, with local governments becoming "federalized" later and under state government frameworks.
- Principles of divided or "compartmentalized" government responsibilities quickly gave way to both jurisdictional responsibility and overlapping powers.
- The basis of interactions among the various units were originally and continue to be rooted in public law and in political processes.
- The patterning and analysis of continuing interactions among political and government actions—that is, the various combinations of interdependencies and influences among public officials representing governments—have come to be known as intergovernmental relations (IGR). Intergovernmental management (IGM) refers to the transactional connections, routine and system defining, that take place within IGR. Thus, IGR is more analytical whereas IGM is more routine or managerial.

vintage, specialized usage, limited visibility and uncertain maturity" (Krane and Wright 1998, 1162) because it includes so many disparate actions: seeking funds from other governments, coping with an expanding regulatory burden and externalization by contract, and developing interlocal cooperative agreements as well as many network-based collaborative activities. Following this observation, in discussing contemporary models of managing within IGR, IGM is useful; however, only *some* of the activities occur exclusively between governments. The rest is highly interactive and involves governments and NGOs. In its contemporary formulation, IGM has clearly evolved as including nongovernmental—nonprofit and for-profit—as well as governmental units as a model for understanding the complexities; thus, IGM has more recently partially separated out managerial activity (Agranoff and McGuire 2001).

Government in Governing

One tenet that is familiar to those who work with programs such as Medicaid is this changing role of the government. Indeed, at the century's turn George Frederickson (1999, 702) concluded that "the most important feature of contemporary public administration is the declining relationship between jurisdiction and public management." A look at a program like Medicaid reinforces that conclusion. Some 4,500 federal employees administer this program, which includes nearly 175,000 contract provider organizations and nearly 80,000 surveyors and management contractors. As an intergovernmental program the small federal workforce masks the fact that 34,000 state government workers are also involved in this program (Social Security Administration 2007). It has led some to conclude that this "disarticulation" of the state through such contracting has "hollowed out" agencies in the same way that many holding corporations have (Milward, Provan, and Else 1993; Rhodes 1997), and to some it has meant that governments are no longer the central steering actors in the policy process as government-NGO connections weaken the effects of government hierarchies (Klijn 1997). Others go even further, arguing that these long chains of multiple partnerships lead to a loss of accountability and weaken the government's ability to perform its most challenging agendas (Bozeman 1987; Frederickson 1999; Kettl 2009).

It is important to look at the broader picture before government is hastily cast aside. Regarding the US federal system, we are talking about considerably more than the federal government. Indeed, 56 state and state-equivalent entities are organized into over 3,000 counties, over 19,000 municipalities, over 16,000 towns and townships, over 35,000 special districts, plus over 13,000 school districts. In turn, all these governments are served by over 500,000 elected officials, 364,000 members of legislatures/governing boards, and over 160,000 other elected boards and commission members (see Stephens and Wikstrom 2007, 36). Light (2008, 195) once estimated that another 4.4 million state and local employees were de facto federal employees working under contracts, grants, and mandates. In addition to these officials, some 2.4 million nonmilitary, non-postal civilian employees are also part of NGOs that deliver public programs.

The intergovernmental influence obviously varies considerably. Administration, one of the state of Indiana's smallest departments, employs over 200 people to oversee the state's purchasing, vehicle and aviation fleet, real estate transactions, and government center campus in downtown Indianapolis. The state's largest agency, Family and Social Services Administration (FSSA), while highly externalized through contracts, nevertheless employs around 5,000 staff members who do everything from determining basic services eligibility to assessing and controlling quality and standards, managing service contracts, overseeing programs, and doing evaluation and policy analysis (Associated Press 2009). Medicaid is but one of the dozens of programs that the FSSA administers.

The FSSA example has two important intergovernmental implications. First, before one reaches the conclusion that the federal government has off-loaded its functions, one must bear in mind that, as with the FSSA, the states (and local governments) are partners in federal programs. They also administer independent state programs through local governments and NGOs. This sort of first order of program collaboration is forgotten when federal, state, or other levels of contracting are highlighted. Second, the FSSA's charge would suggest that perhaps the state has not completely hollowed out. While contractors and other agents are deeply involved in the delivery of services, government remains involved in many nondelivery aspects of programs, perhaps even in operating partnerships with NGO contractors. This is IGM at its basic hub and spokes, so to speak. One must begin to understand what government continues to do along with how it interacts externally as it engages in IGM.

It may be safer to conclude that the jury is out regarding questions related to the extent to which the state has hollowed out versus the administration down the line, so to speak, and which functions remain with government. Indeed, with the ascendancy of IGM, federal and state administrators may have taken on new, important roles. The same issues would be true regarding not only the complexity of contemporary accountability, as Beryl Radin (2006) has indicated, but also the efficacy of government (Koliba, Campbell, and Zia 2011). For these empirical questions, the evidence is scarce and anecdotal, yet it does not suggest that government is going away. Indeed, many programs maintain government delivery rather than contract out for services or external operations for the very reasons that relate to control. Social Security income and Medicare (in contrast to Medicaid) programs are examples of the federal government's exclusive program operational delivery.

In a similar vein, Michael McGuire and Robert Agranoff (2010) have argued, contrary to a body of contemporary literature, that networks of NGOs and government officials working together have not necessarily displaced the power or centrality of government agencies in America (see chapters 8 and 9 of this volume). More accurately the empirical evidence from prior research on American bureaucracy in general, and on contracts and networks in particular, is too mixed to support the more extreme hollowing out contentions. It is in this spirit that IGM should be understood about changing public roles. Until proven otherwise, governments remain at the core of programs, and their roles in IGM deserve further attention.

BOX I.2

- The tradition of jurisdictional autonomy has led to government strategies at all levels that are both independent and interdependent, particularly at the management level.
- Actions of managers representing various governments have become increasingly differentiated and wide ranging, from program design to post auditing, prompting the need for intergovernmental management.
- As respective governments have expanded in functions, an increasing number of nongovernmental actors have become part of the intergovernmental mix, particularly reaching beyond procurement to include interdependent, direct service delivery and agencies.
- Multiple programs, many levels, and recognition of problem complexity ultimately led to networked "governance" among disparate actors, levels, and auspices, mixing sociopolitical actors in different modes and orders.

Externalization

Having suggested that governments may not have been eviscerated by contracts and networks, it is necessary to recognize that the intergovernmental system has moved governments outward toward an increasing number of external agents that do at least a portion of the governments' business. Particularly they have expanded direct service delivery outside of government.

One long-standing force is that of contract seeking, which has been a venerable example of local-federal relations in US history. In the nineteenth century, city officials regularly secured federal government contacts for commerce routes, freight and passenger services, government installations and buildings, waterway and harbor dredging, infrastructure assistance and related internal improvements, tariff concessions for local industries, and other government contracts and subsidies. Most of these federal benefits were immediately externalized into contracts with the nongovernmental sector. This form of interaction became notable in the 1840s, becoming a "significant means of improving government services at both levels and of forging strong, if not informal, cooperative lines between Washington and the localities" (Elazar 1967, 516).

The contract with a broader scope of the nongovernmental sector was the next step. Subsequent chapters demonstrate that domestic program expansion, along with the move toward more efficient and less costly government, has brought on a new era in which the US IGR system must meet those governance challenges presented by all the outside organizations involved in the work of government. As mentioned, national, state, and local programming has expanded to include a host of NGOs, particularly in the delivery of direct services. The primary vehicle everywhere has been through externalization, especially through contracting for services. This has brought NGOs into the scheme of government programming at the delivery and local level, and into the policy stream at the national level, as their interests are advanced by national associations representing subnational governments and NGOs (Salamon 1999). Everywhere nonprofit and for-profit NGOs have become "governments for hire" (Smith and Lipsky 1993).

The result is that subnational governments in the United States, as in other countries, are bound into systems of governance. Among others, Jan Kooiman (2003, 3) has identified the concept as involving mixes of public as well as private "governors":

These mixes are societal "responses" to persistent and changing governing "demands," set against ever growing societal diversity, dynamics and complexity. Governing issues generally are not just public or private, they are frequently shared, and governing activity at all levels (from local to supra-national) is becoming diffused over various societal actors whose relationships with each other are constantly changing. There has, judged against traditional public governing activities, been an increase in the role of government as facilitator and as co-operating partner. As such it is more appropriate to speak of shifting than of shrinking roles of the state.

Governments in most countries face this governance phenomenon, where the effective intergovernmental boundaries are shifted outside the formal confines of subnational governments (Rhodes 1997). For example, this would include contracting with nonprofit agencies for human services delivery, partnering with business associations for economic development, monitoring the environment with green organizations, and working on planning issues with neighborhood associations. Thus, it must be recognized that IGR has highly externalized. Governments do not simply engage in interactions but interact with one another and with external actors that are now involved in government operations and services. Thus, these interactions expand our understanding of IGM.

Pervasive Politics

IGM's last name, "management," does not necessarily remove the politics involved, as government is also at work. It is important to understand the political dimension related to the actions of government officials and operatives. While "large P" party politics sometimes does play a role, more often the "small p" of political actions and moves is involved. Even with externalization and networking, political moves—visible and hidden or subtle—pervade what appear to be routine transactions.

Intergovernmental politics are as old as the federal order. The first secretary of the treasury, Alexander Hamilton, developed a plan for the federal government to assume $25 million of state debt, the famous trade-off for winning votes from the House of Representatives to locate the national capital along the Potomac River between Maryland and Virginia. Assumption sealed the idea of countrywide taxing and spending, according to Hamilton's biographer Ron Chernow (2004, 330), as it "created an unshakable foundation for federal power in America. The federal government had captured forever the bulk of American taxing power. In comparison, the location of the national capital seemed a secondary matter." The federal bonds given to those states that had already retired their debt, along with their own-source revenues from the sale of lands they possessed or were granted by the federal government, allowed states to finance projects that local opposition to tax support would otherwise prohibit. This, in effect, was among the first intergovernmental lessons in politics.

A contemporary example of politics relates to the Patient Protection and Affordable Care Act (known as the ACA), which was enacted in 2010. One provision of the health care reform bill required the states, by 2014, to mandate that their citizens purchase health insurance and that states either expand existing insurance pools or set them up to make access affordable. This politically controversial issue actually goes back to the political debates in Congress over a "single payer" for privately delivered health care, similar to that of Medicare, versus a system of legally regulated private insurance companies. To garner the political support of the health insurance industry, regulated and organized by the states, the latter option was chosen as the most politically viable choice. The political game is far from over, however, as the Republican caucus in the House repeatedly attempted to repeal the entire ACA program, and some nineteen state attorneys general filed suit in federal courts to strike down the purchase requirement as an unfair use of the commerce clause of the Constitution. In mid-2012, the Supreme Court upheld this provision, basing the mandate on federal taxing power. Nevertheless, a new round of politics will likely be brought forward over revision (Joondeph 2011), with the incoming administration's pledge in 2017 to repeal the individual mandate heading the political list. Politics will now shift to the states, where consumer groups, insurance companies, and health lobbyists will fight over the insurance pools. Even then the politics will not stop there, as the state oversight bodies will be lobbied regarding types of individual cases and litigation will be filed regarding the treatment of insurees.

The ACA insurance purchase mandate is not the only intergovernmental political issue. Some state governors are resisting the bill's provisions that require, at risk of losing all federal Medicaid funding, low-income childless adults be added to the rolls of Medicaid, which the states partially finance. This requirement was successfully challenged in the Supreme Court. This decision opened a whole new set of political moves, lobbying, and administrative attempts to contain the fiscal impact of this expanded coverage at partial state expense. Finally, these kinds of actions are by no means the end of politics. With extensive NGO involvement in delivering services under contracts, a new politics of networking has emerged, where providers become engaged with governments to steer programs in their direction, so to speak. In short, virtually every phase of an intergovernmental program such as health care reform carries substantial political dimensions.

In a federal system where each jurisdiction, as William Anderson (1960) suggested, operates within a nonhierarchical framework, every politician has the potential, if they choose to exercise it, to be political and administrative role players in the intergovernmental system. These roles are essential for operating jurisdictions within the federal matrix. Local governments, for example, deal directly with people and are operational focal points in multitiered systems. Working with their citizens and groups in the community, as well as with regional and federal officials, according to Daniel Elazar (1962, 24), local officials play five essential roles:

- the acquirer of external aid for local needs,
- the adapter of government functions and services to local conditions,
- the experimenter with new functions and services (or new versions of traditional ones),
- the initiator of governmental programs that spread across state and nation, and
- underlying the others, the provider of a means by which a local community can pay the "ante" necessary to "sit in the game"—that is, to secure an effective voice in governmental decisions of local impact.

Elazar also factored in the interlocal matrix because local governments operate within their civil communities, which include the other local governments, local services' operation units of regional and federal governments, public nongovernmental bodies, and local political parties. Each of them obviously has a highly political orientation, and it is important for analysts of IGR to constantly remind themselves that these matters do not just entail law or finance or technical detail or administration. They also involve politics.

Plan of the Book

The book is primarily organized around the four themes: law and politics, jurisdictional interdependency, governments' partners, and networks and networking. Chapter 1 lays the groundwork by providing a quick overview of how federal development and IGR (patterns) have framed IGM (transactions), how actors within the system have defined the system, and how the number and type of actors have expanded. Then chapters 2–9 examine the four themes that together frame IGM. Each theme first covers the conceptual development and then overviews the management applications in a sequential and primarily chronological fashion. Thus, chapters 2 and 3 deal with law and politics, as they evolved with the building of the US integral nation-state (Elazar 1962). By the early twentieth century, the Progressive Era, the New Deal, and subsequent domestic programs expanded the federal government's domestic role and led to growing program connections between the levels discussed in chapters 4 and 5 (Skowronek 1982). These changes contributed to the rise of externalization, as governments' partners moved beyond procurement and became involved in more ways (Smith and Lipsky 1993), the foci of chapters 6 and 7. The growing number of jurisdictions, actors, and programs led to more regular interactions, transactions, and collaboration structures, as networks and networking are analyzed and illustrated in chapters 8 and 9 (Agranoff 2007c).

Chapters 2–9 begin with summaries of real-world IGM in action. Each ends with a short summary section that briefly states the key conceptual learning points. They are followed by a parallel set of key practice points that discuss their applications. These points are designed to bring together the many complexities involved in IGM and to demonstrate their operational or managerial utility.

The volume's conclusion pulls the four IGM strands together and identifies future concerns. It particularly focuses on the continuing role of government and how public management is changing in light of IGM's complexity. This discussion highlights the challenges of getting programs to work together—that is, interoperability—plus the digital issues in IGM and the emerging role of open-source technology in IGM. While no one knows exactly where this highly interactive field will go, it will no doubt move with technology and require increasingly new skills that go deeper into these existing themes.

1 FEDERAL FRAMING OF INTERGOVERNMENTAL RELATIONS AND INTERGOVERNMENTAL MANAGEMENT

American federalism has been understood as involving divided but overlapping or interactive powers. Gary Gerstle's (2015) historical work on the federal system looks at two conflicting principles of governance. The first focuses on the importance of limiting the federal government's reach by enumerating and fragmenting powers and then by granting broad powers to the states to shape public and private life and to engage in many types of coercion precluded from general government powers. Second, the system was also built with "an emphasis on improvisation rather than transformation" (5). This development was based on three phenomena: exemption, surrogacy, and privatization. *Exemption* meant approaching the court system for permission to sidestep federal prohibitions. *Surrogacy* involved broadly interpreting and taking actions in using explicitly granted powers into new terrain, thus expanding the system's authority. *Privatization* worked by persuading and working with private groups to do federal government work that would not otherwise be authorized. Regarding the states, Gerstle's work thus sees federation as becoming subject to improvisation and incremental change, a process that would open the "black box of U.S. government—that which combines the particulars about the powers given to the states—and examine its contents." Between these two principles is the way that American federalism frames intergovernmental activity. It will "give individuals of all political persuasions a fuller understanding of how governance in the United States has worked" (13).

Thus, despite the general understanding that federalism somehow divides powers between the general (or federal) government and the states, and through the states' local governments, notable overlaps exist. Cooperation has been in practice since the early days; federal compartments are not as watertight as they may be on a ship (Watts 1999a). In Daniel Elazar's classic work, *The American Partnership* (1962), such intergovernmental cooperation has been an operational theme since the early nineteenth century. As Elazar (26) relates,

This was the case with internal improvements during the early period of American federalism. States were establishing boards of internal improvements in the period between the establishment by the federal government of the Corps of Engineers and the United States Board of Internal Improvement to coordinate activities under some form of national plan. Congress created the United States Army Corps of Engineers in 1802, with the understanding that the corps could be used for civil, as well as military, works. The first federal master plan for internal improvements was prepared by Albert Gallatin in 1808. The debate in Congress over the next two years indicated to the states that a substantial number of the projects contained within the master plan would be undertaken. Despite the delays engendered by the War of 1812, the Virginia General Assembly adopted a policy calling for a major internal improvement program to be developed in conjunction with that of the federal government; and the Virginia Board of Public Works was organized in 1816 at least partly as a result of federal activities in this field. The creation of this and other state boards of internal improvement led to Congressional formalization of the existing internal improvement program of the Corps of Engineers by establishing a national Board of Internal Improvement in 1824.

The situation thus became of interest to the federal government because development concerns for one section of the nation were generally a problem for all sections (see also White 1951).

The internal improvements issue was an early demonstration of federal and state cooperation. By the late 1830s the US Army Engineers developed what amounted to a national master plan for roads, canals, and railroads. Thus, along with the theory of "dual federalism" (Corwin 1934), where it was assumed powers did not overlap and perhaps never worked in practice, came the idea of working cooperation between the levels of government, for governmental activities were collaboratively shared despite political rhetoric and formal pronouncements. Elazar (1962) found evidence of federal-state cooperation at the management stage in several programs that ranged from informal contacts to formal program agreements. He concludes, "A substantial share of American government has been the search for such methods to provide for the necessary collaboration among the various units in the system" (305). And the system does engender a great need for cooperation for two reasons.

First, in his study of the emergence of American-style bureaucracy, Stephen Skowronek (1982, 21) writes, "Sovereignty was to be shared between the new central government and the old regional units of government, which retained their revolutionary designation as 'states,'" thus ensuring their integrity and legal codes. For most of the nineteenth century, he concludes, the national government was passive and left substantive governing to states and, through them, to localities, leading to a "distinctive sense of statelessness in the political culture" (23).

Second, in a United States with subnational governments, as Frank Goodnow (1900) noted early on, administrative officials had inherited from England the idea that allegiance is owed to the law, not to the hierarchy represented by the Crown and later by some distant executive in England of another organization. "The result was to make impossible any state administrative supervision over the main body of officers intrusted with the execution of the law. All the control which could be exercised in the governmental system in the interest of producing coordination between the functions of expressing and executing the will of the state had to be found in the power of the legislature to regulate in detail the duties of officers intrusted with the execution of the law" (101). Enforcement was largely by the courts as statutes were interpreted.

Collaborative Federalism

Coordinating federal-state, federal-local, and state-local programs has provided a venerable stream of findings on intergovernmental, collaborative program management. One stream that emanates from the federal setup is that of the kind of cooperative federalism Elazar (1962) identified as existing in the nineteenth century. Similarly, Jane Perry Clark (1938) recognized the federal opportunities for "political and economic" experimentation. Her study included the many modes of intergovernmental administration: informal cooperation, intergovernmental agreements and contracts, exchange of personnel, interdependent legal action, grants-in-aid, and tax policy. Her work describes such cooperation as distinctly experimental and routine:

> Much of the cooperation between the federal and state governments has been found in the sea of governmental activity without any chart, compass, or guiding star, for cooperation has been unplanned and uncorrelated with other activities of government even in the same field. Nevertheless, a certain number of patterns may be traced in the confusion. Cooperation has frequently been a means of coordinating the use of federal and state resources, of eliminating duplications in activity, of cutting down expenses, of accomplishing work which could not otherwise be carried out, and in the federal system of the United States move more smoothly than would be otherwise possible. (Clark 1938, 7)

Clark's view of collaborative federalism was highly optimistic regarding officials' problem-resolution abilities.

Closer examination of collaboration arose from the 1930s onward because of the federal-state grants programs of the Great Depression. Although they were supportive of cooperative federalism in principle, studies were not always sanguine about their success. V. O. Key Jr. (1937, 228) identified a "gap between policy determination and the task of administration" because the expenditure of money and performance of function have been under the supervision of state agencies "operating in a sphere of and tradition of freedom from central control." Another well-known study by John Gaus and Leon Wolcott (1940), concerning US Department of Agriculture programs, examined the role of cooperating governments. The department recognized the need for strong functioning units outside of Washington that could participate in federal programs but questioned the operating capacity of many (particularly small) governments to be cooperative partners. Regulations and administrative supervision as a whole tend to be greatly modified in practice by the ideas and prejudices of local officials. Edward Weidner (1944, 233) concludes, "State's supervision of local governments is largely determined by a meeting of the minds of state and local officials."

Not all collaborative management across levels of government in the first part of the twentieth century was recognized as being problematic. For example, William Anderson (1955) found in the day-to-day administration of federal programs that administrative officials, many of whom were from similar professional backgrounds, had relatively harmonious relations. "They usually worked together in trying to get changes in standards, rules, budgets and personnel requirements to advance the service" (201). He reported an absence of "crack-down" orders from federal to state agencies; indeed, state and local officials welcomed the presence, advice, and help of federal field officials. In his work, Lawrence Durisch points to the many "new federal-local relationships" (1941, 326) after the Tennessee Valley Authority's "program integrated on the basis of place or territory." These staffs worked together on many issues: dozens of signed memorandums of understanding; legal contracts; special municipal ordinances; multiple conferences regarding the impact of the influx of construction workers on local services; liaisons with local law enforcement agencies; state-local consultations regarding highway relocations and access roads; land acquisition issues; readjustments for water supply, sewage disposal, and other public facilities; property tax loss adjustments; and several administrative improvements in local governments. They recognized the need for sound local governments and the "cooperative nature" of the undertaking as well as the "grassroots approach to which the Authority is committed" (334).

Such a non-centralized approach was fundamental to the managerial experience of David Lilienthal (1939) with the Tennessee Valley Authority. To him the essence of coordination in the field involved the field operatives making the great number of decisions, the affected citizens actively participating and working with state and local agencies, and the state and local governments cooperating as they aimed toward common objectives.

As Dwight Waldo (1948, 149) observed, Lilienthal saw this decentralized collaborative strategy as essential to preserving democracy in a large bureaucratic state and to overcoming the drawbacks of centralization. A cooperative approach was also observed at the state level. John Vieg (1941) analyzed the cooperation of federal, state, local, and private organizations in Iowa's agricultural programs in four areas: research, education, planning, and programming. He suggests that different interests work "physically side by side" while forging out "a rational division of labor and clear understanding of authority and responsibility all the way around; there must be close agreement on all questions" (142).

During World War II, extensive program coordination was required for heavily congested production areas. After consulting with all levels of government and nongovernmental officials, the president's Committee for Congested Production Areas facilitated all types of public services in these local areas. The committee, according to Corrington Gill, provided common meeting ground for "across the table discussion of common problems" (1945, 32).

The Establishment of IGR for Coordination

How does one manage through the maze of multiple interacting governments? Non-centralization and a sort of federal matrix are the established order in the federal system. Elazar (1984) observes that the non-centralized nature of the US system of government is owed to de jure and de facto jurisdictional constitutional diffusion and sharing of powers. Units consequently have a propensity to operate independently. "The model for federalism is the matrix, a network of arenas within arenas" (3). These arenas are distinguished by being larger or smaller rather than higher or lower. This phenomenon of achieving federal goals through state and local action involves coordination with both the federal government and the state and local governments. Jeffrey Pressman and Aaron Wildavsky's landmark study *Implementation* (1973) reveals the myriad steps, negotiations, and trade-offs in a single federal program. "We have learned one important lesson from the [Economic Development Administration] experience in Oakland: implementation should not be divorced from policy" (12–13). Developing the program's initial design and reaching agreements were easy, but the later so-called technical questions did not resolve themselves as the program went along and proved to be "the rocks on which the program eventually foundered" (13).

Frederick Mosher (1980) paints a rather complete picture of the extension of the federal government beyond its own operations into how "the nooks and crannies of our economic, social, cultural and even personal lives seem almost unlimited" (543). He documents that "the problems that the federal government is now called upon to address and try to resolve are more numerous, more complex, more interrelated than ever before in history" (545). Operationally, this means a greater reliance on indirect administration through third parties; an increased dependence on negotiations, collaboration inducements, and persuasion and less on immediate direction and control; and a greater concern for and involvement of the roles of organizations outside the immediate control of the federal government. Calling them devices, Mosher uses a tools approach to demonstrate the rise of federal external programming through income support, grants, contracts, regulations, tax expenditures, loans and loan guarantees, and quasi-federal agencies. He concludes by observing the importance of top public executives—including those personnel who are paid by the US government but work for organizations outside of federal control—who bring to their work "an understanding of the relations and interdependence of the public sector and the private, and of one level of government with others, both above and below" (547).

This need to coordinate throughout develops, James Sundquist and David Davis explain (1969, 12), because the federal system's programs are based on "goals or objectives that are established by the national government, through the actions of other governments, state and local, that are legally independent and may be even hostile." Thus, coordination becomes almost "any change in organization, relationships, policies, practices, projects or programs that will resolve whatever conflict or hiatus in the federal-state-local chain of relationships" (19). It is, they conclude, a matter of mutual adjustment rather than that of central coordination. Similarly, successful federal government supervision of state enforcement activity amounts to the use of communication, financing authority, and organization tools rather than top-down authority.

BOX 1.1

> - The US federalism tradition has always somehow balanced Jeffersonian subnational rights and responsibilities with Hamiltonian-involved general government action.
> - Federal-state action in the nineteenth century displayed as much conflict as cooperation, well beyond the slavery issue, to include trade, property rights, public works, interstate navigation, and other matters.
> - Managing large programs in arenas such as public works and infrastructure first brought attention to the existence of and the need for field-level cooperative interactions.
> - The study of policy implementation reveals the complex orders involved in making programs work, particularly the decisions that are made along the line that range from the national level to the street-level program operative.

The States in Cooperative Federalism

State governments are not restricted in the purposes for which they can exercise power, and can legislate comprehensively to protect the public welfare. They have plenary legislative powers and act in a broad number of arenas. While nationalization and intergovernmentalization have eroded some state powers or become shared in many arenas, a number of exclusive powers remain. The states possess *primary* powers over private property and contract law, public health, roads and transportation, education and higher education, economic development, motor vehicle registration and licensing of drivers, rural patrol and public safety, election administration and voting (including federal elections), regulation of state banks and financial institutions, corporation registration, licensing of crafts and professions, civil law, criminal law, local government, natural resources and conservation, intrastate commerce, weights and measures, food and beverage regulation and safety, mental health and mental disability services, law enforcement and public safety, prisons and corrections, and many other matters.

Many other programs, though, are now shared with the federal government: vocational rehabilitation, job training, assistance payments, health financing for the poor and handicapped, social services, environmental protection, national highways, mass transportation, technical assistance in agriculture, and more. Concurrent powers include the power to tax, not subject to formal preemption, and powers granted to Congress and not prohibited to states (e.g., interstate commerce and economic development) but where preemption is allowed. For example, taxation of intellectual property and regulation of online Internet services were areas of state involvement long before Congress entered these arenas. The states, however, are forbidden to exercise such nationally delegated powers as minting money, operating post offices, engaging in war, and signing foreign treaties (which is changing).

State constitutions are much longer than the US Constitution and enumerate very broad powers under their reserved authority to act in many areas. A clause of the Alaska Constitution (Article 12, Section 8) states: "The enumeration of specified powers in this constitution shall not be construed as limiting the powers of the State" (quoted in Tarr 2000, 9). Unlike the federal constitution, states periodically rewrite their constitutions and regularly add amendments. State constitutions differ in some respects because they more directly reflect the states' distinct political and policy choices and reflect different decisions regarding how they opt to limit governmental power (Tarr 2000).

During the twentieth century, state governments grew considerably from their previously passive, decentralized orientation (to local governments). They too centralized effective policy control over many programs that were previously the province of cities, counties, and special districts. To take one example, public primary and secondary education emerged in the nineteenth century as almost exclusively local in administration, financing, curriculum, and standards. The twentieth century saw state control over schooling gradually increase. Today, there are fifty-plus state systems of education, where local boards have more operational than policy and program control, and state governments determine most standards and provide a majority of the funding.

Likewise, in many policy areas, states have increased their commitment to professionalism, expertise, efficiency, and contemporary management. In his history of state governments, Jon Teaford (2002) concludes the twentieth century was a period of development of legislative expertise, the rationalization and concentration of administrative authority under governors, and the transfer of power from local elected officials to expert state bureaucracies. The states became significant actors in American government (230). He determines that the century proved, contrary to the beliefs of many, that history was made in Albany, New York; Madison, Wisconsin; and Sacramento, California; as well as Washington, DC.

Local Governments in System Perspective

The Constitution neither delegates nor reserves powers to local governments; there is no mention of them (Hills 2005). They were always subordinate to colonial and later state governments to some degree, but over the nineteenth century, states gradually assumed legal control over local governments (Tarr 2000), leaving them to obtain their powers from the states. Since they do not have federal constitutional status, local governments are at the legal mercy of the states, which have imposed the ultra vires rule. A political subdivision can exercise only those powers granted specifically, and those powers came to be narrowly interpreted by state courts (Zimmerman 1995).

At an early period of American history, the states more or less ignored local governments, which were considered small "civil communities" that in many ways combined to form the colonies and later the states (Lutz 1988). Early state constitutions accepted their authority, along with the legitimacy of their prerogatives, and many states offered them direct representation in state legislatures. Based on the American pioneer tradition, they were considered self-organizing and self-governing communities. As Alexis de Tocqueville (1988, 67) observed in the 1830s, "In all that concerns themselves alone the townships remain independent bodies, and I do not think one could find a single inhabitant of New England who would recognize the right of the government of the state to control matters of purely municipal interest."

This pattern began to change by the middle of the nineteenth century as local governments were legally redefined as creatures of state governments. New York was the first state to adopt constitutional provisions regulating cities, and other states soon followed. The constitutional shift moved local governments to a status where their powers are derived from and subject to the sovereign state legislature rather than being regarded as component units of a quasi-federal government (Tarr 2000). This "unitary" relationship of subordinating local governments was solidified in legal doctrine through the well-known Dillon's Rule. It is based on a state court case in which Judge John Dillon ruled that municipalities could exercise only those powers that were expressly granted by the state or that could be reasonably considered indispensable to those declared purposes (*City of Clinton v. Cedar Rapids and Missouri River Railroad*, 24 Iowa 455, 476 [1868]). This ruling clearly ended previous notions of *imperium in imperio* among local governments.

While Dillon's Rule remains in good standing in a legal sense, it has been modified in practice over the years. Most important has been the states' practice of granting home rule, or the authorization of broad discretionary authority to petitioning local governments, particularly municipalities. A home-rule government can draft its own charter, choose its form of government (there are four main types in the United States), organize its administration, tax, regulate, and so on, subject to state law and constitutional provisions. Local governments have also been able to expand their discretionary authority through several other means: those states' "political cultures" that value local governments, constitutional revision, part-time and short-term state legislative sessions, the lobbying strength of associations of local governments and of local officials, limited state oversight and supervisory effects, judicial widening of local authority, and the pressure of rapid population growth, which encourages local officials to exercise their authority to the fullest (Zimmerman 1995,

BOX 1.2

- Intergovernmental relations have been complicated by shifting some program focus from state to federally authorized area-based entities—for example, those in metropolitan transportation—yet planning and operations remain state and local in focus and operation.
- Since the post–Civil War period, local governments have increasingly been drawn into the federal government's orbit. Cooperation and tensions have developed between federal and state leadership, as local governments remain legal creatures of their states.
- Within states, continuing tensions exist between the court-interpreted "Dillon's Rule," granting states major supervision of local governments, and the push for home rule, under which local governments have broader "own source" powers. States vary considerably on home-rule powers. Some are in effect Dillon's Rule states whereas others have liberal home-rule statutes.
- Intergovernmental interdependency has pushed, excluded, and redefined the "boundaries" within which managers in the public sphere have had to work. Today few officials have work confined exclusively to their own governments.

5, 8). In some states, Dillon's Rule has effectively been reversed by legislative actions that authorize local governments to tax, regulate, and deal with matters of local concern unless such matters are prohibited by state statute.

Expanding IGR to Locales

Over the past century or so and based on the aforementioned centralization of state powers and more federal government involvement, a creeping intergovernmentalization in effect has tied the states to local governments regardless of legal doctrine. States have become highly involved in many notable locally administered programs—for example, education, law enforcement and criminal law, land use, food regulation and safety, elections administration, and regulation and licensing of professions and occupations. In these arenas, local discretion is regularly set aside by legislative act, in effect preempting local discretion. A good example is in the area of food regulation and safety. Most cities and counties operate their own inspection units, but the code of regulations is virtually that of their state government. Local units thus primarily implement state codes. As mentioned, education has become increasingly standardized as well in terms of curriculum, achievement examinations, qualifications for graduation, staffing patterns, approved textbooks, and in many other areas. Now it is also tied to federal government expectations since the No Child Left Behind legislation of the 2000s. At the same time, local governments have in effect become federalized, as federal-state programs (e.g., environmental protection, occupational health and safety, unemployment, highways, mass transportation) are extended to local governments. Local governments are also affected by federal decisions arising from Supreme Court rulings in arenas such as franchising and merchandising, hiring practices, wages and hours, accessibility of the handicapped, and tort liability.

Most states have many tiers and types of local governments. Basically, county governments are administrative subdivisions of their states and carry out state functions on the local level. But in large urban or metropolitan areas, they also fulfill municipal functions in nonmunicipal territories. Municipalities hold the status of citizen-initiated public corporations, which under their charters not only provide those services that their citizens choose but also state-mandated services. Townships or towns provide government in most of the rural areas of the country. They now have very limited functions, such as rural roads, emergency financial relief, rural fire safety, and sometimes basic justice. In the New England states, however, towns serve most city and county functions and are the most important units of local government. Then there are numerous special districts, including school districts, water districts, sewer and sanitation districts, transportation districts, and dozens

more. These districts are state authorized but voluntarily created by local officials and citizens. They often (but do not always) cross municipal lines, have
taxing authority, and exist for single or for very limited purposes. Because
they are voluntarily created, they may not be organized in all parts of a state.
They have emerged in the United States for three reasons: to remove certain
service functions from the overt politics of local governments; to "sidestep,"
or avoid, state-imposed tax limitations on cities; and to create economies of
scale in a service function, both in terms of operational efficiency and building a sufficient taxation base to operation economically (Foster 1997).

National-State Debates Continue

The political conflict regarding the federal health reform law, which mandates
that citizens not covered by an employer-sponsored plan or a public insurance
program must purchase health insurance by 2014, once again raises the continuing federalism debate between the founding constitutionalist Hamilton's
view of a strong national government and that of James Madison's for a more
limited federal government. This "split personality," revealed as early as the pre-
ratification *Federalist Papers*, "can be considered the root of the dualism that
became so characteristic of the American Constitution. Hamilton's and Madison's differing views about the character of the federal order largely account
for the Court's oscillation between federalism and nationalism" (Dietze 1999,
273). The true nature of the connective interaction between levels in the federation has been at the core of these concerns (e.g., see Bailey 2000).

National power, combined with respect for the states, has been the thrust
of federal development. In the famous post–Civil War case *Texas v. White*
(1869), Chief Justice Salmon P. Chase, while rejecting the right of secession,
reiterated the right of self-government by the states, "for without them there
could be no such political body as the United States, there can be no loss
of separate and independent autonomy." Other Supreme Court cases such
as *McCullough v. Maryland* (1819) and *Brown v. Board of Education* (1954),
where national power is asserted, demonstrate the interactive and tested and
retested nature of the federal system. National power is real but tempered
by levels of respect for the states. This holds true at administrative as well
as at policy levels. In *New York v. United States* (1992), the court ruled that
Congress could not commandeer state government officials to "enact and
enforce a [federal] regulatory program," and later it said that Congress could
not require local officials to conduct background checks on gun purchases in
Printz v. United States (1997). These rulings are evidence that both Madison
and Hamilton to some degree have held sway.

The story of IGR and its management dimension, IGM, thus tells a part of
the federal story that is less well understood. Generally, it has appeared below

the radar of political battles over federal powers vis-à-vis the states. Continuing cries for states' rights have truly masked the march of federal programming through the states and local governments. As Morton Grodzins (1966, 41) concludes in his study of interactions within the federal system, they are "found outside of the conflict-laden dockets of the courts. The national grant-in-aid programs are an example. They served the common purpose of nation and states and heavily relied on state cooperation in the task. . . . When the national government and the states collaborated to carry out these programs, they renewed old administrative bonds and formed new ones." Decades later Deil Wright (2003, 12–13) continued to echo this theme when he characterized the federal system as wrapped up in "contingent collaboration," which involved the entry of NGOs into the system and placed daunting expectations on state and local officials. He pointed out that these officials face resource restrictions that put a premium on the ability to forge consensus amid diversity, to network across organizational and jurisdictional boundaries, and to find creative approaches to resolving intergovernmental conflicts.

Key Learning Points

The US federal system has evolved in theory and operation to be one based on the legal division of powers among the levels of government (dual federalism) and on the operational crossing of the lines. The boundaries have never been strict, and as government has become more complex, it now not only is involved at all levels but also includes NGO executants. The federal idea has consequently become more complicated and overlapping. Thus, this volume is devoted to exploring how the boundaries are crossed, particularly at administrative levels.

An additional issue, based on overlapping principles, is that there are openings, cracks, and brick walls in the system. On the one hand, with regard to the latter, federal laws and court decisions—for example, in the arenas of civil rights, national security, and the flow of commerce between the states—are rather hard and fast and are not easily managed around. Generally they are rather strictly enforced. On the other hand, with many "cracks" in the system, there is room to maneuver around federal issues, particularly where national influence is regular and broadly defining but open to broad arenas of discretionary application as state and local governments, and more recently NGOs, put their stamp on programs.

In many basic ways, intergovernmental relations programs are in reality some amalgamation of federal framing, state boundary parameters, and local NGO application via intergovernmental management. For example, Neil Kraus (2013) demonstrates that a bottom-up approach to important concerns is taken in cities as the interests of all local citizens and groups are limited. He also emphasizes the connections that form the specific policies that affect programs like housing and schools. The actions of federal entities in Washington—Congress, the administration, and courts—generate the start rather than the end of this process. Federal grants, regulations, and other activities filter through the systems, looking like federal intent via state and local application. In this long chain of events, many hands and minds handle programs today; for example, vehicle emissions provisions regulations are put in the hands of state agencies, local governments, and NGO and private business contractors. These chains of operations place increased emphasis on the management of programs.

Practical Applications

As in the case of most arenas of management, intergovernmental management is an interactive process among government and NGO actors and program clients. IGM carries the legacy of jurisdictional responsibility—law and its interpretation—blended with organizational politics and interunit negotiations and understandings all mixed into the managerial process. It is not easy to combine framework concerns, interorganizational diplomacy, and knowledge-seeking and its application as managers try to accomplish something.

Nor is managing a simple formulaic undertaking where one size fits all. There are light years of knowledge and its application behind facilitating an interstate highway bridge over a river that connects two states or in establishing home-based rehabilitation programs for intellectually and developmentally disabled (I/DD) persons. They both involve heavy doses of interpretation, information, politics, and negotiations but over very substantively different concerns. No *formulaic* method can be pointed to and simply applied to these processes. Indeed, application normally involves trying out ways to address concerns in the face of common yet unique situations. Each represents a long chain of differentially applied applications.

Finally, these processes are both "open" and "closed" as national policy is filtered through state and local governments down the line. The further one gets from the source—for example, national law, standards, and regulations—the less we know about management as a process. The bridge goes well beyond the design, of course, and ultimately involves dozens (or hundreds) of construction industry contractors, inspectors, state highway engineers and examiners, public and private auditors, and many others. The local NGO agency that delivers federally funded I/DD services in and outside of their agency adds many hands to the program, some of which are publicly known but more are not. In the process, the policy or program is modified at the street level. In essence the program is not exactly what Congress says it is, but the sum of what happens all along the line and what is reported as IGM completes its cycle.

Conclusion

Governmental evolution in the United States has expanded the understanding of IGR and IGM. In his 1977 presidential address to the American Political Science Association, Samuel Beer (1978, 9) pointed to the emergence in the United States of meeting "new arenas of mutual influence among levels of government ... as the federal government has made vast new use of state and local governments and those governments in turn have asserted a new direct influence on the federal government." He concluded that operating federalism now comprises vertical bureaucratic hierarchies cutting across different levels of government, not to speak of the intergovernmental lobby of elected officials along the line that influences and operates programs. This regular inducement had the benefit of expanding professionalism at various levels by persons who simultaneously not merely operate branch offices of some central authority but also perform as "vehicles for carrying out programs of central governments and, at the same time, have taken increasingly active role as agents of representation before, and indeed, within those central governments" (19).

As a result, one must not begin the quest for solving the riddles of collaborative public management without understanding some basics about the American administrative system. A way to start is with reviewing Kettl's (2009) chapter "Managing Boundaries in American Administration." He underscores the importance of ever-changing boundaries related to mission, resources, capacity, responsibility, and accountability that, when subjected to today's interorganizational service networks, vastly complicate administration. The US system of federalism and political culture manifests these boundaries, and as such they define what organizations are responsible for doing and what powers and functions lay elsewhere. Kettl argues that "the basic dilemma of American public administration for the 21st century ... [is] devising new strategies to bring public administration in sync with the multi-organizational, multisector operating realities of today's government. It requires a 'collaborative, network-based approach'" (17). However, these realities conflict with the imperatives of American politics: symbolism, reorganization, and restructuring of systems. The *"boundaries that served us so well in the past can no longer solve either our administrative or political needs"* (17, emphasis added).

2 INTEGRATING THE FEDERAL SYSTEM THROUGH LAW AND POLITICS

The focus of this chapter is the first of the four themes that condition IGM—the idea that under the US federal system a pervasive, politically oriented legal system frames relations and connections in American federalism. This chapter takes a deeper look at how jurisdictional politics and legal systems emerged, particularly from federal-state and state-local perspectives. While pervasive over time, law and politics provide the earliest and in many ways the most familiar framework that, to a great degree, preceded any systematic analysis of intergovernmental relations, let alone intergovernmental management.

Most who follow IGR are quite familiar with the previously identified nexus of Dillon's Rule and home rule, a clear intersection of how legal doctrines and political forces intersect to formulate the management of IGR. One force is that, under the law, Dillon's Rule considerably restricts the policy and program roles and powers of local governments within a state. The other opens these strictures, as a result of the political process, to allow varying degrees of local government discretion over their affairs. To those who work in local government, the legal framework established by the states, and later by federal action, sets a context within which intergovernmental action is manifested (Krane 2003).

By the mid-nineteenth century, the legal position of state supremacy over local governments—municipal and others—was established. As identified briefly in chapter 1, what is commonly symbolized as Dillon's Rule was established after two Iowa court decisions in 1868. The first ruled that cities owe their existence to state legislatures (*Clinton v. Cedar Rapids and Missouri River Railroad*), and the second (*Merriam v. Moody's Executors*, 25 Iowa 163, 170 [1868])—made it clear that local inherent powers were quite limited. As Justice Dillon wrote in *Clinton v. Cedar Rapids and Missouri River Railroad*,

> In determining the question now made, it must be taken for settled law, that a municipal corporation possesses and can exercise the following powers and no others: First, those granted in express words; second, those necessarily implied or necessarily incident to

the powers expressly granted; third, those absolutely essential to the declared objects and purposes of the corporations—not simply convenient, but indispensable; fourth, any fair doubt as to the existence of a power is resolved by the courts against the corporation—against the existence of the power.

In later work on the law of municipal corporations, Judge Dillon (1911, as quoted in Zimmerman 1995) continued to make clear that municipalities, or any local government for that matter, possessed no particular rights, privileges, or powers. Also, the US Supreme Court recognized and upheld Dillon's Rule in *Atkins v. Kansas* (191 U.S. 207, 220–21 [1903]), ruling that local governments were creatures of their states and "may exert only such powers as are expressly granted to them, or such that may be necessarily implied from those granted . . . being subject only to the fundamental condition that the collective and individual rights of the people of the municipality shall not be destroyed." In practice, home rule varies from state to state, ranging from prohibition of any form of home rule to very liberal granting of local powers (Krane, Rigos, and Hill 2001).

Political forces in states have nevertheless facilitated notable measures of local control within the context of Dillon's Rule in different ways (Richardson 2011). Historically, the oldest and most familiar method is through municipal home rule, which allows cities to draft their own charters and identify local powers that, unless contravened by state legislatures, are free of state supervision. It gives qualifying local governments the right to make decisions without specific grants of authority on local matters and limits the power of the state to intervene in local matters. The home-rule doctrine was clearly a product of local-state politics and of the nineteenth-century movement by middle-class interests to recapture control from working-class political machines (Griffith and Adrian 1983, 41–42). Its aim was to "create an *imperium in imperio* for municipalities by making them a state within a state and to construct a strict division between state and local powers comparable to the notion of dual federalism" (Berman 2003, 71). In practice, Berman concludes, courts have found it difficult to determine what is local and what is of statewide concern, usually resolving uncertainties in the states' favor (72; also Zimmerman 1995, 27–28). Over time states have eroded local powers. For example, in 2017 the North Carolina State government removed local discretionary authority over regulating transgender restrooms, prohibiting local governments from enacting access protections (Associated Press 2017).

With the American manifestation of building on existing governments to form the nation-state by aggregation of smaller units, often counties (or minor nobility territories) that combined commercial cities into units could provide for a common defense and could protect and promote markets. Nation-state construction was closely linked with related aspects of modernity: industrialism, national markets, liberal representative democracy, and national public administration (Loughlin 2007, 387). Formal territorial division and organization evolved both on the basis of historic minor jurisdictions and later by administrative consolidation. Most important, as multiple units are created and operate with respect to one another, political decisions and agreements lead to constitutional principles and laws that set the rules that frame governmental structures and operations (Ostrom 1985). Thus, to understand IGM one must build on a base of law and the politics that framed the laws, and that is the focus of this chapter.

The legal base of the American tradition obviously emanates from the Constitution and law. For example, the powers of the respective governments are a clear starting point. Then politics enters the picture, as laws are made and enforced. Compounding this story for the United States is the long-standing belief that politics, at least formally, should be removed from the administration of government. This perhaps misunderstood idea that politics and management are separate functions is also a critical notion for misunderstanding IGM. In part as a reaction to problems emanating from corruption and from what were considered inefficient practices and operations when compared to those of business, the "progressive" orientation in the early twentieth century attempted to remove administrative functions—at federal, state, and local levels—from partisan control. Leonard White's (1958) final volume on administrative history, covering the progressive era reforms thematically, makes the point that administration was to be freed from control by politicians. These reforms contributed mightily to the professionalism of administration, bringing in technical and management specialists in practice, but as will be demonstrated, political actors did not remove politics in administration. Politics have become integral components of IGM.

The issue of interaction between units today, along with the integral role of law and politics, is more or less clearly understood compared to the early days of the US federation. For example, recently the Indiana state legislature worked on a plan to repair its unemployment insurance system, which included a $2 billion debt to the federal government and interest payments on that debt, and to make program adjustments to avoid further deficits. Meanwhile, the legislature is dealing with another plan to broaden the way charter schools are formed in the state, to designate public transportation money for charter schools, and to open a public funding line for charter schools that is supported by private gifts and state and federal grants (Associated Press 2011). Finally, the legislature is working on several provisions to strengthen the regulations and reporting requirements regarding general "township assistance" relief payments, as Indiana was one of the last states to administer this program locally under state supervision.

Each of these issues obviously raises the specter of politics as well as law. The unemployment fund issue involves higher employer payments and reduced benefits, thus bringing in state employers and unions as well as others. The charter school issue draws, among others, advocates of school reform versus those who wish to fight them and see them as a force that erodes existing public schools. The township issue pits the 1,008 township trustees and their three-member boards, plus those political interests that fear the costs of the state's assumption of general assistance, against those government leaders—including the governor—who wish to streamline local government by consolidation and efficiency moves. This "slice of legal and political life" demonstrates that despite changes toward governance, law and politics in some combination very much remain in IGR.

This chapter focuses on the developmental features of laws and politics whereas chapter 3 concentrates on their administrative legacies. Beginning with a brief examination of the historical background of IGR that reinforces the idea of independent jurisdictions, this chapter then introduces a synopsis of IGR practice in the early period. Next is an explication of the "national idea" that provided the pre- and post–Civil War beginnings of the United States as an integral state. A discussion follows about the building of state-local relations, from legal control to home rule, and the importance of political forces as integral to the practice of IGR. Finally, "from commission to hierarchy" introduces the idea that administrative agencies play frontline roles in IGR and IGM. These historical developments set the IGR tones that remain and in practice fold into IGM.

Historical Antecedents

Legal supremacy over minor civil divisions evolved over time and was gradually integrated into the nation-state. The situation of cities becoming part of state governments illustrates this legacy. In medieval and Renaissance England, as well as most of Europe, a city was created by the king or some other nobleman through granting a charter that spelled out the rights and privileges of the city and its residents. Although what the king granted could be taken away, the special status and rights and privileges were politically hard to remove once granted. This undoubtedly created some tensions between cities and their creators. Chartered cities were gradually recognized by the king's court as corporations, meaning that they were accepted as having a permanent existence independent of city officials or residents. By law they were considered artificial persons and possessed their own rights, privileges, and duties, including the right to sue and be sued; and by the fourteenth century, these concepts were accepted principles. Later charters became more definite in form, establishing villages, boroughs, and cities as both corporate and political bodies; specifying local powers; and outlining some organizational structure.

The US pattern varied somewhat in that local governments were chartered not by kings but by colonial governors or viceroys who acted in the name of their sovereigns both in the case of New Spain and in what would become the original thirteen British colonies. In the latter situation, royal governors granted the charters, which did not become permanently incorporated units until independence from Britain. Meanwhile, in New England, in the town of New York, and in other places, the township or county occupied a different position. Lacking charters, they existed for carrying out policies established by the colonial governments. This became, then, the legacy of county government. Upon independence, the Articles of Confederation and the federal Constitution automatically gave the states rather than the national government residual powers over local government. In the following period, legally and politically legislative bodies were ascendant. As Ernest Griffith and Charles Adrian (1983, 34) describe,

> The colonial governors had been generally viewed as agents for the King, and hence with suspicion and hostility. The American executive went into a deep eclipse from which it did not emerge for many decades. At the same time, however, the legislative branch emerged as a heroic institution. Having been locally elected, its members were viewed as representative of popular opinion and hence compatible with the spirit of the Revolution. From the time when the royal or proprietary governors fell into disfavor until the newly created states began to select their own, the legislative bodies assumed control over executive functions, including control over municipal corporations. A power that had always rested in the executive, that of creating municipalities and determining their powers, had passed to the legislatures for the first time. Just as medieval townsmen had jealously guarded their special privileges, so did the legislatures now guard their right to control the structure and powers of municipalities.

Of course, this legislative power refers to guidance over all local governments. Legislative powers that deal in policy and program frameworks with the local and federal government were also part of the legislative domain.

The other break with English historical tradition has to do with the American system of elected administrators (e.g., clerks, treasurers) and the "hierarchical" legal independence of higher-level officials. While there was notable administrative borrowing from the English Crown (Carpenter 2005, 46), there were differences. As Frank Goodnow (1900, 100) explains, the English system retained many aspects that date back to when the Crown was more powerful than Parliament and when complete administrative independence of executive officers had not developed. The center—that is, the Crown officials—and local officials were both Crown appointees. In America the people abandoned these principles, basing their governments on popular control. Thus, elected officers and frequent elections became the pattern, at first by legislatures but later in popular elections, at both state and local levels.

This clearly changed the nature of what would now be called intergovernmental supervision. As Goodnow (1900) pointed out earlier, direct supervision became difficult. The control had to be found in the power of the legislature to regulate in detail the duties of officers entrusted with the execution of the law. The courts had to be trusted, on the application, either of individuals whose rights were violated, or of officers who by express terms of statute were given power to make such applications themselves, to force obedience to this detailed legislation (101).

Later, the same could be said of federal "supervision" of state government officials. The control to be found in this power of detailed legislation, concludes Goodnow (103), was exercised by a body that was "confessedly political" and "not possessed of large administrative knowledge" and whose main purpose was to express the "will of the people by whom it was elected."

Another feature of the first federation is the ability of American states under some circumstances to take a different course in administering federal programs or to operationally undermine federal expectations. It is also an important aspect of IGR and IGM. Identified as "uncooperative federalism" by Jessica Bulman-Pozen and Heather Gerken (2009), it occurs when states (and by implication local governments) refuse to enforce certain provisions of a federal act when implementing federal law and instead use their powers to urge federal authorities to take a new position or when states relying on federal funds create programs that erode the foundations of the policies they are being asked to carry out. For example, by mid-2014 a dozen states informed the federal Justice Department that they would not or could not comply with the Prison Rape Elimination Act, jeopardizing up to 5 percent of their federal grant funds. The respective governors argued that compliance is too expensive and is too bureaucratically cumbersome (*Bloomington Herald Times* 2014). Over the years this matter has become contentious as issues of noncompliance, commandeering of state actions, and selective enforcement and implementation have become regular features of intergovernmental affairs at the federal, state, local, and external agent levels while the system of IGR and IGM has become denser. Finding a balance between hewing to federal purpose and encouraging a marketplace of ideas within the "administrative safeguards of federalism" can be a challenge, one that emanates from such legal and political interactions (Grodzins 1966; Bulman-Pozen and Gerken 2009, 1309).

Federalism additionally allows for a type of devolution where subnational governmental bodies can use local majorities to face national policies that they feel are not progressive. These progressive nonfederal actions have been manifested recently at the local level by their legislated actions in increasing voter registration and access, minority and female employment practices, and minimum wages; in approving medical and recreational marijuana use; and in resisting state strict gun control (Rosen 2016, 5). From the perspective of federalism, people in majority positions in state and local governments but who constitute national-level minorities can be empowered to push their more progressive ideas in a Jeffersonian small polity sense. Identified as Progressive Federalism, national minorities constitute local majorities and act on their cases locally (or by state) in the decentralized system. As identified by Heather Gerken (2012, 41),

> Federalism and localism, in contrast, depend on—even glory in—the idea of minority rule. Neither theory requires you to like every policy passed at the local or state level any more than a nationalist has to agree on the assumption that decentralization can produce a healthier democracy in the long term. Ours is a world in which decision-making bodies of every sort (school committees, juries, city councils) are dominated by groups of every sort (Italians and Irish, Catholics and Jews, Greens and libertarians). We don't worry about this representational kaleidoscope—let alone condemn it as "segregated"—merely because one group or another is taking its turn standing in for the whole. Perhaps we shouldn't worry when it is a racial minority group in that position.

Gerken concludes that history suggests a more "muscular" account of what a democracy can do for minorities, giving politics an important role in overall social integration, and enhances minority rights in policy agenda setting in the long term. Moreover, subsequent analysis in this volume underscores the role of operational localism at administrative stages.

Early Federal-State Relations

During George Washington's first term as president, the federal assumption of state war debts identified in chapter 1 was not the first IGR program. One program under the Articles of Confederation actually preceded the federal Constitution. Congress passed the Northwest Ordinances of 1785 and 1787 after the original states ceded their outlying and excess lands to the Confederation, and a system was set up for operating the new territories and ultimately creating new states. The 1785 legislation included the well-known surveying plan that divided the lands into six-mile-square townships, which were then divided into thirty-six sections. Disposition of the lands included a requirement for the sale of one lot per township, with section 16 put aside "for the maintenance of public schools." The program set the tone for many federal land grants during the nineteenth century, using "the superior resources of the central government to initiate and support national programs, largely administered by the political subdivisions" (Graves 1964, 481; see also Onuf 1997).

The ordinance established the precedent for grants to involve reciprocal action on the part of the state and federal governments. Initially the federal government took a direct interest in operating the future states (Ohio, Indiana, Michigan, Wisconsin, and part of Illinois). It administered the territories with federally ensured rights and an elected territorial legislature that worked with the federally appointed governor until a defined population level was reached and statehood was achieved. This represented "a high-water mark for the new nation's mostly dysfunctional central government" (Kluger 2007, 197).

With regard to the grants, Elazar (1962, 32–33) concludes that two IGR precedents were set. First, indemnification lifted the grants out of the gift to the locality category and made it a state grant. The first Ohio Territory leveraged control of the distribution of the grant, and that important precedent led to channeling virtually all funds for local purposes through the states. Second, the move for statehood in the Northwest Territories embodied a desire for both self-government and better access to national councils—that is, "to send representatives to Washington who could speak with the authority and power necessary to back up local desires and actions" (133).

Over the nineteenth century a series of land grants followed that stimulated and financed or partially financed a host of state and local programs. The grants to the states of federal land—that is, ceding lands that could be sold for state financing of the intended purposes—were considered a constitutional means of avoiding federal government interference in the reserved powers of the states. Indeed, until after the Civil War several presidents followed Thomas Jefferson's lead, opposing direct grants until the Constitution could be amended to fund the development of "rivers, canals, roads, arts, manufactures, education, and other great objects within each State" (from the second inaugural address, March 4, 1805, in Larson 1984, 209). Presidential vetoes or veto threats followed many congressional enactments, including those invoked by Madison, Andrew Jackson, James Polk, Franklin Pierce, and James Buchanan. Pierce's veto, subsequently upheld, of a bill to provide grants to the states for supporting mental hospitals stated that "the federal government's purpose was not to dispense charities catering to the indigent whose provision is now confined to the communities to which they belong" (Manning 1962, 46).

Land grants were developed for various purposes and were of different types. One went to the states for education, others for internal improvements and welfare programs, including elementary and higher education, public works, public buildings, river and harbor improvements, public institutions, and veterans' benefits (e.g., Pessen 1969). They were designed to support vital public services and were precursors to contemporary monetary grants-in-aid. Another approach involved land grants for internal improvements and education that went through the states but were then passed to private entities for roads, canals, and railroads and for educational academies and colleges. In these situations the states administered the land sales and the distribution of funds. Finally, a third category did not directly involve the states while disposing of the public domain, which included various mineral and homestead claims, tree-culture laws, grants to railroads situated outside of state boundaries, and some town grants in pre-statehood territories (Elazar 1962, 133–34).

Setting the tone for later years, IGR in the law was manifested from an early period. It materialized through actions taken by the federal and state governments. A lengthy quote by Morton Grodzins (1966, 22) identifies many notable actions:

> The adjustment period assumed an experimental approach toward the coordination of national and state statutes. From the very beginning, Congress left the administration of national elections to the states. In 1790 it authorized federal collectors to assist in the enforcement of state quarantine laws—despite some objections that this form of personnel assistance was an unconstitutional interference with states' rights. The licenses of state auctioneers were accepted as a qualification for federal auctioneers. Lacking jails, the national government entered into contracts with the states to use state jails for federal prisoners at the rate of 50 cents a month per prisoner plus cost of maintenance. National officers were authorized to use state courts in suits to collect fines or forfeitures. National jurors were to be selected in the manner employed in each state to select its own jurors. State laws were adopted as the basis of rules of decision in common law trials. In 1792 the powers of United States marshals were prescribed to include the same powers in executing national laws as the state sheriffs possessed in executing state laws.
>
> From 1789 to 1800 the state government went through a series of adjustments to bring their laws into conformity with the Constitution and the national laws enacted in pursuance of it. Laws regarding coinage, legal tender, admiralty, naturalization, and Indian affairs were amended or repealed. But few men in either national or state governments had clear ideas of how the working relationship should be arranged, and the national government was not yet able to carry out its new powers thoroughly. As a result, in the first few years of the new government, the states performed tasks which violated the theory of the new Constitution. Nor did the busy national government insist on the letter of the law. True, a federal circuit court declared a Rhode Island state law invalid; and Virginia and Connecticut laws conflicting with provisions of the Treaty of 1783 were voided. These were exceptions, however, and the states, for a while, ran up an impressive list of violations.

Grodzins reports that Congress passed laws prescribing cooperation in several areas—for example, between state-licensed harbor pilots and federal customs officers. States followed through by publishing national laws and requiring their officers to carry out national laws.

Another important historical precedent was the establishment of congressionally authorized joint-stock companies to create banks and internal works projects like railroads and canals. In effect, the company was a corporation designed to develop a specific project that was financed by stock purchased by the federal government, one or more states, affected municipalities, and private investors. Control was vested in a board of directors, with voting power based in its articles of incorporation. The federal and state governments proved to be the most influential of the board members. In this way the federal government could supply funds, technical assistance, and equipment to the states for their projects while maintaining a sufficient measure of control over the plans, construction, and use of the improvement without violating what was then understood to be the strict construction of the Constitution (Elazar 1962, 34). Not only was the joint-stock company an early example of federal-state working interaction, it must be considered a precursor to the various contractual and network arrangements discussed in relation to the government partners of the IGR era.

Personnel operations constitute a final example of early connections. In 1802 Congress established the US Army Corps of Engineers and a school of engineering at West Point, New York, the first (and virtually only) source of the country's civil engineers. Lacking private counterparts at the time, the corps became deeply involved in internal improvements, working with the states on projects. In 1824 Congress enacted the General Survey Act, which made official such arrangements and authorized the president to use military and civil engineers for surveys, plans, and estimates for routes, roads, and canals of national importance necessary for commercial, military, or postal use. The act supported the national public improvement program, and before it was repealed in 1838 (because of inattention to military priorities), the corps had created what amounted to a national master plan for roads, canals, and railroads. The availability of the engineers also stimulated state and local activity. By 1838, Elazar (1962, 29) concludes, "the pattern for intergovernmental cooperation was already set and the idea had proved its worth in a national system of communications that was capped by 1,899 miles of railroad, almost all of which had been constructed with the aid of the Army Engineers." In addition, this technical assistance and involvement of the engineers introduced the idea of employing professionally trained expertise in IGR/IGM programs, and this force became increasingly important as it moved into its later phases.

Finally, there was federal support for state militias. Beginning in 1805 Congress appropriated $200,000 to the states to arm and equip their militias. It imposed no conditions of supervision until 1856 when it enacted troop

ratios based on congressional representation. The Dick Act of 1903, or Efficiency of Militia Bill, provided for the standardization of arms and equipment and the inspection of state performance. Nevertheless, as Grodzins
(1966, 37) observes, "While the national government could advise, make
regulations, and threaten to withhold pay, the state governments retained
administration and command."

From the earliest days of the country, federal administrators actively
wielded broad statutory authority, promulgated general rules, and adju-
dicated cases within congressional oversight and direction, particularly on
state building (Mashaw 2006, 1256). One contemporary historian's support
for recognizing the nuances of these connections is in a study of the early role
of the federal government. Brian Balogh's *A Government Out of Sight: The
Mystery of National Authority in Nineteenth-Century America* (2009) demonstrates that the United States governed *differently* but less visibly than other
developing bureaucratic states, noting that the United States had a national
government that was capable of mobilizing comparable resources in the private and voluntary sectors. This ability often yielded more impressive results
than the use of unilateral state power. Other than the postal system, few federal government functions penetrated deeply into the country because the
vision of the early executive officials left little room for powerful, centralized
administrative structures but left plenty of room for states and local governments to mingle public and private interests into mixed efforts. To Balogh
these practices were in great part due to the suspicions of the founding fathers
of a traditional, active, and powerful centralized national government. These
views prevailed in federal efforts to avoid direct taxation, regulate individual behavior, or erect far-reaching hierarchical organizations to administer
national programs. Meanwhile, the federal government was purchasing and

BOX 2.1

- Although appointed administrators were usually politically tied to elected
  executives—president, governors, mayors—they also brought from England
  principles of loyalty to the law. In many ways, law and politics are manifested
  side by side.
- While originally considered to be "agents" of higher-level executives, the American system of multiple elected executives (clerks, treasurers, auditors) thus
  attenuated hierarchical supervision and reinforced the independence of office.
- Land grants to the states for various purposes (e.g., schools, internal improvements, social welfare) led the way to linking governments of all levels. Accompanying requirements departed from uniting state traditions of central directive
  operations at regional and local levels, ushering in federal considerations as well.
- The creation of government–private sector joint-stock companies set the original tone for public-private financing and operation, which was followed later
  by the involvement of nongovernmental charitable organizations.

distributing land, supporting infrastructure provision, and otherwise sub-venting funds to state and local governments. For Balogh the federal government's role was defined as that of an "enabling state" (376).

The Rise of the National Idea

Before the Civil War, as the federal government was reluctant to act as a direct engine of policy and program, non-enumerated areas notwithstanding, an active national government along the lines of Alexander Hamilton's ideas ultimately prevailed. The leading exponent of this view was Daniel Webster, who argued that the general government is not a compact among states, nor is it established by the states but by "the people of the United States in the aggregate" (quoted in Beer 1993, 9). Webster did perceive the prospect of increasing interdependence and recognized that it could fully realize its promise of wealth and power only with the assistance of the federal government toward his grand objective, "the consolidation of the Union" (Beer 1993, 11). In the words of Webster, "Let us develop the resources of our land, call forth its powers, build up its institutions, and see whether we also, in our day and generation, may not perform something worthy to be remembered" (Beer 1993, 13).

The national idea began in a small way in the 1830s when surplus federal funds were distributed to the states, despite doubts concerning the constitutionality of collecting money and turning it over to the states. After Hamilton's earlier war-debt settlement for the states, it was the first real intergovernmental instance of cash payments to the states, a precursor to today's unconditional grants. (Grants for specific programs did not begin until later in the nineteenth century.) The surplus grants were short lived, getting caught up in the economic panics later in the 1830s and in the elimination of the Second Bank of the United States. Moreover, an extension of the program in 1833 was pocket vetoed by President Jackson (Heidler and Heidler 2003, 256).

During the Civil War the national idea was set in motion in several notable ways. In addition to the Emancipation Proclamation, which freed slaves in the rebelling states in 1863, in 1862 Congress passed the Homestead Act, which granted plots of public land to families who settled and worked on them, as a means of promoting migration and crop expansion and of boosting exports. The Pacific Railway Act authorized the Union Pacific Railroad to build west from Nebraska and meet the Central Pacific Railroad, coming east from California, to bridge the continent (Ferguson 2004, 232). The Morrill Land-Grant College Act approved the sale of public lands to set up agricultural and mechanic arts universities in the states. In turn, university staffs were expected to work with state and local officials. This continuing program of conditional grants was the first of many to follow over the next 150 years. The federal government also returned to the banking field. After negotiating with eastern bankers, a series of laws provided for the granting of federal charters, including the right to issue currency, to banks holding specified amounts of bonds. A tax of ten cents on each dollar effectively ended the ability of state-chartered banks to print money.

The times required bolder action. As the foremost historian of Reconstruction, Eric Foner (1988, 23) concludes,

> In their unprecedented expansion of federal power and their effort to impose organization upon a decentralized economy and fragmented polity, these measures reflected what might be called the birth of the modern American state. On the eve of the Civil War, the federal government was "in a state of impotence," its conception of its duties little changed since the days of Washington and Jefferson. Most functions of government were handled at the state and local level; one could live out one's life without ever encountering an official representative of national authority. But the exigencies of war created, as Sen. George S. Boutwell later put it, a "new government," with a greatly expanded income, bureaucracy, and set of responsibilities.

Three post–Civil War constitutional amendments expanded national power by eliminating involuntary servitude, prohibiting types of voting restrictions in all elections, and, most important in the Fourteenth Amendment, by tying the Bill of Rights to the actions of the states (and local governments) for the first time. Significant with regard to IGR/IGM is the overall impact of the due process and equal protection clauses of the Fourteenth Amendment. It has many "nationalizing" effects—in particular, protections against harmful state and local actions, covering the entire Bill of Rights. By the 1920s the Supreme Court began to interpret broadly in such areas as freedom of speech, press, religion, and assembly, and in recent years it has delved into a whole range of civil rights. The Fourteenth Amendment was made applicable to all levels of government, creating "to all intents and purposes a single (and nationalized) system of rights" (Graves 1964, 102). From this point on, the federal government became a more direct actor, often invoking the constitutional changes that brought about the core of national power.

The first Morrill Act of 1862 (one followed in 1890), as it developed over the years, required that the continuing appropriation from land investment fulfill four purposes: higher education in non–liberal arts areas, research on agricultural problems (later expanded) at research stations, dissemination of basic information to people through the work of the Agricultural Extension Service, and vocational training on agricultural problems, home economics, and industrial subjects, including distributive education (see Graves 1964, 490–506). The act began grant requirements to serve national purposes, including annual reporting, limits on certain types of expenditures, repayment if certain actions were not taken, and stipulated curriculum requirements. These heretofore unfamiliar grant provisions, however, should not obscure "the binding character of the entire land-grant measure on the states," mostly enforced by the courts, "in a day before elaborate administrative procedures of the twentieth century" (Elazar 1962, 225). Only when court enforcement was too cumbersome were provisions for administrative enforcement employed.

Along with growth in the economy and post–Civil War constitutional support for a greater federal government role in the economy came the gradual expansion of intergovernmental programs. In 1913 the federal government could finance subsequent programs and thereby ride on the resource advantage of the Sixteenth Amendment, which authorized federal income taxation. In the next year the Smith-Lever Act established continuing state aid to support the county agent program, which previously had been funded locally, with state dollar–match provisions. It ushered in, as will be demonstrated, a national system of conditional and often federal-state programs financed on a shared basis—for example, the Federal Road Aid Act of 1916 and the Smith-Hughes National Vocational Education Act of 1917.

These changes impacted the intergovernmental system in ways that, to date, have never been eliminated. The laws triggered the need for oversight and administrative procedures that carried notably beyond enforcement in the courts to the rudiments of interactive, intensely collaborative IGR. As Grodzins (1966, 37) concludes,

> The historical development of the grant system displays changes in attitude toward the administration of the grant as well as changes in the source, size, and function of the grant funds. In the early years, grants were largesse—primarily in the form of land, cash based on land sales, and Treasury surpluses—from the national government to the states. The national government attached general, simple, and generous conditions to those early grants, sometimes designating the broad purposes for which they were to be used, but left the states almost complete freedom in disposing of their proceeds. Beginning with the first Morrill Act, however, Congress took care to write into the grant enactments an increasing number of administrative prescriptions. These prescriptions assumed and encouraged cooperation between the national government and state governments. The total effect of the growth pattern of grants was to provide a new and important field of collaboration.

The importance of these trends is that despite many conditions, in almost no situation did the federal government assume direct control of programs inasmuch as members of Congress articulated fears of national control and opted continuously for state administration through the inducement of funds to maintain programs and standards. In effect, state administration constituted the only reasonable force of program control. In later years, when the federal government did assume levels of program responsibility in the 1930s for new programs (e.g., unemployment and income maintenance), it opted to work through the states, leaving direct federal programs such as the postal service and veterans' affairs as exceptions rather than the rule. The interactive relationship became the domestic intergovernmental program norm.

State-Local IGR: From Dillon's Rule to Home Rule

State governments are involved in four important legal arenas: as constituent units within the federal government and their ability to carry out legally determined programs; as enablers and operators of its own programs, particularly those reserved and virtually state-run operations (e.g., vehicle licensure); as partners with other states through interstate compacts; and as overseers of local governments in their states. As indicated at the start of this chapter, the latter function takes the greatest focus here. Whereas the largest number of governments are local, they are under their state legal codes, making law-based IGR/IGM a highly important function within the states. Thus, local governments, while representatives of their communities, are also "subjects" of their states. This legal relationship is usually depicted as unitary rather than federal (Briffault 1994, 1335–44).

The evolution of state government over the past two centuries has two important historical strands that help to understand IGR/IGM—its professional and administrative development and the gradual state control of local governments. The first, or professional development, is more indirect. Over the nineteenth century the national government provided promotional and support services, as Skowronek (1982, 23) indicates, for the states "and left the substantive tasks of governing to these regional units. This broad diffusion of power among the localities was the organizational feature of early American government most clearly responsible for the distinctive sense of statelessness in our political culture." Second, during the nineteenth century, state governments did commence legal control over local governments and went beyond the previously identified court enforcement to a more professionalized supervision of local government. Teaford's study of evolving state governments (2002, 7) concludes,

> As policymakers curbed the authority of local, partisan amateurs and moved responsibility up the governmental ladder to state capitals, they greatly expanded the role of the state. This shift from delegation to control was a notable theme in the history of twentieth-century

state government. In the nineteenth century, state legislatures authorized townships, counties, cities, school districts, business corporations, and trustees of educational and charitable institutions to take
action and exercised little supervision or control. In the twentieth
century, state governments increasingly intervened and often took
direct charge. Local road supervisors, township assessors, one-room-
school districts, and justices of the peace untutored in the law were
no longer thought adequate, and the states transferred the construction and maintenance of highways to professionals in state highway
departments, assumed a larger share of the responsibility for levying
and collecting taxes, shouldered a growing portion of school expenses
while also imposing professional educational standards on local districts, and fixed higher professional standards for local jurists.

Over the years states continued their growth and supervision patterns but
were accused of having antiquated constitutions and legal systems, amateur
legislatures, and limited gubernatorial powers and controls over administration. As a result, from about 1960 to 1980, a series of legislative and gubernatorial reforms, along with administrative professionalism, were introduced in
the states (Walker 2000, 264–65).

State control over local governments is a fundamental aspect of integrating the US federal system. It can be understood as both political and legal
in the most profound intergovernmental sense. The political developments
are best captured by David Berman (2003, 54–60). In brief, after independence from Britain, control over charters shifted, as mentioned, to state
legislatures. With ultimate court approval, legislatures abandoned the idea
that charters were inviolable contracts and came to regard them as statutes,
amenable to political will; that is, they could be amended with the tides of
the legislative process. Gradually, an attempt to democratize local charters,
responding to local antielite forces, had the effect of bolstering the authority of the states over local government and gradually transformed municipal
charters into instruments of state policies. In effect, this legally eroded the
earlier tradition of local self-government. Meanwhile, states created counties, which, unlike cities and being creatures of their states, had no such
independent standing.

Increasing urbanization also contributed to state control over cities. State
legislative doubts about the ability of local officials to provide usable streets,
sanitation facilities, adequate water supplies, and competent fire and police
services or to head off epidemics—coupled with doubts about the ability of
hordes of immigrants to govern themselves—reinforced state intervention.
In this time as well, concern regarding corruption in city governments ushered in the establishment of state commissions to operate certain programs
and the beginning of more detailed state requirements. This development, in

turn, led to large numbers of special bills for cities, some politically successful and some not. Also, these special bills became a means of building a voter following for state legislators.

City issues in the 1860s and 1870s then began to divide the parties, making them ever more political. State intervention in some cases involved taking over certain services—for example, police forces—and turning them over to a commission. In effect, state legislatures became supra-city councils, regularly taking away local powers, altering local structures and procedures, and undermining local decisions. They even used their powers to pass "ripper legislation" that gave states the power to appoint and remove municipal officials and dictate pay schedules. In the latter part of the nineteenth century, states followed Michigan's 1850 lead and did away with special legislation but got around this obstacle by classifying cities, normally by population size. Meanwhile, state control of local government was accepted as "the *ultra vires* rule on local governments; for example, a political subdivision could exercise only the powers granted to it, and these powers were to be interpreted narrowly by the courts" (Zimmerman 1995, 4). This ushered in the Dillon's Rule–home rule era identified at the beginning of this chapter.

Another method of state-local legal relations identified by Joseph Zimmerman (1995, 29–34) includes the state's devolution of powers under city charters or by assignment to other local governments, superseding state powers in some cases, as extensions of Dillon's Rule. The problem with this approach is that it does not remove conflicts between governments over the states' exercising their police powers in, for example, public health, safety, traffic regulation, and many other areas. The courts have generally settled disputes in the states' favor. Advisory opinions by state attorneys general or other state officials such as auditors or commissioners of education or counsels for various administrative departments have, in effect, broadened Dillon's Rule. These opinions normally hew closely to related court opinions, but they often have the effect of narrowing local powers. Most important, despite home rule, state legislatures retain plenary power over local governments through the enactment of general laws.

In this regard, David Berman (2003, 76) captures the current practice of state legislation regarding home rule:

> All in all, there are few practical barriers to state intervention into what one might consider local affairs. On the average, about one-fifth of the hundreds of measures introduced yearly in state legislatures significantly affect local governments. State laws extend to several aspects of local governmental operations. Some determine the general level of local authority and the types of governmental structures that local governments can adopt. Other types of state laws concern incorporation, annexation, consolidation, and intergovernmental

service agreements. In recent years, states have also passed a great deal of legislation relating to local governments' finances and personnel management. State laws often set debt limits, mandate public budget hearings, require a referendum for bond issues, and outline property-assessment methods. Most local governments must abide by state laws requiring employee training and workers' compensation. Among the most common types of regulations affecting local governments are open-records and open-meeting requirements. The latter have been particularly controversial, leading to charges that particular laws hamstring local officials and their staffs in doing their work and create unreasonable criminal offenses.

These laws form the basis for state mandates, which are more voluminous than the more visible federal mandates (although some are federal mandates that are passed on) that come in the form of statutes, executive orders, and administrative regulations. Many of these federal mandates are unfunded and, of course, create performance standards. As a state official from North Carolina once related to the author, "The feds do it to us and we complain about their encroachment on state government, and we, in turn, do it to the local governments a lot more. And when their officials complain about state control, we turn a deaf ear."

Systematic empirical research on state-local relations by Ann Bowman and Richard Kearney (2014) reveals a mixed picture of the Dillon's Rule–home rule issue. State restrictions on local governments include various prohibitions on local actions, revenue source restrictions, mandated service standards, preemptions of constraints on local actions, and cost-share shifting. States use the following tools to empower local governments: arranging authorizations to take actions, adopting programs that add appropriations for localities, repealing prior mandates or expenditure requirements, and lifting revenue restrictions. Overall the two-year study reveals a picture of states acting "sometimes in a manner that expands local power, other times in ways that diminish local power" (15). These issues and concerns are continuing forces that link national, state, and local politics along with the politics of local political parties. By extension, these forces also combine into national parties, contesting elections with expanded franchises (Skowronek 1982).

The Politics of IGR/IGM

Political forces are of course implicit in practically the entire development of IGR/IGM and federalism. Legislative and judicial decisions impact government connections, as do many actions of executives. Indeed, the analysis to this point, including the overview of federalism in chapter 1, reveals primary political overtones within intergovernmental affairs. This is not the place to examine the entire scheme of such politics; that task is better left to dedicated works on the political dimension (e.g., Conlan, Posner, and Beam 2014; Posner 1998; Mossberger 2000).

In an era when political parties have considerably weakened in organization and control, it is easy to forget their influence on the US system. Political power was considerable through the nineteenth century, as parties managed the nominations process for federal, state, and local offices. Frequent and regular elections kept the parties highly energetic and enthusiastic. From an administrative standpoint, from the Andrew Jackson period through the early twentieth century, parties had a lock on the staffing and functioning of the administrative agencies, as "administrative staffing through patronage was complimentary to the intensified electoral activities of the new parties. The opportunity to control the allocation of public offices inspired party cadres and allowed national and state party brokers to offer local loyalists influence over appointments allocated from their levels of government" (Skocpol 1995, 22). As party appointees settled in office, they had the effect of bringing together the branches and levels of government. While it is well known that party roots sank deeply into neighborhoods, they also spanned jurisdictional boundaries in a facilitative rather than a hierarchical fashion. The result was "they successfully linked local to state politicians and kept state politicians in touch with one another and with whatever national officeholders their party might have" (23). This situation led foreign observers like James Bryce (1941 [1895], 5) to conclude at the time that in "America the great moving forces are the parties. The government counts for less than in Europe, the parties count for more."

It is nevertheless important to identify the range of key actors and components of the politics of IGR as they impact the system. Paul Posner (1998, 20–26) points to ten important aspects of policy-making in his study of federal unfunded mandates: (1) the difficulty of program enactment in the US multiple-veto pluralistic system; (2) the presence of interest groups that generally represent particular interests, sometimes involving a small number of persons; (3) a party system whose power base is at the state and local levels, where the parties have a profound influence in selecting federal officials; (4) an organizational presence since the late nineteenth century of state and local government interest groups in Washington, bringing a major decentralizing influence on the design and administration of federal programs; (5) the Supreme Court's long-standing view that state and local governments should rely on the political process to protect their interests; (6) the reality of political forces in Congress that maintain measures of restraint with regard to state and local governments; (7) a congressional propensity to protect states in federal legislation, particularly in carrying out programs; (8) the growing propensity of legislators to listen to and act on ideas and program choices proposed by influential experts and policy entrepreneurs, particularly solutions based on the shared values of broad groups of experts; (9) the shift of legislators themselves over time from party loyalists to independent policy brokers as they search for new issues to highlight their visibility to interest groups and the media; and (10) the growth and concentration of media in Washington (and to some extent in state capitols), giving policy makers vehicles to reach the public independent of parties and groups. These political forces, Posner concludes, constitute important components of intergovernmental politics that facilitate growth in the system, initially through fostering grants but later through introducing regulations and other forms and instruments. They are applicable to a broad range of concerns.

One important addition to this list is the impact of administrators themselves in the political mix, particularly at program design and implementation stages. To some notable degree these actions are highlighted in Daniel Carpenter's (2001, 4) historical study as he identifies bureaucratic autonomy: "Bureaucrats take actions consistent with their own wishes, actions to which politicians and organized interests defer even though they would prefer that other actions (or no action at all) be taken. Short of bureaucrats' wishes, their actions can constitute leverage, based on their reputation for expertise, efficiency, or moral protection and a uniquely diverse complex of ties to organized groups, the media, and with political actors." Carpenter found the power of bureau officials lay in the multiplicity of their ties to political organizations. Multiple networks did not refract power. "They rather reduced the dependence of agencies on any one group, putting the agency in the role of broker among numerous interests seeking access to the state" (363). In this respect, with regard to IGR and IGM, federal administrators are able to build powerful local constituencies that protect new programs and regulations and advocate for increased funding or expanded regulatory power (Johnson 2010, 67). Administration is indeed a political as well as a legal-technical process, bestowed by statutes (Mashaw 2012, 291).

Most important, these largely political forces contribute most to the enablement and maintenance of intergovernmental programs. In subsequent analysis the administrative aspects of IGR become the focus, but they also carry important political dimensions. They involve the politics of program execution, or those forces that begin when legislation generates administration (e.g., Pressman and Wildavsky 1973; Pressman 1975). In short, "programs create federal, state, and often local bureaucracies and clientele groups that subsequently become a source of program augmentation and expansion" (Posner 1998, 26). Thus, the politics of IGR must always be in the analytical foreground.

BOX 2.2

- Post–Civil War reconstruction set a lasting tone for extensive federal interaction and oversight of state and local governments. Interaction was linked by postwar constitutional amendments, particularly the Fourteenth Amendment.
- State control over local governments varied from state to state, but gradually cities, particularly the larger ones, were given greater powers to act on their own behalf through home rule.
- Increasingly IGM recognized that public administrators were able to exert leverage—often in the name of expertise, efficiency, or moral protection—in addition to their working connections to local political organizations.
- Appointed administrators also became recognized actors in the system while working both within their agencies and across organizational and jurisdictional boundaries. Indeed, after legislation was enacted, the government's role was largely in the hands of government staff.

From Commission to Hierarchy

Early executive powers were quite limited. In fact, in his textbook on public administration, first published in 1926, White (1939, 49) observes, "The principal historical fact concerning the American chief executive as an administrator is that, until 1900, he had little to do with administration." Not only did the government focus its attention on legislative bodies but also the mayors, governors, and presidents preferred to concentrate on policy and politics.

During the early years, administration was diffused. Pennsylvania's first constitution contained a plural executive. Over the nineteenth century the positions for a number of independently elected officials, treasurers, auditors, attorneys general, city clerks, and so on as well as a series of administrative boards and commissions over programs were created. In most situations the membership and scope of action of these offices were beyond the chief executive's or departmental influence. An example of the latter was at the state level, where legislatures established overlapping commissions whose members often duplicated the tasks of other boards and were not subject to gubernatorial removal or control. "A public health board or agriculture commission could be virtually a government unto itself" (Teaford 2002, 70).

This changed in the late nineteenth and early twentieth century. At the local level the strong mayor and council-manager (city manager) plan recognized the importance of executives as administrators over the various functions of their organizations. Governors began to be recognized as administrative heads from about 1910 on, and the president's administrative powers were enhanced under the Budget and Accounting Act of 1921. Most important for IGR and IGM purposes is that at all levels the work of local, state, and national commissions and boards was being consolidated into administrative departments that were hierarchically under the supervision of their respective chief executives. During this early twentieth-century period, a growing commitment to professionalism, expertise, and efficiency led to concerns for the practice of professional management—including scientific management—which then led to governmental reforms. "Belief in administrative reform and professionalism in government promoted centralization of authority, the creation of a nonpartisan bureaucracy, the concentration of power in the hands of the executive, and the development of legislative expertise" (Teaford 2002, 6). It not only shifted power from commissions and boards to a bureaucratic hierarchy but also took control from federal to state and particularly from state to local levels. This state-level story is well known. For example, with schools, highways and roads, and public health, professional standards imposed on locals had the long-term effect of enhancing professional departments at all levels. Hierarchy then established the potential for greater unity of command, coordination, internal responsibility, and administrative leadership, to use the public administration language of the day (White 1939, 51).

Today the role of bureaucrats working in public agencies focuses on implementing programs. In this respect, in their work, the bureaucrats are accountable both to the law they are implementing and to the hierarchical supervision of politically appointed superiors and persons in line order of supervision (also established in law). John Kingdon (1995, 33) points to three important political resources that bureaucrats have within the hierarchy. First, their longevity in an agency puts them in a position to influence appointee superiors and their chief executives. Second is their expertise, which is based on professional training and in implementing programs, including their experience in dealing with the political forces that have a role in programs. Third are the working sets of relationships that bureaucrats establish with persons who have an impact on programs—in this case, with legislative bodies, external groups, and other governments. These forces have moved administrative and professional personnel into the orbit of programming, including IGR and IGM programs.

Program impact is particularly important with IGR and IGM because of the core features of intergovernmental administration. Steven Rosenthal (1984, 470) once identified them as a form of *indirect management*. In program delivery, public agencies are partially but not fully accountable to the sponsoring agency; those responsible for some aspect of the program are likely to differ, in some important respect, on the objectives of the program; programs are generally ongoing, as distinguished from one-time projects; and activity involves the exchange of resources and information across formal organizational boundaries. What Rosenthal's indirect management formulation suggests is that rather than one hierarchy, two or more hierarchies could be involved and on an interactive basis. The same might be said regarding politics and often the legal IGR underpinning, where local ordinances or rules blend into state legislation and federal law, and where local politics of intergovernmental programs can impact the work of administrators all along the line (Agranoff 1986).

Key Learning Points

From legislative acts to operating bureaucracies, IGR and its administrative companion IGM are framed by organic and specific laws regarding the relevant territorial organization. From the earliest points in history, law has served to integrate the state into an interactive entity. Immediately following the prominent legal establishment of a constitution, virtually every nation-state establishes the levels of government and their competencies in laws that reach into the entire nation. They enable listed powers and duties, reports and audits, financing arrangements, electoral processes, and much more. Paralleling these laws are the political processes that empower and condition their execution. Indeed, beyond most laws are politics of many sorts.

In *The Administrative State*, Dwight Waldo (1948, 2007) developed the idea that public administration in the United States was not "neutral" or "value free" but based on a political philosophy rooted in American and Western culture. Thus, it is important to understand the historical lessons and the philosophy of federal operation and how the past conditions the present. As Mordecai Lee (2011, 97) concludes, "Hindsight improves with age. The greater the distance of the event the easier it is to see embedded values . . . [compared to] more recent management events."

Moreover, beyond there are specific laws, such as particular fiscal subventions or tax sharing and delegation of enumerated tasks. Within the framework of government actions, laws obviously play an intergovernmental role inasmuch as they determine the scope of government activity, establishing the variety of actions and responsibilities that governments can and cannot take, along with the circumstances of agency action. Laws do not determine every IGR action, but they clearly set out guidelines for action. The ambiguities of language and of life inevitably leave much to the discretion of the interpretation of statutes. Most important, a majority of laws are permissive rather than directive (although it may not always be the case in important clusters of Napoleonic countries); that is, "they point to what policymakers or citizens may do, not what they must do" (Rose 1984, 63). Such actions also frame the system that is governing connections among and between governments.

The legal framework and its impact on IGR and IGM are to a great extent "of the political process." Politics and policies shape the environment of government, while the law grounds administrative practices of implementation. Moreover, administrative organizations are part of the playground of politics. As Donald Moynahan and Joe Soss (2014, 325) observe, politics follows policies:

> Politics are objects of action, in administration as in the rest of the policy. A feedback perspective calls on scholars not to reject this insight but to complement it with its reverse. If politics and policy shape each other in a reciprocal relationship, and if administrative organizations are sites of political action, then the study of administration today is distorted by a one-sided focus. The fruitful investigation of how administrators shape policy has blinkered researchers to the ways that bureaucracies are remade by the policies they administer.

In this regard, they conclude that administrative programs follow "a significant force in ordering political relations" (329). Politics indeed shape bureaucracies as well as the reverse.

Key Practice Points

One must operate within the IGR-IGM system by starting with the framing legal code (chapter 3 introduces the regulatory framework that is authorized in law). But the law is only a start, inasmuch as the law's intent and its living interpretations are part of intergovernmental affairs as they come to life through the working interactions of officials. So knowing the legal framework is an important start in the process.

Since it is a process, the politics behind and beyond the law and of the associated court decisions is also important to know. Why did this law come about? Who was behind it, and what expectations follow? To what degree does every provision have to be executed? What are the expectations of compliance and of noncompliance? Who benefits and who loses under specific provisions? In short, understanding the politics of enactment and administration constitutes important steps when working in the system.

Managing across the boundaries of governmental entities then starts but clearly does not end with law and politics. They frame the issues, and to overlook or avoid them is often at the peril of those who are responsible for programs. The difficulty is that rarely are these issues overt. They are seldom part of the written cover story. Those involved must look for and understand the issues and must get reactions to these key concerns. Compounding this understanding is that neither politics nor law will prevail, as each issue or administrative concern is a set of interacting legal and political questions.

Conclusion

During most of the nineteenth century, the federal system evolved into one with proscribed functions. Most federal domestic enactments relied on the states as implementers. Until the Civil War in the 1860s, the Jeffersonians and then the Jacksonians adhered to a limited role for the federal government in domestic affairs. Politically, the states were the program hubs. The Civil War began the breakthrough in substantial federal and state programs, which later enhanced during the Progressive Era's legislation, when the advent of universal suffrage made it more politically feasible to do so. Meanwhile, the states gradually exercised legal and administrative control over local governments and, with certain home-rule exceptions, tied them together in a unitary fashion. Administratively, strong legislatures and weak executives gave way to administrative commissions and ultimately, during the Progressive Era, to stronger executives and executive-controlled agencies, which gradually became important intergovernmental players. As subsequent chapters indicate, executive and administrative personnel are now the primary "carriers" of intergovernmental management.

3 LEGALLY AND POLITICALLY BASED INTERGOVERNMENTAL RELATIONS IN PRACTICE

The administrative practices that emerged from the exercise of law and politics are examined here in greater depth. While among the earliest of IGR-IGM practices, the bureaucratic and management legacies identified in chapter 2 remain, however refined, often streamlined and sometimes expanded. They generally flow from intergovernmental grants and regulatory regimes, along with the federal government's attempt to document and understand the ever-expanding system that defines US-style operational federalism.

The 1950s and 1960s were a period of expansion of the federal grant system, followed by "accelerated efforts to manage burgeoning cooperative relationships" (Conlan 1998, 66). Federal aid for highways began in 1955, triggering the interstate highway system. The next year federal aid for elementary and secondary school construction followed. In the 1950s grants for math, science, and language training began, followed by new grant programs in public health, agriculture, and urban renewal programs. Grants grew rapidly in the 1960s as well, tripling the number from the 1950s (132) to more than 400 in the 1960s, with the dollar amount growing from $7 billion to more than $400 billion (Walker 2000). Most were dedicated project or categorical grants with their own eligibility criteria, application and reporting requirements, specific clientele, and allowable objects of spending. This rapid increase in programmatic complexity "frayed administrative relationships, raised intergovernmental tensions and prompted a redoubling of management reforms and coordination efforts" (Conlan 1998, 66).

This led to several efforts to "manage" the intergovernmental system through White House–level intergovernmental coordination, the exploration of grant consolidations, and the Intergovernmental Cooperation Act of 1968, which encouraged state and local elected officials to be involved in the grant process. Management attempts followed with, among others, the establishment of Federal Regional Councils, management efforts in the Bureau of the Budget (later Office of Management and Budget), and an intergovernmental unit in their Program Coordination Division. Most important from an analytical standpoint was the creation in 1959 of the US Advisory Commission on Intergovernmental Relations (ACIR), which comprised officials from all levels to study and provide practical advice on improving the federal grants and later to shift focus on federal regulations. Among others, ACIR "was among the first to warn of the rising burdens on state and local governments resulting from the multiplication of federal preemptions, mandates, and grant conditions" (McDowell 1997, 113–14). The work of the federal government in scope and depth regarding the management of the system, particularly by ACIR, included federalism in operation, opportunities and barriers to cooperation, federal government system understanding, and tolerance of state and local management practices while maintaining federal purposes and national actions, support for management modernization of state and local partners, and work toward institutionalizing intergovernmental coordination and analysis (Conlan 1998, 66).

This chapter focuses on what has been enabled in law or otherwise legislatively delegated as the law is administered and at later stages audited and potentially enforced through the courts (Benjamin and Young 2008, 2134). With US federal programs, administration is often executed through a series of subnational governments. The case was made in chapter 2 that interactive federal-state and state-local systems—that is, intergovernmental relations— operated throughout US history despite any lingering perceptions of dual federalism or watertight compartments of administration. Morton Grodzins (1966, 26) once concluded that in reality two federal systems evolved—separate, compartmentalized governments and operations that unfolded with interlocking governments and their operations. The operational issues within this interlocking intergovernmental management system are the focal point of this chapter.

Early IGM

The legacy of the law and politics theme gradually put in place the precursors to the present-day system of management practices. For example, in some form early grant standards and reporting requirements, financial reviews and audits, program rules and standards, and contractual arrangements have been in force for more than two centuries. These practices to some degree brought state and local administrators together interactively in their respective federal agencies. In earlier periods, transactions were mostly formal and process sequential—for example, by letter, in mailed instructions, or in submitted report forms. Only in later years did they become more direct and more interactive.

From the earliest days of the federation until the rapid expansion of interdependent state programming after 1950, managers gradually built a legacy that carried into the present. Leonard White's groundbreaking four-volume series on administrative development from the Federalist period to early progressive management reforms of the early twentieth century broadly outlines American administrative development (1948, 1951, 1954, 1958; see also Carpenter 2005). Daniel Elazar's (1962) monumental study of federal-state and federal-local relations concludes historically that there has never been a rejection of cooperation, only of certain methods of interaction. "In a sense, a substantial share of the history of American government has been the search for methods to provide for the necessary collaboration of the various units of the federal system while at the same time preserving and strengthening those units as separate bases for such collaboration" (305).

The now-familiar administrative chain, particularly regarding grants, of federal legislation, rules, guidelines, state plans, and so on—until ultimately post audits were performed—gradually emerged. These practices had the effect of "allowing for voluntary albeit coaxed (i.e., incentivized) cooperation on the part of the states in advancing national preferences in policy, and by carving out protected areas of state regulatory autonomy, these intergovernmental policy tools helped state builders evade the limitations of federalism as they were interpreted by the Supreme Court" (Johnson 2010, 64). These practices became the administrative procedures and methods of those agencies established along the line to accomplish them and included program parameters, particular instruments to carry out programs, procedures and rules in running programs, in monitoring practices and procedures, and in recordkeeping and reporting. As these instruments developed, they led to what one historian called "administrative contracts with agencies of the Federal government charged with policy or administrative functions" (Scheiber 1966, 53). Indeed, they operated long before the concept of IGM approaches were actually identified as distinct undertakings.

These administrative practices are analyzed in some depth in this chapter. Initially the processes and standards related to grants administration are addressed, and the evolution of intergovernmental rules, regulations, and mandates are reviewed. The following section looks at intergovernmental reports and data gathering, practices that date to the earliest days of the federation. They were major federal and state government agency functions but are now overshadowed by other instruments and represent another aspect of IGM. The next section overviews the legacy of the ACIR's 45-year history (1951–96) and the commission's huge contributions to understanding IGM. The final section analyzes cooperative federalism, or the prevailing style of interactive management that developed over 150 years and is related to passive reviewing, maintaining legal integrity, and being mildly enforced by intermittent discussions among officials. It will become clear that many current practices in IGM long preceded its development as a concept. These practices indeed have quite a history and have been ingrained in the system.

Early Intergovernmental Grants Administration

The earliest features of federal-state grants-in-aid management were not stringent. The long arm of federal regulations and their auditors that appear in the news today were not always present. Nevertheless, concern arose over how the involved governments could exert control over rather extensive projects like land grants or joint-stock companies. The prevailing mode followed these processes into direct services as the federation became more deeply engaged in reimbursing veterans and vendors of the Revolutionary War, for the federal government insisted on reviewable documentation and a paper trail of accountancy before issuing reimbursement from the national treasury.

Elazar's (1962) research on the Great Dismal Swamp Canal, an early public works project, is illustrative. As a joint-stock company the federal government delegated its shareholding proxy rights to the treasury secretary, who in turn delegated them to the tax collector of the port of Norfolk, Virginia. The company and the collector were required to file fiscal reports annually with the US Treasury Department and the Virginia Board of Public Works. Many of the federal-state interactions were over matters of personnel, issues on which there was general federal-state agreement. Further numerous and regular interactions were related to canal construction, maintenance and facility improvement, and control over operational administration. The federal government, through the Army Corps of Engineers, provided the initial surveys as well. State administrative personnel not only served as proxies representing the state but also acted as supervisors for the state of Virginia regarding construction and operation. Periodic non-fiscal reports were required by the federal and state governments. As in other projects of its type, Elazar (1962, 53) related that "while federal control over standards tended to grow, state control over processes grew as a counterbalance. All of this was achieved through trial and error."

The process of depositing federal funds in state-chartered banks involved intergovernmental interactions conducted largely by correspondence that related to matters of specific transfers, changes in routing and personnel, and regular depository reports. Somewhat stricter procedures were ushered in in the 1830s when the Bank of the United States was discontinued. This development, suggests Elazar (1962, 91), increased interaction:

> In addition, the Treasury Department attempted to impose even more stringent conditions on those state banks desiring to become depositories for federal funds. The contract between the secretary of the treasury and the Bank of Virginia is a typical example of this new policy. The Bank of Virginia agreed to receive and deposit to the credit of the United States Treasury all money presented on account of the United States. It agreed to provide collateral security, submit weekly returns

of the funds on deposit, transfer funds to other banks at the request of the secretary of the treasury on receipt of reasonable notice, and submit all its records (not only those concerning the federal deposits) for examination by federal inspectors, excepting only personal accounts. Furthermore, it agreed to serve the federal government in all the ways the United States Bank had, to pay the expenses of the federal bank examiner, and to furnish bills of exchange to London at cost.

Additionally, as a precursor to today's "ultimate federal sanction," the secretary of the treasury reserved the right to terminate any arrangement at will if it was in the public's interest to do so.

Land-grant administration during the nineteenth century was similarly reciprocally involved, but it was neither regularly interactive nor highly detailed. For example, a federal grant authorized the state of Ohio to sell land so an asylum could be built in New Hampshire. The sale funds were placed in a permanent fund and the interest used to defer expenses of the asylum. Since the funds were not sufficient for operations, they were matched by those states sending residents there. In return, the asylum made an annual report to the federal government and to the states.

Federal land grants to set up state school systems followed a similar pattern. Proceeds of land sales were put into permanent state school funds. State treasurers managed the funds, investing them and distributing money to counties and school districts according to law. This process not only led to the establishment of a state school system but also began to tie the local schools into a system of state control. One of the first administrative duties was to have state and local officials examine the township's set-aside sections 16 and 36 and determine if they were either mineral lands or previously settled (thus unavailable); substitutes were identified as needed before the land transfer was certified by the US General Land Office. Next came the required filing, claiming, and patenting procedures conducted at the state level. The entire process often involved interactions between state and federal officials regarding land selection, and where differences in potential use existed, federally selected engineers who reviewed the existing survey and state agents who were sent to the federal office to procure a settlement decided the issues. States were required to file lists of the land selected in the federal district land offices for public examination. The General Land Office periodically issued instructions on how the states should make decisions, thus introducing the earliest uniform national rules associated with the grants.

At the state level, all expenses related to selecting, locating, appraising, leasing, and selling the lands were state funded as well as operated. State laws were normally added, such as those related to the price ranges for sales, the structures of rental rates for leased lands, the duration of leases, the mineral royalties where extraction was involved, and the conditions of lease renewal. States generally worked toward standardizing their own procedures by distributing standard forms and registers to the local school districts. Finally, county school superintendents or equivalent local officials were held responsible for leasing arrangements for all state lands in their county and for removing squatters. County commissioners served as rudimentary appeals boards. Elazar concludes (1962, 190) that these administrative procedures brought together local officials, contracted agents of the federal land offices, and surveyors working with state agency officials and occasionally county officials.

The Morrill Land-Grant College Act of 1862 and its subsequent additions, identified in chapter 2 of this volume, are considered the turning points in managing federal-state grants. Funds were disbursed on a continuing basis rather than those of individual land allocations. More stringent restrictions on spending purposes and conditions were also applied. Several thousand acres were conceded to the states, and funds flowed for agricultural testing, research, publications, and dissemination of scientific information on a federal-state basis. Originally no control other than annual audits of the states was imposed. Each new additional function also increased statutory requirements covering many far-reaching activities (Graves 1964, 490–509). Additions and restrictions piled on year after year, well into the mid-twentieth century. Beginning in 1916, an extensive system of local agents and county programs was established that was supported by federal, state, and county funds. Then, as well as now, county agents represented all three levels of government while administering programs under state option for agricultural production, marketing, natural resources, home and farm management, family, youth, leadership and community, and public affairs.

Most post–Civil War federal government intergovernmental programs set similar requirements. These stipulations included determining (1) which public agencies at the state level would exercise program supervision and control; (2) what allowable services and programs would be funded and who were the required recipients; (3) eligible service or program providers; (4) articulated state assumptions of the program and a formal state plan; (5) restrictions on certain types of spending, such as capital expenditures; (6) agreements to submit to an audit; (7) matching funding requirements; and (8) the maintenance of state-level spending requirements as federal funds increase (Graves 1964, 506–7). Clearly, expectations gradually changed from the early years when "grants were largesse," and the federal government attached "general, simple, and generous conditions." The first Morrill Act grants nevertheless contained "an increasing number of administrative prescriptions" that could bind the states but also "assumed and encouraged cooperation between the national governments and state governments" (Grodzins 1966, 37). From the beginning there was some attempt to balance cooperation with the rules.

State-Local Administration

From an intergovernmental perspective, little state administration impacted local governments from the founding period until the Civil War. Administration was under separately elected state constitutional officers—attorney general, auditor, treasurer, secretary of state—who had small offices and performed more formal and less managerial duties. Among others Alexis de Tocqueville (1988, 89) observed, "The state usually employs officials of the townships or counties in dealings with citizens," and there were no state government officials in the European (central government) sense to perform public services. Moreover, "over these local officials acting as agents of the states there was practically no central state administrative supervision. Instead it fell to the state courts, acting in cases brought before them by indignant citizens or local prosecutors, to try to keep the officials within legal bounds and reasonably diligent in the performance of their duties" (Anderson 1960, 103).

This devolution of sorts later came with administrative supervision under the state's powers to control local governments. The best illustration is in the fiscal affairs arena. Regulations and standards in local tax administration, accounting, budgets, and local indebtedness were introduced as far back as the early 1800s. Over the nineteenth century, W. Brooke Graves (1964) reports, states gradually assumed supervision of local finances regarding assessments, tax collection, tax rate limitations, budgets and expenditures, debt incurrence and retirement, accounts and audits reporting, and receiverships and credit facilities. "The scope of the supervisory function involves the setting of standards, instruction of local officials as to their meaning and observance, and finally, inspection to ascertain that they have been observed" (863). Such administrative actions normally proved to be some blend of legal controls, cooperation on the part of state and local officials, the rendering of a state fee-based service (e.g., an audit), an advisory service to local officials, "or even a nominal, perfunctory, and more or less sterile examination of their financial records after the transactions have been completed and it is too late to do any good" (864).

Over the nineteenth and early twentieth centuries, states improved their administrative capacities along with the transfer of some powers from local elected officials to state administrators. Jon Teaford (2002, 6) has identified these powers as professionalization and centralization. Meanwhile, many small, particularly rural governments remained charged with carrying out the primary tasks of government. Responsibilities were gradually shifted "upward" inasmuch as the burden was on "the least competent elements of government with the heaviest duties" (122). In the case of new challenges—for example, emergency relief in the 1920s and 1930s—the state administered them directly. In other cases, public welfare was assumed from townships by the states or became state directed and locally administered. State supervision and control of fiscal matters also increased. Sometimes states even assumed the maintenance of local roads, even in rural areas. Most important, the states tightened their supervision and control of schools. While schools had long been assumed to be state responsibilities, operation had been delegated to thousands of local school districts. Yet in the fifty years from the 1880s to the 1930s, state intervention in terms of requirements and administrative supervision had been building and accelerated at an unprecedented pace by the thirties. In this respect, the more direct involvement in the program arena, the further the states "moved . . . from the nineteenth-century tradition of delegated responsibility and dispersed authority" (130–31). This made local and state officials "working partners" to unprecedented degrees.

State Departmentalization and IGM

The first half of the twentieth century led to the rise of state government departments that over time became either administrative units under their governors' offices or independent departments. Many such departments— highways, state police, institutions, higher education, commerce, banking and securities—were often the previously identified transformed commissions and were subsequently converted into departments. Whereas this set of departments is less likely to be engaged in overseeing local governments and services, another set of departments—health, welfare, finance, education (K–12), fire safety—has major functions in working administratively with local governments. These departments promote, advise, inform, assist, and review the state codes that relate to services in their program arenas. In this latter set of departments, state officials are charged to examine and certify personnel; collect, analyze, and publish data; audit local functions and accounts; inspect buildings; assist local administrators in their functions; and supply information on local government legal powers and procedures related to the administration of state programs. Over the years, a number of states have expanded their units or departments of local finance into more comprehensive departments of local affairs, although the chief line of state-local administrative contact remains among the defined functional officials in state departments with local counterparts.

The extent of state administrative supervision of local administration that developed in the late nineteenth century and the first six decades of the twentieth century can be illustrated through examining the field of primary and secondary education. School inspections began over the process of state accreditation, which in turn involved course content guidelines and course duration and later led to standards necessary for school ratings. Grants-in-aid were used as a means of establishing salary standards, teacher qualifications and certification, criteria for entering teaching, school curricula, improvement programs, and textbook selection (in many states). Also, school buildings were inspected for safety (and security today), exits, emergency lighting, and fire hazards. The latter are usually under the control of a state's building department, while the schooling functions involve interaction with the state's department of education.

The increased amount of interactive state-local administrative supervision is thus a direct result of state government modernization and its inherent exercise of control over local governments. These practices increased as new tasks and statutory expectations evolved. Graves (1964, 862) observes that, at the end of the 1900–50 period,

> it has often been said that nature never permits a vacuum. Likewise, in the field of government, a governmental vacuum, a kind of governmental no-man's-land, does not long continue. If the local units break down, the states must either attempt to do the job themselves, or establish and enforce upon the local units minimum requirements for the performance of the function. The reasons why and the methods by which the power and influence of the states increase in the state-local relationship are substantially the same as those which account for the growth of Federal power in the Federal-state relationship.

The arena of program control and oversight is but one form of IGM. Rulemaking and regulation also have emerged as part of the management fabric.

BOX 3.1

- As the field of public administration emerged around managing hierarchies that existed within federalism, scholars identified and underscored the importance of collaborative modes of operation. They once called it cooperative federalism, on the assumption that the various actors representing different agencies were "all in it together."
- The origin of management practices emanated from the execution aspects of federal and state programs. They ranged in scope from application to audit.
- With federal-state programs, state administration followed a similar pattern to those of federal codes and guidelines, which then influenced local administration. Indeed, administration filtered up and down the system, as well as laterally.
- Federal regulations affecting states and local governmental related NGOs increased, for states proved to be politically and technically unable to meet the challenges of emergent problems as they became increasingly complex.

Intergovernmental Regulation as Administration

The first session of the US Congress enacted laws that delegated to President Washington the authority to issue rules governing trade with Native American tribes. The law itself was not very detailed, relying on the administration to provide substance (Bryner 1987, 10). The Congresses that followed continued to delegate the power to write rules to executive branch officials. Most of these rules related to trade and commerce. For example, in 1796 Congress gave the president authority to develop regulations regarding duties on foreign goods, and they were considerably expanded twenty years later when the secretary of the treasury was granted extensive powers to make such rules. The extension was a clear delegation of rulemaking power to a subordinate official of the executive branch. The legislation stated that the secretary had the authority "to establish regulations suitable and necessary for carrying this law into effect; which regulations shall be binding" (quoted in Kerwin 1999, 8). As Congress chose not to provide important details, a pattern followed in contemporary statutes. In the 1830s federal engineers developed standards that states had to follow when improving rivers for navigation. After a survey of the Ohio River, the Army Corps of Engineers set standards of maximum tonnage and average water depth based on earlier federal canal and river improvement surveys (Elazar 1962, 60).

A *rule*, as subsequently defined and codified by the Administrative Procedures Act (APA) of 1946, is the "whole or part of an agency statement of general or particular applicability and future effect designed to implement, interpret, or prescribe law or policy" (5 U.S.C. 551 [4]). The act was designed to bring regularity and predictability to the decision-making process. Rules, according to Cornelius Kerwin (1999, ch. 1), are first of all products of the bureaucratic institutions to which we entrust the implementation, management, and administration of law. Second, the authority to issue rules can derive only from statutes that establish the mission of agencies and set in the statutes their goals and objectives. Third, rules not only interpret when law and policy are well established but also confront unanticipated or changing circumstances, a process of adaptation to new situations. Fourth, rules affect persons or activities (or governments) in the widest circumstances, in both general and particular situations. Finally, rules, like legislation, attempt to anticipate future situations by creating new conditions, eliminating existing ones, or preventing others from occurring. Inasmuch as federal rules impact other governments through federal programs, just as persons involved in transacting across jurisdictions do, their impact is inherently intergovernmental. The Administrative Procedures Act requires that "interested parties must be given an opportunity to say what they think about the specific changes which he (executives) proposes, and what they say must be given consideration," meaning agencies must be involved in "coordinating administrative policies" (Hyneman 1950, 465–66).

Within the federal government, regulatory action also requires measures of interagency coordination. Such "shared regulatory space" is fostered by legally required coordination. Jody Freeman and Jim Rossi (2012, 78) identify five types of consultation: *discretionary*, where Congress authorizes but does not require such actions; *mandatory*, which requires inputs from agencies; *public response requirements* to respond to interested agency comments; *default position requirements*, where notification of a regulation would affect the rules of another agency; and *concurrence requirements*, which necessitate the action of another agency. Another regulatory approach involves interagency agreements, normally through the memorandum of understanding, that are voluntarily negotiated by the agencies. Finally, joint policy-making coordination tools include issuing policy statements or guidelines, for example, or joint rulemaking, standard setting, and other related collaborated action. These measures are coordinated by executive action at the White House level, are subject to judicial review, and are designed to enhance coordination and improve efficiency in a complex environment at a point even before intergovernmental processes are put in place.

Federal regulation was relatively inactive during much of the nineteenth century outside of enforcing grant conditions. Change came quite slowly. In the 1880s the Interstate Commerce Commission set the tone for other means of reach by the federal government. Gradually regulatory actions by similar commissions were made applicable to state activities—that is, intrastate commerce. Federal-state railroad safety standards followed. In 1899 the Refuse Act required permits to dump in navigable waters (although it was not enforced until decades later). The first Pure Food and Drug Act was enacted in 1906 to protect consumers, and the Oil Pollution Act of 1924 prohibited oil discharge in coastal waters. There followed other enactments in agriculture, livestock production, and wildlife protection. These laws all required that administrators issue rules to implement their important provisions. For public management, legal and constitutional questions were being displaced or expanded by administrative questions. In a now well-known quote on the immediacy and daunting challenges of rulemaking, Woodrow Wilson reflected, "It is getting harder to run a constitution than to frame one" (1887, 484). Regulation in numerous areas became a process of gradual federalization in the face of the states' inability to adequately deal with the political pressures related to social, economic, and health problems. This process moved from the free market to the government and then from local to state to federal levels because "there is every reason for persons and groups to turn to the jurisdiction with authority over the whole area" (Beer 1973, 67).

State regulation of local government activity has deeper roots, as the previous discussion of legal controls over local governmental units from cities to school districts has made clear. From the nineteenth century, the state has exercised its "authority to establish minimum standards for the performance of functions by local governments as well as the authority to require local governments to perform or not perform specified functions" (Zimmerman 1995, 152). The problem of state supervision has been compounded over the past half century by the proliferation of special districts, largely in response to state tax and debt limitations imposed on local governments. These districts provide services that are not being funded or supplied by general-purpose governments and in some cases serve multiple cities or counties. Many rely on user fees (e.g., water and sewer) whereas most rely on property taxes separated from cities and counties as revenue sources. Special districts multiply, as allowed by law and local support, to meet service needs. In 2012 Illinois had 3,252 tax districts; California, 2,786; and Colorado, 2,315, with the latter comprising 57 percent of all local governments (Shafroth 2013, 66).

State oversight involves regulations, supervised by state officials, that have long been promulgated regarding local government civil service, finance, public safety, public welfare, public health, and standards of performance. Detailed rules in most states normally involve finance and local government personnel requirements. States have also long issued rules controlling road construction in local jurisdictions, particularly regarding planning, connections to feeder roads, design methods, flexible usage, and construction methods. In the public health arena, states have historically taken the lead in setting regulations and standards for local government personnel, establishing health standards of prevention and operation, and enforcing state codes locally (e.g., restaurant inspections), along with reviewing and approving local health ordinances. Air pollution control policy has gradually passed from local control to the states as well as regulatory control over the construction and maintenance of sewage disposal systems. Finally, state sanitary engineers have long been responsible for the rules related to beverage bottling plants, to nonmunicipal water supplies, to noise and nuisance abatement, and to the inspection of public bathing facilities, housing, and cemeteries. From an IGM standpoint, each of these state rulemaking and enforcement endeavors not only is a product of state political processes and thus subject to the lobbying and advocacy of state-level groups in their revision but also potentially allows for a cooperative working interaction between local and state operatives during inspection, supervision, and control (Graves 1964, 717, 724).

Information Gathering and Cooperative Arrangements

From the earliest days of the federal system, the federal government has been involved in gathering, analyzing, and disseminating useful program data and information of use to other federal agencies and all subnational governments as well as other interested parties. The first constitutionally mandated decennial census enumeration began in August 1790. Responsibility was initially assigned to US judicial district marshals. That practice continued until 1840 when a Census Office was created in the administration; it was renamed the Census Bureau in 1903 and placed in the new Department of Commerce and Labor. From the 1920s on, special censuses were launched. Today each census is organized by input from users at the bureau's website, census.gov. Of particular intergovernmental interest is the Census of Governments, conducted every fifth year, that documents various units of governments. It determined, for example, that by the early 2000s there were around 88,000 local governments and an estimated 400,000 administrative departments (Stephens and Wikstrom 2007, 25). In addition to its use in apportioning seats in Congress and districting congressional and legislative seats, census data has many intergovernmental uses—for example, in allocating grant fund formulas, locating public facilities, planning transportation, and creating locations for elections, schools, and public services.

Congress authorized some federal agencies to gather information for the states, and over time the agencies evolved into grant-making and standard-setting agencies. The Children's Bureau, politically mobilized by women's groups and social welfare professionals, was created in 1912 to "investigate and report on all matters pertaining to the welfare of children and child life among all classes of our people" (Skocpol 1995, 262). Within a few years, "the Children's Bureau was soon to extend its reach into states and localities and enlarge the scope of its activities to include the promotion of new programs and the administration of large federal grants" (481). In its early years the bureau coordinated efforts that led to the distribution of 22 million pieces of literature, orchestrated 183,000 health conferences, established 3,000 prenatal centers, and arranged for 3 million home visits (262). As a result, the Children's Bureau became "the source of authoritative information about the welfare of children and their families throughout the country and the institutional leader of the child-saving movement" (Katz 1986, 122).

Departments at the state level responsible for information and data gathering—for example, state labor and industry departments—also emerged in the early twentieth century. Most began as factory inspection units, spurred on by the Supreme Court ruling in *US v. E. C. Knight Sugar Refining Company* (156 U.S. 1: [1895]) that manufacturing was not commerce as it was a change of form and not place. Thus, the states moved into this arena. These departments gathered data—once called labor statistics—related to factory worker health, and safety conditions; hours and wages; injuries; and other matters related to the workplace. Over a period these agencies became directly involved in factory inspection, mediation and arbitration, and, of course, employment services, with the latter being in cooperation with the federal government.

Regular state-federal information cooperation began with the enactment of the Interstate Commerce Act in 1887. The commission, enabled by the law, began with a conference of state agencies that met annually on matters of regulation and uniform legislation. In 1897 the commission established a bureau of statistics and accounts that became the primary basis for rate making. It was originally based on voluntary cooperation but was legally sanctioned under the Valuation Act of 1913 (Grodzins 1966, 40). Also, as a precursor to federal involvement in matters of social welfare, in 1914 the US commissioner of labor statistics convened a conference to standardize worker accident forms and statistics and to serve as the secretariat for a new association of accident boards and commissions (Katz 1986, 195).

The Cooperative Health Statistics System follows a similar pattern of data gathering and dissemination for health-related statistics. It operates on an interactive basis between the federal government and state and local public health departments and has been "voluntarily" supported—that is, without federal assistance—since 1980. Launched in 1973 with initial databases in vital statistics, health personnel, and health facilities, the program gradually expanded to include health facilities, hospital care, household health, ambulatory care, and long-term care. Each component cooperatively developed standardized definitions, comparable methodologies, and a core set of data—that is, sets of the minimum information needed at the national level. It led to the creation of a network of statistical gathering and processing agencies (Perrin 1974).

Finally, another long-standing cooperative statistical venture is that of the Bureau of Labor Statistics, now in the US Department of Labor. An enabling law authorizes the secretary of labor to enter into agreements, the first being in 1922, with the states for collecting statistical data. Developed jointly by state and federal officials, the bureau's aim is to create a national system that incorporates common concepts, schedules, and sampling and estimating techniques. Most of the data is collected at the state level from employer reports, and by the 1930s it was linked to the federal-state unemployment program by using employer quarterly tax reports. Technical support for state programs comes through various forms of advice, an operating manual (guidelines), schedules for collection, field visits from representatives of federal regional offices to discuss worksheets and calculations, and, today, work with jointly developed software. Meanwhile, the state staff collects employer schedules and checks for consistency. The bureau's work is an example of cooperation that indirectly affects a great deal of economic action, and while much is written about it in the media, it is not well understood as a "federal-state success story."

ACIR and IGM

Dedicated attention to intergovernmental coordination and management began when the Commission on Intergovernmental Relations—popularly known as the Kestnbaum Commission after its chairman, Meyer Kestnbaum—was launched in 1953 and issued its report in 1955. That led to the enactment of the Advisory Commission on Intergovernmental Relations in 1959 to address the broad range of intergovernmental issues. The commission's twenty-six members included three members from each house of Congress, four governors, four mayors, three state legislators, three elected county commissioners, three members of the president's cabinet, and three private citizens. It was charged with seven tasks: (1) identify common problems in the federal system; (2) discuss the administration and coordination of federal grants; (3) attend to conditions and contacts related to federal grants; (4) provide technical assistance to the federal, executive, and legislative branches in reviewing proposed legislation; (5) study emerging public problems that are likely to require intergovernmental cooperation; (6) examine the most effective allocation of functions and responsibilities and revenues among the levels of governments; and (7) coordinate and simplify tax laws and administrative practices to achieve a more orderly and less competitive fiscal relationship between the levels of government (US Advisory Commission on Intergovernmental Relations 1962).

In its thirty-seven years of operation ACIR published 130 policy reports with recommendations, 194 information reports (approved by the commission without recommendations), 23 public opinion polls on intergovernmental issues, 22 staff reports, and 80 issues of its magazine, *Intergovernmental Perspective*. Throughout the 1960s and 1970s, the bulk of the commission's recommendations were mainly oriented to improve the grant-in-aid system. In the 1980s and 1990s ACIR shifted emphasis toward federal regulations and later to performance concerns.

Among the commission's notable studies of grants was *Fiscal Balance in the American Federal System* (vol. 1–A31), which indicated there were 150 major programs, 400 specific authorizations, and 1,300 federal assistance activities by 1969. Of the 400 authorizations, 70 involved direct national-local dispersements that bypassed the states. The report also covered expanding state activity and state aid to local governments.

Deil Wright (1988, 75) captures the management implications of the proliferation of grants:

> The tremendous increase in project grants over formula grants further diversified the activities supported by federal funds and further increased the autonomy and discretion of program professionals. Finally, the public-participation requirements tied to some grants

increased the complexity of managerial activities and of calculations and occasionally added to the chagrin of officials charged with grant alloca- tion choices. The task of securing and spending federal funds involved extensive administrative skills, substantial resources, and expert timing. Success often was defined simply as getting everyone in on the act but still getting action. In several instances federal funds, especially Office of Economic Opportunity (OEO) antipoverty program funds, were seen as sources of support with which to "fight city hall."

This overview also reveals the local politics involved in grants, as states were often pitted against, or having to deal with, city politics.

Among the ACIR's notable regulatory studies was the 1984 compendium, *In Brief—Regulatory Federalism: Policy, Process, Impact, and Reform,* which distilled hundreds of programs into four categories. First are *direct orders,* where state and local actions are required, for example, in environmental protection and public employment. Second are *crosscutting requirements,* such as nondiscrimination and public employment, that apply to many fed- eral assistance programs. Third are *crossover sanctions* that threaten to ter- minate or reduce aid unless program requirements, such as highway safety and handicapped education, are satisfied. Fourth are *partial preemptions* that delegate to the states the administration and administrative adaptations of federal standards, such as with natural resources and occupational safety and health. The ACIR identified the growth of regulatory federalism as "complex and diverse, belying simple explanations of why [it] grew. . . . Regulatory fed- eralism developed as part of a broader wave of national government activism; it was not precipitated by a single actor or factor" (US Advisory Commission on Intergovernmental Relations 1984, 11). The report concluded that virtu- ally every new regulatory undertaking of the initial law was supported by a broad coalition, reflecting "on the politics, policies, and problems of regula- tion in an intergovernmental framework" (Wright 1988, 373).

During its history several intergovernmental landmarks helped define ACIR. They included amendments to the Anti-Poverty Act of 1964 that gave local officials a role in the program, the Uniform Relocation Assistance and Real Property Acquisition Act of 1970, the Intergovernmental Personnel Act of 1970, and the Intergovernmental Cooperation Act of 1968. The commission also had a major role in monitoring the implementation of the General Reve- nue Sharing program that ran from 1972 to 1986. Related, ACIR was known for its annual two-volume *Significant Features of Fiscal Federalism,* biennial updates on state fiscal capacity, and their opinion poll reports, *Changing Public Attitudes on Governments and Taxes* (McDowell 1997, 114). The last notable, impactful ACIR effort was the 1995 Unfunded Mandates Reform Act (P.L. 104-4, March 22, 1995). Its Title III, "Review of Federal Mandates," required three studies: working with Congressional Budget Office methods to measure the full costs and benefits to subnational governments to comply with federal law, analyzing the impact of existing federal mandates on subnational governments and making recommendations to mitigate unwarranted impacts, and providing annual reports on federal court decisions that impose mandates on subnational governments. The act faced political pushback that led to budget reductions and the government shutdown, which stemmed from political battles between lobby groups that wanted to maintain a strong federal role and protect citizens' rights, and those supporters of the Contract with America who wanted to reduce the federal profile and roll back federal regulation (McDowell 1997, 115–17).

About the same time as the Unfunded Mandates Reform Act, the ACIR began to unravel due to funding reductions and changes in IGM interest, particularly given the shift in emphasis from cooperative to other forms of management. Timothy Conlan (1998, 666) captures this change in focus by identifying four critical trends:

> First, the proliferation of federal mandates, preemptions, and increasingly intrusive grant programs since the 1960s has prompted a shift away from cooperation in vertical relationships within the intergovernmental system. This shift has been only partially mitigated by uneven efforts at devolution. Second, the administrative paradigm in the federal system has been changing from intergovernmental management to performance management, an evolution that holds promise but also carries the risk of further federal co-optation of the policy agenda. Third, there has been an erosion of institutionalized, systemic analysis in the intergovernmental system and a concomitant increase in instrumental advocacy. Finally, federal tax policy making has increasingly departed from a traditional stance of federal deference toward state and local governments to one of federal disregard.

Additionally, as chapters 4–9 of this volume demonstrate, intergovernmental management has moved in different directions. Permeable bureaucratic structures work across their hierarchies in interdependent modes and interactively across "boundaries" of governments to include many different types of NGOs. These structures also seek to network and develop formal and informal operational networks that include more than formal governments to solve vexing problems while reaching out to a host of other organizations and to citizens and clients of public and publically supported services (Agranoff 2014; Conlan 1998). The concluding chapter identifies the success or capacity of IGM analysis after the demise of ACIR. Despite the shifts, "in many respects the federal role has continued to expand by standing on the shoulders of state and local governments, which have solidified their emerging role as the true workhorses of our federal system" (Conlan and Posner 2008, 34).

Administrative Cooperation: Antecedents in Federalism

The formal demise of ACIR does not eliminate a federal analytical presence. Moreover, statistical and information gathering and cooperation are clearly not the only areas of working-level, federal-state and federal-state-local interaction. For most of the twentieth century extensive cooperation continued, for example, in law enforcement (e.g., police training, criminal identification, joint enforcement), with the US Postal Service and state agencies inspecting agricultural products and dangerous materials; in agricultural and conservation programs; and, of course, on "militia"-related matters with state National Guard units and the US armed forces. Although such working cooperation has been in effect for a long time, the period leading up to federal expansion after the 1950s was sometimes known as the period of cooperative federalism, when "complimentary and supportive relationships were most prominent and had high significance" (Wright 1988, 71). The concern here is with the administrative legacy of cooperative federalism.

Its administration initially followed the style identified in chapter 2, where agencies were called on to carry out the funding rules, standards, and financial practices contained in federal and state law. It proved to be a time of more or less informal interactions or shared administration (Walker 2000, 90), with a preference for passive reviewing, concern for legal integrity, and encouragement of legal compliance as opposed to strict and detailed supervision. With a few basic rules—for example, statewide administration and merit services—each jurisdiction had considerable leeway in making programs work generally within their traditions. In this time, before the lead-up to massive expansions of intergovernmental programs, program management tended to be pushed down the line, so to speak, with minimal detailed supervision or oversight.

One of the first to recognize and capture this cooperative management style was Jane Perry Clark (1938), who, as depicted in chapter 1, found cooperation between the federal and state governments as distinctly experimental and routine. Of course, Clark's view of federalism at the time appeared highly optimistic regarding officials' problem-resolution ability, perhaps overlooking differences based on jurisdictional interest and resource constraints and not speaking of administrative capabilities.

Closer examination began during the 1930s with studies of the federal grants programs of the Great Depression. Although they were supportive of cooperative federalism in principle, studies were not always sanguine about its success. V. O. Key Jr. (1937, 228) identified a "gap between policy determination and the task of administration" because the expenditure of money and performance of function had been under the supervision of state agencies "operating in a sphere of and tradition of freedom from central control." Similarly, George Benson (1942) identified the management and performance weakness of state governments as operating partners. While they need to be the apex of the system, he wrote, "at times there seems discouraging evidence the core is rotting" (157).

Clearly the restrictions and procedures passed down the line met modification in practice (and one of the early indications of policy implementation concerns is introduced in chapters 4 and 5). Edward Weidner's study of federal programs (1944, 233) concluded that "state supervision of local governments is largely determined by a meeting of the minds of state and local officials." Nevertheless, cooperation was the aim of management.

Such a non-centralized cooperative approach was fundamental to the managerial experience of David Lilienthal (1939) with the Tennessee Valley Authority. To him the essence of coordination in the field involved the field operatives making the great number of decisions, the affected citizens actively participation and working with state and local agencies, and the work of state and local governments coordinating as they aimed toward common objectives.

As Dwight Waldo (1948, 149) observed, Lilienthal saw this decentralized collaborative strategy as essential to preserving democracy in a large bureaucratic state and to overcoming the drawbacks of centralization. A cooperative approach was also observed at the state level. John Vieg (1941) analyzed the cooperation of federal, state, local, and private organizations in Iowa's agricultural programs in four areas: research, education, planning, and programming. He suggests that different interests work "physically side by side" while forging "a rational division of labor and clear understanding of authority and responsibility all the way around; there must be close agreement on all questions" (142).

During World War II, extensive program coordination was required for heavily congested production areas. The president's Committee for Congested

BOX 3.2

- The rise of cooperative agreements, particularly in the regulatory arena, underscored the importance of the broadened knowledge needed to approach complex problems.
- Systematic concern for the growth, impact, cost, and effectiveness in the federal systems led to the work of the Advisory Commission on Intergovernmental Relations (1959–96), whose work has continued by academia and governmental entities.
- Research on the IGR system over time revealed both cooperation and conflict, although top-down program analyses far exceed extensive research on bottom-up program examination.
- Only recently have observers and researchers begun to recognize the daunting challenges in IGM, and interest in mutual interdependence and networks and networking has prompted sorting out the complexities.

Production Areas, after consulting with all levels of government and nongovernment officials, facilitated all types of public services in these local areas. The committee, according to Corrington Gill, provided common meeting ground for "across the table discussion of common problems" (1945, 32).

Academic Research on Cooperative Federalism

The field-based studies of William Anderson and his associates during the 1950s ultimately led to ten volumes that reported on the intergovernmental relations between Minnesota governments and the federal government. Anderson's *Intergovernmental Relations in Review* (1960) and his earlier *The Nation and the States, Rivals or Partners?* (1955) laid out the essence of management under cooperative federalism. According to his perspective, the role of the federal government is to provide money for state and local governments to fund specified functions, to set certain standards, and to exercise a minimum amount of supervision over state and local planning and the performance of these functions. The states have primary and direct responsibility, some of which is administered within state government and some through local governments. Grants lead to federal-state cooperation (e.g., public welfare policy [Anderson 1960, 37–38]). Anderson also concludes that some degree of national involvement and interest in domestic policy arenas that were considered state centered were the inevitable result of "complexity, the failure in some cases of the states to act, and political forces motivated by the desire to improve standards of living" (14). His study of some eighty-one cooperative (grants, shared administration, and contracts) programs between Minnesota and the federal government was said to have brought about many administrative changes to state government, including the creation of new state agencies and the enlargement of others, the establishment of new state merit systems, an increased emphasis on planning of state services, and more opportunities for interstate cooperation in administration (1960, 62).

The group centered at the University of Chicago under Morton Grodzins's Federalism Workshop also contributed to the study of cooperative federalism. The landmark historical work from this series is, of course, Daniel Elazar's *The American Partnership* (1962). Grodzins's compendium based on his workshop's studies, particularly his volume *The American System* (1966), was the magnum opus of cooperative federalism. His famous "marble cake" analogy was a way of deflecting attention from the layer cake metaphor of three separate levels of government. Multiple overlapping functions, where sharing of administration in many areas beyond grants was the norm, was his core intergovernmental characterization. National supervision occurred with substantial state and local discretion, through mutual accommodation, and by state and local officials participating in setting agendas. Even without joint financing, federal-state-local collaboration was said to be the characteristic mode of action. Although there was some enmity and resistance to mutual federal and state control over local programming, constructive interaction persisted (Grodzins 1966, 373). Grodzins's own work, particularly in recreation administration, led him to conclude that contacts from the federal and state governments led to considerable variation, leaving wide areas for administrative discretion. To a considerable degree, local success depends on local governments taking advantage of what the federal government offers. The opportunity is universal, but all do not partake. "The extension of free enterprise to local-federal relationships produces some communities which profit handsomely and some which get less than an equitable share" (189). Cooperative federalism combines federal assistance with the opportunity for other governments to become "constructively involved in the great public service functions" (381).

Key Learning Points

Not until the twentieth century, long after democratization of the electorate and the rise of large industrial organizations, did the US federal, state, and local governments make managerial progress in the professional bureaucratization of their agencies (Shefter 1978; Skowronek 1982). During the early twentieth century, the greatest changes actually came first at the municipal and state levels. Administrative practices such as formal reports and fiscal audits appeared, largely as a by-product of political reform movements, and gradually moved up the line, reaching the federal government during the Progressive Era, the New Deal, and the federal program proliferation during the last half of the twentieth century. This gradual process muted the excesses of party machine politics and attendant corruption.

This latter period was particularly important as the federal government enacted hundreds of new programs, with accompanying legal parameters and operational expectations, that were "parachuted" into state and local governments. In many ways the transformation from a system known as "federalism" to "intergovernmental relations" began and laid the foundations for dedicated concern for the "management" of programs that crossed jurisdictions in ways well beyond the formal transactions of earlier times.

Inasmuch as these parachuted programs were a product of politics and government, so to speak, the kind of management that emerged was also seasoned by politics. Managing these programs involved much more than filling out a form or submitting a final report. Transactions beyond the routine involved situational interpretations and establishing mutual understandings of how to apply legislated and guiding principles to real-world situations in participating governments. More regular, working interactions thus developed between state and local officials with federal administrators. As these interactions and transactions became more frequent and more identifiably patterned, consciousness regarding the systematic practice of IGM reared its formative head.

It was also a time when the scope of federal-state-local program growth became a concern, perhaps first politically, given the cost and expansion of government roles, but also eventually administratively. Thus, the Kestnbaum Commission of the late 1950s melded into ACIR, which tried to discern a general sense of how federalism was being transformed. During its nearly four decades, the ACIR not only documented proliferation and expansion but also raised the consciousness that programs should be understood as a cooperative combination of expanded managerial techniques, particularly with the commission's fundamental jurisdictional political underpinnings. The work of ACIR triggered the rudiments of what later became intergovernmental management in its fuller dimensions (see chapters 4–9).

Key Practice Points

As the old saying goes with regard to sales, one must know the territory. One cannot seriously engage deeply into intergovernmental programming without a basic understanding of its legal framework and measures of its related politics. The latter would include some knowledge of both the potentially supportive and negative forces regarding the operation of a program. Practice begins but hardly ends here.

Another relevant but not explicitly stated premise is that each program has a technical dimension. Whether it involves building a bridge or educating intellectually disabled children, its professional applications range from setting up the program to assessing its results. Technical applications are real. Federal-state programs normally have qualification requirements that are based on education, training, and experience. The IGM difference is that the professional or specialist is challenged with applying her or his background within the legal and political parameters of a multi-jurisdictional program. Blending people, political, legal, and managerial skills with one's professional or occupational competence is complex, but it has become the only way to build a public bridge or to operate a public special education program.

This sounds daunting, but there is even more, as subsequent chapters reveal. While balancing all these concerns, particularly the professional-legal-political nexus, one can expect different measures of mutual understanding, constructive and entrenched conflict, give-and-take, and so on. With legally based intergovernmental programs, the list of requirements and expectations will often boil down to what is important (and enforced) and what is not. Short of what are called direct orders, managers have to learn what is critical, what can be delayed, and what might be benignly overlooked in the context of performance. IGM has become a protracted process. Again IGM entails some law and politics blended into managerial and professional know-how.

Conclusion

The American style of administration at its basic level remains a product of law and politics. Theda Skocpol (1995, 23) concludes that "the fragmentation of political sovereignty built into US federalism and into the divisions of decision-making authority among executives, legislatures, and courts was reproduced in new ways throughout the twentieth century." These patterns of state formation and their influence on administration have conditioned administrative IGR, hence the IGM dimension gradually emerged out of law and politics.

Management in the intergovernmental sphere thus operates within a federal array of governments, and in later years their recognized agent implementers therefore bring on the need for aspects of managerial collaboration (Metzger 2008; Eskildge and Baer 2008). As Elazar's (1962) groundbreaking historical study of cooperative federalism revealed, collaborative management indeed operates within a federal matrix rather than in a hierarchy or pyramid, for the three levels of government are tiered only in limited respects. Jurisdictions in the United States possess sufficient legal, fiscal, and political interdependence so that, official status notwithstanding (in the case of state-local relations), they can operate, or have the potential to operate, independently on their own behalf (Elazar 1984, ch. 1).

As a result and in many respects, management that crosses jurisdictions is thus indirect. State and local governments as civil societies legally and politically play pivotal roles in making the federal system viable by acting on their own behalf when they participate in broader national aims as part of the system. State governments, for example, operate within the frameworks of their state political systems and cultures, even while they are agents and operators of federal government programs. Thus, they take somewhat different policy stances and differ with regard to intergovernmental postures. To the extent they are able or know how to, states seek to adapt their concerns to federal programs and their own needs and differences, which are rooted in the social and political factors that serve to shape the states and the political settings in which they operate. Each state's political culture also shapes its administrative system, an often-overlooked phenomenon. Federal programs can alter certain tendencies within states, but hundreds of programs nevertheless filter through and are adapted into state and local administrative patterns.

4 JURISDICTIONAL INTERDEPENDENCE

This chapter focuses on the interdependent "joint administration" dimension of intergovernmental relations in the United States as programs have morphed into intergovernmental management, generated by federal-nonfederal proliferation. These practices of intergovernmentalism clearly led to Deil Wright's (1988) overlapping authority model. The chapter begins with an intergovernmental overview of selected programs that set the tone for overlapping management, particularly from the 1930s through the 1960s. For example, many of the non-retirement assistance program titles of the Social Security Act of 1935 involve the states as co-administrators. Indeed, when the nationwide pension system was established, the act also included the incorporation of state unemployment systems and federal aid to the states on some matching basis for dependent mothers, the destitute elderly, and the blind, and added in 1950 the disabled. In addition, many urban programs set the tone as direct federal-local operations that bypassed the states.

Federal aid programs that became visible in the United States began in the 1930s and the severe economic downturn. Subsequent New Deal legislation ushered in programs that were modeled on those in European welfare states and gained full force through the federal government's involvement. Previously President Herbert Hoover had been reluctant to engage the federal government in state and local programs, but in 1932 he did sign a bill that created the Reconstruction Finance Corporation, offering the states $300 million in federal funds to be lent and subsequently deducted from future federal highway grants. The corporation also increased the degree of federal supervision of state administrative personnel, particularly with public assistance practices, in a move that accelerated the professionalization of "poor" relief (Katz 1986, 216). One state-level precursor to the federal aid model was New York State's 1931 Temporary Emergency Relief Administration, which served as President Franklin Roosevelt's subsequent program model for federal relief. As the precursor to the federal program Works Progress Administration and operating until 1937, the Temporary Emergency Relief Administration offered matching grants to localities, with the states supervising how monies were to be spent. The program included professional standards for administrators to avoid increased patronage. While short lived and limited in funds and its impact on the unemployed, the program pointed to the general impotence of state and local government approaches to combat widespread unemployment. State and local officials subsequently reduced their prior political resistance to the enactment of federal assistance programs. Indeed, many mayors and governors lobbied for federal money.

Federal action actually began slowly and less visibly between 1900 and 1920 with new federal-state efforts in vocational education, highways, public health, and child welfare. Programs expanded in the 1960s and 1970s for social welfare, employment and training, housing and urban reconstruction, mental health and disabilities, rehabilitation, occupational health and safety, and environmental protection. All in some ways involved funds or regulations impacting state and local governments. Many of these projects were new grant programs that were later followed by new regulatory practices that set and enforced nationwide standards. These programs were different intergovernmentally from those of the earlier, simpler, less restrictive era that were characterized in chapter 3 as hands-off forms of federalism. Importantly, illustrating the second IGM thematic focus of this volume, the new programs legislatively and administratively reached deeper into the intricacies of government operations at state and local levels, thus making executive branch administrators at the various levels more interdependent.

The 1930s Depression accelerated such intergovernmental efforts, as Roosevelt's administrative and fiscal advisers had to face two IGR realities—the political constraints of federalism and the relatively undeveloped capacity of the federal government to operate such programs. The former concern is directly relevant here since the federal government had to maintain a more indirect role in relief, which until then largely comprised state-led programs. The federal government did so by developing its own public works projects, setting labor conditions for federal contractors, attaching grant conditions and standards for states to follow (as long as they could opt out), imposing regulations on interstate commerce, and largely providing for the "general welfare." Of course, while identifiable grant conditions had been around for some time, they grew more detailed and became the cornerstone of a form of welfare state IGR strategy (Brinkley 1995, ch. 1), launching higher intergovernmental interdependency.

Modeled after New York's program, the Federal Emergency Relief Administration gave federal matching funds for work relief and direct relief, along with set-aside funds for programs of national significance. Lasting from 1933 to 1935, the program touched almost five million families in all states. Importantly, the states also raised matching funds. In 1933 the government launched the Public Works Administration, loaning money to state and local governments and to private firms for construction projects, including the building of important public facilities. Also, the Works Progress Administration, enacted in 1935, employed more than three million people, mostly through projects planned and operated by state and local units. While it lasted in some form into the 1940s, and the projects were always criticized as boondoggles and wasteful make-work efforts, the administration was notable in a time of federal action on numerous related fronts that linked state and local governments in similar interdependent, federally operated, and jointly administered actions.

The accelerated intergovernmental action following the economic downturn of the 1930s reflected the cross-national trend toward unification on a nationwide basis, even in federal states used to devolution. For example, in agriculture and food policy, despite subnational autonomy, nations became concerned with protecting national markets to ensure self-sufficiency in food supplies, especially in times of crisis or emergency. In turn, those efforts led to more regulated national markets and a commitment to maintaining a rural sector. In agriculture, they led to the active involvement of the federal government via a central agency charged with managing food supplies and prices (Rieger 1995). It was one of many policy areas triggering greater interdependence.

As in agriculture, the Great Depression in the United States and in many European countries brought on a series of social policy concerns regarding program integration, a process that involves the interplay of policy makers at national and subnational levels. As such, they involve national and constituent actors as highly autonomous actors operating in common policy spaces while working toward similar aims in different ways (Leibfried and Pierson 1995). That means they "mixed" in policy action and program administration.

This intergovernmental program growth followed international trends. Many programs in the health and social welfare arenas followed the logic of promoting subnational policy nationally (Loughlin 2007, 389). It very much began as a principal-agent model, where regional and local governments were designed to become agents of their central governments. Douglas Ashford (1988, 19) traces most emergent central social policies (welfare, social services, employment, economic development) as being top down or polity-wide because most central governments were politically suspicious of local commitments; thus, national programming was coupled with local implementation. Central governments began to infuse centralized programs into local communities and in federal systems with connecting landings in constituent unit governments—that is, states or provinces. Later in the era came more targeted, broader social welfare programs, covering issues such as drug abuse, child and family abuse, and mental disabilities, plus new efforts in economic and community development and in nonsocial welfare areas like environmental protection and public safety.

The result of program growth over the twentieth century has been extreme leakage from the integral Westphalian state's compartmentalization that was forged in earlier times. Thus, many "overlaps of jurisdiction are unavoidable because it is virtually impossible to define watertight compartments of exclusive jurisdiction" (Watts 1999a, 38). For example, a study of over ninety powers and competencies in thirteen federal and unitary countries (Argullol 2004), including the United States, indicates that around two-thirds are not exclusive powers of one level of government but are mixed. The study found varied mixed patterns: central policy control and subnational administration, central normative control and subnational control over the functions, shared powers, and joint or asymmetrical powers. The study included powers in many areas beyond social welfare, such as employment and economic development, public security, tourism and culture, and environmental policy, all of which are standard components of what is now considered broadened "welfare state" programming.

In terms familiar to American researchers, this form of intergovernmentalization has brought on the overlapping authority model of governmental interaction. In contrast to the high degrees of separation or the coordinate top-down control and authority models of earlier eras, the overlapping model is characterized by substantial areas of governmental operations involving several levels simultaneously. Areas of (complete) jurisdictional autonomy are comparatively small and the power and influence of any one jurisdiction (or official) are limited, leading to exchange, negotiation, and work toward agreements (Wright 1988, 49; Agranoff and Radin 2015). This era gave rise to the very concept of IGR at working levels, particularly in management. It is also a product of the American "aversion of direct national administration, particularly in arenas where federal programs are moving into space previously occupied by subnational governments" (Mashaw and Calsyn 1996, 322).

As it unfolds, this chapter looks at the proliferation of federal grants that followed the earlier income security grants, demonstrating the increasing detail that has linked the federal bureaucracy with subnational agencies. One example is that of standards and targets for Medicaid recipients, now subject to both program and fiscal auditing. Next is a discussion of the patterns of interaction set by the growing number of regulatory programs, previously identified as "unfunded mandates." States and metropolitan areas are now held responsible for attaining predetermined levels of air quality, for example, and upon failing, non-attainment areas are required to take certain mitigation measures for which they receive no financial compensation. The next section then reviews the new interdependencies in the non-grant, non-regulatory IGR arenas. These include the growing programs in government loans, loan guarantees, interest rate buy-downs, and government-backed insurance, as they impact state and local governments. All of this expansion has led to new and now established "enterprise," with government associations serving as lobbyists in the system. Those representing cities and counties—elected officials and specialist administrators—go to their state capitols on behalf of organizations representing these entities, while state government representatives

BOX 4.1

- As the number of intergovernmental programs grew, the focus on the quest for "management of the intergovernmental system" as well as management within the system increased.
- Program growth in terms of numbers of distinctive programs led to widespread understanding of overlapping powers among administering governments as an operational norm.
- Resolving differences between levels generated practices involving joint or at least interactive problem identification and the search for workable operating solutions.
- The forces of jurisdictional complexity and the involvement of multiple entities operationally at several levels, where areas of autonomy are small and complete autonomy is limited, emphasized the importance of exchange, negotiation, and working agreements. They underscore the role of managers within the system.

go to Washington (Beer 1978). Finally, the chapter takes a first look at contemporary intergovernmental complexity, examining those "pillars" that are the hybrid of categorical or specialized programs and how they begin to deal with such situations in the process of solving complex problems. One common practice is that of managing by problem instead of by program; another is managing by place. This chapter introduces the "sunk costs" that lead to the building of the administrative state, which crosses boundaries and is promoted by growing interdependency.

Growing Interdependency: A Jurisdictional Perspective

To take the example of the various social protection programs, government assistance shifted "upward" jurisdictionally over time (Skocpol 1995). Before the Great Depression, states enacted welfare laws from their earliest postcolonial days that normally passed on such responsibility to local governments. Pennsylvania, Ohio, and Michigan had laws similar to that of Wisconsin, passed in 1849: "Every town shall relieve and support all poor and indigent persons, lawfully settled therein, whenever they shall stand need thereof" (quoted in Berkowitz 1997, 1). This was a carryover from the English Poor Laws of 1602, which extended to the colonies as early as 1642. Local governments were also charged with ensuring that children were provided with a decent education, and if they were not, the governments were to remove them from family supervision by public action and rectify the situation. Other services followed. As local governments grew into cities, they had to expand their water and sewer services, street lighting and paving, police and fire protection, and schools. Later in the nineteenth century, those cities that were actually loose agglomerations of area-based councils led by businessmen and professionals and weak mayors faced many social problems: overcrowding, high rates of disease and mortality, crime, threats to the social order, education, and welfare challenges. "All required strong, coordinated, central response, which neither city governments nor political machines could deliver" (Katz 1986, 152).

These problems in turn were accompanied by waves of civil service reform and the granting of greater powers for municipalities, mayors, and city managers in a quest for professionalization and efficiency. Most important here is that the seeds of closer interdependency were sown by the state governments' taking over local welfare supervision (Katz 1986, ch. 6). This eventually led to statewide social programming, for example, in mental health care, which during the mid-nineteenth century was transformed from local almshouses to state-run hospitals. In 1865 New York authorized the first state asylum, effectively removing clients from county to state jurisdiction, and by 1890 virtually all mental care was under state auspices. Meanwhile, counties in Wisconsin in 1881 could build local asylums, but they remained under state supervision. Other states followed with mental health care programs organized by state commissions. The pattern of state assumption followed in other arenas: income support, social services, and education. State program acquisition thus increased because it helped to promote uniform standards of operation and administration throughout the system (Gettings 2011, ch. 1).

As the nineteenth century progressed, the care of vulnerable children moved from private charitable organizations and county-level public protective commissions to the state government level. In the early twentieth century, the proportion of dependent and neglected children in public institutions doubled from 10 percent to 21 percent. By 1929 most states had enacted legislation regulating the operations of children's institutions and child care and foster care agencies. States also began to take interest in child welfare in four areas: education, labor, juvenile justice, and public health. Many early twentieth-century social reformers visited Europe and were "impressed by the capacity of government for social action, with faith in their ability to apply expert knowledge to social problems" (Katz 1986, 122).

Also in the social welfare arena, states attempted to preserve families by authorizing "mothers' pensions" for those families where the "primary breadwinner was absent, normally by widowhood" (Katz 1986, 130). Missouri and Illinois passed the first programs in 1911. By the end of 1913 twenty states had such programs, and by 1919 thirty-nine states plus the territories of Hawaii and Alaska had them as well. Very restrictive (e.g., many states excluded divorcées), not exactly generous, and barely the entitlements they are today, these programs were clearly the antecedents for the federal program Aid to Dependent Children (later the Aid to Families with Dependent Children and Temporary Assistance for Needy Families), as public assistance started when

Congress adopted the Social Security Act in 1935. In all, such programs were responsible for state aid to localities that rose from $52 million in 1902 to $596 million in 1927. In addition to highway funding, most of these grants were in the areas of education and public welfare (Walker 2000, 178).

The Great Depression then accelerated broader federal relief for the states that included social welfare, public works, and other spending. In the 1930s the Economic Security Act in effect "nationalized" some aspects of states' welfare responsibilities. The major social insurance program of the Social Security Act in 1935 was contributory and operated entirely by the federal government. But states also played a role, for added to this large program were matching grants to the states for old-age assistance. The Children's Bureau was also inserted into the act through Aid to Dependent Children, which was administered by grants to the states and known for many years as "welfare." Other programs that ran through the states included Aid to the Blind (and aid to the permanently and totally disabled was added in 1950), along with funds directed to the states for public health services, vocational rehabilitation, and infant and maternal health. Meanwhile, the unemployment insurance program was designed to be self-supporting under federal law but operated by the states through state government–organized employer and employee insurance pools. In effect, these programs under the Social Security Act "froze the distinctions between insurance and assistance into national policy" (Katz 1986, 238).

Unlike other Western nations that had adopted a blend of more universal social policies, including family allowances, universal health care, housing allowances, and assistance that benefited the poor and nonpoor alike, the United States obscured the distinction between social insurance and welfare (Patterson 1981, 76). As a former state governor, President Franklin Roosevelt distinctly preferred the federal-grants-to-states approach. It served to settle many debates and potential conflicts—for example, those over unemployment insurance—between the advantages of uniformity and interstate protection versus leaving states room to maneuver and resolve the more routine and controversial issues. Thus, with the exception of the nationally run pension system of Social Security, the New Deal reinforced the American state and its local welfare and services tradition while adding a new layer of federal involvement, not to speak of accelerated interdependency.

Theda Skocpol (1995) concludes that social welfare reform (and related domestic programs) in the twentieth century began through waves of similar legislation across the states. But national policies that would reach deep into the social fabric did not get enthusiastic support until the 1930s. Programs were largely delegated downward to state and local governments, which followed the already set pattern in US intergovernmental relations and continued for many years (Finegold 1982; Weiser 2001a, 2001b; Hills Jr. 1998). Philip Rocco (2013, 5) studied more than two hundred landmark laws

over this domestic growth era that in effect either implied or mandated intergovernmental collaboration as a product of intense policy conflict. It was diffused by distributing governing authority to multiple venues and buying off
opposition, and it continued to limit "the reach of the postwar administrative
state." Of course, some see this downward flow in the attempt to promote
cooperative means as impinging on local priorities and affairs and as co-
opting potential opposition at the local or community level. However, "they
actually increase the patronage exercised by local elites and retain local elite
domination over beneficiary groups" (Cover 1982–83, 1343). At any rate,
they clearly tie such local interests to administering state and federal interests
(see chapter 6 of this volume, where policy implementation is explored).

When the Social Security Act was passed, it was rooted in prior state-
level laws or legislative proposals under active debate in the 1930s. Congressional mediation of contradictory regional interests ensured that strict
national standards could not be established in most programs. As a result,
"basic structural features of the U.S. state have thus powerfully set overall
institutional limits for social provision in the United States" (Rocco 2013, 25),
a key factor in the evolution of IGR and IGM. Put another way, the national
system of many programs in assistance, public works, employment, and so
on was grafted onto state and local programs already in existence.

Intergovernmental Expansion

The rest is history, as the overview of the Advisory Commission on Intergovernmental Relations reveals in chapter 3. Accounts of federal growth and its
impact highlight the grant-in-aid as the primary feature of post-1930s development (e.g., Conlan 1998; Dilger 2009; Walker 2000; Wright 1988; Stephens
and Wikstrom 2007). Program development has grown and changed with
visible federal expansion, not only in funding and authorization but also at
the services level, particularly as "large unitary or centralized governments
must decentralize the administration and delivery of many regulatory activities and public services" (Stephens and Wikstrom 2007, 29). In addition,
state aid to localities also expanded in many categories, including education,
highways, public welfare, health and hospitals, and even for general support,
rising from $801 million in 1932 to $8.2 billion in 1958.

Post–New Deal expansion of federal programs in many new areas highlighted intergovernmental activity. During the Harry Truman years (1945–
53), programs assisted agricultural marketing, hospital construction, mental
health, disaster relief, cancer control, urban renewal and slum clearance, civil
defense, aid to the disabled, fish restoration, and school construction in federally impacted areas. Aid outlays passed the $2.4 billion mark in 1952 for
seventy-one separately authorized programs. The Dwight Eisenhower years

(1953–61) produced sixty-one new programs, mostly in the same areas but with major new outlays for interstate highways and defense-related educational grants totaling $6.8 billion in allocations. However, three-quarters of the dollars were for highways, old-age assistance, aid to dependent children, and employment security (Walker 2000, 99). The states were the primary recipients of these grants (Galle 2008).

Virtually all these programs were based on what were called categorical or conditional grants. Their main features included open-ended matching disbursements, formula allocations based on congressionally determined amounts, formula-based project grants dividing money among competing applications, and pure project grants with no constraints in distribution (Walker 2000, 102). The latest phase of this programmatic building culminated in the 1960s. David Walker (2000, 124–25) identifies this period of IGR growth as involving (1) a doubling of grant-in-aid outlays; (2) a shift in emphasis to urban and metropolitan areas; (3) an enactment of more grant programs—210—than in all prior years, dating back to the first grant in 1789; (4) a host of new grants that greatly expanded the range of public purposes, from antipoverty programs to Medicaid; (5) a move to more panoramic partnerships, particularly with federal aid going to local general and special-purpose governments as well as to a range of nonprofit organizations; (6) an introduction of the regulatory era, where states and the localities became both the objects and the first-line implementers of federal regulations; and (7) a launching of concern for improving grants management in the areas of federal and nonfederal relationships and communication. As Timothy Conlan (1988, 6) concludes, this IGR expansion "not only made the system far more complex, but also upset the temporary balance of intergovernmental power." As the federal government became involved in virtually all fields of governmental activity, the locus of policy initiation and leadership shifted to the national level. It increased state and local fiscal dependence on federal funding, and federal programs increasingly relied on services that required the use of professionals in service delivery.

Through the stepping up of federal conditions and expectations, system growth and change had a corresponding impact on administration. It clearly moved IGR beyond the earlier legal and political concerns and ushered in IGM as a prominent concern. Walker (2000, 102) concludes that requirements for professional qualifications and political neutrality of agency personnel, plus "single state agency" provisions to establish an administrative focus to isolate managers from political pressure, and merit system requirements and political activity restrictions all reinforced the professionalization of programs. It meant a de-emphasis on legislative bodies and the attempt to neutralize the administrative role of chief executives in favor of agency specialists and professional managers. Intergovernmentally it marked the expansion of a more apolitical core of agency administrators—generalists and specialists—who served their jurisdiction and their program, accelerating the collaborative dimensions of programs and placing more emphasis on management, albeit without completely removing political concerns.

Grants: An Administrative Perspective

The evolved grants-in-aid program has substantially contributed to the changes in the nature of traditional public administration's predominantly hierarchical orientation. As depicted, from the earliest years, grants amounted to fiscal or in-kind assistance to the states through land grants that had few program restrictions and in many ways reinforced dual federalism (Dilger 2009, 8–10). Modern grants adhered more to the post–Civil War ideas that the Union was more than a compact among the states; thus, the grants opened up greater nationwide action. Grants have now become principal administrative tools of government action; today grantors provide guidance and direction but leave operational discretion to grantee governments. Finally, as David Beam and Timothy Conlan (2002, 343) conclude, "Grants are much more restrictive than they once were, for example under the more cooperative times identified earlier, as rules attached to them have been more directive, even coercive, and increasingly entangled with federal social mandates." Several works have outlined the types and shapes of grants (Beam and Conlan 2002; Conlan 1998; Stephens and Wikstrom 2007; Walker 2000; Wright 1988), along with how they are designed and allocated. Most important for understanding management is that of the hundreds of federal grants to state and local governments, all but a few are categorical—that is, *specified in purpose* and either automatically distributed by *formula*, where legally or administratively funds are dedicated to states or subdivisions, or are of a *project* nature for fixed periods and for specific purposes.

In addition to federal grants, state aid to local governments includes some pass-through funds from the federal government that the states distribute to local governments. State aid also comes from state treasury–originated funds. The former amounts to an estimated 30 percent of funds whereas state funds supply about 70 percent. At one point, in total, state aid to local governments normally exceeded federal aid by a slight margin, with about 8 percent of the total in general aid and the remainder for specific grants (Beam and Conlan 2002). In some states, local aid is designed to adjust fiscal disparities among communities. Most state aid to local education is provided in a block grant (but with increasing restrictions), while other aid is categorical and intended for such uses as highways and roads, social services, and capital projects. Also, pass-through federal Community Development Block Grants for Small Cities (administered by the states) have been used for local infrastructure construction. For example, by the early 2000s state aid had comprised about a fourth of county budgets, about a fifth of municipal budgets, and just over half of local school district budgets (Berman 2003, 103).

Grants have generated levels of administrative interdependency that were virtually unheard of in the nineteenth century. For example, just one of the nearly six hundred federal programs of aid to state and subnational governments is Title III of the Older Americans Act of 1965. It provides various types of services to needy senior citizens through a network of regional Area Agencies on Aging and ultimately through their service contractors. The act is on a renewable cycle. Each part of Title III is subject to multiple pages of program regulations and subsequent guidelines that fill many booklets. The federal government's Administration on Aging must approve and later monitor each of fifty-six (states and territories) "state plans," which have gradually moved in appearance from pure grants to increasingly look like contracts. Many cross-program requirements have been added to the detailed program requirements—for example, nondiscrimination measures, protected category business set-asides, the ways federal programs are to be organized, and categories of expenditures, such as capital versus operational.

The states have put their own legislative and administrative procedures on Title III (e.g., service priorities, purchasing, travel and reimbursement) as they contract with the Area Agencies on Aging, which in turn make plans and arrangements to deliver home nursing, nutritional, day activity, home help, visitor, and other services to seniors in need (see chapters 6 and 7). At each stage of the process, fiscal and program paperwork is compiled and sent from the contractor to the agency and then to the states, because the state is subject to a dual (program and fiscal) post audit some two years after the close of the fiscal year in which services are delivered. In such a process, lots of interactions and transactions take place, requiring cooperation and some measures of conflict resolution as well. Programs such as Title III have ratcheted up the administrative quotient of IGR and have exponentially expanded such transactions.

These complications expand over time as more and more detailed expectations can be and are piled on as experience with programs grow. One example is related to the states' responsibilities under the Medicaid Home and Community-Based Services (HCBS) Waiver program guidelines for quality management that the federal Centers for Medicare and Medicaid Services (CMS) promulgated in 2000. In an initial phase (the early 2000s), six major areas of assurances were at the guidelines' core: level of care, plan of care, provider capabilities, health and welfare, financial accountability, and administrative authority (Gettings 2003, 227–32). Literally hundreds of detailed provisions and expectations were listed under each of these categories in the CMS *State Operations Manual*, a set of regulation-oriented guidelines of "compliance principles" and "facility practice statements"

(Hayes, Joyce, and Couchoud 2003, 206). These concerns have expanded exponentially over the years.

The problem of federal supervision in this arena is that CMS possesses a thin statutory-based regulatory authority considering the state administration of Medicaid grants. Within such constraints of program assurances, CMS has become more prescriptive on how states manage their HCBS Waivers, including requiring each state to have a set of performance measures for each category of assurance, subassurance, data sources, reporting schedules, and evidence of remediation. Thus, the states have had to develop more intentional quality assurance systems, to make data-driven decisions, and to build in quality improvement. As a result, in states that have been loose with their substate areas, local governments and providers have had to tighten their requirements, standardize data collections, and reform their subcontract procedures. The whole thrust is in a new approach to HCBS Waiver applications that requires states to describe the various processes, which in most cases require specific indicators of performance, measurement parameters, and responsible parties to be pre-identified. States are also encouraged to be more transparent, involve stakeholders, and post data on websites (Bradley 2009). Most important, these changes have clearly complicated and extended interactive activity between CMS regional offices and state Medicaid and state intellectual and developmental disabilities offices, while the state agencies have had to increase substate contacts. Clearly the HCBS guidelines have raised the interdependency quotient, but HCBS is far from an isolated example of more involved managerial concern.

Management by Regulations and Mandates

The era of regulatory federalism further tied governments by levels. Lester Salamon (2002, 118) refers to three types of regulations that emerged on the scene: the familiar rules governing the implementation of a program; the economic regulation governing the entry and exit of firms, prices, or output (e.g., entry and price controls), a carryover from the earlier era; and the social regulation, or those rules governing the effects of economic activity or health, welfare, or social being of citizens (e.g., pollution and workplace safety). The primary intergovernmental regulatory interest is the growth of regulatory federalism, which the ACIR identified and is discussed in chapter 3 of this volume.

In addition to grant expansion, Congress adopted new forms of regulatory statutes, including ones that directly impacted state and local governments. They involved regulations targeted at jurisdictions as separate entities, affecting everything from their employment practices to the operation of municipal sewer systems, along with efforts to enlist states as agents in regulating the private sector—for example, in areas of environmental protection and occupational health and safety. These regulatory programs went beyond the traditional regulations attached to grant programs. As Conlan (1998, 86–87, 192) identifies, four different types were regularly employed: direct order mandates, crossover sanctions, partial preemptions, and crosscutting requirements (see also Posner 1998, 13–14; chapter 3 of this volume). Of all the expanding intergovernmental regulations, crosscutting requirements were the most common. Thus, regulatory federalism not only locked in an enhanced federal role but also created a "senior" federal collaborative role that was "permanently established" (Conlan 1998, 91).

Social regulation further reinforces jurisdictional interdependency. Initially regarded as state functions under their "police powers," they increasingly were subject to federal legislation over the twentieth century. While a few national programs—meat inspection, food and drug safety—were enacted early in the century, the period from 1968 (Fair Housing Act) to 1990 (Americans with Disabilities) saw a proliferation of such legislation. Among others, the social regulation movement included the Clean Air Act (1970), Clean Water Act (1972), Consumer Product Safety Act (1972), National Environmental Policy Act (1970), Nutrition Labeling and Education Act (1990), and Occupational Health and Safety Act (1970) (Meier and Garman 1995). These laws authorized federal agencies to set rules and enforce provisions of the laws, including holding states responsible for enforcing federal standards in grants. In many cases—for example, safe drinking water—state governments are held responsible for enforcement. As Peter May (2002, 158) identifies, each social regulation program has four key elements: rules governing behavior and outcomes, standards that serve as benchmarks for compliance, sanctions for rule noncompliance, and an administrative agency or setup that enforces the rules and administers sanctions.

State and local government involvement in social regulation is also longstanding. Their roles include action in consumer protection, occupational licensing, educational standards and regulations enforcement, child care and nursing homes, building construction and building safety and health, and environmental regulations that parallel federal regulations. Local governments, in turn, deal directly with zoning and land-use regulations, housing codes, traffic safety, signage, noise levels, and property management. What links these state and local regulatory functions intergovernmentally is that many are now tied to the new federal programs and accompanying mandates. For example, state and local governments are subject to and responsible for enforcing the Asbestos Hazard Emergency Response Act of 1986 and the Age Discrimination in Employment Amendments of 1986 (Posner 1998, 233–37).

Regulatory federalism has thus remained as an IGM tool. Beginning with the Ronald Reagan administration of the 1980s and beyond, regulatory expansion survived and was reinforced for two reasons. First, to the degree that such programs are consistent with Congress's broader ideological and economic aims, they are more convenient than funding programs. As federal fiscal deficits mounted, regulating state and local governments became a substitute for new program funds. As mentioned, in 1995 Congress passed the Unfunded Mandates Reform Act, making it somewhat harder to enact direct-order mandates and selected conditions of aid based on estimated fiscal costs, although it had many escape clauses (Posner 1998, ch. 8).

Intergovernmental regulation, as with grants, thus also boosted interdependence. In the process, federalism questions that relate to appropriate roles seem to have been set aside. As the federal government has expanded its role in such policy arenas as state and local employment practices, wastewater and water supply, access to public services, and working conditions through indirect means, concerns over issues such as the federal power and federal presence have largely been set aside for more focused concerns over a program's substantive concerns. Paul Posner's (1998, 27) study of unfunded mandates indicates that federalism concerns have been largely deferred for broader policy or program purposes. In this regard, Hugh Heclo (1989, 312) concludes that once the thresholds of legitimating federal activity are crossed in a range of policy areas, policy conflict moves from ideological to instrumental points involving program design and implementation. This form of regulation has clearly shifted the grounds of interdependence deeply into management, or matters of design and implementation.

Intergovernmental Loans and Borrowing

The federal government has extensive programs that lend money to borrowers and service those loans, along with backing up guarantees for other loans that are made in the private market and ensuring that lenders are repaid if loans should default. While many such loans do not involve subnational governments, a notable number of them actually do involve state and local units in some, albeit often indirect, way. As chapter 2 revealed, historically state and local governments were often partners in ventures that built roads, canals, bridges, and railroads. Federal loans and loan guarantees for local governments date back as far as colonial days, and the federal government continues to loan funds for infrastructure and physical improvements.

During the Great Depression of the 1930s, many municipal buildings, county courthouses, public libraries, park pavilions, and new schools were financed by a combination of direct subsidies and loans. The federal government "sent a message to the towns: Washington is there to help when the town is in trouble, and yet will not intrude on the community to do it" (Shlaes 2007, 262). Since then federal loans support not only local government buildings but also housing purchases, urban and rural development projects, water and wastewater treatment plants, and disaster recovery. From the late 1960s, federal loan guarantees have grown while direct loans have stabilized. By 2000 guarantees exceeded loans by over five times (Stanton 2002, 388). Guarantees include mortgage insurance, municipal loan credit buy downs and guarantees, and guarantees of loans for municipal infrastructure and environmental compliance (e.g., water plants). Such federal loan guarantees facilitate the citizens of local governments to enter the housing market and of local governments to enter the credit market for various long-term projects.

Loan guarantee programs, rural electric and telephone development loans, rural community development, rural and urban housing, and disaster assistance, among others, involve state and local governments as investment partners, often combining state and sometimes local programs. For example, the US Department of Agriculture Rural Development state-level offices facilitate direct and guaranteed loans for utilities services, business development, housing, community planning and development, and infrastructure. In facilitating these programs, Nebraska's state office of this federal agency works closely with the Nebraska Department of Economic Development, local governments, rural cooperatives, and lending institutions (Agranoff 2007c, 74).

The Intergovernmental Lobby

The growth of federal programming and the corresponding increase in multiple source funding and interlinked operations have also given rise to governments advocating on their own behalf and for their jurisdictions collectively before other governments, particularly funders, regulators, and lenders. The proliferation of programs and many branches of the federal money tree, plus regulation, has brought in both specialist officials and program heads and government generalists: mayors, governors, legislators, and other state officials who work the political system across government lines. This form of public interest advocacy, or intergovernmental lobbying, involves working the system at all stages of programming from advocating for enablement and regulatory relief to providing oversight and input into program administration. These advocates or lobbyists are somehow referred to as public interest groups (PIGs), inasmuch as they claim to represent the general interests of particular constituencies.

State and local governments, particularly of large cities and counties, normally have a lobbying presence in Washington, DC, and before federal offices located around the country. Virtually every state government has a Washington office and has other lobbyists on retainer (Jensen and Emery 2011). For example, Cincinnati, Ohio, maintains lobbyists in Columbus, the state capital, where many federal field offices are also located, and has a lobbyist on retainer in Washington, DC. At one time it also had a city representation office in Washington that it shared with other city governments, but now Cincinnati places more focus on its state capital, which can be reached in a one-hour car trip. City officials nevertheless are in email contact with federal offices regularly—for example, with its department heads about once or twice a week, and the city manager's office several times daily. All this effort is to support the city's active intergovernmental program based on council-adopted policy and to pursue funding opportunities and negotiate its regulatory obligations (Agranoff and McGuire 2003, 10–11). This active pattern is not unusual for large cities.

Jurisdictional lobbying can also include developing contacts with trade and professional associations among the large number of functional associations located in Washington; establishing federal program coordinators, or home-based intergovernmental contact and programming offices within the government; and hiring consultants, public relations specialists, lawyers, or lobbyists to pursue specific interests or programs. All this work is to keep on top of the heavy linkages that develop among groups and federal administrative personnel who work outside of the legislative process. Donald Haider (1974, 88) once observed that close links evolve over time between persons working in professional programs in government and advocacy groups representing related service areas. Traditional lobbying in this sense—that is, legislative contact by state and local government interests—extends considerably far beyond enactment stages to extensive and involved administrative agency–group interactions over program-related or "professional" concerns. Haider's landmark study of governmental representation in Washington by associations referred to this practice as involving vital and vibrant partners in the governmental process. Moreover, he maintains that groups that represent governments have greater legitimacy than other interest groups that represent narrower and special interests. As associations of elected officials, Ann Marie Cammisa (1995, 16) argues, "there exists a level of understanding between members of Congress and the government groups that is not present with other groups. The government groups are lobbyists who themselves have been lobbied, and this gives them special status."

Of the state associations, three of the most important generalist bodies include the National Governors Association (NGA), the Council of State Governments (CSG), and the National Conference of State Legislatures (NCSL). The NGA was founded in 1908 and is perhaps the most powerful. It operates through standing committees and staff activities, and it takes policy positions. The most active members are the governors of the smaller states. As Haider (1974, 30) concludes, "What began essentially as a center for information clearance, keeping the nation's governors abreast of federal developments in Washington, matured full force into a gubernatorial lobby." Serving as an umbrella organization that generates information and provides assistance, primarily for legislators, the CSG also serves as a national secretariat for many affiliate organizations of state specialists such as information officers and constitutional offices (e.g., state auditors). Headquartered in Lexington, Kentucky, and with an office in Washington, DC, the CSG is not directly involved in lobbying, although its affiliate groups—for example, the National Association of Attorneys General—regularly are. Headquartered in Denver and with Washington offices, the NCSL staffs national committees, provides direct services to member-state legislatures, and conducts lobbying activities affecting states. Policy positions are taken by a state/federal assembly that meets three times a year and whose members are appointed by each state's two (except Nebraska) houses (Cigler 1995, 136). From the 1930s to the 1980s, federal spending and regulatory powers brought in the states as federal partners and enlarged the federal system, which sustained new structures, links, and support groups connecting Washington and subnational governments (Haider 1974, 2).

Five local government generalist groups also stand out: the US Conference of Mayors (USCM), which represents large cities; the National League of Cities (NLC), which focuses on medium and small cities; the National Association of Counties (NACo), which represents rural, suburban, and urban counties; the International City and County Management Association (ICMA), which does not formally lobby but takes positions that affect its council-manager members and links in numerous non-advocacy ways with other local government groups; and the less visible National Association of Towns and Townships (NATaT), which champions the thousands of small governments, particularly state township associations. Other groups include the National Civic League (once called the National Municipal League), dating back to the nineteenth century, that promotes citizen involvement in local government, and the National Association of Regional Councils, which represents metropolitan areas (Flanagan 1999; Gunther 1990). Together with the identified state associations, these groups are also considered PIGs because they represent not only generalists in government but also their members claim to serve the interests of all their citizens, adding a "spatial or areal dimension to the national decision-making process" (Cigler 1995, 138).

Intergovernmental Activity of the PIGs

To varying degrees, general government groups are involved in what Donald Menzel (1990, 401–3) calls "collecting, conveying, and convincing." In other words, their functions include organizing and conducting research on national and local problems and fostering knowledge networks. Their work also involves preparing numerous reports and other written materials to convey to their members, the legislators, the media, and the general public. Indeed, much of the groups' effectiveness, according to Haider (1974, 286),

BOX 4.2

- The number and scope of grants have led to widespread "shared administration," setting off familiar chains of standards, recipient plans, administrative procedures, and oversight. It clearly makes intergovernmental program administration a distinctive endeavor.
- Many federal and state programs are administered through long chains that work their way through states and to regional bodies, case managers, and a host of for-profit and nonprofit NGO delivery agents. This pattern is particularly true regarding direct services, for example, in human services delivery.
- Program expansion and complex administration contexts have also led to increased involvement by lobby groups, which are active at all levels from program adoption design to various program administration stages.
- Federal and federal-state program expansion has accelerated the growth and greater reach of associations that work on behalf of subnational jurisdictions, as well as programs organized on a statewide basis. Collectively they are known as public interest groups.

is an outgrowth of their information and feedback functions, as they provide officials with information and research related to operational problems, management concerns, and perceived defects in federal programs. Moreover, policy specialization and expertise enable these groups to participate in drafting and amending legislation, pre-legislative clearance, and post-legislative rulemaking (Agranoff 2014).

Lobbying by the active groups (all but ICMA and NCSL) is based on policy statements, which are periodically reviewed and modified, that articulate association policy goals and serve as guides for their staff and key member representatives before Washington legislative and administrative circles to track legislative proposals and to monitor federal programs in the executive branch. In one study of PIGs in the policy-making process, congressional staff and association members rated the USCM and NLC second and third behind the National Governors Association in overall influence. The NLC and USCM have always had active and visible spokespersons, whereas NACo has not been as visible, perhaps because of the divisions of views among its members and its state associations (Cammisa 1995, 120). The influence of these groups and their impact on the programs' management concerns are additional testimony to the rise of IGM, not to speak of its political nature.

Specialized Group Contacts

Functional specialist contacts between state, local, and federal governments increased from the 1930s to the 1960s and remain highly important (Nownes 2014). These include a wide range of groups—for example, city engineers, city attorneys, and county planning and county highway administrators. Most are organized into statewide associations, which can coordinate easily around their particular concerns and, similar to the generalist groups, provide technical and educational functions as well as lobbying. Beverly Cigler (1995, 140) relates how these groups tap into the system: "The specialist associations fit well within the functional policy networks at the national level, sharing knowledge and interest with similar professionals at all government levels, as well as with non-profit public interest groups that specialize in particular policy areas. The special associations work through vertical and horizontal ties within the political system, including those with private professional organizations . . . [and] they come in frequent contact with general state organizations." A number of these groups, particularly NACo, NLC, and NATaT, are affiliated with the PIGs.

Cammisa's (1995) research reports that intergovernmental lobbying has changed with the decline in federal funding and the shift in emphasis on the states beginning in the 1980s. Local groups now face federal deficits, cutbacks in funding, and consolidation of some programs, while the National Governors Association has ridden the tide of emphasis on the states and its members' experiences as experts in social programs. "The direct federal-city connection is loosened, and the local groups have less clout" (129). This trend has accelerated in the second decade of the twenty-first century. Federal programs that in 2010 amounted to 26 percent of state and local spending, or some $654 billion in federal grants, are ripe targets for federal deficit reduction. Those programs that are proposed for reduction will "unleash a political fight far too large . . . [since] state and local governments are deeply tied to federal finance" (Peterson 2011, 46). It will certainly spur lobbying campaigns for mitigating and absorbing the shock.

If one adds the specialist groups to the PIGs, since the 1930s intergovernmental groups representing local governments have enjoyed recognition and a measure of public legitimacy as pursuers of the "public interest," which enhances their legitimacy as well as their traditional ability to influence policy and administration. In this sense group activity contributes mightily to IGM in practice. In particular, associations representing elected generalists appear legitimate and as having the right to speak on behalf of their constituents. However, as claimants before the federal government, concludes Haider (1974, 256), "they have no real formal standing as federal actors." Their position has, he observes, a "certain political devaluation in transference" (256). The question then is, to what degree does Washington view state and local governments as just other interest groups—and not as partners in implementing public policy (Wogan 2014, 55)? These visible intergovernmental groups cannot expect the White House and Congress to automatically embrace their positions; instead, they must spend more effort gathering economic and financial data and explaining why they have taken certain positions.

Key Learning Points

The sheer volume of intergovernmental activity—led by nearly six hundred domestic state and local government aid programs—plus the growing involvement in program implementation detail have led to two important public sector IGR-IGM legacies. First, contemporary programs now need to be organized and managed at all stages of the process. From jurisdictional perspectives, contrary to the earlier period of written reports and fiscal audits, this development has occasioned the need for increased intergovernmental operations. Second, given the number of programs and potential programs, often they need to be "managed" on two- or multiparty bases interactively at the delivery level. This produces challenges of coping with complexity that are addressed in chapter 5.

As a result, post-enablement actions in the implementation and assessment of programs need to be taken into account. These are the "micro processes" of IGM actions, largely hidden from public view as officials work out policies on a day-to-day basis. Practice has indicated that IGM involves solving problems through clusters of actors and is primarily the work of administrators. As a sub-activity of IGR, IGM is a means of coping and working within the existing system while handling regular and routine contacts and transactions, and it entails the joint actions of officials who deal with multiple political and management forces as some project or task is being accomplished (Agranoff 1986).

It is also important to bear in mind the conditions under which IGM operates: the partial accountability, the likelihood of differing objectives held by the various jurisdictions, the ongoing or continuous nature of the programming, and the exchanges of resources, information, and power across organizational boundaries (Rosenthal 1984). In these respects IGM is a different form of management.

Key Practice Points

Intergovernmental management involves many different kinds of managerial behaviors. Early in the development of US policy implementation research, the game was known as dealing with grants and regulations, along with "bargaining and negotiation" over some core questions to make programs work (e.g., Williams 1981; Ingram 1977; Pressman 1975). Later in the research stream, it was discovered that many, many transactions occur along the line that require continuing interaction, if not other aspects of cooperation (Elmore 1985). Empirical examination of IGM activities reveals that they are considerably more involved than the earlier studies suggested. Agranoff and McGuire's (2003) study of city economic development cooperation identifies twenty-one distinct IGM actions. As programs have moved beyond the boundaries of governments, the actions are both vertical—that is, they work with state and federal governmental officials—and horizontal, or with other local governments, NGOs, and the private sector. The vertical IGM instruments are of two types—those that try to make some form of adjustment to the system within the boundaries of the programs' policy intent and those that are designed to determine information or joint understandings. The horizontal instruments either serve particular investment projects or help develop or maintain networks of officials. The frequency of these actions is reported in the full Agranoff and McGuire study (2003, 108, 113).

Given the myriad of intergovernmental programs, one is often challenged to manage by problem while using several programs interactively. For example, states now cope with putting together several federal and state programs that serve to integrate intellectually and developmentally disabled people into community settings while providing a balanced set of opportunities and services. This process includes accessing and combining many services, organized around various types of needs and challenges, that range from limited timely services to full residential and occupational opportunities.

Overcoming complexity and achieving intergovernmental-oriented system-building and integration-related activities thus constitute core IGM challenges. One might call them compound intergovernmental exercises. Such challenges occur in many arenas—for example, mental health, disabilities, emergency management, economic development, long-term unemployment, water quality, and homelessness, to name a few.

Conclusion

Interdependency in IGM illustrates how IGR has changed the face of "constitutionalism," where overlapping powers are an operating norm. Some have referred to IGR as a "fourth branch of government" (Wright 1988). Program expansion clearly puts its imprint on an intergovernmental system, and in the United States it accelerates and interlocks governments. Instead of three distinct pillars of federal, state, and local governments, social welfare and other programs have ushered in *interaction on massive scales* on many program, financing, and administrative fronts. It also launched a massive intergovernmental "establishment" of public officials, program specialists, delivery agents, clientele groups, and advocacy associations that over time has developed deep stakes in program ideas, resources, and management. Moreover, as this volume shows, there is even more to come from the armies of contract service operators outside of government and the networks of working officials (Agranoff and Radin 2015).

Despite more recent leveling of some programs from the 1930s to the present, domestic programs pervade the entire system from Washington ultimately to delivery NGOs. This pattern is unlikely to go away, despite political attacks and budget cutbacks. In a profound assessment of welfare state retrenchment, Paul Pierson (1996, 174–76) maintains that "there are powerful political forces that stabilize welfare states and channel change in the direction of incremental modifications of existing policies" (174). This path dependence includes the status quo nature of programs, affording them attendant political advantages; their protection due to the high political costs associated with retrenchment initiatives; the introduction of newly organized interests as defenders, particularly as consumers and providers of services; and the emergence of configurations of clients, providers, and subnational governments that adapt to particular arrangements. Under these conditions, any retrenchment in welfare and other programs could be at the margins, at least until clear political signals, moments of budgetary crisis, and the visibility of reformers are lowered, and rules of the game such as trade-offs between taxes, spending, and deficits are able to shift the balance of power. Moreover, new programs are bound to surface when the political forces are in the right direction. Such was the case in 2010 when the Affordable Care Act was enacted with all its political and intergovernmental dimensions.

5 MANAGING INTERDEPENDENCY

This chapter outlines the more extensive administrative developments and operations within the managerial concept of intergovernmental relations—that is, the emergence of intergovernmental management as a product of increased working interdependency—and takes a more operational approach with those practices identified in chapter 4. This chapter begins with an encapsulated background overview of the key research focus that led to a broader consciousness of the interactive and operational steps involved in unfolding the programs through the system. These forces are critical to the policy implementation stream as program and operational concerns appear up and down the line, so to speak. Then the chapter looks at how bureaucratic organization has changed to include a more indirect style of management and operation. The analysis elaborates on the major interunit administrative tasks: grants administration, loan transactions, audits, reports, program monitoring, and regulatory compliance. Next the chapter briefly identifies and examines characteristic IGM transactions from the literature, such as information-seeking, adjustment-seeking, and other standard managerial behaviors, along with joint agreements and joint projects, services exchanges, and many established approaches such as negotiating, strategic planning, and capacity building. For those who do not work in this arena, these approaches to IGM are among the least visible processes, but they have become part of the workings of the system in the field and down the line.

The Children's Health Insurance Program (CHIP), adopted in 1997, provides a picture of the grant rulemaking and implementation process. Michael Doonan (2013, ch. 3, 4) paints a picture of the administering agency, the Centers for Medicare and Medicaid Services, working closely with the states. But over time the partnership fell apart under the weight of the rulemaking process, which provided some national protections at the cost of state autonomy. At this stage, state flexibility was harnessed, yet there emerged avenues of flexibility "within federally defined corridors" (42). Nevertheless, the CMS negotiated directly with different states, demonstrating that federal money and regulations together with latitude for state innovations made major inroads on broadening coverage gaps between the states and the federal government. The CHIP rulemaking process also "demonstrated that state flexibility can be harnessed to reach national health insurance goals" (31). Doonan concludes that unlike the ACA health care reform of 2010, political support all along the line for CHIP—coupled with its negotiated state flexibility, program knowledge, and smooth implementation—proved essential (55–56).

Many cities, large and small, also become quite active in reaching intergovernmental accommodation when dealing with federal officials. Woodstock, Illinois, engaged in substantial interaction with the Environmental Protection Agency regarding a Superfund unilateral executive order that designated the city as the "potentially responsible party" of a municipally owned landfill containing contaminated materials. After reaching an agreement with Allied Signal Corporation, the major responsible party, to pay the major out-of-pocket costs for the cleanup, the city hired a consultant who prepared a proposal containing over fifty of its own mitigation measures and sent it to the EPA. The EPA rejected the city's solution out of hand and maintained the original order. Then the city's attorney requested a face-to-face meeting with the consultant, city manager, the city attorney, and EPA officials in Chicago. Several meetings and detailed negotiations followed until an agreement was reached months later. The city agreed to absorb the costs of the initial site preparation and clearing and the subsequent "pump and treatment of the waste and maintenance of the site" for twenty years. City crews, instead of a private contractor, were allowed to do the work. Thus, repeated exchanges led to a solution that was estimated to cost the city a little less than half of the initial EPA order.

As these vignettes suggest, program expansion in the period of intergovernmental growth has produced the need to "manage" intergovernmental programs in ways that bring administrative personnel more directly into the operational concerns of other governments. Legal scholar Larry Kramer's (2000, 283) study of the "political safeguards of federalism" concludes that "we have long recognized how the interdependency of the legislative and administrative process gives administrators a voice and a role in lawmaking." These administrators' actions reinforce the manifestation of Deil Wright's (1988, 49) aforementioned overlapping authority IGR model, where substantial areas of governmental operations involve many units simultaneously, arenas of exclusive autonomy are comparatively small, and respective jurisdictions share power within the system (Agranoff and Radin 2015; Burke 2014). Thus, the CHIP and Woodstock examples demonstrate that IGM has come into full force (Wright, Stenberg, and Cho 2010).

Virtually everything related to the evolution of IGM during the expansion of intergovernmental programs points to the need to manage *within* the system and to manage *the* system. In this respect IGM follows the administrative tradition of officials being subject to the law as a first principle, followed by professional concerns, but not necessarily to some hierarchical organizational link to another jurisdiction in a non-unified nation-state structure. Programs have simultaneously become more specialized and technical in nature and require greater numbers of subject matter experts who can combine their specialties into dual roles as IGM program managers. Thus, given the degree of program rules and expectations of accountability, more regular interaction and program oversight are required now than in earlier times. As chapter 4 indicates, the emphasis on jurisdictional interdependence has led to IGM consciousness as the forces combine to raise the cross-jurisdiction managerial quotient.

The Legacy of Policy Implementation

The long tradition of studying how federal programs are administered has brought out in bold relief the tensions and contradictions of managing within the federal system. These studies are critical to understanding interdependence because the primary foci on federalism and IGR do not ordinarily examine management but emphasize fiscal patterns, structures of government, and constitutional requirements and legal constraints (Radin 2012, 131). Those who have studied policy implementation, which involves "the vexing challenges of converting policy intent into efficacious action" (O'Toole 2000, 265), are aware of this next step, so to speak. To a great degree they are bound up in the "shifts in intergovernmental relations, and the movement of policy responsibility to the states in recent years" (265). Since implementation is so associated with interdependent action (as this chapter and those that follow depict), implementation, along with the increased number of actors now involved in the process, is at the core of understanding IGM.

One of the landmark studies is *Implementation* (1973) by Jeffrey Pressman and Aaron Wildavsky. In examining the federal Economic Development Administration's development program in Oakland, California, they approached policy as a hypothesis containing initial conditions and predicted consequences. For example, if X is done at time T, then Y will result at time $T2$. The degree to which predicted consequences take place encompasses implementation, "a process of interaction between the setting of goals and actions geared to achieving them" (5). Intergovernmental policy involves connecting actions, linking actions, and objectives similar to those of operations management in a manufacturing business, which combines supply chains and manufacturing operations, but with politics mixed in, of course. Public policy implementation depends on the ability to forge subsequent links in the causal chain to obtain expected results. As Pressman and Wildavsky conclude, "The study of implementation requires understanding that apparently simple sequences of events depend on complex chains of reciprocal interaction" (1973, xvii; see also Reed 2014, 252–53).

Throughout the legacy of implementation studies, there has been a basic dichotomy between so-called top-down and bottom-up approaches. The former began with national programs and followed them down the line on an agency-to-agency basis (Mazmanian and Sabatier 1983; Nakamura and Smallwood 1980), in a more or less "command and control" focus (deLeon and deLeon 2002). A subsequent generation looked at the process from the ground up, not focusing on agencies but starting with street-level bureaucrats and directing their analysis upward (Lipsky 1980; Hjern 1982). A third, democratic approach has been proposed that reaches "back in the policy process framework to include the policy formulation deliberations as a means to help define policy goals by talking with the affected parties well before the policy is adopted by the authorized policy maker" (deLeon and deLeon 2002, 483; see also Matland 1995).

Yet another important wave of implementation studies focuses on the sequential aspects of implementation. This involves a more detailed look. Walter Williams (1981, 5), in his analysis, shifts from the glamour of making decisions toward the detail of putting them in operation: "The central focus over time is on the slow, hard task of raising management and staff capacity through institutional investment so that [social service] organizations will be more likely to make reasonable judgments at the point of service and to respond appropriately to yet unspecified future implementation demands." In this regard, Robert Montjoy and Laurence O'Toole (1979) suggest that implementation can be explained on organization-to-organization bases, both intra- and inter-, as they deal with external mandates and their resource bases and focus on the notion that interorganizational problems arise from the difficulties of coordinating several units. These issues persist, as more recent research on energy policy indicates. It found key concerns in successful implementation were the interactive effects of federal government guidance and governmental capacity. Given the complexity of many programs, guidance and capability need to be approached interactively (Carley, Nicholson-Crotty, and Fisher 2014, 123). In the same respect, Toddi Steelman's study of environmental change found that no matter how much agendas are set and policy windows are open, adaptive strategies are needed to operate "within overlapping and interconnected governance frameworks" (2010, 4).

Old and new implementation studies point to deeper activity in explaining IGM. For example, the author once broke down a seventeen-step sequence—from initial discussions to reporting and consultations—involved in a local jurisdiction's engaging in a tax increment financing program to expand its industrial park (Agranoff 2007c, 275). Others, such as Douglas Reed (2014, xiv), have introduced the idea of "operational localism" in education policy, where political, technical, and managerial forces constrain their ability and willingness to respond to federal directives. As a result, implementation in education produces a "hybrid education state" in which the traditional intergovernmental state blurs multiple actors' claims of authority. In addition to these interorganizational concerns, Anat Gofen (2014) reminds us that in another step, discretion is exerted by street-level bureaucrats within local operations. Thus, street-level operatives, as shared policy makers as well as policy takers, play key roles in policy implementation. In her research on welfare state organizations, Evelyn Brodkin (2013, 23) concludes that frontline workers also make policy and engage in politics through the "adaptive responses to their organizations' environment that indirectly construct policy on the ground." Given the multifarious pressures, for example, the teacher, social worker, job trainer, or auto license bureau employee may take an adaptable action that is different from the intended action.

These issues were once incorporated into what Paul Sabatier and Hank Jenkins-Smith (1993, 16–17) identified as an "advocacy coalition framework," which incorporates policy-oriented learning and the interaction of various actors on intergovernmental dimensions that include belief system–value priorities and cooperative expectations in policy implementation. Sabatier and Jenkins-Smith's work demonstrates constantly that implementation involves considerably more than meets the eye, as this chapter, along with subsequent chapters on governments' partners and on networked activity, explores. What are considered the routines of IGM are adaptive; involve heavy doses of communication, interaction, and cooperative aims; and include multiple programs and uneven participation within legal and political contexts. It is part of "playing the game" (Agranoff 2007c, 281–82).

Changing Bureaucratic Operations

As Thomas Anton (1984, 45) suggests, program interdependence or "dependence in multi-organizational systems is a two-way street." Regarding federal program influence, it "is a variable, not a constant, and cannot be understood if the interactions between federal program managers and thousands of local or state implementing agencies are ignored." For example, in a multijurisdictional study of local implementation of energy efficiency programs, it was found that differences in the support and direct involvement of local elected officials and managers impact the timeliness of program implementation whereas direct city council involvement increases implementation time (Terman and Feiock 2014). As suggested by the preceding policy implementation discussion, the administrative challenges between the sectors are considerable. Managers at one level cannot execute across the boundaries of another's organization, for example, by controlling another level's internal organizing or making cross-agency staff decisions, by exerting direct managerial leadership, or by introducing internal financial control systems (see Ansell and Gash 2008; Ring and Van de Ven 1994; Van de Ven and Walker 1984).

Management of intergovernmental programs is instead, as suggested earlier, "indirect." Steven Rosenthal (1984, 470) once identified four indirect dimensions of the process, since responsibilities for producing a service or seeking compliance must be accomplished through organizations that are not under the managers' (at any level) direct control. Rosenthal suggests that such indirect management can be understood as operating under four conditions:

- Partial accountability—The program's delivery requires that state or local (public or private) agencies be partially but not fully accountable to a federal agency.
- Mixed objectives—Those who are responsible for some aspect of the program are likely to differ, in some important respect, on the objectives of the program.
- Continuity—The program is expected to continue, as distinguished from a one-time project.
- Interorganizational activity—Mechanisms or devices are specified for exchanging resources and information across formal organizational boundaries.

Such familiar IGM devices as proposals, award letters, prohibitions, standards, requirements, assurances, reimbursement procedures, plan reviews, contract negotiations, monitoring audits, and evaluations become prospective and, in many situations, actual interactive norms of operation. In these ways the shifting objectives, limited resources, multiple interests, and diffusion of authority are approached across jurisdictional boundaries. Importantly, these methods include reciprocal activity and negotiated adjustment.

Reciprocal administrative action is a result of the matrix-like character of the American federal situation, coupled with localism and the absence of a large federal bureaucratic presence. Inevitably many actions, such as those with the Woodstock landfill and the CHIP programs, must be worked out administratively as programs unfold across jurisdictions. Actors working in

BOX 5.1

- The broadening of federal-state programs and their different applications mean that state flexibility and national aims need to be balanced, in some situations, on a case-by-case basis.
- Administrators, both appointed and civil servants, at all levels who are familiar with the substantive issues and their legal and political expectations have become the primary intergovernmental managers.
- Analysis of policy implementation has revealed the realities of those reciprocal actions involved in moving programs from enactment to operations.
- IGM not only involves interorganizational transactional activity but also tends to be continuous over the life of programs and seeks to identify and solve problems posed by such interactivity.

the same spheres implement federal and state programs but not always with the same commitments to policy and program aims down the federal, state, and NGO line, so to speak (Bulman-Pozen and Gerken 2009). Intergovernmental disputes do not constitute the totality of reciprocal action. As the Woodstock example indicates, they can also be based on interactive accommodation and negotiated adjustment. IGM thus involves the two approaches that invite cooperation as well as conflict.

Negotiated adjustment is often a normal state of outcome. As in Woodstock, the inherent differences in interests often engender more extensive managerial action. Many jurisdictions play the IGM game of "bargaining and negotiation," as the early policy implementation literature labeled it. Such activity occurs in many different contexts and for many different purposes. The most common types of on-the-ground intergovernmental activity take place within the context of grant or contract programs, although they are also present in regulatory and other programs. Negotiating over differences can be large scale, where stakes are high and political action parallels the administrative action. For example, compromise can occur over different interpretations of the use of targeted grant funds. No less significant for the manager, jurisdictions also interact over daily, routine problems such as whether to include specific city blocks in a targeted low- and moderate-income area in the Community Development Block Grants program or those neighborhoods that are traditionally racially segregated. Grants management has thus provided the primary focus and locus of intergovernmental management (Pressman 1975; Ingram 1977; Liebschutz 1991; Williams 1980).

A local government IGM study by Agranoff and McGuire (2003) provides empirical examples of this kind of bargaining behavior over grants. The administrators of the Cuyahoga County Community Development Block Grant program observed that the city of Garfield Heights, Ohio, submitted more than its limit of two local project applications for federal money year after year. When they asked the mayor and city grant coordinator to reduce their requests from as many as six to the required two, Garfield Heights officials took the opportunity to ensure in advance that they would receive both grants (whereas other cities normally had one of two submissions approved). The city officials then proceeded to negotiate the most favorable terms for each.

In a more lighthearted example, Ithaca, Michigan, once allowed the US Environmental Protection Agency to do some experimental water testing that the federal agency had requested be done locally. After the testing, the EPA in Chicago wrote city officials a letter informing them that the testing was completed, that they would hear the results in some months, and that the agency "might charge the city a fee for the testing." The mayor and city manager fired back a letter that included the following sentence: "Ithaca reserves the right to charge EPA for the water run through the testing source, as metered by our public utilities department" (Agranoff and McGuire 2003, 15). Other than the test results, the EPA had no further contact with the city.

Cincinnati became heavily involved in both political and administrative bargaining and negotiation with its state government while under pressure in the mid-1990s by both of its major professional sports franchises (baseball Reds and football Bengals) to build new playing facilities and to improve financial arrangements with the city. When the city government, including the city manager, was pressured to broker a deal that would keep both franchises in town, it saw the opportunity to negotiate with the state regarding capital improvement project (CIP) funds. The CIP program is primarily designed to help communities revitalize their physical infrastructures, particularly those of public use and those that connect with state projects through the Division of Natural Resources, the Building Authority, the Board of Regents (universities), or agencies in the governor's administrative cabinet. Although the CIP is not explicitly designed for stadia infrastructure, city staff initially proposed to add local funding criteria to existing state criteria and then sought local public input on projects. Though the original public hearing list of nine priorities included an aquarium, a park, and conservatory improvements, in the end the city heavily emphasized those projects that were designed to retain the sports franchises, particularly for riverfront improvements near the proposed stadia and for nearby downtown recreation and entertainment. The next stage involved extended back-and-forth negotiations with state officials, who were not initially receptive. After a great deal of give-and-take, they approved a total of $13.9 million in CIP money, the largest award in the city's history. City officials then directed a substantial proportion of the state funds, primarily intended for other purposes, toward their most pressing priorities at the riverfront site. It would not have happened without their mobilizing local political and managerial support, sublimating other priorities, and, most important, confidently formulating their proposals as well as the city's managerial capacity—that is, its experience-based ability to engage in protracted bargaining with the state government. This form of interactive, indirect management has now become part of the working core of IGM.

Grants, Regulations, and Other IGM Specialties

On the core notion of indirect management, the interactive processes of key interdependency-generated IGM—particularly those related to grants, regulations, and other core operations such as loans—are examined. Left out of this chapter is one major formal government-to-government transaction—namely, contracts, which in an increasing number of situations also involves the NGO sector (see chapters 6 and 7).

FIGURE 5.1. Typical Federal Grant Statute

Sec. 1. Short Title
Sec. 2. Table of Contents
Sec. 3. Findings and Purposes
Sec. 4. Definitions
Sec. 5. Establishment of Administering Office
Sec. 6. Authorization of Appropriations
Sec. 7. Authorization of Assistance
Sec. 8. Allotment Formula
Sec. 9. State Plan Provisions
Sec. 10. Discretionary Grant Provisions
Sec. 11. Conditions of Assistance
Sec. 12. Accountability, Audit, Monitoring Provisions
Sec. 13. Sanctions and Incentives
Sec. 14. Rulemaking Power
Sec. 15. Administrative and Judicial Review Provisions

Source: Administrative Conference of the United States (1990), 57–58.

The first step in grants management involves the statutory identification of the administering agency. For example, the Medicaid HCBS Waiver
program, discussed earlier, designates as follows: "Section 1915(c) of the
Social Security Act (the Act) authorizes the Secretary of Health and Human
Services to waive certain Medicaid statutory requirements so that a State
may offer Home and Community-Based Services (HCBS) to State-specified
group(s) of Medicaid beneficiaries who otherwise would require services
at an institutional level of care" (US Department of Health and Human Services 2011). Designating the agency is important because the agency usually
has considerable discretion in program operation. This includes not only
project grants, where selection is usually in the hands of the agency, but also
formula grants, where program guidelines are enforced (see figure 5.1 for an
outline of a grant statute).

For federal programs, David Beam and Timothy Conlan (2002, 354–58)
identify the following critical management stages:

1. Identify and negotiate supported activities.
2. Establish eligibility of various classes of recipients.
3. Determine how funds are to be distributed.
4. Set conditions of assistance, such as pre-applications, application
   deadlines, matching funds and other financial requirements, duration of assistance, and eligibility for renewal.
5. Specify rules to operate the program and ultimately the regulations
   spelling out such rules.

6. Inform recipients and potential recipients of the availability of funds and the procedures that the agency will use to distribute funds.
7. Announce the application in the *Federal Register* and the submission of an appropriate form—for example, Application for Federal Assistance (SF 424).
8. Review applications and process awards.
9. Implement recipient program.
10. Monitor, evaluate, and conduct fiscal audit by granting agency.

In short, these administrative phases follow a program's authorization and involve administrative decisions related to allocation, execution, and assessment.

Recipient grant management concerns include seeking and operating grants for implementers that involve much more than handbook tips on grantsmanship or how to seek money. It is a rather involved internal management process that, in effect, involves the entire public agency, its politics, and its publics. Many well-run agencies begin by asking five types of questions, such as those raised by Ralph Brody (1982, 171–72). First, will the time and effort—holding meetings, garnering group support, writing drafts, obtaining bureaucratic clearance—of preparing and negotiating a proposal yield benefits? Second, does the agency have the staff capability and technical knowledge to deliver on the projected program? Third, to what degree will the funders' demands impact agency autonomy and internal operations, inasmuch as the lure of funds always contains conditions and restrictions? Fourth, what are the potential consequences of program discontinuation or time limitations on funding and possibly only year-to-year funding? Fifth, are there negative consequences regarding potential cash flow problems along with the level and extent of financial compensation? Regarding the latter issue, sometimes the administrative costs and burdens can exceed any funding benefits. In this respect, the city government of Cincinnati has a council-adopted intergovernmental grants policy. The city manager's office regularly applies criteria similar to those that Brody raised, particularly the fiscal ones, before it decides to seek state or federal funding (Agranoff and McGuire 2003).

From the recipient manager's standpoint, Rosemary O'Leary (1996) offers several pieces of useful advice. Initially, consider the financial implications, service enhancement, impact on other programs, client needs, political support, internal objectives, continuity of services, and potential legal issues and impediments. Each of these factors should be weighed before getting a jurisdiction deeply involved in a grant from another government. A special effort must be made to see that political support is forthcoming from the appropriate legislative body, community groups, and potentially impacted citizens. Next, if there are subgrantees or delivery contractors, encourage competition, check the reputation of each potential agent, and put the agents first in line to report waste, fraud, and abuse. Then, be sure to monitor and review all overhead costs—subcontractor's design and management, monitoring, reporting, and expenses—and compare them with projected expenses. Also, investigate and communicate all applicable laws and regulations, ranging from administrative requirements (e.g., purchasing, travel) to mandated processes and client-handling procedures. Finally, subcontracting raises the need to take advantage of micro lessons from the literature: determine the appropriate format (e.g., fixed price, cost reimbursement, cost sharing); set clear and unambiguous sub-grant terms; clearly think out and delineate activity sequences; set target dates for services, monitoring, reporting, and auditing in writing; delineate performance assessment measures; and ensure that sub-grantees engage in regular communication with the grantee jurisdiction. All of this seeming process "detail" may appear to be beyond (and to some beneath) the core of learning about grants, but issues and questions such as those raised by O'Leary set the parameters for the real IGM work.

Managing within Intergovernmental Regulatory Regimes

The increase in regulatory programs and mandates attached to federal and federal-state assistance means that state and local governments are increasingly becoming regulatory arms of the federal government, as implementation and enforcement are normally passed on to state and local governments. Peter May (2002, 170) points out that intergovernmental rules and standards are different from those of private sector regulation in that they normally specify deadlines and the format for developing regulatory programs but pay limited attention to specifying what constitutes full compliance. He cites the example of state growth-management programs that establish planning requirements but are devoid of high-quality plan standards.

From a regulatory standpoint, management begins with setting standards, a process that is heavily dependent on technical expertise. This process can come in some combination of the research- and testing-based and industry or services arena with consensus-based standards, legal expertise concerning appropriate rulemaking procedures, economic analyses such as cost-benefit assessment, and, of course, the managerial ability to blend these three types of data into rulemaking and adherence to legislative intent. Next, built in are penalties for noncompliance that range from imposing fines, seizing products, or ultimately removing the authority to regulate. As a corollary, rewards or incentives to comply—for example, different forms of public recognition—are sometimes used to induce compliance. Then the process also must set design issues of surveillance and inspection that entail decisions regarding procedures to address violations and priorities for targeting inspections. Coupled with detection are methods to invoke sanctions, which often begin with informal communications and violation citations but also include civil and criminal penalties. Finally, enforcement systems require reporting mechanisms for tracking inspections, violations, and dispositions (May 2002, 166–69). In a hands-on way, the entire IGM enforcement system usually involves direct oversight of state and local compliance machinery as opposed to the type of complaint-based surveillance or self-regulation that is typical of private sector standards enforcement.

Management is also based on managerial mandate politics. Indeed, regulations are hardly apolitical; they often follow the political process of enactment. The voices heard on regulation are mixed. Paul Posner (2008) has raised several dynamics related to the politics of regulation. At one level the federal regulatory regime and mandates attached to aid have been difficult for subnational officials to oppose. Posner concludes that many such regulations and mandates have developed as a result of lobbying or input from the regulated, as they have neutralized or championed some programs while seeking some level of predictability. In some situations, lobbyists for the regulated have urged friendly members of Congress to introduce very "extreme" amendments to pending bills, knowing they will not survive committee markups. The purpose in these situations is to send the message to the bureaucracy that it should "go slow" on stringent regulations.

Normally, regulatory lobbying has two or more sides, as other state and local interests have often either supported or opposed the same measures. As a result, state and local groups are disarmed by their lack of political cohesion and are often reluctant to articulate a position. Also, political leaders and top elected officials are sometimes swept away by the compelling appeal of national debates on these regulatory issues. It is also true that "state leaders have come to endorse certain preemptions and mandates to address collective action problems stemming from intergovernmental competition that can undermine states' incentives to assume policy leadership in key areas" (Posner 2008, 300–301). Nevertheless, if agreement can be reached, states and localities can have a substantial influence on regulatory politics, especially when they are politically cohesive in articulating their position and can mobilize their membership to advance their interests.

The greatest political influence nevertheless lies within the IGM process because regulatory programs are in the day-to-day hands of state and local governments. As Posner (2008, 302) concludes,

> Perhaps more fundamentally, state and local governments gain bargaining leverage when considering implementation issues because the federal government critically relies on them to achieve its policy goals. Simply put, the policy ambition of the federal government far exceeds its administrative, legal, fiscal, and political capacity to

implement federal programs, mandates, and preemptions. Accordingly, states and local governments, as well as a wide range of nonprofit and private corporations, are brought in as third parties to carry out federal initiatives through a host of governmental tools, including grants and loans in addition to regulatory tools.

In this sense, regulatory interaction follows Michael Reagan's (1987, 194) managerial political bargaining model. To get something done, those charged with achieving results must negotiate and compromise with those from whom compliance is sought. In turn, the top policy group of "federal enforcers" must accept some compromises that the implementers sell to them as necessary to achieve target group compliance in a broad sense. As a process, regulatory implementation is one of give-and-take across governments.

As regulators apply rules, they manage regulations from below. The regulated managers are increasingly involved in what Deil Wright (1988, 428–29) identifies as calculating costs and benefits. He points to extensive calculations that the regulated must make: estimating the dollar and compliance costs and the benefits of getting federal grants, assessing the risk of noncompliance with regulations and mandates, and selecting appropriate standards and rules (that is, arranging for partial compliance, since programs have so many details of compliance that all cannot be met). As an IGM strategy, Wright observes that calculating involves thinking before acting, forecasting or predicting the consequences of anticipated actions, and counting, figuring, or computing in a numerical sense the dollar or resource-commitment costs.

Successful implementation of regulatory programs thus becomes a political as well as a technical process. The arena deserves considerable further study. Regarding state-imposed regulation on cities, one study found that "state rules curtailing local discretion on policy substitutes for cooperation change the decision calculus among cities considering cooperation" (Krueger and Bernick 2010, 709). State-imposed rules thus dictate the transaction costs, discourage linkages, and attenuate home rule, in effect reinforcing Dillon's Rule.

Reagan (1987, 194–95) maintains that the degree of workability of the managerial approach depends on the prior success of political bargaining. He identifies three key elements of success. First, a program can work only if adequate political support can be generated and maintained. The more an implementing jurisdiction supports the aim of a program—for example, employing women—the more effort will be put into getting the desired results. Second, along with political support, a "sound theory" of regulation must embody appropriate action. Some programs are based on flawed theories of regulation—for example, recycling regulations based on duration without costs or penalties. Third, diverse participants must share a harmony of values, or belief integration, in a form of joint action. If one agrees with the program's ideas—for example, in waste recycling—then one is more likely to act and support it. The latter element requires elaboration. Reagan (1987, 195) refers to it as the concept of value integration, which applies to implementation as a whole and, importantly, to managing regulations at the operating level. Success is based on "harmony of values among diverse values held among diverse participants." Under such value congruence, it becomes easier to "forge the conditions of acceptance" of regulatory management (195).

Within these contexts, the management of regulations involves the routines of enforcement authorized by law in relation to the regulated parties' adherence to standards. The approach is difficult and sometimes successful. One chronicled success is the federal government's enforcement of school desegregation in the South through regulatory actions related to compensatory education (Peterson, Rabe, and Wong 1986, 190; see also Reed 2014). The federal government also used program regulations to move the state of Massachusetts to change its welfare program from a locally administered to a state-administered program (Derthick 1970). Some provisions, however, are harder to enforce. Jane Massey and Jeffrey Straussman (1985) found that regulatory enforcement of fair housing provisions was variable, with spotty performance and compliance. They concluded that the impact of federal mandates is overstated.

What kinds of activities do enforcement jurisdictions, primarily state and local managers, engage in while dealing with regulatory concerns? The author once compiled a list of some eighteen activities either reported by various publications of the International City and County Management Association or derived from field research over the years in working with state and local governments. They are displayed in figure 5.2. While undoubtedly no jurisdiction engages in all the activities, managers claim they are the core regulatory management activities at the field level. Clearly, they go well beyond simply reading the rules, making up a compliance plan, monitoring, and reporting. Also important, not all of these regulatory management activities are in house; thus, they require substantial collaborative reaches to other governments and NGOs.

Loan and Loan Guarantee Management

From the federal and state lenders' standpoint, establishing a lending program begins with program development and concludes with repayment or writing off losses. In the early phases, statutory-based regulations and contractual agreements and paperwork (forms) that will be used in processing loans are developed. Loan guarantee programs are also required to establish procedures to certify and decertify lenders' eligibility. Then the program can

FIGURE 5.2. Regulatory Activities

A. Standards
1. Reading, digesting, explaining, and circulating regulatory information to governmental and nongovernmental parties
2. Holding workshops and information meetings on regulatory programs, standards, guidelines, compliance
3. Developing operating standards and guidelines for the "point source"/regulated agency or program
4. Working with jurisdictions and other entities on creating appropriate operating policies
5. Promoting preventive and long-term solutions
B. Compliance
1. Working with jurisdictions and organizations to draft compliance plans
2. In enforcement, developing a (short-term) system for compliance monitoring
3. Working with in-house (or out-of-house) legal counsel on issues of compliance, liability limits, feasibility of actions, and other questions of law
4. Coordinating in-house and consultant preparation of permit applications, compliance plans, and any waivers, exemptions, and variances (e.g., National Pollution Discharge Elimination System permit involved 17,184 person hours in Columbus, Ohio)
5. Conducting outreach, education, and awareness activities, including providing information regarding new technology
6. Coalition building with other jurisdictions to create demonstrations and innovative methods of compliance, for information and training, and for state and local compliance
7. Networking with professional and technical associations
C. Rewards and incentives
1. Working with budget agency and task force on compliance costs and long-term set-aside costs for major problems (e.g., storage tanks, inaccessible public buildings)
2. Conducting studies of particular problem areas and the feasibility of long-term compliance and mitigation
D. Sanctions
1. Working with the most serious violators to encourage changes in practices and actions and to pay for mitigation
E. Surveillance and inspection
1. Coordinating local responses to proposed regulatory legislation, regulations, and guidelines
F. Reporting
1. Establishing working relationships with federal and state officials through agency contacts (including organizing visits to local governments, sites)
2. Serving as a resource center and information line on regulatory program information

be marketed to potential lenders, and in some cases government-supported businesses to handle loans can be created.

Then comes origination. This contractual agreement exists between borrower and lender, which is either a direct government agency, such as the Small Business Administration or US Department of Agriculture Rural Development, or an intermediary, such as a university or school. In the case of a guarantee, usually a private lender is involved, in effect as a third-party subcontractor; with direct loans, the government maintains considerable control; and with guarantees, more control is delegated to the lender, as the government is normally the guarantor. What follows is disbursement. Funds are transferred either on a one-time basis, such as with mortgages, or over time, as in the case of many infrastructure loans that support construction occurring for a period (Stanton 2002, 392–93).

From the government-as-borrower standpoint, repayment according to the terms is a part of servicing, which also includes accounting for the loaned funds. For direct loans, for example, it requires the local government to regularly interact with the state or federal government lender, and for guarantee loans it must do so with the borrower. In both cases government increasingly contracts with outside firms to service these loans, and these firms are then in contact with lenders. Loans are sometimes repackaged and securitized, then borrowing jurisdictions have to deal with them. Assuming a completed repayment, a final audit is usually required of loans to jurisdictions. Those jurisdictions that default on loans raise many political and legal problems, but normally the lending government has the right to seize any property and reduce the amount lost on the default.

Thomas Stanton (2002, 399) concludes that government loan and loan guarantee programs always have to balance "mission and risk." "Achieving a proper balance may require an agency to try to manage its political environment. Credit programs often have political constituencies that have interests that conflict with the management of a program in a cost-effective manner" (400). Often compounding the situation are capacity problems, particularly short staffing, and issues with monitoring and keeping third-party agents accountable, as well as reducing the levels of adverse selection of risky borrowers. It requires financial soundness as well as attention, concludes Stanton (406), to matters of managing the agency that is administering the program.

IGM Transactions

A number of approaches and techniques have developed over the past five or six decades as further managerial approaches—operative tools of IGM, so to speak—related to how officials interact to solve routine or particular IGM problems. As most of these approaches are covered in the public management

BOX 5.2

> • Federal grants have been vertically standardized to a considerable degree in formal processes, but horizontally they reach across to many related programs.
> • At one time bargaining and negotiation were considered the essence of managing across organizations and jurisdictions, but now problem identification, political support, and belief in joint or mutual problem resolution are also seen as contributing to important and routine transactions.
> • Program capacity, or the ability to understand and operationally manage internal needs and to transact one's internal concerns, both politically and technically, is a core IGM skill.
> • Program capacity also involves mobilizing political and technical support to set programs of IGM in action. Few programs are successfully implemented without this capability.

literature, they are only identified here. They include, first, *strategic planning, leadership,* and *related visioning* (John 1991; Bryson 1988). Next, as expected, an obvious mainline activity is *direct and indirect contact* with officials in state and federal offices, ranging from seeking information to proposing and making adjustments (Agranoff and McGuire 2003; Agranoff 1986; Kettl 1987; Rosenthal 1984; Bardach 1977; Brown 1983).

More indirect approaches involve *leveraging local funds or other resources* to move applications or projects in the works from one's jurisdiction (Eisinger 1988; Posner 2008; Stanton 2002; Ross and Friedman 1991) or *leveraging the resources of one's partners* in the community (Agranoff and McGuire 2003). *Capacity*—or the ability of governments to understand extant challenges and anticipate change, to attract and use resources, and to guide future action that enhances interactive management processes—is also key (Honadle 1981; Noh and Krane 2014; Carley, Nicholson-Crotty, and Fisher 2014; Howitt 1984; Mead 1981; Brown and Glasgow 1991).

Program leverage is also important. Jurisdictions often have the option not only to seek program waivers, or the legal authorization to suspend certain rules, but also to propose that they undertake model program effort—that is, request some form of asymmetrical treatment that is not technically in the rules, standards, or guidelines but still forwards the program's purpose and meets jurisdictional needs (Agranoff and McGuire 2003; Eisinger 1988; Thompson 2012; Agranoff 2013). Related, some seek forms of deregulation or *negotiated regulatory flexibility* to make the burden on a jurisdiction lighter or to move program purposes along (Agranoff and McGuire 2003; Posner 2008; Stenberg 1992). Another IGM tool is for the involved levels of jurisdictions to engage in some type of *formal or informal "shared" decision-making* to enhance a broader purpose for a program (Agranoff 1992; Hanf 1978; Agranoff and McGuire 2003; Howitt 1984). They can also make mutual attempts, through consultation and bargaining, to *reduce the scope of higher-level monitoring* or other forms of oversight, often with various aspects of agreed performance parameters to be met (Metzenbaum 2008; Radin 2006; Eisinger 1988; Davis 1990). Finally, of course, there is *recourse to adjudicate enforcement*, or, in the case of subnational governments, to seek judicial relief from what they consider difficult, costly, and unenforceable regulations (Keleman 2004, ch. 3), not to speak of pre-regulation interest group participation and lobbying regarding proposed regulations (Kerwin 1999, ch. 5).

IGM techniques highlighted in the literature suggest that the successful managing of programs involves the ability and the capacity to operate in a complex system of rules, regulations, and standards, and, most important, to take advantage of opportunities. In practice, empirical research indicates that successful management is much more than reading through catalogs of assistance and filling out sets of applications. It entails considerably more than sitting at a training workshop and being bombarded with a variety of program opportunities. Further, more than the usual "grantsmanship" talk, it requires mobilizing political and nonpolitical forces in the community to build support, setting a course of action, learning about the system of development, reading funders' ever-changing signals, and successfully operating within that system. It is essentially about politics and administration. Some jurisdictions, large and small, are extremely successful at this process, whereas others struggle because they do not possess the critical implementation capabilities needed for effective development (Agranoff 1986; Wright, Stenberg, and Cho 2010; Carley, Nicholson-Crotty, and Fisher 2014). IGM has arrived as a distinctive approach to "politico-administrative action" based on direction, knowledge, and interaction—in short, managerial capacity.

Performance: An Intergovernmental Perspective

Given the nature of the federal system, the concern of holding subnational governments responsible or accountable is problematic. Beryl Radin (2008, 244) observes, "Efforts to hold federal government agencies accountable for the way programs are implemented actually assume that these agencies have legitimate authority to enforce the requirements that are included in performance measures." Most often the use of performance measures realistically involves collaborative efforts between federal agencies and the states, then between the states and their implementers. In her work on performance, Radin (2006, 2012) identifies the difficulties of the federal government's two major performance programs—the Government Performance and Results Act of 1993, a bottom-up agency–initiated program, and the Performance Assessment Rating Tool, a top-down, one-size-fits-all review that attempted to apply performance measures geared to efficiency outcomes. The problem with these efforts is that they tend to assess programs that were not really outcome oriented. In addition to states as recipients and partners that have their own agendas, as Posner (2002, 548) observes, using third parties such as contractors, nonprofits, and universities introduces a whole new set of actors. In turn, they influence the setting of goals along the line, with their "voluntary participation in the process, and often possess inside knowledge that creates information asymmetries that favor them" (548). These providers are deeply involved in the complex implementation chains where federal activity is only one of many actions.

As a result of such challenges, several different efforts have been taken to work around these seemingly formidable obstacles. In *Challenging the Performance Movement* (2006, 167–78), Radin identifies them as follows: (1) performance partnerships that employ the grantor and the grantee more or less coequally and emphasize reaching mutual agreements—for example, in environmental programs—as opposed to supervisory-oriented, principal-agent relationships; (2) incentives, such as matching fund requirements in Welfare to Work, and funding bonuses as a reward for reaching certain outcomes; (3) performance goals that are based on core indicators in areas such as employment and education that are negotiated by states and the federal government; (4) established standards that states can voluntarily meet, such as in education programs; and (5) waivers, or experimental approaches tied to research and development strategies in areas such as welfare, Medicaid, and job training, that in effect allow states to establish their own approach to eliminate or modify input or process requirements and normally in a budget-neutral process. These more flexible approaches represent an attempt to deal with the realities of performance in programs that extend from the federal government to the nonprofit or for-profit delivery agency. Reform efforts need to account for the limits on the one-size-fits-all approach, the federal government's design to minimize the exertion of concentrated power, the high diversity in program approaches, the ways in which governments separate the role of the executive and legislative branches, the differing expectations regarding appropriate performance information, the lack of federal expertise and resources for the different types of performance measurements, and the problem of the detachment of performance information from the real federal budget process (Radin 2012, 151–55).

Key Learning Points

Intergovernmental management has come to focus on the need to manage at more detailed levels of high-level interdependency and beyond the enactment of programs. Now it reaches to the daily transactions, or "working out of relationships," between component governmental elements—bureau to agency—in a system of governments. It emphasizes the goal achievement embedded within the process (Agranoff and McGuire 2001, 2003) since management is a *process* in which cooperating officials *direct action* toward goals.

IGM is also an eminently political as well as managerial process. For example, the persons administering the programs and the involved "groups clearly co-evolve with government in a dynamic progression that leads each to affect the other" (Leech et al. 2005).

In addition, Wright (1988) once attributed three special qualities to IGM. First, it focuses on problem-solving—that is, "an action oriented process that allows administrators at all levels the wherewithal to do something constructive" (450). IGM also provides a means of understanding and coping with the system *as it is*, including strategic perspectives that address how and why interjurisdictional changes occur as well as guidance on how to cope with the system. Last, it puts an emphasis on contacts and the development of communication networks. Intergovernmental management thus involves multiple parties in a distinctive form of interactive government and politics.

Key Practice Points

IGM involves parties developing joint solutions while recognizing the importance of, and making accommodations among, the jurisdictional-legal, political, and technical questions involved. IGM is therefore depicted as a complex and involved process of joint action while working managers search for feasible courses (Agranoff and Lindsay 1983). As managers work in the real world of IGM, all three guiding forces are in action and to varying degrees are applied to concrete situations or problems.

The accelerated pace and complexity of intergovernmental affairs have brought attention to managing across boundaries on a continuing basis. They are both political and managerial. Advancing one without acting on the other is thus really difficult. These forces arose from the evolution of the federal grant-in-aid system, coupled with increased national regulation and integrated tax systems, that has led to greater complexity and overall interdependence between governments. The process of coping with these new and expanded functions has generated a need to handle these relationships systematically, hence the increased attention over the past several decades to management in intergovernmental analysis and in the practices needed to facilitate operations.

Conclusion

Three major reasons lead to IGM growth and complexity: (1) increased *calculation*—for example, the need to weigh the costs and benefits of federal grants (and regulations), to determine who benefits by formula distribution of funds, and to assess the risk of noncompliance with requirements (and regulations) versus the cost of compliance; (2) the game of *fungibility*, or the ability to shift or exchange resources received for one purpose in order to accomplish another purpose; and (3) *overload*, which leads to excessive cost, ineffectiveness, and overregulation (Wright, Stenberg, and Cho 2010). The core roles of public managers in IGM are highlighted when meeting these conditions (Agranoff and McGuire 2003). They are now understood to be mainline features of IGR or US federalism in operation. While normally invisible to the public, even to those who are civically active, the largely behind-the-scenes activities identified in this chapter are the building blocks of contemporary IGM.

The era of cross-boundary interdependency among government jurisdictions arrived decades ago. Now IGM must cross governmental boundaries and include NGOs as partners and as participants in the networks.

6 INTERGOVERNMENTAL MANAGEMENT PARTNERSHIPS WITH NONGOVERNMENTAL ORGANIZATIONS

Deep and continuing involvement with nongovernmental organizations, both nonprofit and for profit, has changed the nature of intergovernmental management in program managers' politics, policy, and operations. Actions through the intergovernmental chain to NGOs "render the traditional concerns of public administration if not irrelevant, at least far less germane," observes Lester Salamon (1981, 261), as the patterns emerge. For example, the people who work at the direct operations level are less likely to be public employees, generating the need for new tools of public action that emphasize coordination and guidance on how government program managers can "shape the behavior of the erstwhile allies on whom they are forced to depend" (261). Steven Smith (1999, 206–7) concludes that coordination and guidance first impacts the delivery by NGOs themselves, the kind of services offered, the type of clientele, the orientation of the organizational program, the political orientation, and, most important, the formal and informal relationships with public agencies. It has also caused a rethinking of public and private boundaries within the policies themselves and the nature of IGM itself. Finally, Smith suggests that government-NGO contracting and similar means of interactions (e.g., vouchers, tax credits, donated assistance) are complicated and raise difficult trade-offs and dilemmas for nonprofits, for-profits, government administrators, and legislators. This consequence arose out of the exponential growth and transmission of programs through the intergovernmental chain and is the focus of this chapter. As a new or more visible form of IGM, it requires focused and detailed analysis.

The rise of formal, organized intergovernmental connections with nonprofit and for-profit organizations outside of government is clearly on the increase. For example, the New York City–based P-Tech program, which focuses on high school and technical college combined, was developed by IBM in partnership with New York City government and the City University of New York in 2011. The partnership funds the six-year program to avoid the burdens of high student debt. The curriculum focuses on science, mathematics, engineering, and technology, along with liberal arts subjects; provides mentors and paid internships; and leads to high school and associate degrees. Most P-Tech students come from low-income and minority homes and are the first in their families to attend college. The program has an open admissions policy and operates within the local school budget. As an NGO sponsor, IBM is particularly interested in filling open technical positions (*Economist* 2015).

Beloit, Wisconsin, is one of the many medium-size cities engaged in economic development partnerships. Since the 1980s it has operated through the Beloit Economic Development Corporation (BEDCOR), which primarily involves the city of Beloit; the township of Beloit; the city of South Beloit, Illinois; and several private businesses and industries, with the Beloit Area Chamber of Commerce as a major partner. BEDCOR has become the major conduit for federal community development block grant programs and Wisconsin Economic Development Corporation's Enterprise Zone assistance. During a typical year BEDCOR works with local jurisdictions in administering between forty to fifty state and federal grants; maintaining an active presence in Madison, the state capital; seeking development assistance; and helping locally with potential business start-ups or expansions and in regulatory permits and adjustments (Agranoff and McGuire 2003, 11–12). In 2005 BEDCOR merged with the Beloit Economic Development Advisory Council and became the Greater Beloit Economic Development Corporation, still maintaining its focus on business retention and expansion and on attracting new businesses. The corporation continues to facilitate "professional partnerships with local government agencies, utility companies, realtors, and public and private entities" (Greater Beloit Economic Development Corporation 2014).

The NGO sector has also become more directly engaged in public service in various partnering arrangements. In early 2011 IBM's consulting arm announced a $50 million Smarter Cities Challenge in which the corporation plans to help a hundred cities worldwide improve their data analysis and make a wide range of city services more effective. The program was piloted in Baltimore, Maryland; Austin, Texas; and Mecklenburg County, North Carolina (Charlotte). Its focus is on using intelligent technology to reduce costs, improve coordination, and enhance productivity. The IBM challenge illustrates the growing partnerships now engaged between both nonprofit and for-profit organizations that are not part of some governmental entity.

The relevance of these partnerships to IGM is that participating government agencies and NGO partnerships have become more "conductive" as they work back and forth with external interlocutors such as P-Tech, BEDCOR, and Smarter Cities in activities that go far beyond acquiring goods and contracting for "simple" services like security or meal catering. They are now in the direct services and public administrative support businesses that impact people, including at the end of intergovernmental program chains that are related to grants, regulations, and loans. This work not only ratchets up the connective idea but constitutes the rather complex and involved dimensions of IGM.

Fiscal year 1979 was the high-water mark of federal domestic aid to state and local governments, and it saw an increased emphasis on actions "out of government but funded by government," as NGOs gradually became regular agents and partners of government. Through contracts and a limited number of grants, the government accelerated its links with nonprofit service agencies and for-profit vendors of services. While nonprofits have been around for decades, particularly in some human services programs, the boundaries of the state have expanded considerably to include them. These NGOs operate more interactively in aspects of administration and direct service delivery in a sort of government "for hire" (Smith and Lipsky 1993, 5).

For-profits have always been part of government procurement, and certain basic services such as facility security and road building were regularly contracted out. This externalization now includes basic services for public health care (the latest being Veterans Administration health services), the disabled, vocational rehabilitation, mental health, substance abuse, and family violence as well as health and human services case management, finance and accounting services, and other management support functions. For-profits bring a new dimension to the delivery of services inasmuch as they are linked not only to government programs and the clients they serve but also to their operating partners and shareholders (Wade 1999, 324).

In the 1980s and 1990s, contracting out was expedited in more management-related support sectors: information management, transportation support, public marketing, and legal representation. As a result, new sets of connections developed between governments at all levels and a host of public and private bodies: nonprofits and private businesses, law firms, finance specialists, banks, and insurance companies. Thus, "the public administration problem has spread well beyond the borders of the government agency" (Salamon 1995, 2). These forces have been bound up in a more involved and, one could say, protracted IGM.

The key institutional and policy impetus for this IGM dimension includes or is based on beliefs, in the United States and in many countries, in the primacy of market forces, the reduced importance of the public sector, the deregulation of state controls, and the abandonment of the principle of equality (Loughlin 2007, 390). A prevailing political view in turning outside of governments was thus one of a more "minimalist" state with less direct government intervention in the economy and society. Some believed "market" superiority, or a market model of government services, could provide for the needs of people and achieve greater efficiencies than a public operation could. These ideas, of course, were the Reagan and Margaret Thatcher credos in the United States and the United Kingdom, respectively (Loughlin 2000), and to a lesser degree in the rest of western Europe (Wright 1994; Micklethwait and Wooldridge 2014). With the introduction of nongovernmental players, the IGM game greatly extended to more than governments at different levels. In a complimentary fashion, with heavy borrowing from the private sector, it also was the era of the new public management. Its benchmarking, performance targeting, competitive bidding, outsourcing, and the like, all reinforced IGM by increasing foci on levels of government and NGO partnerships (Hood 1991). In a sense the game changed "from an arrangement with a government producer to one with a private producer" (Savas 2000, 104).

To some degree IGM issues are bound with broader questions of government cost-based performance. In the United Kingdom, for example, the movement started in local government in the 1960s and 1970s but later became a core ideology from the 1980s. The basic questions, posed by Christopher Hood and Ruth Dixon (2015, 4–5), relate to whether government works better and costs less as a result of management reforms such as outsourcing, citizen-driven programs, and the business- and performance-oriented reforms of the new public management movement. They take a broader view of "management as the key to better government" (9). Building on an earlier view (Hood 1991), their empirical research reached the conclusion that the United Kingdom's central government "cost a bit more and worked a bit worse" in contrast to the "heady drumbeat of political and managerial rhetoric surrounding successive makeovers of central government" (Hood and Dixon 2015, 183). Indeed, Hood and Dixon conclude that with externalization and information technology (IT) notably using consultancies, raw cutting of personnel costs is not enough. The costs of private contracts and IT also lead to inconsistent cost and performance measures that are hard to secure and maintain. Thus, Hood and Dixon (2015, 197) conclude that "tracing out how well government works and what it costs will and should continue to be a central issue in public management."

The result of these forces then led to the turn to privatization and NGOs as a feature of IGM, or the focus of this chapter. The chapter begins with a historical sketch of the rise of NGOs in service delivery, a movement that is not new but clearly has become more visible and more prevalent in public programs in the past few decades. Next comes a discussion of "extensive partnering" between the federal and state governments in social service programs. Then the chief mechanisms of the era, particularly contracting but also vouchers, are examined. The politics of IGM by partnering, as well as small and large politics, are viewed from the standpoint of NGO lobbying and advocacy. Next, administrator-to-administrator interactions, particularly around IGM contracts, are explained. That is followed by a discussion of the legislative imprinting of private sector ideas on the management of these intergovernmental programs, including the rise of the performance movement and its challenges with the long intergovernmental chains of actors involved in programming. Finally, the analysis looks at how judicial interpretations of government-NGO control have become increasingly involved in the details of administration. This dimension's emergence demonstrates that NGO partnering has clearly made IGM ever more protracted, intractable, nettlesome, and accountability challenged, but nevertheless it remains legal, political, and technical in orientation.

Historic NGO Involvement in Public Programs

The US government has a long legacy of procuring from the private sector various goods—office supplies, military equipment and uniforms, munitions, food, and other commodities—and by mode of procurement contracts or other arrangements, complete projects: roads, bridges, canals, and ships. The contracts and agreements were always to some degree legally and administratively monitored, but the extent is not clear. Also, the government engaged in a number of NGO partnerships—for example, joint-stock companies and railroad construction agreements—throughout the 1800s (see, e.g., Elazar 1962), and the practice is prevalent in infrastructure provisions today. Government support for NGO services thus did not begin in the 1980s when, as noted previously, contracting out accelerated. One must examine the antecedents of these partnering practices.

Beyond infrastructure, the story of direct government-NGO service relationships begins with the voluntary or charitable sector, particularly for social help. While there were many different types of voluntary associations in the eighteenth century—libraries, fire brigades, security watch, hospitals, and schools—the nonprofit social and health sectors notably developed in the colonial years. Hospitals such as Pennsylvania Hospital, founded in 1751, and New York Hospital, opened in 1791, offered health care for indigent patients with expenses paid by local governments. Private institutions for the mentally ill, such as the Hartford Retreat in Connecticut and McLean Hospital in Boston, used state and local government funds to provide care for indigent mentally ill persons. In the early nineteenth century, many nonprofit child and family services organizations were founded, normally to supplement the services of public almshouses and what were called reform schools. These organizations provided short-term relief, crisis intervention, and long-term custodial care for orphans and dependent children, and they sometimes received public subsidies (Smith and Lipsky 1993, 47). The service organizations' facilities included institutions for the handicapped, homeless refuges, settlement houses, summer camps, seamen's missions, and similar groups.

With an English heritage and tradition, "private charity and poor law existed side by side for hundreds of years . . . each developing at its own pace and with gradually increasing influence over the other" (Kramer 1981, 57). The era of the voluntary human services agency predominated in the United States until the 1930s, when governmental programs in social welfare massively expanded. From the earliest days, however, the voluntary organization was a sectarian or humanitarian expression of dissatisfaction with inadequate public resources, and its supporters sought to supplant the government. The voluntary agency also filled the vacuum due to the absence of any form of deep government involvement. As Ralph Kramer (1981, 59) concludes, the two most important factors that conditioned these relationships were the public sector's subsidy system and the efforts of the coordinating body Charity Organization Societies (COS) to eliminate "outdoor relief" locally—that is, financial aid to persons not living in institutions, for which the public sector was ultimately responsible.

Outdoor relief was rooted in the eighteenth-century practice of boarding and contracting for the care of the poor and handicapped, and it was extended by the 1820s to agreements between state governments and private entities as state institutions for certain populations—blind, deaf, mentally disabled—were being established. Yet by the late nineteenth century, public sector financial subsidies prevailed due to political pressures from the voluntary sector; individualistic, moralistic, and religious views that held the government was somewhat responsible but unsuited to deliver services; and a pervasive distrust of government operations, particularly where the partisan-oriented spoils system was prevalent (Kramer 1981, 61–62).

The COS movement mostly operated in large urban centers. Its approach, which came to be known as "scientific philanthropy," was based on the conviction that poverty was a result of individual character defects and that the dependent poor needed interpersonal supports as much as monetary supports. Frustrated by the operation of local political organizations and local governments, the COS movement concentrated on eliminating public institutional relief as a municipal function and on allocating assistance to persons in their own homes and through private charitable organizations. This movement, successful in a number of cities, created "a strong link between private philanthropy and social reform was forged toward the end of the nineteenth century and strengthened the advocacy role of the voluntary agency" (Kramer 1981, 64).

Steven Smith and Michael Lipsky (1993, 50) observe that hostility toward government led the Progressive Era reformers to campaign against public subsidies to nonprofits. By 1930 twenty-six states had constitutional limits on public funding of nonprofits, although those restrictions were often circumvented. The floodgates of public support opened during the Great Depression of the 1930s, as noted in chapter 4, but the ambivalence of deep, public operational support existed until the programs grew in the 1960s, the era of federal expansion of nonprofit funding. Notably the Office of Economic

Opportunity was established to oversee the War on Poverty and channeled money to state and local governments, which distributed most of it to private agencies that targeted their programs to poor persons and families (Smith and Lipsky 1993). Federal funding of social welfare services rapidly increased such that by 1980 the federal government funded 65 percent of all spending at all levels of social welfare services as compared to 37 percent in 1960 (54). A large proportion of this increase was expended through nonprofit agencies, on the backs of new federal policies that encouraged such involvement. For example, the 1967 amendments to the Social Security Act (Title IV-A), or Temporary Assistance for Needy Families, specifically encouraged states to enter into purchase-of-service agreements with private agencies, and that amounted to about half of all services funded by the late 1970s (Smith and Lipsky 1993, 55). Thus, funding of nonprofits had come full circle, in many respects, from modest subsidies for private charities to extensive purchase-of-service contracting on a widespread basis.

The two sectors—public and NGO—continue to have a dynamic and shifting relationship. Dennis Young (1999, 34–40) observes that to comprehend the government-nonprofit relationship, one must take into account three distinct analytic views. First, think of nonprofits as filling in with supplementary actions to government programs. Nonprofits provide variety, faster responses to changes in society, collective goods on a voluntary basis, and important influences on public sector action. Second, one must consider the partnership or contractual connection involved. Governments largely finance public services and nonprofits deliver them, despite a series of transaction costs and an occasional reversal of roles (e.g., private agencies in short-term disaster relief). Third, be aware that nonprofits act as adversaries and advocates. Because of different goals and philosophies, they sometimes collaborate on and sometimes oppose legislation and become increasingly involved as adversaries or advocates in the administrative details of programs. This latter role also develops as a function of government monitoring of nonprofit operations and performance and sometimes through negotiating changes between the NGO and the government.

The purchase-of-service contract with nonprofits parallels the tenets of localism that has been maintained for so long in the United States. Theda Skocpol's (1995, 23–24) observation regarding schools pertains as well to nonprofit social welfare agencies:

> Early democratization of the U.S. white male electorate ensured that masses of ordinary Americans could support public schooling as a right of democratic citizenship rather than warily opposing educational institutions imposed from above by officials and upper classes, as happened in Europe. In the United States, moreover, no national bureaucracy existed to regulate, finance, or serve as a central magnet

for educational development, and no single dominant church served as a prop of a counterweight to the state. Thus local and voluntary forces, including Catholic parishes and a multiplicity of Protestant and Jewish sects, took more initiatives than they did in other nations. In a democratic political context, "participatory localism" encouraged many such groups to support free public schools, while others built and defended private schools. Decentralized federalism allowed local, state-level, and private initiatives to compete with one another—and often to imitate one another as well, in waves of analogous institution building.

As in the case of schooling, social welfare became more of a public function from the 1930s to the 1980s, but these programs were already rooted in both state and local traditions along with prior connections with the NGO sector. Thus, a mixed system continued earlier traditions, like schools, while other services were considered to be part of the community.

Extensive Partnering: Disability and Health

Nonprofits are not the only groups that have a partnership or contractual relationship with government. Today the for-profit sector, ranging from the large health care conglomerates to small solo practitioners of counseling or other services, has emerged as a major vendor of services financed by government, primarily the state and federal governments. In addition to medical and hospital services, among the public services contracted with the for-profit sector are family counseling, employment and training-related services, senior citizen day care, child day care and preschool, foster care services, youth mentoring and activity programs, substance abuse counseling, housing assistance, immigrant settlement services, nursing home care, residential services for the intellectually and developmentally disabled, and day activities for a host of clients. In some situations for-profit services may be the only providers in a community, whereas in others they are in competition with other for-profits serving the same clients (Frumkin and Andre-Clark 2000).

The first large for-profit intergovernmental breakthrough began when disability insurance was added to the Social Security Act in 1950. State government–supported vocational rehabilitation programs made the initial determinations of disability eligibility for the federal Social Security Administration. State administration was operated by rehabilitation counselors who were public sector employees. Other than transacting assistance payments, however, all direct client counseling, training, rehabilitation services, and medical care were purchased by the government and largely from the for-profit sector. It set a pattern for other services, with the government as the payer and NGOs as the providers.

Medicare and Medicaid opened the floodgates for this type of purchase of services from the for-profit sector. Enacted in 1965, Medicare became a federal government responsibility. While it is not a federal-state intergovernmental program, financing for the program is conducted through contracted "private intermediaries," who in turn deal with health care providers, hospitals, and more recently prescription drug vendors. The classic intermediary is a large for-profit like Automatic Data Systems or Anthem/BlueCross Blue Shield. Most important, these intermediaries purchase services mostly from private for-profit and nonprofit hospitals, paying the vendors for their "reasonable" costs.

Medicaid, also adopted in 1965, is a federal, state, local, and private program that is quite different. The government's grants to the states are allocated on a cost-sharing basis (for many years, 40–60 percent came from the federal government, depending on a formula using the states' economic conditions). The health care program is for medically indigent persons, dependent children, the elderly poor, the blind, and the disabled. Instead of an intermediary, the states themselves handle the contracting for services, which are largely purchased from the private sector. The 2010 Affordable Care Act's reforms serve only to reinforce the private sector and for-profit purchase of services given that more persons hold partially government-supported or subsidized health insurance, vended largely through the private sector, and millions more are included in the Medicaid program through state option eligibility extensions to those persons above the Medicaid eligibility line.

The ACA maintains the Medicare-Medicaid divide (Starr 1982, 320). Some states have refused to expand Medicaid despite the incentive of heavy federal funding ratios, and in 2014 the US Supreme Court upheld the states' voluntary participation. Also, Medicaid reimbursement rates remain low in comparison to those for Medicare. Through different models both programs nevertheless represent extensive purchase-of-service contracting from broad elements of the private for-profit sector, using the Medicare intermediaries and state governments for Medicaid. Clearly, they represent the largest and, some would say, the most complicated aspects of government partnerships.

The Scope of Partnering

Intergovernmental partnerships extend well beyond economic development, education, and health and human services. Three additional examples provide greater depth to comprehending this arena: environmental management, rural development, and road construction. Together they broaden understanding of the range of public-NGO connections.

In the environmental arena, the Darby Partnership focuses on the public and NGO agency information exchange related to the Big and Little Darby

Creek Watershed in central Ohio. Launched in the early 1990s by the Nature Conservancy of Ohio and six local soil and water conservation districts, the protection effort has since expanded to include some sixty state and federal agencies as well as NGO conservation groups. Darby also receives technical assistance from several state and federal agencies and the Ohio EPA. Darby partners decided early in making their connections to go beyond their formative agricultural land-use issues and include agricultural practices, wastewater treatment, residential and industrial development, and citizen education (Koontz et al. 2004). Darby has a limited agenda, inasmuch as it does not take formal action itself but is primarily geared to listening to partner reports at quarterly meetings. The partners or other participating public or voluntary agencies are expected to take the decisions or actions. Darby is a public-private partnership that is basically a clearinghouse for many projects and for watershed organizations that take actions that serve the US Department of Agriculture's hydrologic unit area project (Agranoff 2007c, 52–55).

Many rural development partnerships have emerged in the states. The department's rural development office in each state uses its twenty USDA grant and loan programs to partner with various NGOs within its state. For example, a rural state such as Nebraska is involved in numerous partnerships with universities, community organizations, and statewide associations. Together they promote value-added agriculture and agribusiness and market state products. The state's Department of Economic Development also is in separate partnership with the Nebraska Regional Development Network (regional planning associations) and the University of Nebraska Center for Rural Research, among others (Agranoff 2012).

Many state and local jurisdictions have established partnerships to build physical infrastructure: roads and bridges, correctional facilities, solid waste facilities, stadia, and wastewater systems, to name a few. For example, in recent decades Indiana turned over toll- or revenue-generating public facilities to privatized arrangements of different sorts that lend themselves to user charges. Virtually all of the state's road construction is done by private contractors whereas maintenance in most areas remains a government responsibility. These arrangements lend themselves to partnerships because they provide easier access to private capital, thus reducing the need for public borrowing, and often with many operating costs paid by users.

E. S. Savas (2000, 241–45) identifies a series of alternatives to government-built and operated infrastructure: public-private authority; service contracting; operations and maintenance contract and lease; formation of a nonprofit, voluntary cooperative association; lease-build-operate framework, when private firms lease and operate facilities and collect user fees over a set period; build-transfer-operate, when private firms finance, build, and operate a facility but ultimately transfer it to a sponsoring government agency while still collecting fees; build-transfer-operate framework, when private firms finance and build but after a time transfer to a public authority while still collecting fees; buy-build-operate framework, when private firms purchase an existing public facility and collect all fees; and build-own-operate framework, when private financing, building, ownership, and operation are in perpetuity, subject to regulatory constraints on pricing and operations. Savas explains, "Many of these models are extremely complicated and time consuming to arrange, and they may call for explicit or implicit guarantees from government, of volumes (of traffic, for toll-road projects or of water usage, for water and wastewater projects, for instance) revenues, input prices, and so on, so that the government is left with significant contingent liabilities after all" (245).

Infrastructure thus has provided many partnership models. While the benefits represent ways of providing notable extensions of public services, they also involve both vertical federal, state, and local public funding and regulatory sources as well as horizontal connections with partners.

Governments Contract with NGOs

Contracting for services has become big intergovernmental business. Although it has been a major activity of local governments for decades (Ferris and Graddy 1986; Morgan, Hirlinger, and England 1988), the overall scope of activity may be narrower than commonly understood. On the one hand, surveys by the International City and County Management Association have demonstrated that such privatization peaked at less than 20 percent of all service delivery commitments in 1997 (Warner and Hefetz 2004). Indeed, surveys have shown that intergovernmental cooperation of no-contract-for-services or partial contracting is considerably more common than that of complete contracting out (Agranoff and McGuire 2003; Warner and Hefetz 2009). On the other hand, Nicholas Henry (2011, 221) reports that the federal government is "a contractor-dependent environment." He reports that all types of contracting, procurement, and purchase of services now amount to about 4 million distinct contract actions through some 160,000 contractors and involving nearly 5.17 million NGO workers in this "indirect" form of operations.

A contract, in its simplest form, is an agreement between parties—in this case, between governments and NGOs—to deliver goods or to perform certain services (Cohen and Eimicke 2008, 4). Jeffrey Brudney and associates (2005, 394) observe,

Despite the apparent heterogeneity of the privatization concept and the various methods for achieving privatization, in the U.S. context especially, this term is usually taken to mean government "contracting out" or "outsourcing" with a for-profit firm, a non-profit organization,

BOX 6.1

- Governmental units increasingly partner with NGOs far beyond their earlier, primary supply and infrastructure roles, and extend to various clients such direct services as contractor first-line case management as well as service delivery.
- A growing number of NGOs involved in intergovernmental programs are non-profit organizations, particularly in the human services, with many becoming implementation partners for delivering direct service programs.
- Partnerships in direct services make NGOs more than agents for national and state programs. They are also actively involved in comanaging programs in their design, organization, service delivery, and reporting phases.
- As government has externalized, the management challenge has increased, particularly given the need to coordinate various programs serving particular populations, whose many problems are served by agencies carrying out multiple missions.

or another government to produce or deliver a service. Although the job of delivering services is contracted out, the services remain public, funded mainly by taxation, and decisions regarding their quantity, quality, distribution, and other characteristics are left to public decision makers.

This type of contract activity is sometimes referred to as "third-party government" (Goldsmith and Eggers 2004, 19). Because the sometimes-used term "outsourcing" also connotes moving private sector jobs overseas, it is preferable in this context to use an English translation for the Spanish term for contracting out, *externalización* (externalization). Indeed, the reference is to governments moving functions and services to external operators and does not necessarily have exportable connotations.

Contract Basics

Ruth DeHoog and Lester Salamon (2002, 320) point out that service contracts differ in several respects from simpler procurement contracts. First, many are directed at assisting or changing the behavior and circumstances of disadvantaged populations, leading to complex service configurations, uncontrollable factors, and uncertain outcomes. Second, as highly labor-intensive services, they make cost control and employee supervision problematic. Third, performance is often difficult to assess, requiring extensive monitoring and review of investments. Fourth, the potential for competition is usually heralded as an advantage of contracting, but some service arenas will not necessarily have competing providers, whereas too much competition in other arenas may lead to subsequent difficulties in coordination. Clearly government-contractor relationships are critical and present a very large contrast between this type of *complex contracting* and the less complicated purchase of goods or clearly defined services (Brown, Potoski, and Van Slyke 2008b).

Service contracting is generally understood to entail a set of rather well-established processes. With regard to IGM, a first principle would be judging who is lawfully authorized to have a financing and operational role in the service: a federal government fiscal intermediary, state governments, state government and nonprofit combinations (e.g., aging services), direct NGO contractors, state and local governments with NGOs, local governments and NGOs, and so on. In some cases the law permits the first-level administering agency as well as others down the line to determine whether the service is eligible or worthy of purchasing. After making these types of decisions, the bid solicitation process begins, normally through announcing a request for proposals and advertising through media that will reach appropriate service delivery agencies. Next within the context of process fairness, the proposals are reviewed and the contract awarded, avoiding corruption, collusion, fraud, favoritism, and conflict of interest. When operations begin, contract monitoring also starts, with evaluations established to ensure that services are delivered, are within cost parameters, and are meeting expectations. These assessments may include regular site visits, periodic reports, random file probes, documentation of financial costs, and reviews of client feedback. Finally, after a period of execution, renewal or termination decisions are made (DeHoog and Salamon 2002, 324–26; Cohen and Eimicke 2008, chs. 5, 6).

Regarding government-NGO relationships in contracting, contract experts often warn public agency managers to treat some contractors as "treacherous thieves" and others as "trusted partners." Academics normally call for some form of "relational contracting," grounded in both firmness and specificity of expectations along with trust and reciprocity between the government and the NGO partner (Williamson 1984). The problem, argues Trevor Brown, Matthew Potoski, and David Van Slyke (2008b, 5), is that this advice is not only contradictory but also misses the mark. The missing element, as identified, is making a distinction between simple, or product-oriented, contracting and complex, or service-oriented, contracting. The former can be easily and carefully defined, whereas those that involve services are hard to spell out and difficult to verify. With complex contracts, they conclude:

> Complex products are challenging targets for contracting. Markets for complex products tend to be "thin" (there are few buyers and few sellers), which means the market provides little information about the product and its price, quality, and quantity tradeoffs. It is consequently difficult (and expensive) to define precise terms of exchange

and ambiguous contract terms are often left to be negotiated as the product is produced and delivered. The result can be a risky combination of a government under-informed about the product it is buying, depending on who is contracting with a vendor unconstrained by competitive market pressures and able to exploit contract loopholes and ambiguities for its own advantage. (5)

In *complex contracting*, the buyer and seller do not fully know the performance parameters and costs until the exchange takes place. The exchange also requires *ex ante* (before the event) investments in assets that lose value should the exchange not be fully executed. The contract for the exchange is also incomplete, so the parties have room for discretion. This leads to a payoff uncertainty that provides further chances for two-way payoff uncertainty, thus opening the possibility for negotiations regarding potential cooperative behavior (Brown, Potoski, and Van Slyke 2016, 300). Brown, Potoski, and Van Slyke conclude that in this process, the fruits of trust and cooperation in contracting are among the highest in demand for complex products. The downside risks when trust breaks down and contracts fail are considerable.

Thus, the collaborating managers and program officials need to understand the two most basic theoretical approaches to the contracting relationship—*agency theory*, based on the general idea that the government funder is the "principal" and the contractor is its "agent," and *stewardship theory*, based on the idea of mutual goals and high levels of trust. Figure 6.1, summarized from an empirical study of the two approaches in social services contracting (Van Slyke 2007), highlights each. Agency theory is clearly control oriented, premised on the assumption that there is goal divergence between the principal and the agent, and tight controls and monitoring must be imposed to eliminate situations where contractors might pursue opportunistic behavior. Stewardship takes more of a joint goal orientation approach with greater mutual trust, places less emphasis on strict provisions and monitoring, and assumes fairly mutual agreement on process and goals.

Van Slyke's (2007, 182–83) study of social service contracting reveals the presence of both models in the real world and calls for a better understanding of relational contracting and perhaps for some sort of IGM principal-steward in contracting. At first in contract relationships, public managers act consistent with agency theory, while the initial disposition and desire of nonprofit executive directors are consistent with stewardship theory. It turns out that a lack of financial incentives and inconsistent use of monitoring are incongruous with the agency theory. The use of trust and reputation is clearly consistent with the tenets of stewardship but may also be consistent with an evolved principal-agent relationship. In practice the two

FIGURE 6.1. Theoretical Tenets and Applications of Agency and Stewardship Theory

Main theme	Agency theory	Stewardship theory
	Goal incongruence: Assumes goal divergence based on self-interested rational actors. Initial disposition is to distrust. Control-oriented management philosophy. Theoretical assumptions are from economics. Uses incentives and sanctions to foster goal alignment: • Risk assigned to the agent to ensure goal compliance • Monitoring • Reward systems • Use of bonding, threat to reputation ✓ Eliminates opportunistic behavior ✓ Provides the level of incentives and sanctions that reduce the threat of information asymmetry ✓ Corrects, through specific contract requirements, for asset specificity and moral hazard ✓ Uses reputation as an incentive and sanction ✓ Ensures goal alignment	Goal alignment: Mutual goals and objectives achieved through initial trust disposition. Involvement-oriented management philosophy. Theoretical assumptions derived from organizational behavior, psychology, and sociology. Empowers workers through: • Responsibility • Autonomy • Shared culture and norms • Personal power and trust • Other governance mechanisms ✓ Aligns goals based on shared goals and trust ✓ Rewards workers through nonpecuniary mechanisms ✓ Reduces the threat of opportunistic behavior through responsibility and autonomy ✓ Decreases the threat to the organization of information asymmetries, moral hazards, and asset specificity ✓ Reduces dependence on legal contracts to enforce behavior ✓ Uses reputation as an incentive and sanction

Source: Van Slyke (2007), 167. © Oxford University Press. Reprinted by permission.

theories, when used in concert, are complementary. Stewardship theory captures the state of what actually emerged regarding what principal-agent contract management practices might look like between government and nonprofit organizations.

Van Slyke concludes that the contextual characteristics that color much of the application of public management contract practices are not well accounted for in either theory. The theories explain only part of the government-nonprofit relationship, and to some degree it is because program operations often involve long IGM chains. He determines, "More work is needed on the evolved principal-agent relationships and on the development of principal-steward relations. The variables that comprise the set of contextual conditions are a very important set of factors to be considered and controlled for if these theories are used to explain how government manages its social services contracting relationships with non-profits. In this respect, the line between an evolved principal-agent and principal-steward relationship is less precise than desired" (183). This research suggests that the contract relationships indicate the importance of working toward an evolved principal-agent relationship. Clearly, contracting is a relational and interactive process that has elements of looking out for gaming and thievery as well as elements of trusted partnerships. In this respect, both the mechanics of contract management and network-oriented, integrated service markets are IGM goals (see chapter 9 of this volume).

The evolution and frequency of purchasing services in complex contracting mean that whichever way a contracting model leans, toward agency or stewardship, there is a situation where joint "production" among many actors for the provision of government services might be inadequately specified. Moreover, clientele groups receiving service may have varying levels of motivation for and acceptance of service intervention. For example, many recipients of substance abuse or mental health services are not eager service recipients, and providers are sometimes reluctant to serve the most difficult clients. Some families of persons with intellectual disabilities who are in institutions hesitate to remove their family members, fearing that their needs may not be met in the community, that their personal risks will increase, or that greater personal burdens will be placed on the families to support their disabled family members. Some welfare or income support clients resist education and training that will move them off welfare for fear of losing their related health benefits, child care, or housing support. Thus, in addition to difficulties with specifying contract provisions and contractors gaming the system, reluctant clients must be factored into any process that compounds the relational contracting process.

Despite the many obstacles, managers on all sides of contracts are pressured to work together to build the kind of relational contract model that is somewhere between the agency and stewardship approaches. Relational models normally involve agencies and contractor providers in long-term negotiated relationships that involve trust, discretion, joint problem-solving and information exchange, and efforts to contribute to mutual goal alignment and reduce measurement difficulties and intractability in service provision. Trust is built through extensive interaction and involvement focused on communicating one another's goals and approaches to service intervention. This investment in front-end transaction costs builds alignment. These concerns are raised in greater detail in chapter 7.

Vouchers

A *voucher* is a subsidy that grants limited purchasing power to an individual to choose among a restricted set of goods and services. It provides choice to the beneficiaries of government programs (Steuerle and Twombly 2002, 446). Four of the five largest federal voucher programs—Child Care and Development Block Grant; Supplemental Nutrition Assistance Program (formerly Food Stamps); Women's, Infants, and Children supplemental nutrition program; and Workforce Development Initiatives—are distinctly federal-state or federal-local programs. The fifth, Pell Grants, are federal-university scholarships. The well-known Section 8 housing support program also operates through vouchers. State and local governments have other voucher programs that, for example, help move persons off welfare, provide child care assistance, assist local firms with "buyback" exchanges of goods for vouchers, and, of course, subsidize tuition when parents want to enroll their children in nonpublic schools. Vouchers differ from grants and contracts because they vest more control to the ultimate beneficiaries of public programs, particularly in choosing vendors or service agents (where a choice exists), rather than to the suppliers of goods and services. While choice is in the hands of the beneficiary, vouchers normally limit what can be purchased, and their purchasing power always has a finite value.

From an intergovernmental standpoint, vouchers are similar to contracts in that they shift control from governments to consumers or NGO providers. The government normally sets eligibility, payment levels, and program restrictions, avoiding direct government service (goods) provisions. Clearly, the private market (with the exception of public universities) is the provider of the government-sponsored voucher program.

Those who tout the superiority of voucher programs, such as David Osborne and Ted Gaebler (1992, 181–86), believe that that this form of "putting clients first" is efficacious for seven reasons. First, these programs force provider accountability because clients can seek alternative providers. Second, vouchers can depoliticize government-provider interaction when contracts are let to more than one competing provider, thus reducing potential problems of corruption. Third, when funds are disbursed based on client choice, providers have more incentive to innovate. Fourth, voucher systems offer more opportunity for choices not only among various vendors but in some cases (e.g., job training) between various types of services offered. Fifth, voucher programs make aligning client demand—for example, for housing, food, nutrition, and workforce training—with the available supply somewhat easier because suppliers move to meet funding expectations. Thus, shortages rarely occur. Sixth, vouchers reinforce the ability of clients to choose in service selection, increasing their sense of empowerment. Finally, vouchers promote equity to the extent that separate institutions for the poor or other service recipients are normally not created. Clients can utilize vouchers in the normal marketplace of services.

These so-called advantages have their downsides. For example, without entering a protracted debate regarding their merits, school vouchers are divisive politically. Despite the choice levels that they may create, many opponents of school vouchers feel that they weaken public school systems as some of the best students go to the private sector; that they drain resources—for example, state support payments—from local school districts; and that they are a subsidy for the well-off, inasmuch as even with a voucher most parents cannot afford private school tuition. Another issue with many types of vouchers, school and nonschool, is that head-to-head competition among potential providers is not always possible, leaving few alternatives. Vouchers also often fall short of equity expectations. Sometimes there is only a single government voucher provider, thus creating a sort of "welfare provider" vendor. This situation is particularly true with regard to housing, child care, and food institutions. Clearly choices are simply not available. Even if competition is present, vouchers assume that in all cases consumers are able to make intelligent choices among accessible goods, services, and providers. To many who follow the politics of voucher programs, this is an open question (school vouchers are paramount here). It suggests, conclude Eugene Steuerle and Eric Twombly (2002, 455) that "vouchers are easier to implement for products that are easier to assess (e.g., food), or where information on quality is readily available or where beneficiaries have the strongest incentives to invest the time and effort to acquire the information they need to make wise use of their vouchers."

Regarding voucher administration, Steuerle and Twombly (2002, 452–54) have identified a series of eight generic administrative tasks for handling vouchers. First, define what will be subsidized and devise parameters that ensure the program's resources are restricted to those items. Second, identify recipients and certify their eligibility through client screenings and determination proceedings. Third, devise payment and distribution methods, particularly if payments go directly to the producer or to the clients. Fourth, establish modes of communication between the distribution system and the eligibility process, as client eligibility status changes and needs to be continually updated. Fifth, arrange a process of informing, certifying, and in some cases recruiting suppliers, along with some administrative apparatus for communicating with suppliers. Sixth, launch an information system, including marketing and counseling, so that less educated potential and actual clients can efficiently use vouchers. Seventh, put in place systems of enforcement, monitoring, and evaluation, including occasional audits. Finally, set up budgeting and provisions for coordination with other programs (e.g., food stamps, supplemental nutrition programs, and Medicaid) using both formal and informal means. Throughout this step-based administrator sequence, it is important to remember that the ultimate policy "selection of vouchers vis-à-vis other policy tools takes place in a broader political environment" (454).

The Politics of Partnerships: New Forms of Lobbying

Legislative bodies and political interests caught up with market-oriented philosophies have obviously encouraged shifts from grants to the purchase of services contracting, or vouchers. By the early 2000s, all but four states contracted out a portion of their correctional services and in some cases portions of education and health care, while some chose complete externalization of these programs (Nicholson-Crotty 2004; Price and Riccucci 2005). For example, both mental illness and developmental disabilities and service areas have signaled a notable public externalization even of public agency field operations and management, programming, and facilities, and favored delivery by for-profit and nonprofit sectors. In vocational rehabilitation and in substance abuse, the bulk of services came from nongovernment agencies. In this case the shift is merely from grants to contracts.

As the dominant paradigm became market-based connections with NGOs, the emerging intergovernmental actors became private vendors and nonprofits, which are now part of the "public enterprise." For example, most institutionalized long-term care for the elderly is no longer provided by government institutions (e.g., county homes) but by private owners of large nursing or residential homes. Noninstitutional, or community, services for these populations not in long-term care are now supervised by state governments under federal Medicaid funding through a host of nongovernmental case managers, activity and employment programs, supervised living and group homes, and other medical and social support services. Nonprofits and for-profits provide virtually all of these programs externally on a government-funded basis. As the government still funds these programs, a new politics of trade and vendor NGO associations has emerged amid these changes.

Externalization has accelerated the need for public administrators to become more directly involved in IGM political matters and deal with big providers and associations. Partisan and electoral politics also follows. In collaborative activity "public administrators may be more acutely aware of, and more affected by, the larger political conditions of their environment" (Dormady 2012, 754). These larger political constructs impact not only the major political issues of who is in office or who receives high-level appointments but also the dealings at the program implementation stage—over rules, standards, limitations, and authorizations—along with the ongoing feedback on program design and operations from a host of external organizations, clients and their advocates, legislators and legislative commissions, and external

BOX 6.2

- In contracting for services, externalization has called attention to relational contracts involving technical, political, and managerial concerns that are interactively transacted. One might call them the nonmechanical components of contracting.
- At the operational level, coordinating among services that many clients need calls for joint production that works across programs. In the human services, this process has been identified as services integration.
- Voucher programs that allow eligible clients to choose services from an authorized range of providers also enable the clients to engage and assess these providers and to review funder assessments.
- Program growth has led to the proliferation of jurisdictional and program support government interest groups. For example, the National League of Cities and the National Association of Rehabilitation Facilities are now important IGM actors at all stages of their respective programs' cycles, from program enactment to service delivery.

program assessors. Regarding rulemaking, Cornelius Kerwin (1999, 260) observes that the process operates within a variety of constraints including those of a legal and administrative nature: "Politics permeates the rulemaking process, bringing strong pressures to bear on those developing rules." Indeed, going beyond rules, the greater the externalization of programs, the more this type of politics will also become part of the IGM political game but not necessarily always to serve constructive problem-solving interests (O'Toole and Meier 2004).

Just as subnational governments use public interest group pressure to lobby central governments, associations of different kinds of nonprofit and for-profit providers now interact with governments over the administration of intergovernmental programs. They do more than visible lobbying at legislative levels. As demonstrated in chapter 7, these trade associations try to, and often do, sit at the table with governments and negotiate nettlesome and costly contract provisions or what they perceive as loss-bearing cost reimbursements, unreasonable standards, or loss-bearing and protracted procedures. These actions are not always negative or work against government interests. For example, associations also work with government agents to determine complicated per diem funding allocations and reimbursed costs for various types of residential services, like contracted group homes. Similar IGM behaviors follow in other areas, as NGOs try to change the nature of their contract provisions and the interpretation of funding rules. Meanwhile, NGOs play external politics by contacting legislative representatives and persuading them to increase budgets and to ease legal restrictions. A new IGM politics of NGOs has thus arisen as a result of externalization and as lobbying and administration have become intertwined IGM processes.

The Courts Enter the IGM Arena: *Olmstead,* the States, and NGOs

The courts have entered the era of government partners with rulings affecting cases related to intergovernmental programs that are largely administered by the states and through the states and to NGOs. The courts have long upheld the public sector's rights to regulation over financial and program restrictions, reporting and monitoring, and the like, as conditions of funded services or otherwise extending contract conditions and due process (Malatesta and Carboni 2014). The courts are now using other legislation—for example, those related to civil rights or due process—to guide intergovernmental programs that involve third-party service delivery. Whereas this judicial impact could take up a whole volume, it is illustrated by how the US Supreme Court's *Olmstead* decision on developmental disabilities has impacted the states and contractors with NGO services.

The Supreme Court ruling *Olmstead v. L. C. and E. W.* in 1999 directed states not to institutionalize persons if they were clinically ready for community-based services and if the individuals chose these options. Keeping such persons in institutions, the court found, is in violation of the 1991 amendments to the 1990 Americans with Disabilities Act that state that "a public entity shall administer services, programs, and activities in the most integrated setting appropriate to the needs of qualified individuals with disabilities" (28 C.F.R. § 35130 [b][7], [d]-[e]-1). *Olmstead* requires states to make "reasonable modifications" to their programs, yet they do not have to "fundamentally alter" these programs and services (Rosenbaum and Teitelbaum 2004). This case has moved state programs considerably in the direction of building stronger connections with NGO service providers (Fox-Grage, Folkemer, and Lewis 2003), and it has triggered many suits in lower courts that interpret "reasonable progress" and "fundamental alteration." The courts have not been shy about prescriptive behavior regarding how states treat their NGO client intermediaries.

Two implications are important for understanding the nature of the government partners' dimension of IGM. First, many *Olmstead* follow-on suits have put the federal courts into the details of the federal, state, and NGO provider program administration. Judgments have been made primarily regarding the chief *Olmstead* funding mechanisms, Medicaid and HCBS Medicaid waivers, "on the ground" factors such as funding evening services, refusal of home care after minor adjustments to income standards, limits on prescription drug benefits to five per month, changes in eligibility criteria, states' waiting list sizes, clients' time on waiting lists, funding levels for waiver services and numbers of waiver slots allocated (states are allowed to set caps and targets), types of "optional" community services, and administrative time taken to process applicants (Agranoff and McGuire 2005; Rosenbaum, Stewart, and Teitelbaum 2002; Human Services Research Institute 2005).

Olmstead puts the federal government and state governments via the courts right in the details of state programming with NGOs, more or less using Medicaid "carrots" to create "sticks" while building relationship-based partnerships and working toward systems of services.

Olmstead has also influenced the states to move toward compliance actions designed to incorporate NGO partners into more integrated services. With some small federal grant incentives under Executive Order 13217 Community-Based Alternatives for Individuals with Disabilities in 2001, at least thirty-nine states developed *Olmstead* plans that not only included direct services but also attempted to connect various NGOs involved in related services: housing, transportation, legal services, and health services as well as data collection on persons with developmental disabilities, waiting list reduction plans and actions, education programs regarding services options, and quality care assurances (Fox-Grage, Folkemer, and Lewis 2003). Real Choice Systems Change Grants, funded nationally at about $100 million per year, have supported these programs for several years. These efforts are not designed to replace state systems but to encourage the pace of states' progress in linking providers or integrating services within the parameters of existing state designs, for example, in Indiana, Ohio, and North Carolina (Agranoff and Pattakos 1979; Agranoff 2013). In conclusion, *Olmstead* is but one of many examples of how the federal courts have become involved in intergovernmental partnering and have entered the thicket of IGM in deep and operational ways that exceed what are thought of as broad policy issues.

Key Learning Points

The era of externalization is not without its public sector consequences inasmuch as many public agencies have gone through some levels of administrative capacity disinvestment. With many externalized programs, the further one moves down the line, so to speak, the more indirect government becomes. While it is probably somewhat of a stretch to say that the hubs of the intergovernmental system—the federal and state governments—have "hollowed out" (Milward, Provan, and Else 1993), they have changed, moving away from direct operations. Many state agency offices have thus become shadows of their former operational or service selves. Others outside of government are doing what agencies once did or have taken on new functions.

Much work remains in the state or federal agencies, albeit it is increasingly intergovernmental. As they have progressively transferred many of their operations to a series of administrative and data systems contractors and provider agencies that do initial intake and case management, systems development and oversight have become key government agency functions.

Meanwhile, field or regional operations have fallen away or are at risk. Programs and budget agencies, for example, now share intergovernmental negotiations. These changes are among the new marks of IGM partnerships.

The tenets of partnership along with intergovernmental concerns nevertheless continue to focus somewhere on quite minute details of program orientation. In practice, invoking relational contracting may be admirable in program goals, but the involvement of so many actors—from designated administrative agencies, with budget instructions to public or contract case managers and NGO delivery administrators, to service provider–client interactions and not to mention regulations and court rulings—makes these relationships complex, involved, and problematic. They are the new dynamics of "multi-partnering," so to speak. This development has led to the protracted complexity of the IGM externalization phenomenon.

Key Practice Points

Under this "divested" system, the IGM style of operation now includes federal and state officials negotiating with contractors, reporting upward through the system, and conducting downward auditing of contracts. Intergovernmental programs remain held together by law and financing, for example, through Medicaid and other federal funds transmitted to the states and through federal Community Development Block Grants to local governments.

The external operation of government programs also raises important value considerations that had not been widespread issues of concern until they were introduced in the debates regarding public sector support for charter schools. In a far-reaching article concerning privatization, Martha Minow (2003) discusses many concerns about this trend, particularly how it affects people's ability to take part in communities, to act as citizens who care about the welfare of others, to know about or participate in actions promoting the issues of others, and so on. Privatization reduces people's option to be engaged citizens. Contracting out public services such as education and human services thus runs the risk of threatening "public commitments to meet basic human needs, redress inequalities, and strengthen democracy" (1254).

Conclusion

This IGM focus has brought into the operational discourse the point that many intergovernmental policy and program arenas now include nongovernmental partners. Now one must think both vertically, through the chain of governments, and horizontally—that is, between governments at the local level and with nonprofit and for-profit NGOs. More and more these new organizations deliver public programs and services that go well beyond the procurement of goods. They are linked up the chain of governments, and their legal authority, mainly by contract, and NGOs at the delivery level are at the end of a long and increasingly protracted intergovernmental chain. They experience operability challenges and strains that compound IGM well beyond the confines of governments and are the focus of chapter 7.

7 MANAGING INTERGOVERNMENTAL MANAGEMENT PARTNERSHIPS

A broad range of intergovernmental working partnerships has emerged in the past few decades. Two underlying forces undergird an evolving IGM as the government partners' domain becomes increasingly operational, particularly at the service or implementation level. First, government may be reduced in scope but not necessarily in authority. It has not exactly been hollowed out or reduced to a shell of its former self; instead, government is assuming new and expanded roles. Second, new means of collaborative managing are consequently emerging, with government or the grantee/contractor moving from *supervising* NGOs toward *managing with* NGOs. Regarding authority, government retains most of the legal, fiscal, enforcement, and supervisory powers, while NGOs now have more of the day-to-day responsibilities of organizing and managing direct operations that require higher, more interactive coordination. This arena produces a new or essentially refocused public management.

Increasingly the era of externalization involves more than contracting or vouchering. The depth and extensiveness of these transactions often lead to more regular and formalized government—namely, NGO contracts. Two such examples emanate from the Medicaid partnerships and the National Interagency Fire Center known as the Incident Fire Command. Each leads to sets of regularized connections that extend the partnership approach.

First, in addition to the Affordable Care Act's private insurance subsidies that the federal government supports, the legislation also boosts Medicaid (Thompson 2013). The difference between ACA-supported private insurance and Medicaid is that the latter is the quintessential intergovernmental federal-state partnership program. Adopted in 1965, by 2010 Medicaid accounted for over 90 percent of all federal health grant dollars. It serves four main populations: people with serious mental or physical disabilities, elderly people who do not qualify for Medicare, low-income children, and low-income nondisabled adults who lack insurance. The state governments operate this federal program within coverage parameters set by the federal government, but the states have considerable discretion to determine eligibility, payment rates to providers, services covered, and related issues. Medicaid is an entitlement;

for each eligible client, the federal government must match a specified rate chosen by the states, ranging from 50 to 75 percent, depending on their relative wealth. Now at a state's option, under the ACA, Medicaid can cover a new group of persons living just above the poverty line.

Most important, Medicaid-financed services are carried under state contract via partnership by provider contracts with private firms and nonprofit organizations: hospitals, physicians, nursing homes, managed care organizations, community health organizations, home health agencies, community health centers, and many others. Also, a series of private providers, again in partnership, manage overall care cases in several states. For example, Anthem/Blue Cross Blue Shield operates in nineteen states. At one time the states mostly served as check writers to these providers, but now they face extensive negotiations and monitoring of contracts. As Frank Thompson (2012, 17) observes, "In sum, state bureaucracies that receive grants from the federal government to operate Medicaid face formidable implementation issues." The primary vehicle for such state operations in most states is through a series of partnership arrangements.

Second, the National Interagency Fire Center's Wildland Fire Management Strategy involves five federal agencies, multiple state governments, state-based NGOs, and large private forest holdings to combat large-scale fires. Along with the US Government Accountability Office, the center sees the challenges as identifying and defining problems; establishing coordinated goals and standards that respect state, regional, and local differences and needs; and defining the roles of federal, state, and local governments and other entities. The fire center's collaborative policy involves ten broad, overlapping goals: bringing together disparate resources and agencies; documenting agency and organization sequences and procedures; developing a command-and-control structure; establishing an agreed-on management strategy; finding a resource redeployment sequence; setting an agency-"donated" staffing sequence; agreeing on and setting common standards, policies, and procedures, including equipment deployment; settling incident response policies and procedures; forming and operating a council, or networked organized structure; and negotiating and setting interorganizational policies and procedures (US Department of Homeland Security 2005). From the perspective of the federal Homeland Security Department, William Jenkins (2006) notes the difficulties that independent organizations have in compelling such behavior. He also calls for structures and processes "that provide incentives and rewards for collaboration, consultation and support for implementing key goals," particularly clear problem identification, establishment of collaborative goals, and definition of respective roles (321).

Has externalization by such interactive working partnerships eliminated, attenuated, or reduced the role of government, or has government changed? Regarding public agency authority, Michael Walzer (1998, 138) reminds us that government frames the nature of the public sector-nonpublic sector paradigm, or what he identifies as civil society. In other words, government both establishes it and occupies space within it while fixing the boundary conditions and the basic rules of associational activity. In relation to collaborative management, government-NGO interactions, in turn, have led to new nonhierarchical means suited to "addressing problems that often transcend organizational boundaries"—that is, "initiatives deliberately undertaken by government to accomplish public goals, with measurable performance goals, assigned responsibilities to each partner, and structured information flow" (Goldsmith and Eggers 2004, 7, 8). Indeed, there are few examples of direct service delivery leading to increasing operating discretion on the part of third parties. "Yet there is little acknowledgment of the impact of these differing roles in the three levels of government" (Radin 2012, 69). Despite such shifts in the locus of services, it is important to understand the emergent processes and that the "visible hand of managerial hierarchy" still remains (Frederickson and Stazyk 2010, 363).

The primary IGM concern involves the powers and roles of the public sector as it operates through NGOs. The process, however, does not stand alone as a management entity. It is intertwined with government rules and procedures. Government regulations and standards, often passed from federal to state governments, are also enforceable in contracts or grants or other means of tying in NGOs. These other means are always under operational law, transacting standards, and collaboration at this stage. The same powers of oversight ascribed for funder governments in grants, for example, have been applied to NGOs that operate under government contracts, such as in Medicaid. Rules and standards are enforceable in contracts in the same ways as those of grants. This has been particularly acute with decisions relating to the civil rights and equal protection of clients who are served by NGOs under public auspices. While NGOs have argued that as nonpublic entities they are not as tightly subject to the same standards and rules as those of governments, rarely do courts accept these arguments. For example, as vendors or contractees or even as recipients of funds, NGOs must not only abide by the rules but also afford the same protections to clients and citizens as those held in publicly operated programs. For example, the rights of appeal or eligibility hearings are maintained. Although not widely understood, the protective concerns of public programs carry over to NGO delivery, thus extending public management.

This chapter looks behind these concerns at new influences on public management, where there is another, usually nongovernmental, step in the operational details of IGM—that is, management through externalization. First is an examination of how IGR and IGM have changed as a result of the contracting process and how NGOs stand as the primary direct service operational agents of government. Second follows a look at how the government partners' IGM paradigm works by reviewing three mini cases that focus on how states have moved their mental disability programs out of state-operated facilities and largely to contract systems. Next, the basics of contract management operation, government to NGO, are identified, and the aspects of management that go beyond the signed contract are raised. After noting the influences of the new public management movement on IGM, the chapter examines basic government-NGO dynamics in contracting, ranging from supervisory or interventionist models to trust-based stewardship behavior. This is followed by a demonstration of how the US Forest Service and the federal Bureau of Land Management (BLM) promote stewardship connections through to local levels. Finally, the chapter considers the issues and prospects of the IGM framework that are related to building evolving partnerships between governments and collaborating NGOs.

Government under the Contracting State

There is clearly an administrative shift from operational in-house delivery to oversight or contract monitoring in the public agencies that deliver services externally. As mentioned, George Frederickson (1999, 702) observes that "the most important feature of contemporary public administration is the declining relationship between jurisdiction and public management." At the federal level, contracting to third parties, according to 1992 instructions from the Office of Management and Budget, is supposed to preclude inherently government functions that are "'so intimately related to the public interest as to mandate performance by government employees' ... [and] involve exercising discretion in the use of government authority or ... in government decision makings" (as quoted in Burman 2008, 41–42). However, the author of this letter later stated that the instructions provide "no bright line test of allowability" but must be based on the circumstances while taking into account many concerns, including consideration of politically sensitive issues (Burman 2008; Minow 2004–5; Radin 2012, ch. 4).

As program delivery moves out of public agencies, the remaining and normally downsized staff works inside and outside the agency offices involving tendering, reviewing, enforcing, auditing, and evaluating contracts or grants, all while ensuring that laws, regulations, standards, and contract provisions are followed—at least to the extent that this is possible. These tasks can be daunting, because where once hierarchical-based public employees were supervised, now they are non-organizationally connected agents who are expected to deliver. The challenge is that normally there are few contractees (those left in the bureaucracy) and many contractors in the NGOs, with numerous employees of many types. Since the programs under examination are usually intergovernmental as opposed to direct federal contracts (e.g., procurement of goods), the federal and state government legislative provisions, mandates, and rules must be translated and enforced all the way down the line to the point where the "vendor" employee meets the service client. While reviewable, this transactional process is often long.

The major mode in the transaction involves the various required fiscal and program reports. They begin with the NGO employee–client contact paperwork exercise, which the contractor agency then compiles and transmits ultimately to some intermediate public agency. These reports and other contract performance data—program and fiscal—are aggregated, summarized, and transmitted to executive agencies and later in summary or analysis form to legislative bodies and commissions, all as means of public accountability. These materials are almost always output oriented—including, for example, numbers of clients served, costs, waiting lists, services rendered—and only recently are government program outcomes or cost and efficiency studies involved. A final but crucial step is the post audit of the contracting government's or funder's fiscal program, which often comes years after contracts are completed. These audits can and do provide important policy-making input, for example, at legislative program reauthorizations time. The federal government, particularly the Government Accountability Office, has been more actively engaged in these post-program assessments.

Contracting has also generated a set of potential and actual managerial problems that either did not previously exist or at least were not as visible in the earlier grant-oriented era: poor coordination, inconsistency in applying the rules, inefficient paperwork procedures, long lead times for contractor amendment or payments, and changing political climates that affect funder-contractor relationships (Bernstein 1991, ch. 3). Moreover, state and local agencies do not always have the administrative capacity for contract oversight and other aspects of managing externally (Romzek and Johnston 2005; Van Slyke 2003). Also, in this IGM mode, ironically while fewer government employees are directly involved in the actual delivery of services, contracting out does not always reduce the total public-serving workforce by much, for a cadre of public paper handlers (either in government or by administrative contractees) normally substitute for government direct service workers (DSWs) and supervisors. Indeed, as a result of contracting to NGOs, the vendor staff workers and public agency oversight paper carriers are the new public "foot soldiers," or white-collar workers, of intergovernmental programming.

It is said that these changes have reduced some public agencies to shadows of their former selves. For example, the state of Indiana not only shifted its intellectual and developmental disabilities programs largely out of state government but also cut its administrative presence to points that make oversight difficult. A state-level policy review body found that this disinvestment had several important consequences (INARF 2005, 17–18):

1. Workflow related to administrative issues concerning serving routines has slowed, as fewer people in the various state offices can review and approve program changes.
2. Many information systems have come, in effect, under the control of contractors, not the program agency they are serving.
3. The lead program agencies within the state's Family and Social Services Administration have lost a number of talented administrative leaders, many of whom have gone to the NGO or business sector.
4. Consequently, virtually all of the DSW and administrative program leadership resides in the nonprofit or for-profit provider sectors.
5. Routine administrative delays, a lack of personnel, and an absence of leadership undoubtedly affect the quality of services, not to speak of the services' timing.
6. While nongovernment associations such as Arc (advocacy), Indiana Association of Rehabilitation Facilities (INARF, a trade organization), and Indiana Institute on Disability and Community (research) at Indiana University–Bloomington are willing to participate in program leadership and implementation, fully staffed and operating Family and Social Services Administration (state government) entities also need to be present in advancing programs for the developmentally disabled.

This Indiana brief does not reflect a particularly unusual situation. The potential or actual I/DD IGM leadership axis has thus moved out of state government, particularly among direct service workers. From the standpoint of the potential to build networks of various types, a more distributed leadership is undoubtedly beneficial and what an Indiana Association of Rehabilitation Facilities report ultimately suggested.

Not every state agency has taken such draconian steps in dismantling its public presence. Paul Castellani (2005) indicates that New York's successful experience in building a full array of I/DD services in partnerships between institution-community agencies is due to management capacity. Despite cutbacks in some other areas, enhancing state agency and regional staff made working with nongovernmental agencies and local governments easier. In New York regional offices and "comprehensive local authority allowed [the state I/DD office] to deal with problems as they arose, to provide the technical and other assistance to the private agencies in their early stages of development, and to effectively manage deinstitutionalization" (280).

In this external paradigm, what roles do public agencies maintain? Chapter 4 noted that states' Agencies on Aging administer federal pass-through Title III funds to the area agencies, which in turn contract with providers for services for the elderly. What do the state units do? They develop operational plans within federal regulations and guidelines; negotiate grants upward with federal government funders and downward to contractees; monitor grants to states' area agencies; collect and analyze program and fiscal data; report and monitor the quality and frequency of services; check the appropriateness of area agency subcontracts; meet and oversee state purchasing and travel standards; prepare for federal post audits; and engage in literally thousands of bilateral and multilateral connections with federal agencies, area agency personnel, and contractors. All of this occurs while the states are internally planning, staffing, organizing, and budgeting for the agency itself (Agranoff 2007b) as well as dealing with inquiries from interest associations.

As in the case of state aging agencies, other public agencies are also in the business of operating programs beyond the process of IGM contract managing. They must also manage within the aforementioned games of law and politics (e.g., compliance) and interdependency (fungibility) as well as maintain partnerships with associated local government agencies and NGOs. The politics of contract management are also involved. All of this requires executive leadership and management that can meet many challenges at the federal and state levels. Most of these policy and implementation functions present challenges to be exercised both inside and outside of government (Agranoff 2007c, ch. 9; Castellani 2005).

The Contracting State and Evolving Programs

Three different state-level service system examples from I/DD programs, heavily funded by Medicaid, illustrate the nature of the contracting state. The Indiana 317 Plan (Senate Bill 317 in 1999) introduced person-centered planning, redirected funds from congregate settings to integrated residential day services, developed quality assurance measures, promoted community capacity, and began to reduce its large waiting list for services. This plan was financed by eliminating its state developmental disability hospital beds over time and increasing funding of nongovernmental agencies. The 317 Plan has been largely supported by the Medicaid HCBS Waiver (see chapter 8 of this volume) and an 80 percent increase in state community spending (Braddock, Hemp, and Rizzolo 2004, 2008). The state does not have a substate I/DD operations system, as is the case with its aging programs through the Area Agencies on Aging. It works by directly contracting with NGOs, particularly rehabilitative facilities and programs that provide small residential and day services, and partners in planning and system development through a network of provider groups, state associations, and an Indiana University–based I/DD center for excellence supported by the federal government (Agranoff 2007c). The core of the system at the operating level is the state agency–provider contract. The Indiana system is built on the interaction between the state's Family and Social Services Administration, Bureau of Developmental Disabilities Services, Rehabilitation Services,

Office of Medicaid Policy and Planning, provider and advocate associations, and the providers themselves. Most important, the service contract between the state and providers links planning and financing to the service delivery system (Agranoff 2014).

The North Carolina model, adopted in 2001, more directly institutionalizes the government partners theme through contracting and recognizes the challenges of building collaborative service systems (see chapter 9 in this volume). Adapted in 2001 the state converted its county-level service entities to local management entities (LMEs), which are responsible for contracting out services in their respective (single or multicounty) areas. The expectation is that the contract system will be ultimately transformed into "a unified community-based system" (Lin 2007, 1). Programming through North Carolina LMEs blends mental health, substance abuse, and I/DD. LMEs are responsible for the following:

- Planning—including identifying service gaps and efficient and effective use of all funds for targeted services
- Provider network development—ensuring available, qualified providers to deliver services based on the business plan
- Service management—implementing a uniform portal process, management of state hospital and facilities bed days, utilization management, case management, and quality management
- Financial management and accountability—carrying out business functions in an effective and efficient manner and managing resources dedicated to the public system
- Service monitoring and oversight—ensuring services provided to consumers and families to meet state outcome standards
- Evaluation—conducting self-evaluation based on statewide outcome standards
- Collaboration—working with other local service systems in ensuring access and coordination of services at the local level

The LMEs are also responsible for ensuring that core services to all consumers, within the state and local resources, are provided. They include screening, assessment, and referral; emergency services; service coordination; and consultation, prevention, and education (Lin 2007, 13–14). In brief, North Carolina has taken the initial steps with its state Division of Mental Health to transform its contracting system and establish networks of services. Again, Medicaid is the major funder of these services, which also receive matching state funds.

Ohio began to reform its system in 1988, when local boards were established under its Mental Health Act (Senate Bill 156). I/DD services involve approximately fifty-five separate local boards, with some being multicounty.

This state stands out among others because, in the eighteen states that require some local government public funding for I/DD, Ohio provides the highest local financial support. Whereas most states require funding of 10 percent or less, Ohio funds around 41 percent of all I/DD services with local funds. In 2006 this amounted to $950,564,266, of which $176,651,749 was for Medicaid matching, and the remaining $773,912,517 funded other programs (Braddock, Hemp, and Rizzolo 2008, 27). The boards are responsible for managing both care under state supervision in an I/DD agency, where local boards decide on hospitalization partially paid from local funds, and community care, which is partially funded by shifting hospital funds downward to local boards. Medicaid stands as the major federal funding partner, as it is in most states. Community services boards thus fund *both* state hospital inpatient services and contracts for community services provided by local agencies. Local boards are also charged with local planning, promoting local financing, purchasing services, developing community-based services, auditing for compliance with state regulations, and ensuring quality assurance. Ohio is one of the few states that has county tax levies and local levy campaigns, including one for I/DD services; thus, it brings citizens into concerns regarding the local system (Lin 2007, 24–25).

These three snapshots illustrate how federal-state programs are moving into the contract state while employing varied IGM models. Using the various federal funding programs, particularly Medicaid and its HCBS Waiver, in partnership with private agencies, states are adjusting their substate systems while shifting institutions into programs that finance and purchase services models. Chapter 9 demonstrates that the emergent array of funders and providers are also in search of networked systems, the most recent and pressing approach in IGM.

Contract Management 101

The service contract both legalizes and legitimizes the government-NGO partnership. The public agency enters into a business and legal arrangement with a nonprofit or for-profit entity where, in exchange for payment, certain products or services are delivered to and for the public agency (Keleman 2004, 282).

This type of contract is a fiduciary arrangement that has considerable collaborative potential, particularly in the purchase of service contracting. The latter involves agreements under which "a government agency enlists a private organization to deliver a service to an eligible group of 'clients' in exchange for money" (DeHoog and Salamon 2002, 320). The literature on public sector contracting is broad and deep, although not all authors take the kind of IGM perspective taken here (e.g., Behn and Kant 1999; Krueger,

Walker, and Bernick 2011; Fernandez 2007; Keiser and Miller 2013; Marvel and Marvel 2007; Perlman 2013). The arena of purchases of service contracting is thus one of considerable IGM interest today.

Procurement by the states is not always thought of as an integral part of IGM, yet state governments are in the middle, so to speak, of many federal, state, and local programs and federal, state, and NGO programs. Highway construction, Medicaid services, state ACA health exchanges, research grants to state universities, the Supplemental Nutrition Assistance Program, mental health services, and many more come to mind. A comprehensive study of state procurement, ranging from fleet vehicles and photocopier ink to major services, displays great variation in the governments' ability to purchase wisely. Procurement often faces a labyrinth of rules, normally in response to some scandal, and they limit the decision maker's and manager's discretion, rendering the process protracted without clear evidence that fraud and abuse have been prevented. In particular, there is greater interest in reforming the system for more flexibility, for increased vendor performance, for improved tracking of contract execution, and for the use of emergent technology (Farmer 2016).

A Governing Institute survey identified several criteria for improving procurement management. Among the most important issues follow:

1. Relationship management between purchasing departments, state agencies, and vendors, receiving interactive feedback with administrative unit
2. Sourcing, when possible, access to a variety of potential vendors and the authority for procurement officers to negotiate contract terms to get the best deal and to factor in past performance in future awards
3. Contract administration, delineation of clear lines of responsibility, the ability to monitor cost overruns or question expenditures, and, in some states, contract oversight offices
4. Technology beyond the usual digitization and automation to include analysis of outcome data, to help better handle vendors and agencies, to improve transparency, and to make procurement more flexible and innovative
5. Use of information technology to overview the process, working between IT and procurement to understand industry trends, and to incorporate particular industry trends into draft solicitations
6. Workforce training and certification to bring state workers current knowledge and skills to improve performance (Farmer 2016)

In addition, some states promote communities of practice to develop and share contract management knowledge, and most states now provide training to promote diversity, particularly to small, emerging, disadvantaged, and women-owned businesses. According to the study, states that lead in procurement have been working for more than a decade on modernizing their technology, increasing "engagement" between purchasing and departmental officials, and gaining support from high-level officials to move beyond rule enforcement and to make procurement reform important state goals (Farmer 2016).

Although not technically intergovernmental, an example of direct procurement by the federal government is in Trevor Brown, Matthew Potoski, and David Van Slyke's (2008a) study of the US Coast Guard's Deepwater Program. Designed to acquire new ships and to integrate all of their command, control, communications, computers, intelligence, surveillance, and reconnaissance systems, the program provides a prime illustration of what is known as complex contracting. The authors view the program as involving the acquisition of a complex product because, unlike the simple procurement of goods or specifically defined services, "its specifications, performance standards, costs, and mission impacts were difficult to identify before acquisition of the system" (14). They define this interactive process as between many sellers and the buyer, the Coast Guard. The key to handling complex contracting requires involved parties to keep addressing costs, risks, and technical issues; to encourage heavy collaboration among the parties—buyers and sellers—by creating venues of informal negotiation; and to space out decisions about design standards, performance requirements, and costs expended to take advantage of mutual learning (24). In IGM the core of federal, state, and NGO funding and programming of direct services—for example, I/DD in Indiana, North Carolina, and Ohio—also fall into this complex contracting mold. Thus, similar measures of collaboration, negotiation, and spacing of decisions appear to equally apply.

BOX 7.1

- The links in the chains of governing have been extended through grants, contracts, and vouchers to nongovernmental organizations, yet governments remain pivotal and focal actors in the management of intergovernmental programs. In this respect, government has not hollowed out but has changed its roles.
- With most service operations, where programs meet clients and citizens and make jurisdiction and management more separate entities, governments shift roles from agent to partner but within the context of legal definitions and political constraints.
- Contract management entails more than what is commonly thought of as a "sale-purchase agreement." It can and often does bind government and contractee in a lasting relationship, which leads to more regular interactions.
- The contract state involves protracted reciprocal relationships, and particularly regarding direct services, contracting reaches deeply from policy enactment to subnational governments', NGO agencies', and citizens' involvement.

The hows and whats of different types of contracting can be left to the growing literature (Goldsmith and Eggers 2004, 21; Cohen and Eimicke 2008; Van Slyke 2007; DeHoog and Salamon 2002; Brown and Potoski 2004). The primary focus here is on the IGM contract as it demonstrates partnership interaction in government agency and contractor relations. It is important to note, however, that the latest IGM trend in the purchase of services is the *contingency fee contract*, where an outside firm is hired to increase different forms of revenue enhancements: recovered tax dollars, increased federal reimbursements, recaptured Medicaid overpayments, litigation, and other agency administrative reductions. These contracts are in their infant stages. Generally, the firms that hunt for such dollars work for a fee of around 10–20 percent of collections or savings (Barrett and Greene 2010, 41). Many questions about these relationships will no doubt be raised in future contract cycles.

When does the government choose to contract services? Ruth DeHoog and Lester Salamon (2002, 327) raise a thoughtful set of questions regarding this concern:

1. Are competition and choice among agencies present in the service environment?
2. Are reputable agencies available with specialized expertise, good administrative staff, and trusting relationships with clients and the community?
3. Does the government have enough information and expertise to understand the service, agencies, and client populations?
4. Do the government and contract agencies have sufficient resources to operate the contracting process effectively?
5. Are there any legal or administrative prohibitions about this tool?

From both parties' perspectives, these are among the more important "make or buy" decision questions that launch the interactive nature of contracting.

The contract itself is at the heart of forging the relationship. Stephen Goldsmith and William Eggers (2004, 185) agree with the Coast Guard's Deepwater lesson: integrating partners effectively needs to become a core competency of government when most direct service work is delivered through these contractors. Some years ago, Kenneth Wedel (1983, 190) articulated several principles of contract specificity:

1. The legal base—The service contract must conform to the various federal, state, and local laws and regulations.
2. The client management responsibilities—The roles of management and administrators for the two partners and the contractual agreement must be made clear. This includes the role of the contractor and its

responsibility in assigning, reviewing, and terminating each individual client's services.

3. The sponsor agency's role—Clarifying the role of the sponsor agency in terms of the administrative review and monitoring of the program involved and the contracting procedure is equally important.

4. The service to be provided—To the extent possible, services should be defined in terms of intended client outcomes.

5. The standards involved—When performance standards are expected, contracts require additional specification of quality standards and the means for determining whether they are actually met.

6. The unit of service and cost structure—Units of service and costing for them should be spelled out in detail and specified in the contract.

7. The program and fiscal audit—Procedures and criteria for the monitoring process should be as detailed as possible, clearly delineating who actually does the monitoring and auditing and under what certification requirements.

8. The service delivery—This special area of concern addresses whether service delivery conforms to agreed-on plans. Both the sponsoring and contracting organizations share this concern, as the public sponsor must assure constituents that the contractual terms are being carried out and the contractor must guarantee a continued capacity to engage the service delivery market.

Wedel's venerable list appears still relevant. These issues underscore the basic framework of the government and NGO contracting relationship, from the parties' legal dimension to their shared management obligations.

Beyond the Signed Contract

Contracts need to be managed as a process as they go beyond the formal drafting and signing of a document. Steven Cohen and William Eimicke (2008, ch. 7) identify twenty problems that can emerge in the process of operating by contract, including challenges related to the letting of contracts, issues of communication, internal management dynamics of the contractor, dynamics of the government managing agency, and political and other operational issues. The authors discuss each and provide a reference point for every issue. Clearly to contract involves maintaining constant lines of communication, directing and interacting, staffing and training, and handling issues of politics and conflicts of interest (see also Hall and Jennings 2012). Also emerging in the literature is the relevance of providing performance incentives in contracting (Davis, Girth, and Stazyk 2013; Dinan 2013). The contract has become the new IGM tool, somewhat equivalent to the grant, with its more prevalent use in connecting governments and clients of various services.

In this regard, Barbara Romzek and Jocelyn Johnston (2002, 423–33) identify several important challenges in contracting for services that raise new and important issues of the previously identified *relationship* aspect, such as the availability of competition, the contractor's capacities, the funder's ability to make sound assessments, and the theoretical rationale for contracting. They are summarized in a "top ten" list of contract management matters:

1. Healthy levels of provider competition provide market incentives for strong performance at the lowest possible cost. It may mean the potential loss of a contract to more cost-effective competitors.
2. Resource adequacy reflects the capacity of the funder to fund staff and other expenses related to its accurate cost projections, analysis of contractor capacity, and training for new contract staff.
3. In-depth planning for measuring contractor performance facilitates the evaluation of the provider's performance and cost-effectiveness.
4. Intensive training for contract management staff often requires retooling and reinvesting in converting staff from service delivery to service oversight duties.
5. In evaluating the contractor's staff capacity, funders must ensure that the contractor has the capability to staff up adequately and in a timely fashion so as not to compromise performance.
6. Funders must access the contractors' potential to manage the financial side of service delivery.
7. In addressing the theoretical integrity of the rationale for contracting, one must ask, does the undertaking meet the social problem or program need? Other than economic and efficiency reasons, a policy reform based on a flawed rationale is probably doomed.
8. The political strength of the client advocacy groups—that is, their influence with officials such as legislators—can lead to situations where contract managers' enforcement authority is undercut.
9. The subcontractor relationships are complex. Effective implementation in human services arenas normally requires cooperation, if not the integration of services, among separate contractors, thus making accountability more difficult.
10. Funders will shift risks downward to the contractor. In programs such as managed care, where prepaid or capitated payments are involved, the contractors are exposed to losses that cannot be covered by agreed payments; consequently, the contractors resist expensive clients or cut back on higher-paid staff.

As numbers 7 through 10 in particular suggest, the most important problems and issues for IGM are those related to the need for cooperation within complex relationships. They reinforce the notion that contracting is clearly a relational process in IGM.

The first challenge is that only a small number of providers—if any—in the competitive markets for governments that contract have been investigated. The research of Jocelyn Johnston and Amanda Girth (2012) reveals that, indeed, several areas and levels of the government they examined have problems. For example, when staff must engage in competition enhancement strategies, government staff time and energies increase and transaction costs rise. As programs—even contract design and monitoring—are contracted out, a corresponding loss of in-house expertise occurs, eroding capacity. "Contractors are now overseeing other contractors with growing frequency, and the role of government in public service provision is shrinking" (19). It also is clear, contrary to some people's assumptions, that the private and nonprofit sectors are considered superior in potential performance. That is not necessarily the case. Competition, therefore, should be regarded neither as a panacea nor a guarantor of enhanced performance. Competition can also undermine other government aims related to service quality and program performance, for example, in continuity of services in many social welfare programs (Fernandez 2009). In many cases "managing markets" thus drains administrative resources by promoting competition. Most important, it entails real costs that need to be taken into account (Johnston and Girth 2012). With regard to public sector contracting, administrative capacity for contract oversight has been a long-standing issue (Girth 2014; Romzek and Johnston 2005; Van Slyke 2003).

The Contract and New Public Management

The rise of externalization also coincided with a market-oriented approach to administration known as new public management (NPM). Oriented toward the emphasis on markets rather than bureaucracy, it is sometimes associated with performance measurement, the use of market-like mechanisms in place of command-and-control regulations of competition and choice, and the devolution to staff with better matching of authority and responsibility (Organization for Economic Cooperation and Development 1998, 5). In a number of ways, the I/DD situation in North Carolina identified earlier in this chapter reflects, to a great extent, an NPM approach. While not without controversy, that a market-based approach can substitute for politically and legally based management in the public sector, NPM thinking has duly influenced IGM as government increasingly engages NGO interlocutors.

NPM in the United States was initially associated with Steven Osborne and Ted Gaebler's (1992) *Reinventing Government*, where they called for a more indirect, market-oriented, mission-oriented, and decentralized government. Similar to Osborne and Gaebler, Christopher Hood (1991) identifies seven features of NPM that underscore a new way of government doing its business: hands-on professional management, explicit standards and measures of performance, greater emphasis on output controls, shift to disaggregation of units in the public sector, greater competition in the public sector, emphasis on private sector styles of management practice, and greater discipline and parsimony in resource use.

Among the NPM instruments are movements to encourage privatization of services, increased managerial flexibility and deregulation, competitive bidding for service delivery by government and nongovernment agencies, performance-based contract management, citizen input into management decisions, municipal or public companies that are self-sustaining and off budget, institution of performance benchmarks, performance evaluation, imposition of national minimum standards of service, internal devolution of power and decision-making to services departments, and strategic (cross-entity) local management. Generally imprinted from business, NPM focuses on inside operations. It includes three major shifts: from government to governance, invoking a host of nongovernmental organizations in the work of government; from direct service provision, or "rowing," to enabling outside competition by government involvement in guiding operations, or "steering"; and from focusing on government itself to the "customer" and "user" of services (Snape 2004, 63). Public management experts believe that a number of these NPM approaches—performance measurement, control of results, benchmarking—along with management information systems will become increasingly valuable (Prueller 2006, 21).

NPM has left an important imprint on IGM. As programs at the administrative support and the service delivery levels have moved out of the confines of government direct services, it has led to greater flexibility in contracting. Some contract funders have experimented with competitive bidding (Goldsmith and Eggers 2004), although the North Carolina experience would suggest that multiple bidders proved not to be available in many situations, particularly in rural areas. NPM has slowly moved to performance in contracting, again with varying degrees of success, but this seems to be a lasting legacy of this era. Off-government public "companies" at the local level—for example, local utility companies sponsored by municipalities or special districts—have existed for some time, but NPM has stimulated this movement into new arenas, including quasi-public or public-private partnerships that operate enterprises that are funded by intergovernmental programs. Examples of the latter would be companies that provide intake, eligibility, and payments processing of client claims under Medicaid or the

Supplemental Nutrition Assistance Program (food stamps). In essence, both federal and state programs extend joint stakes to these new administrative overhead companies. Performance has clearly become the hallmark of Medicaid transactions; as described earlier, "guidelines" transformed into "standards," then to specific "measures," and ultimately to rules, particularly for persons with I/DD and many who are physically disabled. These metrics in many ways are what NPM would call performance benchmarks. Performance evaluation is a different situation. Given the extreme difficulties in assessing performance in intergovernmental programs (Radin 2006), measuring performance has been more self-driven (see e.g., Koliba, Campbell, and Zia 2011) or, in the case of disabilities in many states, has been left to third-party accreditation bodies.

Undoubtedly NPM-aligned consumer orientation has had a considerable impact on intergovernmental management. For example, today service clients no longer simply provide after-service information on customer satisfaction surveys. They instead supply individual and group input on operations and client improvement to providers. Consumers or clients now can participate in planning their services as well, eschewing the idea that the provider always knows best. Currently the assumption is that within the guidelines and legal parameters of the program, the provider and the client collectively can produce a better service course of action. In some human services areas, this is called self-advocacy. Finally, in many situations management has been decentralized, with decisions often made at points closer to delivery and on a shared basis between the implementing public agency and the NGO service agents or their representatives.

NPM and its market orientation in a number of ways are manifestations at the managerial level of the IGM government partners' movement. It has no way removed the public from public management. Government remains. As Christopher Pollitt and Geert Bouckaert (2004, 100) maintain, it did not evolve as the prophets of NPM envisioned, as "an entrepreneurial, market-oriented society, with a light icing of government on top"; instead, the state is "the irreplaceable integrative force in society, with a legal personality and operative value system that cannot be reduced to the private sector discourse of efficiency, competitiveness, and consumer satisfaction." In an extensive and balanced review of NPM, Alan Lawton and Frédérique Six (2011, 420) conclude that while NPM has perhaps been overhyped as a panacea for public management, it has contributed to services' efficiencies, has pushed programs closer to their targets, and made some services more user friendly. With managerial operations, they caution academics and practitioners to focus less on the NPM value orientation and more on its role in implementation, making clear that emphasis should be placed on what works under certain conditions. Moreover, Lawton and Six observe that this emphasis on public sector reform is only recently coming to terms with the practice of public-private collaboration, the essence of this transformation of IGM. "It is a recognition that most societal challenges cut across organizational boundaries" and that there are "three possible regimes for organizing public tasks: hierarchy, markets, and networks" (421).

Formal and Informal Contract Supervision to Contract Partnerships

Government-partner relationships are normally legally bound by their respective contracts, and as suggested in chapter 6, they range from close rule-bound supervision or agency theory to negotiation-based interactive stewardship approaches. In most cases, behavior is somewhere between the two poles. Noncontractual or less legally bound contractual partnering arrangements can also run the range from loose, informal, and occasional connections to very close relationships. The collaborative arrangements in the Ohio Darby Partnership and the National Interagency Fire Center's arrangements, for instance, are noncontractual in nature.

The relationships developed in this section are similar to those of signed contracts. Beth Gazley's (2010, 71) study of NGO contracts concluded that "once [survey] respondents are engaged in partnerships, their attitudes will be shaped by another and potentially stronger set of variables related to partnership characteristics, including the size of each partnership, its goals, its accomplishments, and its demands on respondents." (See also Gazley 2008a). In this respect, Goldsmith and Eggers (2004, 106) suggest that moving toward a true partnership or closer to the stewardship pole rests on the three-legged stool of communicating with partners, coordinating activities, and relationship building. Cohen and Eimicke (2008, 86) add that a true stewardship or working partnership goes beyond the details of the contract or formal agreement, but the transaction assures that "contractors act as the agents of a representative system where the directions they receive are designed to both respond to public views and ensure that government functions effectively." It is therefore useful to look at how IGM managers can build such contracting or relational partnerships.

In a general way, Wendell Lawther (2002, 34–35) suggests that the parties in formal contracting build in some of the tenets of public-private partnerships:

1. Both parties should reduce the uncertainty involved in producing the service or product.
2. Partners have discretion to identify ways and means of reaching goals.
3. Analysis and awareness of the risks involved by both parties—particularly regarding performance, reputation, and financial resources contribution—need to be explicated.

4. Both parties should consider the genuine cost-sharing as part of the partnership, even if the NGO partner contributes in-kind or overhead resources.
5. They must work to understand the expected long-term connections and relationships.
6. Overall, the reasonable expectation is that the partnership is based on trust, on a commitment to problem or conflict resolution, and on the recognition that flexibility is necessary and that the relationship will evolve and change over time.

Lawther concludes that in contracting, relationships are built as the connections move from traditional "customer relationships toward these six partnership principles" (35; see also Fernandez 2009). In many ways these working approaches help build lasting connections in the same fashion that local governments working with local community organizations and citizens build mutual rapport over time. A Cincinnati police chief once referred to this effort as "relationship collateral" (Blackwell 2015).

Whether a contract exists or not, among the most important front-end relational investment process costs involve well-established types of collaborative management. Managers who work in contracting require training on contract design and agreements, solicitation, and management. They must understand the trade-offs among service, client, and agent characteristics as well as market competitiveness. Their training in contractual collaboration includes determining how and when to involve working partners in the joint formulation of goals, objectives, quality standards, reporting mechanisms that all parties understand and agree to, modes of oversight that meet substantive and legal aims, and evaluation tools that can indicate service effectiveness, accountability, and program success. Each of these appears to be open to joint development by the funder and contractor in drafting a set of interactive training goals (Goldsmith and Eggers 2004; Romzek and Johnston 2002).

In IGM the process calls for fostering what some regard as new intergovernmental skills—that is, developing persons who can advance both public purpose and relational programming. At a minimum, contract/partner management requires new, different, and, some would say, nontechnical talents: bargaining and negotiating; communicating policy and program goals to a broad set of publics; working with aligning partner goals with agency goals; conducting oversight activities that include contract or partner and program details; providing technical assistance on the contract, or relationship, and on the service; and evaluating program and client outcomes. These competences all constitute various forms of collaboration-based skills (Brown and Potoski 2004; Agranoff 2007c; Cohen and Eimicke 2008; Agranoff and McGuire 2003; Van Slyke 2007).

Regarding implementation, Goldsmith and Eggers (2004, 171) conclude that those who work in this area require broad knowledge of processes and organizations and a deep appreciation of the importance of open information to a continuously learning organization. Those skills that the contract or other partnership overseers need are closely related to contemporary public management as applied to IGM. Cohen and Eimicke (2008, 213) capture the overall picture with respect to contracts cogently:

> Effective contract management requires skill at the use of all the tools of standard and innovative management. Managers must understand human resource, financial, organizational, information, performance, strategic, political, and media management. They also need experience with quality management, benchmarking, re-engineering, and team management. But the effective contract manager must do more. In addition to deploying those tools in problem solving, today's effective public manager must learn how to elicit contract bids that result in appropriate and well-priced services and goods. They must learn to monitor contractor performance and write contracts that allow them to develop informal networks that reach deep into contractor organizations, just as they have done within their own organizations.

Concerning the development of collaborative partnerships and monitoring, Goldsmith and Eggers (2004) point to the need for integrators to establish communication channels, to coordinate activities between network participants, to share knowledge, to align values and incentives, to build trust, and to overcome organizational as well as client cultural differences. "Consummate behavior is more likely when buyers and sellers are engaged in repeated

BOX 7.2

- Relational models of public services involve shared administration: planning, network-building, service coordination monitoring, auditing, and many other jointly agreed-on and shared management tasks.
- The contract nevertheless involves a series of transactional concerns, such as legal responsibilities, specified services, costs and reimbursements, data gathering, and post auditing.
- The new public management approach to efficiency, performance, and consumer involvement influences contemporary capacities to manage as these concerns are increasingly built into programs.
- In recent years contracting has oriented toward a "stewardships" model, focusing on building relationships, mutually changing rules to enhance collaboration, jointly building incentives to collaborate, and making investments in capacity building.

interaction with the opportunity to demonstrate their consummate behavior, when there is ample information about mutual understanding of what constitutes consummate and perfunctory behavior and when buyers and sellers care about the future and their reputations and thus behave consummately" (119). The authors conclude that a combined system of cooperative governance rules and repeated interaction provides venues and opportunities to sort out differences and reach understandings. Contracting and partnering include but go well beyond the procurement-oriented mechanics of agreements between principals and agents to encompass a rich interactive process between the agency and the contractor in a true stewardship relationship (see chapter 6 of this volume).

The Essence of Stewardship Contracting

The BLM and the US Forest Service have seriously engaged in stewardship contracting to implement forest and watershed restoration projects and to create local community benefit. The contracts' focus is on building federal and state connections with the nationwide three-thousand-plus, county-level conservation districts. Beginning in 2010 the Forest Service shifted to stewardship contract templates that encourage relationships and local participation along previously identified lines. The joint goals are to identify common ground and barriers and to seek solutions (Moseley 2010, 11). Rather than the old system of "timber sales," which allowed for timber harvests and service activities in a single contract, it permits the value of the service to pay for other service activities—for example, restoration and soil conservation.

Cassandra Moseley's (2010, 30–35) study of several pilot projects in stewardship contracting highlights four common strategies to building such partnerships. First, build the relationships over time and space. Through conversations, meetings, and field tours, partners found common ground and identified barriers that over time evolved into more formal financial relationships. Government senior managers involved in mission-area management, budgeting, and performance worked with staff to create the space in work plans to accomplish joint objectives.

Second, change the rules to encourage collaborative work. Moseley suggests several ways: fund the implementation of those agreements that truly are collaboratively reached, create the decision space for frontline operatives to make adjustments and agreements, and continually update all procedures and remove any that are barriers to cooperation.

Third, create incentives for agency or organization staff to work at collaboration, and establish negative consequences if they do not. The BLM and the Forest Service emphasized a local circumstances imperative to collaboration, and it has since become an agency-wide priority. Guidance to frontline staff on how they can build partnerships is also valued. Leading by example—that is, having mid-level and senior staff engage in collaborative management—is also helpful. Building partnerships, moreover, should become part of the conversations about performance measures and, in some cases, creating targets for respective units for stewardship contracts.

Fourth, invest in building the capacity of both governmental and nongovernmental partners in the stewardship. This effort includes creating a cadre of personnel who are willing to use the tools of stewardship in supporting the organizational health of partner organizations (e.g., giving up-front seed money to fledgling NGOs), training staff and partners in modules specific to the process, and developing peer-to-peer learning processes to facilitate process and information sharing.

The Forest Service and BLM processes have important implications for long-term IGM contracting and partnering. Stewardship required, as Moseley (2010, 36) concludes, concerted efforts on the part of government officials:

> Many of the changes needed to encourage greater use of collaboration came from places in the agency that do not initially appear to have much to do with the collaborative process, such as budget formulation and allocation and performance management, which also need to support frontline collaboration. Moreover, successfully supporting collaboration requires that senior executives themselves engage in collaborative and iterative learning by creating systems to take lessons from the frontline staff and stakeholders and turn them into new guidance, which improves practices and procedures and reflects innovations and changing conditions on the front line.

The stewardship partnership arrangement suggests that working at contracting reinforces the idea that inward-looking models of administration are not well suited to address problems that cross organizational boundaries (Freeman 1997; Goldsmith and Eggers 2004, 7; Fernandez 2009). Its process orientation calls for new and different sets of IGM skills.

Key Learning Points

Governments now extensively engage with NGOs through program externalization with agencies normally linked by formal contract and process partnering. The NGOs do a great deal of the "heavy lifting" involved in direct connection services or the production of complex products and services. For example, at one period in the United States, those persons who either were so disabled that they could not function on their own or were perceived as harmful to themselves or others were confined to state-run institutions staffed by small armies of public direct service workers and professionals. Today, few such institutions operate, or they are severely reduced in population and staffing, having given way to many types of NGO services in the community under federal Medicaid–funded and state-funded contracts. This development has changed public policy, as it makes the NGO providers working partners and contractors under federal and state law.

Governments nevertheless remain involved on one side of these new connections. Any production of services outside of government is done within the context of delegated operational authority, ultimate government legal authority, legally enforceable regulations and standards, predominate public fiscal capacity, public sector operational oversight, and public fiscal auditing authority. The federal and state governments' status also makes them "principals" versus the NGOs' status as "agents."

Despite some people's feeling that government has resultantly hollowed out, it has not. It has changed. Government's ability to participate with contractors and partners in the process of planning and organizing services is sometimes understated (McGuire and Agranoff 2010, 380). The stewardship examples provided are notable in this respect. Both federal and state (and some local) governments interact regarding federal and state plans and operations, negotiate regulations and service conditions, monitor their agents, collect and analyze fiscal and program data, and so on. These roles are not insignificant, nor do they render government inoperable. Simply government is less directly involved in day-to-day operations.

Having emphasized partnerships and contract management throughout, the introduction of performance management under NPM has reduced some agency or delivery-level discretion down the line (Schram et al. 2010), in contrast to the partnership approach emphasized earlier. At the other end of the spectrum are contracts that involve government moving into completely new territories—for example, performance information and systems, where the contractor has virtually all of the relevant knowledge and control (Johnston and Girth 2012). Settling these issues has become a public management focus in recent years and is expected to continue for some time.

Key Practice Points

The introduction of public programs that cut across federal, state, and local lines that are then externalized raises very different management considerations than those found in traditional hierarchical management. Supervision, for example, gives way to cooperative forms of two- or multiparty collaboration. The earlier discussion of policy implementation—from the NGO agency control over the day-to-day operations down to the street-level bureaucrats who exercise discretion—changes the management operations game. Inter-governmental management is heavily invested or has many hands in multi-party administration.

Since so many parties play roles and program and operational control is diffused, new or more relationship-based managing is called for. Whereas the basic tenets of law and court decisions still apply to relevant public programs, and the processes and procedures within one's particular organization are extant, IGM remains ever more relevant, for new demands on two- and multiparty connections need to be established, nurtured, and maintained. These connections inject respective responsibilities and roles into the mix. They are clearly "people processes" blended with technical approaches that overlay responsibilities and program methodologies. The new IGM is heavily interactive as it crosses boundaries.

Along with government comes politics. The politics of program enactment is only the start. As programs move down the line, more politics are injected at state and local government levels. Although elected officials normally have almost nothing to do with day-to-day program operations, they will still make inquiries and provide advice and sometimes approval. Then at NGO agency levels are politically involved and influential governing board members and sometimes deep-pocket contributors. If the program involves education, health, or human services, there are also clients and client families involved. One might ask, where do the politics stop? Maybe they never stop.

The lists of key contracting and partnership considerations are not in any way how-to-do-it, manual-like prescriptions. They are introduced to raise concerns and issues that practitioners face and may have to address in the real world. In many instances, they suggest how agencies are horizontally managed along with any informal vertical or hierarchical connections in IGM. These points represent quantum leaps from the days when an end-of-the-period grant report was filed or a later-day fiscal audit was performed.

Conclusion

The applied partner arrangements between NGOs and government have produced a new political and lateral system of relationships that adds to prior political and managerial connections. Along with network activity, they form the emergent core of IGM thinking. The contracting partnership state under NPM influences but does not remove the politics of IGM. However, as Beryl Radin (2012, 177) reminds us, "It is the political system that legitimizes the authority and power of the management structure. We might seek neutral information to justify reform activity but rarely does information escape the determination of who benefits and who loses from decisions." She concludes that despite the emphasis on the managerialism in IGM, the political forces, considerations, and influences are truly here to stay. Following on what Larry Kramer (2000, 293) identifies as the "Wechsler (1954) tradition" in the federal system, programs always contain long-standing "political safeguards" that have a long pedigree and strong claims to constitutional legitimacy.

Within this overarching concern, management in the era of partners with programs such as Medicaid and the National Interagency Fire Center are beginning to raise new dimensions to managing across levels of government and within and between program partners. The old hierarchical tenets are not eliminated. Agencies still have administrators, program directors, and operating staff. But reaching across, joining managing within, is the new external paradigm. As more is learned about these emergent concerns, a body of relational knowledge is being built and added to the core of IGM theory and practice.

Over time even more knowledge will be developed about IGM behavior while multiple parties interact horizontally and vertically and as groups of government agencies and NGOs form networks of formal status. How they form and operate within IGM is the subject of chapters 8 and 9.

8 THE NETWORK ERA

This chapter and chapter 9 indicate how complexes of public, NGO, and delivery agencies work together to solve problems that no single agency or program alone can solve. Indeed, since the dawn of the twenty-first century, "'network' is probably the single most widely used metaphor in the analysis of modern governance" (Peterson and O'Toole 2001, 300). While the present may be the "era of the network" in intergovernmental management, the various entities work *alongside* government often at the same time they are working *for* government. They are by no means replacing government or their component organizations' hierarchies. Indeed, they are differentiated by functions and are nonhierarchical and self-functioning, but they are nevertheless managed. They often become knowledge builders, as with the Department of Homeland Security (DHS) fusion centers and the Lower Platte River Corridor Alliance, which are highlighted here. Managers devoted to their primary purposes can make a difference in terms of advancing disparate types of public value.

While they change the way public agency managers work with nongovernmental organizations, networks do not control public agencies. What is most interesting about the emergent set of intergovernmental networks—and what makes them different—is the way officials from federal government, state governments, local governments, public and private universities, and NGOs representing the nonprofit and for-profit sectors sit down with one another at the same table to discuss, explore, negotiate, and solve issues (Margerum 2011; Radin et al. 1996). In earlier times intergovernmental transactions were more bilateral, focused on government-to-government or government-to-NGO matters. The network approach is not only more interactive but also clearly multilateral and collaborative. Networks attack issues that transcend bilateral intergovernmental concerns at both policy and service delivery levels. In recent years, collaborative arrangements in IGM have transformed into more stabilized arrangements through cross-organizational networking. In this way IGM serves to link multiple organizations—public and NGO—on a more regular basis.

One network is the Lower Platte River Corridor Alliance (LPRCA), a consortium of three natural resource districts and seven state agencies in

Nebraska. The US Army Corps of Engineers and the US Geological Survey (USGS) joined together to encourage local natural resource management issues in the LPRCA area. With the passage of an interlocal agreement, the LPRCA was established in 1996. Members contribute to an administrative fund, initially totaling $65,000 annually, to support a coordinator's position for the alliance, and they agree to provide technical and other assistance within their authority to the coordinator. Quarterly meetings are convened to share progress reports on programs and projects of all involved.

The alliance assists counties and communities spanning a hundred river miles to become fully informed about the impact of their decisions on natural resources and to promote their conservation in the river corridor area. The alliance also provides a forum for concerned, interested citizens and local elected officials to bring their different perspectives to the table and seek common solutions. The goals of the alliance are to foster an increased understanding of the Lower Platte River's resources, to support local efforts to achieve comprehensive and coordinated land-use planning to protect the long-term vitality of the river, and to promote cooperation among federal, state, and local—both private and public—organizations to meet the needs of the many and varied interests in the river corridor.

The alliance furnishes easy access to relevant information on key issues and proposed projects, opportunities for dialogue and discussion for individuals wishing to influence the decision-making process, and a forum for consensus. Community participation is an integral part of this process. Opportunities for public involvement include river tours, the Water Quality Open golf tournament, stakeholder summit meetings, and regional planning workshops and *charrettes* (intensive planning sessions).

Over its twenty years, the LPRCA has provided many fact sheets and guides, public policy analyses, web-based geographic information system videos, water and wastewater studies, and conservation and mitigation proposals (Agranoff 2007c, 133). Recently the network partners with USGS to provide real-time water quality information, and with the Nebraska Game and Parks Commission, it has developed a comprehensive recreation plan. Other projects include joint efforts at conducting an environmental suitability assessment, establishing a water quality-monitoring network, developing a watershed management plan, supporting a sandbar monitoring study (with USGS), and running a cumulative impact study. The alliance also works with cities and counties on coordinated land-use planning.

Other networks are more directly inspired by federal action. After the federal government published the 9/11 Commission's report in 2004, DHS promoted fusion centers to facilitate data sharing across government agencies and NGOs. These centers support frontline law enforcement, public safety, fire emergency response, and private security and provide links to local and national intelligence. DHS aids the fusion centers through personnel training and technical assistance, support activities, security clearance connectivity to federal systems, technology, and grant funding. Some fusion centers were newly created, DHS-funded entities, whereas others emerged from existing law enforcement organizations—for example, the Federal Bureau of Investigation's Joint Terrorism Task Force—and from state and local antidrug trafficking programs. Between 2004 and 2009 the Government Accountability Office estimated that states' centers accessed around $426 million in DHS grant funds. About 60 percent of fusion center funding comes from federal grants, 30 percent from state funds, and 10 percent from local funds (US Government Accountability Office 2010).

Although counterterrorism was the original impetus for the fusion centers, "they quickly mutated their missions to include all crimes, and in some instances, all hazards" (Regan and Monahan 2014, 477–78). Together the fusion centers' partners have established an auspicious activity reporting system that emphasizes information gathering, reception, analysis, and dissemination, along with communications outreach (US Department of Homeland Security 2016). The fusion center program is evidence that regional-based networks are important in crossing jurisdictions and providing foundations for "picket fence" regionalism, where the three levels of government work across a range of functional areas "that build from working ties into broader understandings" (Regan and Monahan 2014, 481).

Contemporary connections between persons and organizations have obviously accelerated due to increased information and communications technology (ICT) (Castells 1996). IGM is no different. Both the fusion centers and the LPRCA are prime examples of ICT-based networks and represent increasingly prominent ways to conduct intergovernmental operations (Raab and Kenis 2009). Actually teams of local governments, business associations, and economic development agents have regularly networked for some five decades, and these entities have had extensive links with higher-level governments to secure support and promote local economies (Agranoff and McGuire 2003; Rhodes 1997). Currently people do even more as they also connect in electronic-based social networks via the Internet, which can link millions of end users by satellite-transmitted narrowcasting. These networks operate for varied purposes, such as manufacturing and uniting transacting parties in a host of ways. Public agencies and NGOs similarly network for four broad purposes: exchanging information, enhancing one another's capabilities, smoothing service interactions, and solving policy and program problems (Agranoff 2007c).

Thus, a baseline for understanding IGM by networks and networking is examined here. It begins with an introduction to what organized networks are and how they operate in bridging organizations intergovernmentally. Following is a discussion of why formal networks so rapidly and easily became part of the intergovernmental scene. It next identifies who the main actors in IGM by network are and how they operate. Networks in IGM are not all alike, as their public functions range considerably from exchanging information to making decisions that impact their participants; so their different foci are explained. Next, the chapter demonstrates what networks actually do by illustrating how they work with governments and NGOs on a set of problems—in this case, with Medicaid Home and Community-Based Services for intellectually and developmentally disabled persons. Finally, the potential and actual roles of citizen engagement in network operations—that is, how these activities touch multi-organization enterprises—are discussed. Chapter 9 then assesses how these IGM networks work.

On Networks and Networking

The signature organizational feature of the information age is said to be the network. In IGM *network* is an umbrella term for a host of connections between public actors (e.g., political leaders), governments, and NGOs. In this sense it is a loosely held expression to describe representatives of different organizations working together on issues and concerns that potentially or actually interact. Chris Ansell and Alison Gash (2008, 543) characterize networks as decentralized, team-based organizations using strong lateral communications and coordination that cross functional boundaries within and between organizations, which are linked by cooperative exchange relationships. In relation to IGM, multi-organization networks are in many ways outgrowths of accelerating contacts between NGOs and government, spurred particularly by contracting and by the rising importance of multi-entity responses to emergencies and to service fragmentation (Wise and Nader 2002).

In practice, networking is more commonly applied to a variety of situations where organizational boundaries are crossed; thus, a broader conceptual handle would be that of regular and highly involved collaborative management, or "the process of facilitating and operating in multi-organizational arrangements to solve problems that cannot be solved, or solved easily, by single organizations" (Agranoff and McGuire 2003, 4). Formal networks such as the LPRCA or a fusion center then are more organized and formalized versions of *collaboration*, which Laurence O'Toole (1997, 45) defines as "structures of interdependence involving multiple organizations or parts thereof, where one unit is not merely the formal subordinate of others in some hierarchical arrangement." In an update, nearly two decades later, O'Toole (2015, 361) adds that these structures do not replace bureaucratic organization; instead, "they add one or more layers of structural complexity as public agencies are interwoven with counterparts" from other multiple entities. Networks, in this sense, tackle rarely solved or wicked policy problems that cut across boundaries of agencies and programs, deal with ambiguous policy goals in contexts of dispersed power, face political demands for inclusion and broader influence, and deal with second-order effects (such as the unemployment, education, and job training nexus) and layers of mandates from federal and state governments (Rittel and Webber 1973, 160).

Usage of the term "network" in an IGM context preceded O'Toole's treatment by several years. Donald Kettl (1981) was among the first public management scholars to use the term, arguing that network-like changes in American federalism were brought on by two block grants from the Richard Nixon era—the Comprehensive Employment and Training Act (CETA) of 1973 and the Community Development Block Grant (CDBG) for Small Cities programs. Although these programs have many implications for local administration, Kettl's study of Richmond, Virginia, highlights the contracting in the direct administration of numerous projects to non-city agencies. He notes that the "complicated administrative *networks* that manage CETA and CDBG have simultaneously streamlined and muddied the problem of accountability" (371, emphasis mine). This use of the term "networks" thus predates its contemporary twenty-first-century connotation.

Robert Gage (1984) offered a prescient early look at the role of networks in administering federal programs in the late twentieth century. Presenting a critical analysis of the creation and demise of federal regional councils, he observes that the positions of actors and organizational units can be represented pictorially as nodes, or "junctions when there are multiple interconnections" (137). He emphasizes the role of politics in networking and the necessity of formulating strategies, bargaining, and negotiating in administration across governmental levels. His in-depth depictions of national and local councils offer some of the early representations of network structures in the IGM literature.

Since the term "network" is currently used to capture a variety of activities, more precision is required (Rhodes 2003). To begin, the prior definitions of collaboration and network imply *organized* action. Catherine Alter and Jerald Hage (1993, 46) consider *networks* to be social forms that permit interactions of exchange, concerted action, and joint production through nonhierarchical organized clusters. By contrast, they define the act of *networking* as involving individuals' actions of creating or maintaining cross-organizational arrangements that are conducted by *boundary spanners*, or those who engage in networking tasks and employ modes of coordination and task integration across organizational boundaries. Networks and networking are of intergovernmental concern. The important work of O'Toole and Kenneth Meier (2004) and Meier and O'Toole (2003)—along with that of Keith Provan and Patrick Kenis (2007), Provan and H. Brinton Milward (1995), and Joop Koppenjan and Erik-Hans Klijn (2004)—have led the way in illustrating managers' "networking behavior." During the same period

Robert Agranoff (2007c); Michael McGuire (2002); Koppenjan and Klijn (2004); Myrna Mandell (2001); Christopher Koliba, Jack Meek, and Asim Zia (2012); and Aleksey Kolpakov (2014) all focused on network processes.

Moreover, Malcom Kilduff and Wenpin Tsai (2003, 91) point out that while some networks are serendipitous—that is, their goals evolve through random variation, selection, and retention processes, and their actors participate based on shared ties—others are goal-directed networks, which are formed to reach agreed-on aims, measure success against those aims, and have actors who participate based on the shared goals. In this respect, the focus within IGM is on mutual goal direction, not on some nonfunctional or analytic shared tie without a concerted purpose. IGM therefore is based on real-world organized actions of multiple entities that attempt to solve intergovernmental problems caused by the emergence of complex interdependencies involving multiple levels and types of agencies and organizations.

Networking: Collaboration without Operational Networks

An operating goal-directed network, as defined, does not always make the most managerial sense, but it does when the issues faced are ongoing, complicated policy problems and need multiagency responses (Rittel and Webber 1973). Examples that come to mind are the challenges of using the Medicaid HCBS Waiver to integrate persons with I/DD into their communities, of mitigating a polluted urban watershed, of responding to natural disasters, or of facilitating employment for persons who have modest educational achievements. For these concerns, no one agency or program is in charge of them, goals are uncertain, dozens of often-conflicting federal and state standards and regulations pertain, and political forces with many interests demand solutions. This type of interactive work can be thought of as articulation work; that is, various parties are trying to reconfigure organizational representatives' capacities (Strauss 1988). Emergency management, for example, involves multitasking that encompasses three design principles: tracking of resource requests, incorporating multilevel and private resources, and adapting specifications as the process unfolds (Brooks, Bodeau, and Fedorowicz 2013, 939–41). These types of "externally oriented 'networking' efforts on the part of public managers can perform a number of functions ... contributing to the management of multiorganizational efforts, exploiting opportunities, protecting the core organization from challenges or threats" (O'Toole 2015, 361).

Under these circumstances, persons representing different organizations then need to think about a series of core issues when transforming networking into a goal-directed network formation: a clear purpose as a driving force, an established participation criteria, a need for political and financial support, a ready-made agreement on the type of decisions and actions that will be made as well as how those decisions will be made, and a sense of the resource pool that might be called on (Vandeventer and Mandell 2007, 33–34; see also Weber and Khademian 2008; Alam, Kabir, and Chaudhri, 2014). This would appear to be the case with the multiple actors involved in homeland security and in environmental governance (Clayton and Haverty 2005; Gunningham 2009). Agranoff (2012) has identified some sixteen criteria that point to the need for forming some type of network. Among them are problems that have become the domain of many programs, political and management support from top administrators and the potential to gain resources, and participants who are willing to confront difficult and conflict-prone issues. If such issues and concerns indicate concerted action by a set of organizational representatives is appropriate, then it may well be appropriate to establish a more formal, operational network.

Establishing a network is not always necessary, however, to work together across boundaries and solve the interagency issues. This is where "networking" without networks comes in.

Paul Vandeventer and Myrna Mandell (2007, 20–22) present realistic criteria for when connective actions short of forming a network may be in order. Among the more important ones are the following:

- The problems or issues are minor and can be resolved by dyadic or triadic interorganizational contact and accommodation, thus deflating expectations.
- The focus or orientation—for example, to coordinate some unspecified shared problems—is vague or meaningless.
- Top administrators or decision makers withhold their support or pay lip service to the endeavor.
- Potential activist administrators and specialists are unwilling to commit their time, energy, and resources to the undertaking.
- Key potential activists refuse to confront core conflict-producing issues and related competitive or historic tensions.
- Expectations are that issues can be resolved in a short time frame instead of an orientation to small yet essential "wins."
- From the outset, participants frame problems or issues based on their individual perspectives instead of on new perspectives based in deliberative-based agreements.

Organizations working together on a protracted basis, such as the Lower Platte alliance and the fusion centers, face considerable risk, can expend great resources, and chance potential conflict. Solving many agency-to-agency problems often does not require the protracted commitments that large networks do, not to mention the workloads that goal-directed networks have.

There are fortunately many other collaborative "fish in the sea," so to speak. Networking actions can address less overarching problems and be resolved, as identified, by dyadic or triadic interorganizational contact and accommodation. Some years ago Roscoe Martin (1963a) introduced a scheme of structural and procedural accommodations that are commonly used in metropolitan cooperation that fall short of the usual reorganization proposals or government consolidation that perform designated functions across cities and counties (see also Walker 2000, 286–95). This author has expanded Martin's original list in figure 8.1, which is organized into three different categories: informal practice linkages, collaborative tools of government, and formal public and NGO arrangements. Note that although they are major means of generating collaborative behavior in IGM, figure 8.1 does not include those IGM instruments already covered in this volume: grants, regulations, loans, vouchers, and contracts for services. They have already been identified as the major modes that generate interdependence, and the pervasiveness of these instruments clearly call for various forms of linkage.

The other networking actions or collaborative modes identified in figure 8.1 demonstrate the rich options that have emerged in collaborative management practice. Many have emanated from the bounded jurisdictional practices of intergovernmental behaviors of earlier, less complex, and less interdependent years. They can now be employed to engage in collaborative networking without necessarily building a network. For example, the parallel, or agreed-on, action (I.C) is one of the most frequently used and common approaches to collaboration. Likewise, initially dedicated task forces (II.A) begin to address cross-sector problems, which can often lead to subsequent actions by two or more agencies. Finally, councils or federations of agencies (III.B) exist in hundreds of communities to exchange information and often recommend individual agency action related to respective funding or projects or programs. Thus, the arsenal of collaborative possibilities in the real world is quite extensive (see also Stenberg and Morse 2014).

Engaging in such collaboration clearly does not constitute a formal goal-directed network. While all of these actions serve collaboration by facilitating essential links for managers, they fall short of what has been identified as multiparty agency and organization involvement "in regularized, organized multiagency/multiorganization bodies," or nonhierarchical meta-organizations, "that exchange information, build mutual capabilities, build collaborative services strategies, and solve programming/policy problems at points of service" (Agranoff 2012, 39; see also Koppenjan and Klijn 2004; McGuire 2002; O'Toole 1997). Too often those in academia, in particular, confuse the many practitioner acts of collaboration with organized networks that serve some purpose. In IGM the collaborative arsenal thus includes both networks and various collaborative acts of networking to face contemporary complexities.

FIGURE 8.1. Acts of Networking: Public-to-Public and NGO Agency Collaborating Modes

I. Informal practice linkages

   A. Informal discussions and sharing of information—nonbinding exchanges by personnel of two or more agencies* focused on some program purpose.

   B. Informal cooperation—a nonbinding connection (required by law, contract, written exchange) between two agencies to improve programming services.

   C. Parallel action—an agreement, usually formally adopted, between two or more agencies or operations to pursue a common course of action. The decisions are agreed on jointly, but their implementation requires individual action by the agencies or organizations involved.

   D. Continuous, public, open-source facility use—one organization makes sustained noncontractual use of another public facility, such as public schools, libraries, and museums; small city governments and county planning agencies; community organizations and public buildings; small town leaders; agricultural extension services; chambers of commerce; and small business development centers in colleges.

   E. Conference approach—a bringing together, at regular intervals, of representatives of given agencies or organizations within an area to discuss common problems, exchange information, and develop agreements on issues of mutual interest.

   F. Shared staff—specialists and professionals on loan from another agency perform certain tasks or services for a cooperating agency while remaining on the payroll of the sending agency.

   G. Outreach and liaison staff—employees of one organization assigned to work primarily or exclusively with another agency: police in schools, social workers in mental health centers, occupational health and safety specialists in shipyards, ambulance crews in fire stations, and so on.

II. Collaborative tools of government

   A. Dedicated task forces—multisector, ad hoc bodies charged to examine, study, and research a particular problem and to propose tentative solutions that cut across multiple populations, jurisdictions, communities, and so forth.

   B. Interagency agreements—written collaboration support between two or more code departments or agencies within the same government: social services and parks and recreation departments, economic development and tourism, and the like.

   C. Joint venture—two or more agencies seek to invest in and launch an auxiliary operation (for example, a business or spin-off café or service station) based on shared risk capital and with shared liability as part of their respective programs while maintaining the rest of their operations on an independent basis.

   D. Joint-stock venture—similar to a joint venture but the participating agencies raise capital by selling stock in the operation, and their liability is limited to the joint venture.

E. Joint commissions—private multi-organization bodies that evaluate standards of operation, entry and exit to a field, and sometimes outcomes that are licensed or "franchised" under public auspices, such as the accreditation of hospitals, rehabilitation facilities, geographic information systems specialists, and social workers.

F. Limited powers and intergovernmental public-private organizations—area-based multi-government or super municipal or county representative bodies that have limited or no formal powers over aspects of planning or programming. Examples are transportation metropolitan planning organizations, Area Agencies on Aging, workforce development boards, regional planning boards, rural development councils, and museum or zoo authorities.

III. Formal public and NGO arrangements

A. Advisory boards—citizens, community leaders, service clients, students, and parents representing different organized and non-organized interests meet with public officials, provide advice, respond to proposals, and actively participate in plans and proposals.

B. Councils or federations of agencies—information sharing, information creation, and sometimes pooled fund-raising, with no or few decisional controls over an agency's operations.

C. Compact—two or more agencies or organizations undertake mutual obligations, such as serving clients from neighboring communities where no services are organized.

D. Transfer of functions—shifting an agency's particular service, such as nursing, intake, or case management, to another agency with more adequate knowledge, experience, and resources.

E. Limited partnership—two or more agencies or organizations formally agree to work together and integrate certain functions, such as fund-raising, public relations, financial management, or supportive health services, while remaining separate in their core operations.

F. Formal agreements with a philanthropic body—written compact to work with a philanthropic entity for research, funding, and public relations purposes.

G. Integrated services and partnerships—two or more agencies or organizations contractually, or legally, agree to unify one or more of their services into one operation while operating separately on other functions. Normally it involves intake and assessment, case management, evaluation and assessment, support, or management services.

* The term "agencies" in this figure refers to both NGO organizations and government agencies.

Source: Author's adaptation and expansion of Martin (1963b).

Forces behind the Emergence of Formal Networks

The network mode of organizing is well suited for collaboration as complexities and interdependencies exponentially expand and converge in implementing policy while the resources to meet them become more scarce. Many reasons are behind the emergence of networks as a form of IGM activity. One is the transformation of societies from a labor to a knowledge orientation and the need to integrate human capital into collaborative problem-identifying, strategic-brokering, and problem-solving activities (Drucker 1995; Reich 1991). A second is the change in government roles, which have shifted from direct operations toward steering, partnering, and contracting (Kooiman 2003). This, in turn, has led to the emergence of intergovernmental programs that work on the second- and third-order problems and of issues raised by these shifts in governmental operations (Agranoff and McGuire 1998; McGuire 1999; O'Toole 1997, 2015; Radin et al. 1996).

Related gaps in clear-cut solutions to these problems lead to knowledge collaboration both outside of governments involving NGOs and intergovernmentally between the levels of authorization and operation. This promotes various potential or actual vehicles of collaborative behavior—such as knowledge exchange, shared resources, coordinated strategies, task forces, coalitions, and many other forms of connection—along with associated network structures (Campbell and Gould 1999; Mandell and Steelman 2003).

Next, in organizational structures that become more internally interactive and thus more hierarchically flexible (Clegg 1990; Saint-Onge and Armstrong 2004), their employees are more "positioned" to accept interorganizational collaboration along with managing across their own departments. Finally, these forces lead to a world of multiple overlapping connections in which managers must meet the challenges of increasing complexity amid uncertainty; thus, they are often motivated to operate collaboratively so they can move from the edge of chaos to reasonable solutions (Koliba, Meek, and Zia 2012; Sherman and Schultz 1998). Moreover, recent research on a large database of public managers reveals that participating in networks and actively engaging partners help them clarify goals in their home organizations, and these defined issues are communicated downward in their organizations (Davis and Stazyk 2016, 443). These forces now make IGM networks prevalent engines of management.

Various forces within the intergovernmental scene, as previous chapters have indicated, have also moved IGM toward networking and networks. First is the rise of welfare states since the early twentieth century. Welfare states initially bureaucratized, centralized, and managerialized social welfare, but in the long run they put hundreds of different types of programs administered by multiple agencies into the hands of subnational governments with their own multiple agencies and engaged NGOs as joint policy

BOX 8.1

- Developing less permanent, formal operational connections between organizations—dozens of them—are considered networking activities rather than engaging in formal networks.
- Voluntary and mandated networks in the intergovernmental arena are manifestations of the greater complexity of the levels of government and NGOs that are involved in an increasing number of program arenas, which range from design to direct service operation.
- Comprising parts of various organizations, intergovernmental networks operate in a nonhierarchical fashion while working largely on problems and seeking solutions at their margins.
- Networks do not replace bureaucratic organizations; they work across organizations on issues that involve substantial doses of exchange, concerted action, and joint production.

makers and implementers (Ashford 1988; Wilson 1975; Flora and Heidenheimer 1981). Second, this subvented interdependence led to a greater concern for understanding intergovernmental patterns and IGM as multiple agencies and levels became involved in problems. Third, as explained in chapter 5, managers working between governments and NGOs had to learn how to operate within this system and to solve the everyday problems in making programs work. Finally, these intergovernmental phenomena have shifted "operational centers" over time, moving somewhat away from provision by governments to the nongovernmental sector on a shared administration basis. There, a host of public-private partnerships, shared service delivery administration, marketization, privatization, and decentralization are the norm (Frederickson 1999; Loughlin 2000). These forces in both the organizational and the management spheres have generated greater networking activity and led to the formation of an increasing number of networks (Koliba, Meek, and Zia 2012; McGuire 2002).

Network Actors and Actions: A Demonstration

When working in a formal network, the only way to begin to understand the complications of the intergovernmental connections is to overview the myriad of agencies and concerns that might be brought to bear on the networked actions. Chapter 7 identified the long chain of federal, state, local, and NGO connections that link services under Title III of the Older Americans Act: the Department of Health and Human Services, state units on aging, area-based agencies on aging, a host of contractors and service providers, and ultimately families and clients. In a similar fashion, transportation-focused metropolitan planning organizations (MPOs), such as the Kentuckiana MPO based in Louisville (see chapter 9), are involved in networks that include federal and state transportation (mass transit, highways, and more) and environmental officials, city and county and transit officials, local government elected officials, planners, engineers and managers, airport authorities, citizen advisory boards, special task forces (e.g., freight, open space, databases), and support services contractors (e.g., modeling, accounting, legal). In emergency management, the networks can be even more complicated, as they include the Federal Emergency Management Agency, counterpart state homeland security agencies, local government law enforcement, and emergency services through local first responders and nonprofit charitable organizations. In many aspects of IGR and IGM in the network era, such chains of program operation are the reality of how to understand and where to begin to manage.

One of these networked program chains is illustrated in detail in figure 8.2, which focuses on the Centers for Medicare and Medicaid Services HCBS Waiver for residential and nonresidential services for I/DD populations in a hypothetical state. The figure demonstrates how the various agencies are faced with the difficult problems that cross agency and program boundaries, involve ambiguous policy goals in dispersed power arrangements, present political pressures, and have second-order effects. It is divided by the major network components: public agencies, secondary NGOs, primary service agencies, and their support services and subcontractors. Each of these entities is identified along with their primary roles, followed by the network's systemic aims.

At least seven different public agencies are potentially involved in this IGM network. Because they really authorize HCBS-allowable services, the program is triggered by the federal Medicaid funding stream, and this is where program guidelines and standards are generated. The federal I/DD agency (A.2) and Civil Rights Division in the Department of Health and Human Services (A.4) also have interests. Most important at the state level are the state Medicaid office (A.3), which develops the state planning and financing rules; the state I/DD program office (A.3), which provides contract program oversight and assessment; and the health department, which generates and monitors health and safety regulations and oversight for residents. Other state agencies include the attorney general's office (A.5) for legal questions and actions; the federally funded, state-based governor's planning council (A.7) for system study and recommendations; and two legislative commissions—one for I/DD and one for Medicaid (A.6)—for program-related reviews. At least seven public agencies and bodies are thus in the identifiable network.

Five different secondary-level NGOs constitute the core working network members. They include one or more contractors (B.1) who provide support in matters of claims and claims processing, eligibility determination,

FIGURE 8.2. The IGR Network in Residential and Nonresidential Services for I/DD under the Medicaid Waiver

A. Public agencies	B. Secondary NGOs	C. Primary services and client-contact delivery agencies	D. Support services and subcontractors
1. Federal CMS regional office (authorization, oversight performance review)	1. Administrative support contractor(s) (eligibility, claims processing, case referrals)	1. Nonprofit and for-profit nursing homes	1. Medical and health
2. Administration on Intellectual and Developmental Disabilities	2. Advocacy group 1 (Arcs, families, clients, client advocates, interested citizens)	2. Nonprofit and for-profit group homes and supported living arrangements	2. School systems (under 21)
3. State homes and services agencies, division of I/DD (program), Medicaid policy offices (financing), Department of Public Health (standards)	3. Advocacy group 2 (trade ARF, service delivery agencies)	3. Nonprofit and for-profit day programs and workshops (vocational, activity)	3. Dental
			4. Legal
	4. Advocacy group 3 (state associations for rights and interests of the disabled)	4. Home-based client service agencies (training, habilitation, medical support)	5. Transportation
4. Federal justice and issues of client rights (protection)			6. Vocational rehabilitation
5. State attorney general (represents state interests)	5. University-based center(s) for excellence (research, demonstration, training)	5. Assistance for clients living with their families	7. Assistive devices
6. State legislative commissions (I/DD, Medicaid)			8. Pharmacies
7. Governor's I/DD planning council			9. Others

Source: Author.

waiting list management, and case referrals. Three advocacy groups (B.2–B.4) are organized in most states and represent the following groups: clients, citizens, and families (Arcs); trade associations of rehabilitation facilities (ARFs) and contract service providers; and state associations that advocate for rights of the disabled. Also in this category are federal-, state-, and foundation-financed University Centers for Excellence in Developmental Disabilities (B.5). Normally located in universities, they not only engage in basic rescarch but also conduct research on state-oriented delivery systems and deliver research-based training and demonstrations.

The next group of network participants involves those agencies responsible for the core services for waiver clients. Foremost, they are the primary points of contact for families and individual client advocates. They include both for-profit and nonprofit agencies: nursing home and extended care facilities (C.1); group homes and supported-living programs (C.2) with one- to three-person apartments; rehabilitation-oriented day vocational and activity program agencies and workshops (C.3); home-based client services support agencies (C.4); and agencies that provide assistance and support for clients who are living with their families (C.5). Many of the larger agencies combine two or more of these services, and some area-based mega agencies can deliver all five direct services. These Medicaid HCBS services are under contract with the state agency (or substate agencies, as in North Carolina and some other states) and work directly with the state agency on program and finance issues. They are primarily represented both legislatively and before the state administrative agencies by the state trade ARFs (B.3).

That leaves the providers of nonschool multiple support services—medical, dental, legal, transportation, and so on—who are subcontracted under the payments to the delivery agencies (D.1–5) for support as needed. The state program normally lets the delivery agency manage the clients' budget and allocated payments and secure those services deemed clinically necessary. In some states, the package of these services are built into a service-by-service rate payment system whereas in other states they must be absorbed into a daily or monthly rate. The exception here is public schooling for persons younger than twenty-one years of age, who by federal law must be included in regular schools; thus, the D.1–D.5 agencies and programs must coordinate with the young persons' respective school systems on all matters ranging from transportation to the type and level of instruction. At any rate, while less directly involved in the overall collective management concerns of the network, these support service organizations add another tier.

What then are the collective concerns of this network? They are those issues that transcend respective agency and organizational roles in regulating, financing, enabling, operating, and evaluating service delivery. At least eight systemic or network roles appear to be important in this Medicaid HCBS waiver for I/DD persons:

1. Performing the primary review and oversight of the multifaceted system of operations and services, or the orchestration of the system
2. Checking that federal regulations, state statutory provisions, and third-party (e.g., accreditation) standards are disseminated and followed
3. Ensuring partner contributory maintenance of the interactive, partner-generated system of legal norms, financing practices, services coordination, and system maintenance is followed
4. Participating in the interlocutory software(s) that support the system—for example, data gathering and analysis, system statistics, and information and communications systems
5. Developing the human resources (e.g., direct service support staff) necessary to play interactive roles in networked services
6. Jointly determining effective and fair means of assessing real costs of services and developing reimbursement rates based on cost findings
7. Expanding the continuum of services to include all the life amenities for clients (e.g., particularly expanded occupational opportunities)
8. Assessing the changed life and growth opportunities of clients and of programs as a result of the HCBS waiver as expected by the federal CMS Medicaid program agency (Agranoff 2014)

These network functions can best be collaboratively performed on a regular basis since they go beyond any one organization's mission, capacity, knowledge, and resources. Together they clearly surpass any agency's or organization's direct service role in this highly intergovernmental program. They are collective because the intergovernmental system has exponentially expanded beyond the confines of government's multilevel responsibility and interdependence. Not only are many public and private NGOs operating for the same programs and purposes but also they are operationally linked in ways that include but go beyond traditional "respective roles." In short, their operations call out for forms of communication and to be integrated (Agranoff and Pattakos 1979). That makes the IGM network considerably more real than some analytical construct derived by academics that is based on surveyed or sets of reported shared ties. Rather, the IGM network entails real, goal-directed, and increasingly operational parts of a networked system that are conductively interactive (Saint-Onge and Armstrong 2004).

The Range of IGM Networks

Network activities involved in intergovernmental programs have quite diverse functions. As with other types of goal-directed networks, the intergovernmental networks under analysis are either formally chartered or not chartered. Both types of networks share certain characteristics: permanent status, regular formal meetings, definable communications system, leaders and participants, task forces or work groups, identifiable partners and governance structures, and some form of division of labor or task allocation (Agranoff 2007c). *Chartered networks* are formally established as organized entities, often by intergovernmental agreement, and registered as a 501c(3) nonprofit organization by an act or resolution of a state legislature, by a governor's executive order, or through corporate registration with a state government representative, such as the secretary of state. *Non-chartered networks* do not have such a formal legal status, but their continuing presence and operations, regular meetings, concrete problem-solving actions, websites, newsletters, and the like are testimony to their existence. Non-chartered networks are often harder to locate in the "yellow pages" of telephone directories, but they appear often on websites. Nevertheless, those without chartered status can prove to be equally viable bodies.

Some IGM networks are a direct function of federal or federal and state legislation and programming, while others emerge out of the complications and challenges presented by federal and federal, state, and local programming. Figure 8.3 provides an illustrative list of two types—the mandated, or federally sponsored, network and the non-mandated network. They involve a variety of players from different levels—federal, state, and local—of government or NGOs or a series of locally based public and private organizations that come together to address common problems, to seek solutions, and to attempt to bind their separate missions and mandates into new and practical courses of action and, for some, decisions.

For example, area-based workforce investment boards, under the federal Workforce Investment Act of 1998, oversee employment and training programs on an area basis. The board members include local government officials, members from local area higher education (particularly vocational and technical) and public school systems, employee representatives, and workers from counseling and training NGOs that provide direct services, along with state and federal representatives serving in a liaison capacity. They work collectively to promote local employment and match the workforce opportunities with employer demand. Examples of the non-mandated networks are the small town water resources networks that are state based but include federal program representatives who are based in the state (particularly the US Department of Agriculture Rural Development and the Commerce Department's Economic Development Administration), state program officials (public works, water boards, Small Cities CDBG), local officials (water boards), representatives from statewide water associations, technical consultants, and university USDA/state land-grant university extension representatives. The network's role is generally threefold: to provide information and assistance regarding funding so that small town water systems can be renovated to meet federal and state regulatory compliance, to educate and train

FIGURE 8.3. Public Agency Networks

Mandated, or federally sponsored, networks	Non-mandated networks
Area Agency on Aging (planning and services)	Watershed protection and mitigation
Workforce investment boards (job training)	Small town water resources
Metropolitan planning organizations (transportation)	State geographic information systems
Soil and water conservation districts (federal, state, county)	Emergency management first responders
Rural development councils (federal, state)	Small and home-based businesses
Substate planning bodies (in some states)	Economic development corporations
Homeland security fusion cities (federal, state, local)	Telecommunications and data exchange
Fusion centers (disaster management)	Landscape conservation cooperatives

personnel on matters of operations and compliance, and to facilitate technology transfer and sometimes technology adaptation for challenging local problems. With time, as the presenting complexities that IGM produces constantly increase, so will the types of networks that will play integrative roles.

Network Roles and Missions Differ

Not all networks are engaged in the same level of decision-making or operations. Contrary to the common understanding, at least by some observers, not all networks engage in the type of policy and programming adjustment and funding decisions that transportation MPOs and Area Agencies on Aging do. Following closely with Alter and Hage's (1993) identified exchange, concerted action, and joint production scheme, this author found four different types present in his field study of fourteen networks:

1. Information—Partners come together primarily to exchange agency policies and programs, technologies, and potential solutions. Taking any action is long term and entirely up to the agencies on a voluntary basis (e.g., the Lower Platte River Corridor Alliance).
2. Development—Partner information and technical exchange are combined with education and member services, and they increase members' knowledge and their capacities to implement solutions that

are not made jointly but within home agencies or organizations on a medium-term basis (e.g., fusion centers).

3. Outreach—Partners exchange information and technologies, sequence programming, share resource opportunities, pool client contacts, and enhance access opportunities that lead to new programming avenues. Whereas decisions remain in the agencies and programs, implementing blueprinted programs takes place within an array of public and private agencies. Actions are medium term (e.g., HCBS networks).

4. Action—Partners make immediate interagency adjustments, formally adopt collaborative courses of action, and deliver services as well as exchange information and technologies (e.g., transportation MPOs) (Agranoff 2007c).

This formulation suggests that the commonly assumed direct "program adjustments" are not a part of all networks and that for three of the four types of adjustments, any action that might be taken is more indirect, is either of long- or medium-term duration, and is usually within the scope of other decision makers' mission and powers, particularly within the various participating agencies and programs. These distinctions would appear to be as critical as the missions of participating agencies are (Fleming, McCartha, and Steelman 2015), for they normally condition a network's scope.

Network Politics: A Case of Agencies and Groups in the Management Sphere

The I/DD Medicaid HCBS waiver network, mapped in figure 8.2, involves both administrative and political actors. It represents the new politics of intergovernmental actors as they network. This network now extends to all I/DD and its array of interested and involved publics in order to demonstrate their politics through a real-world example, the broader state of Indiana HCBS network. It also introduces a political window into IGM.

Although not all of the Indiana actors may be involved in the details of network administration, most are. In Indiana, the Indiana Association of Rehabilitation Facilities (INARF) and Indiana Arc regularly design major moves with state agencies, such as the Family and Social Services Administration, Division of Disability and Rehabilitative Services (DDRS), and Office of Medicaid Policy and Planning. In 1997–99 the members of the agencies, INARF, Arc, and several other I/DD representatives drawn from the network developed a "person follows the funding" plan to move clients from state hospitals to community settings. More than $39 million in state institutional support dollars moved, along with Medicaid funds. This 317 Plan was the first

BOX 8.2

- Formal networks are very much products of the information age; they face complexity that transcends organizational boundaries. These networks go far beyond exchanging information as they become joint producers of knowledge across organizational and jurisdictional lines.
- Some networks operate deeply, from program design to direct service operations, and involve different levels of government, multiple agencies, gatekeeping contractors (e.g., case managers), administrative support contractors, and private direct service agencies.
- Networks exist for different purposes: to share information, to mutually develop partner knowledge and service capacities, to sequence and blueprint strategies carried out by relevant partners, to adopt network-level actions and programs, or to pursue some combination of these purposes.
- Network processing is both administrative and political, ranging from high-level administrative connections to citizen and client engagement.

of several network-derived program changes. In 2009 Arc, INARF, and the disability and Medicaid policy representatives worked together on several administrative changes, particularly to review and revise an FSSA-generated resource allocation model called OASIS (developed by a contractor). During the negotiations, they suspended OASIS and agreed on a different means to move potential clients off the community services' waiting list, negotiated a new allocation model for day services, maintained funding levels for behavior management services, and made adjustments to expand funding for individuals needing twenty-four-hour coverage.

The four groups also agreed that proposed OASIS rate reduction changes would be held until after one full quarter of billing experience. Finally, they put the OASIS uniform rate methodology in permanent suspension. One of the key players in this scenario then related that "we have accomplished enough work with our small group and reached a point where we can begin bringing more people into the process. . . . Within the next few weeks work plans to address the major issues related to retooling the model . . . [including] opportunities for consumer, family and provider input in several key areas" (INARF 2009).

In the area of high connectivity, IGM politics plays out this way. The "devils of the administrative details" not only are at the center of the issue but also prove to be very high stakes for the providers, industry associations, and advocates as well as for the government agency. As long as this type of management operates via an intergovernmental network, the expanding politics of programs remain at the forefront of or blend in with routine management. The 317 Plan experience is a prime example of how politics and government are intertwined in IGM networking.

The 317 process also demonstrates how externalization plus the impera- tive for networking in Indiana have therefore opened up intergovernmental politics to more external players. Clearly IGM politics involve more than the traditional legislative lobbying. Instead, participants exert political pressure through network participation and joint decisions and administration, often in a very detailed way. In the old days of grants, for example, it was enough to know the decision points in the two or three levels of government agencies, make one's wishes known, and hope for the best. For HCBS and many other programs, the stakes are too high to stay out of administrative details. Now a whole spectrum of actors and organizations are involved. In the Indiana I/DD case, eight state-level interests (see figure 8.2) were involved in the 317 Plan politically, and they represent hundreds of interests and over twenty major actors in the system. On many issues such interactions occur regularly. This places an emerging and new considerable burden of political understanding on the intergovernmental manager, particularly, to have a working familiarity with subsystem politics and administrative operations, two linked concepts under networking.

Citizen Engagement and Networks

The more or less long-standing federal requirement of providing evidence of citizen involvement and some degree of citizen agreement for program approval now extends to various forms of citizen engagement (that is, beyond holding hearings) in an era when direct services are increasingly delivered by government grantees or contractors, and networks are involved in fostering and making key program adjustments. In the network era, citizens and cit- izen groups do more than interact and petition the public agency; they are part of the network. As "complex adaptive networks" (Booher 2008), citizens and citizen groups place their issues in the public sphere everywhere from the point of program decision to the point of service delivery. For example, the Americans with Disabilities Act of 1990, as interpreted by the federal courts, has led to the strictly enforced rights of handicapped individuals, their advocates, and their families to have a direct role in the disposition of any course of treatment and residential placement. Thus, at the point of service, the client or advocate not only must have a role in developing the course of treatment or action but also must agree to any recommended services. Poten- tially the client as a citizen directly becomes a part of the service network, at least at the street level (Gofen 2014), and involved in intergovernmental programs. It has led to a new issue about participation: How do we achieve citizen empowerment—both for individuals and the group—when the issues have become so nuanced and detailed yet the problem-solving now cannot be left to government alone (Solo and Pressberg 1998, 83)?

The problem of citizen involvement is, of course, compounded with the externalization of services and the rise of intergovernmentalization by network. Privatization raises additional burdens on engagement. For example, third-party organizations such as managed care firms that contract with the government or garbage collection firms have little incentive to involve citizen and community interests. Many are part of the large for-profit chains that make the relationship between government and citizens more indirect (Smith and Ingram 2002). Consequently, engagement and influencing decisions are difficult and put extra burdens on citizens' organizations despite that such contracting makes the public agency more involved externally.

It is also important to recognize that nonprofit contracting, voucher programs, and other linkages of government-to-community–based organizations enlist new constituencies in public service delivery. Many nonprofits and community organizations have developed, as Steven Smith and Helen Ingram (2002, 57) observe a "keen stake in government funding and regulatory policy." As the Indiana I/DD HCBS example indicates, their interest, in turn, led trade associations of service providers, particularly those having an investment or role in policy development, to organize politically on individual and collective bases. To varying degrees, they are now actors in the intergovernmental network as well.

Citizen involvement means that leadership is more distributed and pluralized. It has moved from policy advocacy to program arrangements along with program implementation. No magic formulas exist for organized interests to deal with the new public sector network elements. Citizens now do more than provide advice; they and their groups participate in key program and operational decisions as part of the network of involved program participants. Albeit informally, they sometimes sit as part of the "administrative team," so to speak. At the very least, many citizen representatives and client family members serve on NGO agency boards. In the era of the network, citizen activity thus is included in intergovernmental activity, reaching deeply into program management.

Key Learning Points

The era of the network has shifted intergovernmental operating power, including politics, outward to external agents, their interest associations, and, to some degree, service delivery staff and citizens. Today, relying on existing networks at state and local levels places program services in hands far from the agencies that are put in charge of these programs. The distance, for example, between the federal and state Medicaid waiver authorization and the client receiving an array of services is now quite long.

There are also increasing degrees of power interdependence among network partners, and while governmental agencies retain important roles, they may yet be steered or sometimes controlled by dominant coalitions. This appears to be the case with the Indiana I/DD network illustration, where strategies are used within the rules of the game to regulate the processes of exchange (Rhodes 1997).

In the twenty-first century, government by network at the program or IGM level is a hallmark of policy implementation. In government by network at the program level, the focus is on the construction of meanings given by government managers and their interlocutors as they work within organized entities that involve parts of organizations nonhierarchically (Posner, Conlan, and Regan 2013; O'Toole 1997, 2015). They are primarily administratively operational and interoperable but also politically framed and influenced.

IGM networks are not directly referring in this situation to the broader issue of "democratic network governance"—that is, cross-sectoral efforts based in civil society involvement where issues of deliberation and citizen responsibility, as well as questions of equity, accountability, and democratic legitimacy to serve public purposes, are at stake (Bogason and Toonen 1998; Skelcher 2004; Sørenson and Torfing 2007). Although the IGM network is a central part of network governance and impacts it in many ways (for example, it could limit participation and representation), the IGM focus has been more directly on those managerial arrangements and behaviors that contribute to public management theory within the larger but less direct issues of democratic participation and governance.

Key Practice Points

The common usage of the term "networks" is a complicating factor in IGM. It has been emphasized here that formal networks, chartered or not chartered, have an identified permanence, although they may be hard to locate outside of a website's home page or communication with visible actors. Nevertheless, they are available if one makes the effort to locate them through their program-related activities.

Despite the contemporary appeal of formal networks, a huge variety of collaborative activities that connect agencies and programs without forming a network also remain as viable linkages. Networks take extensive commitments, operate on longer time frames, and sometimes cannot overcome long-standing problems. Thus, their alternatives also need to be explored.

Locating a network is simply not enough, however, as networks perform different functions. Here we have identified four: exchange mutual information, study and identify varieties of potential actions taken by partners, develop potential connected activities taken by partners, and undertake joint actions on behalf of the network. Some perform a combination of the four. It is important for the practitioner to understand just what a given network does—its mission—and what it may be unable to do.

The managerial activities of networks combine practical operations issues, laden with organizational and program politics, and must blend legal and organizational constraints with program goals and the interests of agencies. These challenges are complex.

Conclusion

The term "network" thus refers to formal structures involving multiple nodes—agencies and organizations and clients—with multiple linkages, ordinarily working on cross-boundary collaborative activities. They constitute one of several forms of collaborative activity (Agranoff 2012). An IGM network includes governmental and nongovernmental agencies, citizens, and clients that are connected through their involvement in public policy-making and administrative structure—either program or service delivery—through which information and public goods and services may be planned, designed, produced, and delivered.

Networks or "networked power," observes Anne-Marie Slaughter (2009, 97), flows from the ability to make the maximum number of valuable connections. The next requirement is to have the knowledge and skills to harness that power to achieve a common purpose. Indeed, she concludes that networks exist above the state, below the state, and through the state. Power today, particularly what is called soft power in international relations, means that the measure of power is connectedness (95).

In intergovernmental activity, particularly at the program operational level, networks cannot operate as managerial concerns alone. Previous dimensions of IGM—law and politics, growing interdependency, and government-NGO partnerships—remain as IGM considerations brought forth through the lenses of networking and in networks. In other words, legal prescriptions and proscriptions, political forces, growing program interaction, and program-to-program contacts (and contracts) remain as viable forces that are brought to bear on network activity. In IGM the network is formulated and executed within these contexts. Clearly, to network is to forge understandings and agreements within multiple complexities.

9 ORGANIZED INTERGOVERNMENTAL MANAGEMENT NETWORKS

The focus of this chapter is management as a process as applied within networks in an IGM context. It introduces some of the leading-edge ideas in multiagency managing across boundaries. These ideas include actions beyond old-fashioned cooperation involving informal interactive networking as well as what often becomes regular and more involved in the formation of working networks. The discussion begins by positioning the organization in the network—that is, the public agency that is involved in networking and networks—and looks at the conductive public organization. Next the chapter identifies some of the major requisites of IGM network leadership: adaptive organizing, broadening interjurisdictional politics, promoting networks, managing knowledge, and handling other challenges that arise while taking on what appears to be overwhelming complexity. Then after introducing the emergent requisites of in-network processes, an introduction to interoperability, or sequential interunit operations, follows.

Formal networks have been identified as organized, ongoing, multilevel structures of interdependence. They involve parts of organizations working together. In IGM some are top-down operations; that is, they are legally authorized, chartered by federal or federal and state legislation. One example is the Kentuckiana Metropolitan Planning Organization, one of some four hundred MPOs in the United States. As defined in federal transportation legislation (23USC134[b] and 49USC5303[c]), an MPO is the designated local decision-making body under the Transportation Equity Act for the Twenty-First Century (TEA-21) that is responsible for carrying out the metropolitan transportation planning process. An MPO must be established for each urban area with a population of more than fifty thousand people. Kentuckiana includes three Kentucky and two Indiana counties in the Louisville metro area. The network operates through its Transportation Policy Committee, which directs federally generated activity under the federal transportation act Moving Ahead for Progress in the Twenty-First Century (MAP-21), and the Technical Coordinating Committee, which is responsible for giving technical advice and assisting the policy committee. Kentuckiana is part of the Kentucky-Indiana Regional Planning and Development Agency, whose board of directors is represented by each local government's chief elected officials, state officials, transit officials, and other agencies.

In practice Kentuckiana is structured by five distinct layers: agency staff; federal, regional, and state officials; technical planning, engineering, and research staff; a Transportation Advisory Committee, consisting of interest groups and citizen representatives; and the chief elected officials of each unit of local government. This MPO is highly involved in a number of activities that culminate in a transportation improvement plan and a long-range plan. Along with this work, TEA-21 reserves a substantial portion of federal surface transportation block grants to MPOs in those urban areas with populations greater than 200,000 people, so Kentuckiana qualifies for this kind of grant. In integrating their transportation needs, the staff and officials become heavily engaged in decision-based research tools such as travel model development, air quality analysis and consultation, congestion management, and long- and short-range transportation studies for particular jurisdictions. They also consider data collection and database maintenance on traffic counts; bicycle and pedestrian facilities; socioeconomic, geographic, and travel model data; and project management information. In addition Kentuckiana agency staff oversees a ride-share agency responsible for administering a regional carpool, vanpool, and transit promotion and services program. At policy committee meetings, presentations focus on special studies and workshops, followed by both transportation improvement and long-range planning action.

Other IGM networks are the result of bottom-up activity that is formulated by local action to meet community challenges and is not necessarily tied to federal legislation. One such network is Metro High School in Columbus, Ohio, a science, technology, engineering, and mathematics (STEM) network entity of public and private agencies. Metro's major partners include the Educational Council (alliance of sixteen participating Franklin County school districts), the Ohio State University (OSU), Coalition of Essential Schools (KnowledgeWorks in Ohio), and Battelle Corporation, a research entity. However, there is much more to this operation, including important learning sites where students have internships, projects, field placements, and classes: the PAST Foundation, an independent research NGO that organizes research, field learning, and dissemination of STEM learning to the sixteen county school districts; and the OSU library as the Metro Library. Contractual arrangements allow for student counseling with OSU staff. Metro's students also have the benefit of OSU leadership and educational resources and such other community resources as industry and educator curriculum task forces.

Metro's governance includes the Educational Council upon the advice of the Metropolitan Partnership Group, an administrative network steering group that is managed by Metro's administration and the Educational Council staff. The school admits about a hundred students for each class, by interview and lottery and apportioned by school population among the districts, and it operates on an accelerated basis. Students normally master the eighteen subject-related credits required for Ohio high school graduation in their first two years, after which they attend for-credit classes at OSU. In addition to the network that undergirds the operation of the school, a community of students, teachers, and parents are involved in many aspects that round out the school experience. Metro is a formal, networked, decision-making organization that has a clear structure and mission-defined goals as well as detailed, jointly developed procedures. Also, beyond any formal arrangements, the individuals involved are in a collection of informal relationships that transcend organizational, governmental, and sectoral boundaries. By design, Metro unites numerous network actors who have multiple connections and are engaged in various collaborative activities that require constant negotiation and communication.

The Kentuckiana MPO and Metro High School reflect contemporary networks that are organized decision bodies. It means that as the tools of governance work to increase the spheres of public and NGO connections, the search is on for prevalent management models other than those command and control models that are hierarchically based. Moreover, it includes a partial rejection of the intergovernmental ideas that multiple grants, complex contracts, and layers of regulations are self-administering. In the field of practice, they require aggressive interorganizational management, the emergent aspect of IGM. Thus, it is important to examine how contemporary public management is organized conductively to operate within these contexts across the organizations and sectors, in effect as extensions of IGR into more focused IGM (Burke 2014, 73). How does one manage within networks involving the legitimacy and authority of governments and their NGO partner executants?

As programming moves externally, public administration must pay considerably more attention to the external role of the public manager. Thousands of city and county governments not only engage in community and economic development activities but also work externally with services-oriented citizen boards and service contractors, and they partner with other governments and nongovernmental entities (Abels 2012). For example, at the state level, most highway construction is completed by private sector contracting let by state transportation agencies, and highway planning is shared with MPO networks, which in turn work with multiple local governments and citizen groups. State environmental management agencies administer federal legislation through local governments and regulated industries and organizations. At the federal level, more and more agencies—for example, the Department of Housing and Urban Development's housing programs and Community Development Block Grants, the Department of Commerce's Economic Development Administration and Small Business Administration, and those with the Department of Health and Human Services (e.g.,

Medicaid and other groups under the Older Americans Act)—operate by intergovernmental grant and contract with subnational governments. Their grant intermediaries at the first stage, along with NGOs, then make the programs potentially interactive. For example, under the public assistance Temporary Assistance for Needy Families program, an increasing number of states have privatized what were core public administrative functions: case management, child care, transportation, and job training and placement. Consequently, "the new array of contracts has produced a more fragmented network of local agencies and private providers" (Freeman 2003, 1308).

Conductivity: Positioning the Public Agency for Networking

The ongoing march of IGM, from the integral state to developing jurisdictional interdependence to partnering with NGOs to networking and network activity, has important administrative implications for those who remain in government agencies that work within and across the boundaries. Public administrators and program specialists who work in public agencies are more attuned to internal organizational experiences that are less rigid, cross divisional boundaries of their own structures, reach out to other agencies of their government, and involve an increasing number of cross-sector and intergovernmental experiences. Also, this exposure and experience, with a changing hierarchical paradigm, have produced certain levels of comfort with cross-boundary transactions.

Public agencies and organizations encounter different approaches as they increasingly operate "outside" government, and they often expend a similar amount of effort to what they use "inside." Network activity requires that public officials connectively engage other organizations or representatives of other organizations. As previously identified this phenomenon has been captured by a number of observers, most cogently by Hubert Saint-Onge and Charles Armstrong (2004) in *The Conductive Organization*, where the importance of collaborative partnerships is at the core:

> The capability to effectively manage complex partnerships is growing in importance as organizations are reconfigured. Organizations are becoming more and more involved in complex value-creation networks, where the boundaries between one organization and another become blurred and functions are integrated. Being able to create and leverage participation in network-designed and -delivered solutions is becoming a critical organizational and leadership capability. Trust fosters this commitment and cements the network partnership. By forming value-creating networks focused on fulfilling customer requirements, true customer calibration can be accomplished. (26)

Whereas this particular reference is to managing businesses through such partnerships, public agencies have also become increasingly conductive as well. Saint-Onge and Armstrong define the *conductive organization* as one "that continuously generates and renews capabilities to achieve breakthrough performance by enhancing the quality and the flow of knowledge and by calibrating its strategy, culture, structure, and systems to the needs of its customers and the marketplace" (179).

To Saint-Onge and Armstrong, the conductive organization operates through a balanced organizational structure, working both horizontally and vertically. It has a cohesive culture and systems, structures, and strategies that support a constructive leadership context. It seeks high-quality internal and external relationships, feeding the creation, management, and use of knowledge. As an inherent part of resolving issues and meeting challenges, its capabilities are enhanced (Saint-Onge and Armstrong 2004, 16). Leadership is key in the conductive organization:

> Leaders articulate the common objectives and values to which the network commits and around which it can coalesce. Control must be replaced by empowerment through self-initiation, with the network members being given the freedom to find the most appropriate route to achieve project goals.
>
> The network will be held accountable for delivering its objectives. Leadership's responsibility is to ensure that systems and structures are in place that enable the members of the network to collaborate, learn, share knowledge, and execute their responsibilities. The network's output is the generation of capabilities. (Saint-Onge and Armstrong 2004, 191)

In such cross-organizational endeavors, leaders are instrumental, particularly those champions who sustain organizational commitment and those alliance managers who enable people to work together efficiently and model trust and collaboration (Holbeche 2005, 179). Leaders, then, are responsible for generating capacities, promoting the flow of knowledge within the organization and with other entities, synchronizing the key collaborating organizations, examining mutual capabilities, and calibrating internal organizing structures to external needs (Esteve et al. 2013).

The Conductive Public Agency

The emergent condition of conductivity for public agencies is illustrated in figures 9.1 and 9.2 (author drawn), concerning hypothetical federal and state agencies that are highly conductive. The first is a US Department of Agriculture

Rural Development (USDA/RD) state program, which provides grant, loan, and technical assistance through its state offices. Most of its loan services are offered by direct service delivery but in partnership with lending institutions (banks, savings and loans, and sometimes with state government–sponsored lending programs). These direct operations are depicted by the core operations circle A and the box B.6 USDA/RD home and facility loans. Figure 9.1 indicates that more conductive activity than "meets the eye" occurs in the core loan program, including links with other federal departments (B.2), many links with state government agencies (B.3), local government links (B.4 and B.5), and numerous NGO links, either in networked partnerships or by contract. It is also important to note that formal network involvement (B.7), which tends to be extensive in the case of USDA/RD, is one of several collaborative linkages. Indeed, USDA/RD is heavily engaged in many forms of networking and other intergovernmental linkages, along with its network participation.

The same would hold for the hypothetical state agency depicted as a unit of a larger, comprehensive human services agency in figure 9.2. In this division the focus is on aging, I/DD, and vocational rehabilitation services—all federal and state programs in operation. This conductive agency also demonstrates its core programs (A) and direct services by contract, particularly in all four programs: for the aging program (A.1) by grants to thirteen Area Agencies on Aging, which purchase services in turn; for vocational rehabilitation programs (A.2), whose state counselors arrange to purchase externally delivered services; for persons with I/DD who require nursing home care (A.3) and are directly contracted; and for I/DD clients in day programs, home supports, supported living, and group homes (A.4), based on a contracted case management gatekeeping function and purchase of services from some eighty-three NGOs.

Beyond direct service organizations, figure 9.2 identifies important federal liaisons with several programs in the US Department of Health and Human Services (Centers for Medicaid, Office of Vocational Rehabilitation, Administration on Aging, Office on Disabilities) and the Department of Justice (B.10). Other key state agencies would be public health (B.8), the office of the parent department secretary (B.7), state attorney general (B.9), and Medicaid policy office (B.1). The unit also operates with numerous standing, external working links, including university affiliations (B.2); advisory boards, study groups, task forces, and networks (B.3); third-party accrediting bodies (B.4); and planning councils and legislative commissions (B.5). The agency also operates one external contract to develop and operate information, accounting, and performance systems (B.6).

This obviously makes the Agency on Aging, Disabilities, and Vocational Rehabilitation highly conductive, with connective work that far exceeds grants, contracts with NGOs, and formal involvement in networks. It includes them all but also requires extensive working interaction and networking

FIGURE 9.1. A Conductive Federal Agency: USDA/RD Office

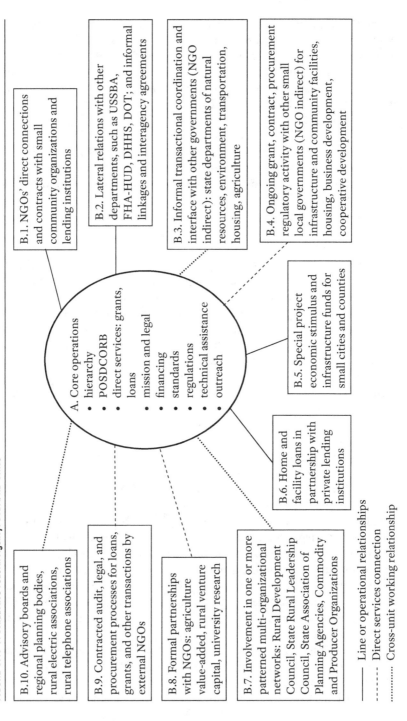

B.1. NGOs' direct connections and contracts with small community organizations and lending institutions

B.2. Lateral relations with other departments, such as USSBA, FHA-HUD, DHHS, DOT; and informal linkages and interagency agreements

B.3. Informal transactional coordination and interface with other governments (NGO indirect): state departments of natural resources, environment, transportation, housing, agriculture

B.4. Ongoing grant, contract, procurement regulatory activity with other small local governments (NGO indirect) for infrastructure and community facilities, housing, business development, cooperative development

A. Core operations
- hierarchy
- POSDCORB
- direct services: grants, loans
- mission and legal
- financing
- standards
- regulations
- technical assistance
- outreach

B.5. Special project economic stimulus and infrastructure funds for small cities and counties

B.6. Home and facility loans in partnership with private lending institutions

B.10. Advisory boards and regional planning bodies, rural electric associations, rural telephone associations

B.9. Contracted audit, legal, and procurement processes for loans, grants, and other transactions by external NGOs

B.8. Formal partnerships with NGOs: agriculture value-added, rural venture capital, university research

B.7. Involvement in one or more patterned multi-organizational networks: Rural Development Council, State Rural Leadership Council, State Association of Planning Agencies, Commodity and Producer Organizations

——— Line or operational relationships

- - - - Direct services connection

·········· Cross-unit working relationship

FIGURE 9.2. A Conductive State Public Agency: Aging, Disabilities, and Vocational Rehabilitation

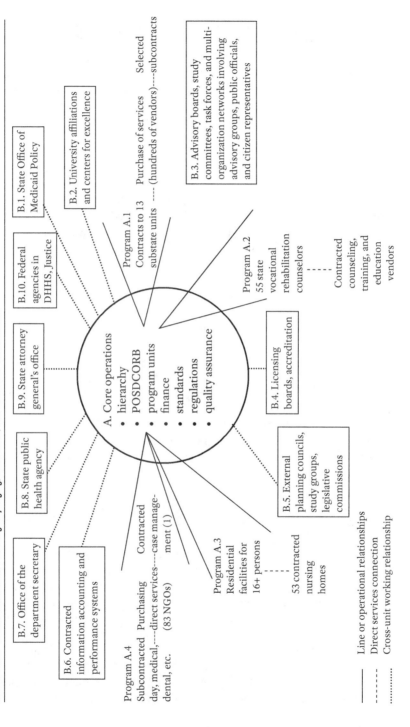

with a host of other agencies, organizations, publics, and—in the situation of program A.4—subcontracted day, medical, dental, and other services. This department, indeed highly conductive and networked in operation, is far more than a hierarchy containing impermeable silos.

Together these internal and external connections better define bureaucracy in the era of IGM by networks and networking. This structure is not unusual for an increasing number of public agencies. Some would argue that to have such external relations and connections is not really new, and that is true. The concept of *boundary spanning*, or the adjustment to constraints or contingencies not controlled by organizations (Thompson 1967) and interorganizational relations (Galbraith 1977) as a managerial activity, reaches back for decades. Most important, James Thompson (1967, 111) reminds us that boundary spanning occurs at points where the task environment is heterogeneous and shifting and requires the exercise of discretion to meet contingencies. Moreover, these highly discretionary jobs are "involved in political processes" as well as boundary-spanning tasks that are necessary for this purpose as managers participate in coalitions (131). To Henry Mintzberg (2013, 27), the management literature has given insufficient attention to lateral relationships in managerial work, yet numerous studies have shown that close to half or more managers interact with external entities "with whom they have no direct reporting relationship." Now not only the existence of linkages but also the degree and intensity of such working or operational conductivity inside and outside of government are relevant. These interactive demands to manage together are what make contemporary IGM operations challenging and require management to take new approaches.

Boundary spanning is a core concept in understanding IGM networking and networks. Standard texts on public organizations like Harold Gortner, Julianne Mahler, and Jeanne Bell Nicholson's (1987) *Organization Theory* conclude the following:

> The boundary spanner's communication links outside the organization relate the organization to its environment. Organizational openness, the degree of information exchange between an organization and its environment, is provided to a considerable degree by boundary-spanning communications. . . .
>
> Boundary-spanning activities are an essential feature of interaction between bureau and environment. They significantly affect the organization's ability either to adapt to or to exploit and control its environment. From a communication standpoint, the boundary-spanning individual plays a liaison role, linking internal bureau networks to external ones. In the sense that they control or filter the flow of communication and information coming into or going out of the organization, they are like gatekeepers. (176)

Today's complex ties would also include bureau-to-bureau connections in this concept.

The Process of Managing in Formalized Networks

Although the network literature base is constantly expanding, our knowledge regarding how managers build multiagency, multi-program, goal-directed networks and operate within them is based on somewhat limited evidence. For example, there is emerging interest in network partners' characteristics in network formulation and their impact on collaborative outcomes (Herranz 2010; Ryu 2014; Kolpakov 2014). As nonhierarchical entities, networks normally involve the exchange of resources and thus are highly based on exchange relations. The problem that managers face is that no readily agreed-on set of dynamically changing functional activities exist that are hierarchical equivalents of standard POSDCORB (planning, organizing, staffing directing, coordinating, reporting, and budgeting) theory, or hierarchical administrative theory (Olsen 2008, 32). To Evert Lindquist (2009, 48) a new set of narratives is needed, including an understanding of disaggregated and loosely coupled, multi-organizational, public service systems. Eugene Bardach (1998) suggests that collaboratives are built on two platforms—one of trust, leadership, and an interactive communications network; the other of creative opportunity, intellectual capital, implemented programs and agencies, and advocacy groups. These two platforms mutually build improved capacity to steer or guide the system toward objectives, which lead to a network that operates subsystems and to continuous learning. Moreover, these functions appear to build on interorganizational equivalents of Peter Senge's (1990) well-known "learning organization," a form of continuous improvement of information and knowledge as jointly applied to problems and challenges.

Walter Kickert and Joop Koppenjan (1997) identify network management as the steering of interaction processes, which comprise three elements: intervention in an existing pattern of relations, consensus building, and problem-solving. Koppenjan and Erik-Hans Klijn (2004, 10) see the interaction process as "searches" in which participants "jointly learn about the nature of the problem, look at the possibility of doing something about it, identify the characteristics of the strategic and institutional context within which the problem-solving develops. Hence, cooperation presupposes learning between actors, crossing the boundaries of organizations, networks and coalitions." Building on these basic ideas, Michael McGuire (2002, 602) suggests that there is both an operational and strategic character to networks and networking that depends on managerial action. Managers' behavior in such goal-directed collaborative activities involves four identifiable processes: activation, framing, mobilizing, and synthesizing.

First, managers bring the partners together to work on problems, thus beginning the interaction:

> One class of behaviors undertaken by network managers is . . . *activation*, which managers in the field suggest may be the most important activity of managing networks. I use the term "activation" to refer to a set of behaviors employed for identifying and incorporating the persons and resources (such as funding, expertise, and legal authority) needed to achieve program goals. The single-organization parallel to activation would be personnel issues of staffing. Activating involves identifying participants for the network and including key stakeholders in the process. . . . The skills, knowledge, and resources of these potential participants must be assessed and tapped into. (McGuire 2002, 602–3)

Next, managers then must provide structure and organize the resulting network:

> Other network management behaviors are employed to help frame the structure and the norms and values of the network as a whole. *Framing* is defined as the behaviors used to arrange and integrate a network structure by facilitating agreement on participants' roles, operating rules, and network values. Like activation, framing is used both during the formation of the network and when network effectiveness diminishes or is suboptimal. Network managers must arrange, stabilize, nurture, and integrate the network structure. Framing involves facilitating the internal structure and position of the participants, as well as influencing the operating rules and the norms of the network. (McGuire 2002, 603)

Then managers strive to hold the network together and keep its elements motivated:

> Network managers must also induce individuals to make and keep a commitment to the network. *Mobilizing* behaviors are used to develop commitment and support for network processes from network participants and external stakeholders. Mobilization in this regard is a common and sometimes ongoing task for achieving network effectiveness. Managers build support by mobilizing organizations and coalitions and by forging an agreement on the role and scope of network operations. (McGuire 2002, 603)

Finally managers build the interactive relationships into productive results.

Managers must also employ *synthesizing* behaviors to create an environment and enhance the conditions for favorable, productive interaction among network participants. One critical behavior of the network manager is to build relationships and interactions that result in achieving the network purpose. The strategies of each network participant and the outcomes of those strategies are influenced by the patterns of relations and interactions that have developed in the network. (McGuire 2002, 603)

These functions, McGuire suggests, are discursive. They do not necessarily operate in sequential order, and they considerably overlap in practice. His four propositions are based in contingency logic as a way to test ideas—particularly, when, why, and how managers undertake these behaviors as they strategically match behaviors within their governing contexts. Originally they were distilled from a large-scale study of local governments and their economic development activity (Agranoff and McGuire 2003), and they have been empirically tested in a number of settings (e.g., Page 2008; McGuire and Agranoff 2014).

Managing in a network therefore means working with and going beyond the hierarchical formalities and rules to develop collaborative-based processes and operations that hold such endeavors together, break down the work tasks, and operate based on joint strategies. In other words, networks have structures. This is where the participants—for example, various agency and organization staff, champions, political supporters, and a technical core—come in, giving networks the needed stability and order to command respect, identify problems, and allow knowledge work to proceed. Another plank in this platform is the network's strategic operations as problems are investigated and solved. This involves problem task forces and work groups or technical subcommittees. Only this entity, which develops as a result of work that is concrete and collectively agreed on, keeps people serving with others outside of their own organizations. The network therefore needs organizational representatives to be more than signatory participants; they must delve into and deliberate on the technical work. Moreover, today's electronic contact through email, video chat and call services, web posting, and so on, keeps connections among the physically distant participants from multiple organizations more regularized and involves more players than before these electronic venues existed (Agranoff 2012, ch. 6).

An often overlooked aspect of network operation is the network participants' regular interactions with the elected politicians who authorize programs, can raise alternative solutions, and are normally the ultimate decision makers. It is the political officials who "initiate the process directed at creating a variety of directions toward solutions that do justice to the multi-interpretability and complexity of the problem situation" (Klijn and

BOX 9.1

- In today's complex intergovernmental arrangements, the law enables some networks to recognize overlapping challenges in given policy areas. Other networks are voluntarily vested by the area's government and NGO representatives, who recognize that some problems require concentrated efforts across their boundaries, missions, and jurisdictions.
- Administrative officials now network as they conduct their managerial tasks related to conductivity or boundary spanning. These activities add to but do not necessarily replace the role of the public agency.
- As government and NGO representatives work jointly in networks, their process is guided by their search for useful knowledge and attempts to solve cross-boundary problems.
- Participating agencies and organizations incorporate the execution of network agreements and actions in their normal processes.

Koppenjan 2000, 383). Carrying out the various roles of networks—activation, framing, mobilizing, and synthesizing—also depends on these strategic interactions. Together, these social forces are important for developing collaborative capacity, instigating changes, and engendering "cooperative dispositions and mutual understanding of the individuals who are trying to work together in a common task" (Bardach 1998, 307). Thus, in many ways networks are self-managed *collaborarchies* (Agranoff 2007c, 123), which Chris Silvia (2011, 70) finds are rooted in five interactive pillars: teamwork, resources, understanding, stakeholder support, and trust. Indeed, networks are clearly not randomly or haphazardly organized or structured, nor do they necessarily work without definable processes.

Comprehensive IGM Networks: The Rural Council Movement

A sustained rural development initiative in the 1990s emerged from various administrations and has not disappeared as subsequent administrations left office. According to several of its participants, the effort was an example "of what can be achieved through a modest investment, coupled with determined action to bring about a new way of conducting the public's business" (Radin et al. 1996, 3). The initiative was the creation of state-level rural development councils (RDCs), which would coordinate rural development efforts among federal departments and agencies and establish collaborative relationships with state and local governments and the private sector. The initiative established six elements: a President's Council on Rural America, a Working Group on Rural Development as a subgroup of the cabinet-level White House Economic Policy Council, a Rural Development Technical Assistance Center and Hotline, a rural development demonstration program, and an effort to target rural development programs on specific activities.

The RDCs were then set up as pilot programs in eight states: Kansas, Maine, Mississippi, Oregon, South Carolina, South Dakota, Texas, and Washington. By mid-1994, despite a change of administration, RDCs were operating in twenty-nine states and were being organized in ten others. In addition, the National Rural Development Council—a Washington, DC-based interagency activity that also began in 1990—had representatives from sixty agencies involved in the process. This movement merged two extant perspectives—the enhancement of IGR and IGM and the promotion of more integrated rural development policy (Radin et al. 1996, 2–5).

Each state's RDC, in effect, represented systematic efforts at IGM networks and networking. They broke down the barriers that impeded not only policy and program action but also inter-level public and private action, providing fora to establish collaborative strategies and outcomes. Thus, the focus of the RDCs was on collaborative problem-solving. As networks the RDCs focused on the following activities (Radin et al. 1996, 155):

- Changing rural development policy
- Statutory relief
- Regulatory relief
- Management improvement systems
- Demonstrations and development projects
- Database development
- Community information improvements
- New funding sources
- Cooperative ventures
- Outreach activities
- Leadership development

Rarely did RDCs set out to change basic rural policy or to seek major new program initiatives. Their primary instruments appeared to be seeking existing program relief, improving the operation of programs, developing databases, providing information, and mounting experiments to assist in rural development.

As networks the RDCs engaged in numerous IGM activities. As the council's study revealed, they included (1) strategic planning, leadership development, and visioning; (2) direct and indirect intergovernmental contacts, including information seeking, guidance, and interpretations of standards; (3) acquisition and administration of grants; (4) regulation handling and management, from learning about applications to seeking implementation adjustments; (5) working through waivers, model program efforts, and related forms of special programming while trying to advance the program's purpose over impediments; (6) joint or collaborative policy-making, involving shared investigation, strategy development, and decision-making; and (7) use of network-wide or council-wide state and efficiency approaches that represent intergovernmental cooperation, such as services consolidation, decentralization of services, cooperation agreements among entities, and governmental consolidations (Radin et al. 1996, 181–84).

As formal networks, the RDCs, of course, are both vertical and horizontal intergovernmental bodies in that they include representatives of all three levels of government and the private sector. Their focus is problem oriented; but as they are charged with handling rural development, one would have to say that their potential scope is broad since their policy focus involves so many programs. Clearly, their primary network domain includes programs of an intergovernmental nature, meaning their managerial activities demonstrate how certain problems can be cooperatively solved and some impediments can be removed.

The RDCs' most essential work is that of convening the actors. An initial and often necessary task or step is to get the right persons involved in a problem arena or in course of action to meet. Rural development clearly has multiple stakeholders: the community or communities impacted, local governments, and the private sector; statewide nonprofits and interest groups; and state and federal governments. The RDCs provide fora for bringing all these actors together. They are particularly helpful in convening federal and state officials, who often are called on to make critical program adjustments, and in assembling local officials and the private sector with state and federal officials to network and to explore problems of rural development. The RDC network movement provides a living template for comprehensive IGM action within a given policy arena.

IGM Network Management and Network Leadership

How does one begin to take on the emergent challenges of managing externally with other agencies that have varied network participants? What are the approaches and techniques that support the need to operate externally and conductively? At least six themes appear to be relevant for public agency administrators who strive to meet the "working with others" challenge of networking and working in networks: organizing conductive structures, broadening the scope of jurisdictional politics, promoting and partnering in networks, building creative bases for human resources, handling joint knowledge and its management, and constructing communities of practice. Since each is derived from the adaptive management literature that deals with collaborative management, the themes are briefly identified with major references that apply to IGM.

Organizing Conductive Structures

Agencies working on public problems that are heavily involved intergovern-mentally have already considered or need to contemplate the many boundary-spanning organizing moves indicated by Saint-Onge and Armstrong (2004, ch. 8): creating cross-functional teams, establishing functional as opposed to departmental units, and broadening performance criteria across units. Several states, for example, originally set up Medicaid policy offices to oversee pay-ments processing, but now Medicaid also funds a broad array of medically related services for the elderly, the physically disabled, I/DD persons, and other social groups that cut across several programs in different units. Therefore, these Medicaid offices do more than approve eligibility and write checks. They work with external providers in creating databases and information systems, oversee federally required performance expectations, study potential linkage systems, and network with larger providers and state associations interactively to assess and improve joint managerial concerns expected by Medicaid.

The Medicaid office also uses an enhanced form of contract management. Contracting for services involves complex forms of linkages that require planning for performance assessment, staff training, evaluating contractor staff capability and contractor financial management activity, and under-standing contractor and subcontractor relationships and policies (Brown, Potoski, and Van Slyke 2009; Romzek and Johnston 2002). Also, emerging concerns include quality improvement (measuring the client's achievement of goals against the program aims) and contract data reporting as additional challenges (Bradley and Moseley 2007).

These emergent Medicaid functions suggest important organizing themes. First, since intergovernmental work is both highly multi-actor dependent and connective, it almost always invokes the need for coordinated federal, state, and sometimes local programming and multiple external provider activity. Second, intergovernmental work has a policy and programming dimension that combines regular federal program input with state administration and regulation, but the policy now must incorporate the reality of its implemen-tation by new armies of providers and contractors. Third, each connection involves working understandings and assessments from at least two levels of government and a series of NGOs, and they must be made *before* services, which are configured on the basis of extensive interaction, meet clients. Finally, the public agency now must deal with heavy doses of shared admin-istration in a service arrangement and assessment protocol that is replacing the end-of-program reviews of an earlier era or some external or contracted-out service delivery oversight role. This style of networking involves more "outside" agency work on shared information, knowledge, and assessments and less "inside," or top-down, running of programs, with IGM emphasis on reaching agreements as well as on giving direction.

Broadening Interjurisdictional Politics

Understanding and using political knowledge have always been part of the intergovernmental game. In the 1980s the author's study of metropolitan human services bodies revealed that "governmental actors appeared to be successful when they recognized the political nature of their task. In the process of working out solutions to problems, politics—both partisan politics and interorganizational politics—must be explicitly acknowledged" (Agranoff 1986, 7). A contemporary example from the Metro High School in Columbus illustrates the pervasiveness of the political factor. The network's original designers wanted Metro designated for students gifted and talented in STEM subjects only, but the sixteen superintendents protested that they were unwilling to see all their best students transfer. Holding to this design aim threatened the entire network, so a more modest compromise of "ratioed" admissions was reached. With externalization and operation in networks, the game of interorganizational politics is notably expanded to include not only new service provider agencies but also a host of industry representatives who are the administrators as well as the program advocates for their service providers' members and affiliates.

The politics of IGM today includes that of the long-standing federal agency (for example, the state or regional office), state program administration, grantee, contractor, and much more, inasmuch as the delivery system has become part of the "managerial political subsystem." In the case of I/DD in many states, network leadership at the state level is assumed by state officials, legislative leaders, industry lead associations, and statewide advocacy groups working together on problems, solutions, and services operations. One could make a similar lineup of potential political actors in most other policy arenas—for example, in emergency management, transportation, economic development, and rural development. They cannot be factored out of the network equation. As long as this type of IGM operates via networking, it must be understood that the politics of support groups and delivery agents are blended into management (Agranoff 2014), raising constant needs for monitoring the actors' "political radar."

Promoting and Partnering in Networks

One emergent managerial transformation to government agencies is an expectation of a shift from the more passive grant-related review roles of earlier years to active network promotion and involvement. Network activities build on previous procedures involving preparing and reviewing grant applications, informing potential grantees and checking awardees on legal compliance, and overseeing grantee program intent, program and fiscal auditing, and the like (see chapters 3 and 4 in this volume). Externalization in networks brings the government and the NGO manager directly into much closer operation (Kapucu and Hu 2016).

For example, previously if there was no locally generated controversy, then it was acceptable for public involvement provisions to unfold at the community level and be included in a written summary report on the process that was forwarded to compliance officials for review. Now that process involves delivery agencies, some of which are in direct competition with one another and some of which have different missions, public and NGO managerial passiveness is no longer appropriate. Dealing with mission incompatibility, for instance, can become a political issue. As the I/DD and stewardship contracting example in chapter 7 suggests, networks are complex and do more than carry out the guidelines established by funder governments. Actors, including executants, participate in operationalization and make policy program adjustments in the field as they approach problems. It is at this stage that the (legal and other) input of government must be injected, promoted, and often protected. Hence, the government manager now not only is involved in IGM networking and all its interactive moves but also is expected to be *in the network* both as an organizer and as a party to any agreements reached. This is clearly the situation that Julia Wondolleck and Steven Yaffee (2000) found in their study of environmental collaboration, where federal and state administrators were routinely and directly involved in IGM networks, normally in some lead role.

Intergovernmental networks need to be held accountable for delivering on their objectives, and their leadership's responsibility is to ensure that systems and structures are in place that enable the members of the network to collaborate, learn, share knowledge, and execute their responsibilities. In this mix one core support element is the perception, development, and maintenance of trust across organizational lines. Summarizing the literature, Peter Oomsels and Geert Bouckaert (2014) define *trust* as "a subjective evaluation made by boundary spanners regarding their intentional and behavioral suspension of vulnerability on the basis of expectations of a trustee organization in particular interorganizational interactions" (600). Such trust is said to have both functionalities and disfunctionalities in public administration.

Leaders are also important, particularly those champions who often are the heads of key government agencies. They represent and sustain organizational commitment, along with alliance managers (heads of major organizations), who help people work together efficiently and are role models for trust and collaboration (Holbeche 2005, 179). Such network leaders are responsible for generating capacities, promoting the flow of knowledge within their organizations and between organizations, synchronizing the key organizations, examining mutual capabilities, and calibrating organizing structures to external needs. Finally, for agency staff program managers working across boundaries, this set of skills is essential: a flair for dealing with ambiguity, an open and flexible attitude toward different management styles, a capacity to build on another's expertise, an experimenting spirit, a competence to create a negotiated and understood means of communication and decision-making, and an ability to build trust and to take judicious risks. In the management literature, these faculties constitute the working manager's collaborative skill set, which serves as a well-established repertoire for working across organizations and jurisdictions (Holbeche 2005, 180–81).

Leadership in networks and networking also calls for an integrative style of operation, bringing in multiple actions and nodes with multiple linkages, while working across boundaries. Examining some thirty-five such behaviors in emergency management, Silvia and McGuire (2010) classified themes as *people, task,* and *organization oriented.* In this regard they found the most important leadership behaviors proved to be treating all "network members as equals," sharing information among network members, and creating trust among network members (275). Overall, the integration behaviors of network leaders among the 417 county-level emergency managers studied proved they were less apt to be task masters and generally avoided making assignments, setting expectations, and scheduling work to be done. In addition, they found these IGM behaviors revealed substantial differences between leading within one's own organization and leading in networks, demonstrating that some leadership behaviors are more central to integrative leadership whereas others are more central to agency leadership (see also Bryson and Crosby 1992; Edner and McDowell 2002).

Building Creative Bases for Human Resources

Network champions and alliance managers require operating staff members— namely, program managers and technical specialists—who can go beyond their focused program interests and narrow specializations and work across the boundaries of their jurisdiction or organization to investigate difficult problems and discover and adapt solutions. At one time, a specialized professional ability in a given program was the primary concern for managers in intergovernmental roles. Mental health and disability professionals in psychiatry, psychology, social work, rehabilitation, or special education were key operatives. Engineers and planners who administered transportation, public works, planning departments, and so on, were also highly valued. This is unlikely to change in great measure when staffing specialized programs; however, now these positions face new demands. Networking and working in networks involve what Robert Reich (1991, 229–32) calls symbolic analytic work, where people interact more and learn from one another. He identifies four critical skills for today's type of problem-solving: the capacity for abstraction; the faculty for systems thinking, or seeing reality as a system of causes and consequences; the willingness to engage in experimentation; and the ability to collaborate. To Thomas Davenport (2005, 65), symbolic analytic work is crucial in this interdependent world because this most recent phase of managerial work has "an interactive, collaborative approach to work in which patterns (of observation and supervision) are more difficult to discern. They may deny that this work has any structure at all—'every day is different.'"

The guidelines for supervising this type of knowledge worker are also different. According to Davenport (2005, 192–201), they entail (1) having managers participate in the work instead of overseeing it, (2) organizing communities rather than organizing hierarchies, (3) retaining workers rather than hiring and firing them, (4) building knowledge skills rather than manual skills, (5) assessing invisible knowledge achievements instead of evaluating visible job performance, (6) building knowledge-friendly cultures instead of ignoring culture, (7) fending off bureaucracy rather than supporting it, and (8) relying on a variety of human resources, wherever they may be located, instead of relying exclusively on internal personnel. The new intergovernmental manager thus represents the aims and requirements of the home agency's program, builds the interagency community, and works with staff to create new knowledge-based solutions.

Handling Joint Knowledge and Its Management

Learning—that is, both knowledge acquisition and its utilization—is at the core of network management. A great deal of the interactive work in networks among intergovernmental partners normally involves deliberating and seeking new ways to reach solutions to the most intractable problems (Leach et al. 2014). It requires not only the best problem-solving work from managers and specialists representing different organizations but also the best prior work of participating organizations in designing and operating various forms of knowledge. For example, in the area of environmental management, effective, interactive multiparty land-use planning and zoning normally follow extensive studies of regulatory policy, current use, environmental threats, agricultural practices, water quality management, and many other areas of information (Margerum 2011).

The key is the handling of relevant knowledge, "a fluid mix of framed experience, values, contextual information, and expert insight that provides a framework for evaluating and incorporating new experiences and information" (Davenport and Prusak 2000, 5). The aim of knowledge management is "identifying, extracting, and capturing 'knowledge assets'" to fully exploit them to accomplish some goal (Newell et al. 2002, 16). Knowledge is broader, deeper, and richer than data or information. It is highly mutable and highly contextual but has greater utility in that it incorporates experience, insight, and contextual information. Knowledge is thus more than facts or data. It is within people; thus, knowledge is an asset of the human capital that is so important in contemporary activities, including all types of management. Indeed, knowledge is intrinsically human. "Knowledge derives from information as information derives from data. If information is to become knowledge, humans must do all the work" (Davenport and Prusak 2000, 6). In effect, knowledge is both a process and an outcome. In the public sector, we use knowledge to solve problems and thus add some public value (Moore 1995).

Interagency networks in the intergovernmental sphere are important knowledge management vehicles. Knowledge production normally depends heavily on collaborative action, or what social network analysts call connectivity. Problem-solving and creative discovery hinge heavily on dynamic interaction among people, particularly at strategic points in social networks (Cross et al. 2003, 8). Michael Schrage (1995, 33) defines *collaborative activity* as shared creation—that is, people working interactively on a process, product, or event. As one network activist related, "Workgroups on various technical issues is [*sic*] the way we learn and grow; integrate new people into our process ... and while we don't codify process we rely on the institutional knowledge of a lot of people" (Agranoff 2007c, 173).

In a study of fourteen government agency and NGO networks, Agranoff (2007a, ch. 7) found that most followed a three-step order for managing interagency knowledge when looking for existing information and converting data to explicit knowledge: look for informal or tacit approaches used, create jointly derived knowledge management programs, and use derived knowledge in the participating agencies and programs or for the network as a whole. Public agencies and NGOs have a huge "knowledge stake" in this game, because the sources of data and information are widely distributed in the network, influence actions, and guide many decisions. In the studied networks, intergovernmental actors sought new ways to discover, organize, and adapt approaches to the thorny problems that they were addressing.

Constructing Communities of Practice

In another form of shared creation, network participants must convert knowledge into practical interorganizational solutions. Building high-quality intergovernmental relationships now comes, in part, through establishing interdisciplinary groups of problem solvers. Interacting agencies commonly deliberate by building communities of practice with people available from different disciplines who have shared outlooks. For example, the USDA/RD state program office studied in Agranoff (2007a, ch. 7) broadened its loan, grant, and housing development programs for small towns and included participation in working groups with state government and NGO officials in such key problem areas as value-added agriculture/agribusiness, adaptation and transfer of technology, and venture capital sourcing for business development. To a great extent, these rural development groups operate as a community of practice.

Etienne Wenger (2000) defines *communities* as self-organizing systems that share the capacity to create and use knowledge through informal learning and mutual engagement. Most communities are self-organized and bring in new knowledge bearers when needed from wherever they can be found. With regard to intergovernmental programs, they normally involve participants from all three levels of government and the nongovernmental sector. For example, the thirty-plus state intergovernmental RDCs, which started in the late 1980s, operate similarly to communities of practice (Radin et al. 1996). In Indiana, the HCBS Medicaid Waiver Rate Reform Workgroup has operated for several years to mutually discover and reach reimbursement payment levels. Maintaining such communities, however, requires concerted effort to keep the different types of knowledge bearers. Retaining busy people to solve important public problems, by calling on their experience and know-how in an interdisciplinary manner, poses yet another emerging challenge.

Peter Haas (1992, 3) suggests that these individuals can represent a variety of disciplines and share normative and principled beliefs that provide a value-based rationale for social action. They also tend to share causal beliefs, notions of validity, and a common policy focus. Such an epistemic community thus normally works to produce various forms of consensual knowledge (55). Even in the face of anomalous data, the community may suspend judgment to maintain its scientific legitimacy and, for the moment, its power resources. For example, Mark Imperial's (2004, 17) study of collaboration in three estuary management programs found that each group of interdisciplinary actors, most of whom were technical staff, was able to not only reach key mitigation agreements based on shared goals but also to secure jurisdictional commitments, to synthesize monitoring information on threatening conditions, and to establish joint reporting processes that assessed the partners' collective programs regarding shared goals.

Such experiences demonstrate that interdisciplinary communities can be important knowledge sustainers for two reasons: They can have a disproportionate effect on organized learning and behavior, and even though such participants may not always be the most powerful decision makers, they "are well situated to provide a driving logic for cooperation" (Thomas 2003, 41). These communities are often extended to what are known in the literature as network administrative organizations (NAO). It has also been found that the street-level administrators—in this case, teachers—are influenced by the network structure and composition within which they find themselves. They are not totally independent responses (Siciliano 2017). NAOs govern some networks and their activities, operating primarily on their interactive bargaining power. One clear measure of the NAO's strength is whether it is mandated or voluntary. The former is more "contractually" based (Saz-Carranza, Salvador, and Albareda 2016).

Thus, it appears one must position IGM activities outward for managing across all organizations. Who among the many potential IGM actors might be asked to take the lead and be supportive of these networking activities? Figure 9.3 looks at the possibilities. All six identified IGM challenges are arrayed by the different potentially involved actors, ranging from governmental agencies to operations or service delivery bodies, including associations and research aims. Potential involvement clearly varies, but two important conclusions stand out. First, government agencies, particularly at the state level, have primarily potential leading roles in meeting each of the six challenges. Second, service delivery agencies—nonprofit and for profit—also carry important primary or supportive roles, particularly in execution. Figure 9.4 makes clear that a multi-stakeholder host of actors, at least eight distinct types, may play some role in interactively promoting

FIGURE 9.3. Network IGM Features and Practices

Feature	Practice
1. Organizing conductive structures	Positioned for external work, internal operations recognize externalized direct services and their nonhierarchical structures for developing, monitoring, and assessing partnering arrangements.
2. Broadening interjurisdictional politics	Familiarity with and engagement in subsystems of politics and externalized program operations are now fused concepts; one must know the network as well as the program and requirements.
3. Promoting and partnering in networks	The public agency executive becomes the network champion and supplies the alliance manager, who assumes responsibility for rule compliance and other oversight activities.
4. Building creative bases for human resources	The new intergovernmental manager represents the home agency, builds an interagency community, and participates in the creation of new solutions.
5. Handling joint knowledge, knowledge management	Network participants seek new ways to use learning and applied practice to find, organize, and adapt ways that interagency problems may be solved.
6. Constructing communities of practice	Intergovernmental managers work together to discover solutions, to administer programs interactively, and to resolve difficult problems.

FIGURE 9.4. IGM Network Actors and Actions—Administering Agencies

Actions	Federal administrative agencies	State agencies	Industry associations	Nonprofit delivery agencies	For-profit delivery agencies	Administrative support vendors	Citizen groups, associations	Research planning and study bodies, universities
1. Organizing conductive structures	N	P	P	S	S	S	P	N
2. Interjurisdictional politics	P	P	S	S	S	P	S	N
3. Promoting and partnering in networks	P	P	P	P	P	S	P	P
4. Building creative human resource bases	P	P	S	P	P	P	S	P
5. Joint knowledge, knowledge management	S	P	P	P	P	S	S	P
6. Communities of practice	S	P	P	P	P	S	S	P

P=Primary role in the network of actors
S=Supportive role in the network of actors
N=No or minor role in the network of actors

IGM by network. In sum, it points to the complex challenges of sharing across boundaries, creating new collaborative cultures, and empowering staff (Tapscott and Williams 2010, 344–57).

Network Interoperability

When networks go beyond reaching agreements on a course of action, they normally need to pay attention to a number of implementation steps. Participating organizations must go beyond sequential operations and work at their interfaces to apply the needed knowledge for actual service delivery or problem resolution. These networked undertakings have been identified under the rubric of interoperability (IOp). As a core aspect of collaborative management, *interoperability* has been defined as reciprocal communication and accommodation to reach interactive policy and programming (Jenkins 2006, 321). IOp is also part of what one might call meta-networking, where management operations and programs interface.

For an example related to emergency management, Charles Wise (2006) identifies how communities network with the federal, state, and local governments while working with NGOs to make their policies and procedures interactively serve similar or common aims—that is, to avoid the more devastating effects of disasters like floods, hurricanes, and forest fires. IOp also became known with the serious Amtrak derailment in mid-2015 that led to eight deaths and multiple injuries. The investigation showed they might have been prevented had automated safety mechanisms using IOp principles been installed.

BOX 9.2

- The process of investigating network problems and finding workable solutions does not remove politics from the enterprise. It pervades all stages, including the execution, or operational, process.
- Network management involves integrating approaches that maximize values such as participation, community building, knowledge seeking, and human resources. Most important, this knowledge development should tap collective experiences, values, and contextual information and convert it to new experiences.
- Interactive network operations usually need to be integrated beyond sequencing into interoperable forms—that is, adapted strategies or reciprocal communications and accommodation to reach interactive policy and programming.
- Network organizing is similar to cross-departmental management in single organizations, including employing cross-functional teams, setting up multi-agency units, designating liaison officers, and utilizing cross-unit records of decision, agreement, and joint data management.

A key government report for US Department of Homeland Security concludes that the principal challenge in developing effective IOp communications is not technical but cultural and organizational (Jenkins 2004b). The report outlines three principal challenges: clearly identifying and defining the problem; establishing national interoperability performance goals and standards that balance nationwide standards with the flexibility to address differences in state, regional, and local needs and conditions; and defining the roles of the federal, state, and local governments and other entities in addressing interoperable needs. These points represent the quintessential issues of IGM networks in their operational stages.

The core elements of network IOp are similar: establishing structure, developing management strategies, identifying and deploying resources, devising policies and procedures, and redeploying partners' resources. Wise (2006, 313) concludes that IOp efforts need to engage in "adaptive models" whose work includes defining and articulating common outcomes, establishing reinforcing or joint strategies, identifying needs and leveraging resources, agreeing on agency roles and responsibilities, establishing compatible policies and procedures, developing cross-agency monitoring mechanisms, reinforcing agency and individual accountability, and involving an array of intergovernmental and NGO actors. In the arena of Internet interoperability, for example, the work of the Internet Engineering Task Force dates back to the 1980s. Its mission is to draft Internet protocols that eventually lead to common standards. In its processes, agreement "does not involve formal voting but is based on what has long been termed in the ITEF as 'rough consensus and working code,'" which is developed through a series of working groups (DeNardis 2014, 69). In his report on developing interoperability, Jenkins (2006, 321) calls for structures and processes "that provide incentives and rewards for collaboration, consultation, and support for implementing key goals."

The use of IOp extends well beyond the Internet, emergency management, and disaster response and recovery. For example, the Denver area's MPO has put a great deal of emphasis on planning for land use, growth control, and coordination of local use of space, balanced with multimodal transport, while using a consensus-based IOp approach (Margerum 2011). Also, with few exceptions, Medicaid-funded programs are normally operated by the states through contracts and purchases of services—ranging from externalized and contracted case management to a series of subcontracts for medically related direct services (e.g., dental, vision, physical therapy) that buttress the work of primary private health care agencies and practitioners—all of which must be connected around the client (Thompson 2012). In another example, since the mid-1990s, CALFED, a federal-state partnership, has evolved into an operating multi-sector effort at safeguarding water quality that emphasizes science-based standards. It has attempted the difficult task of integrating the Sacramento River and San Joaquin River basins while looking at operating problems and attempting to deal with large water suppliers (Kallis, Kiparsky, and Norgaard 2010). Finally the author's involvement in the Metro High School network found IOp to be an integral part of the project's planning and operational phases (Kolpakov, Agranoff, and MeGuire 2016). While the interest in IOp is quite recent in focus and understanding, it is based on an awareness that interdependency has become formalized. Interdependency must often go to the next step beyond "planning," where implementing operations involves multiple levels of governments and organizations.

How Do Networks Perform?

The public administration journals notably feature articles and research studies on whether networks do the job(s) they are expected to perform (e.g., Henderson and Bromberg 2015; Wang 2016). Network performance involves unique challenges because networks have mixed structures, many of which remain operational by command and control. In network analysis Christopher Koliba (2014, 90) points to three features in the "black box of network management capacity": network structure determinants, performance management analysis, and organizational learning and knowledge management analysis. (See also Koliba, Campbell, and Zia 2011; Moynahan 2008; Meier and O'Toole 2003).

Taken together, Koliba (2014, 98) proposes that network performance be viewed as combining "a network and systems logic that distinguishes between network structures and network management roles, performance management functions, and the integration of them into a knowledge management and learning context." He continues:

> The picture of network performance provided here is one predicated on the assumption that governance networks are complex adaptive systems. A complex adaptive system is, "one whose component parts interact with sufficient intricacy that they cannot be predicted by standard linear equations; so many variables are at work in the system that its overall behavior can only be understood as an emergent consequence of the holistic sum of all the myriad behaviors embedded within" (Levy 1993, 34). Network structures, network managers' actions, the uses of performance data, and the capacity of networks to learn from performance data provide a basic architecture for describing network performance as an integral feature of a complex system. These systems are stochastic, meaning that they are inherently nondeterminant; e.g., nonlinear. (Koliba 2014, 98–99)

Koliba concludes that when networks are viewed as being complex and dynamic, the challenge of nonlinearity of systems are present, combinations of variables have multiplier effects, and both positive and negative feedback loops exist. This type of nonlinearity may be captured by computer simulation using modeling social network analysis and qualitative comparative analysis. In this respect the nonlinear approach can incorporate all these interrelated features and focus on both structures and functions and on how "performance knowledge flows, and how complex systems evolve, adapt, and perform" (100).

Will Networks Become Bureaucracies?

Although networks represent horizontal parts of organizations, some increasingly perform administrative functions for the collective, so to speak. Indeed, some network activity is clearly bureaucratic, as are statutory bodies like the regional planning organizations and metropolitan planning organizations. They represent multiple organizations with statutory authority. For example, the MPO's responsibility for preparing the transportation improvement plan is based heavily on staff-prepared and drafted information. While most of the larger MPOs thus have extensive planning staff and clerical operations and are hierarchically organized, their ultimate decisions and plans are formed by boards representing multiple intergovernmental actions. Bureaucratization would bring the opportunity for more standard organizational and managerial activities to networks (Klijn 2008). This at least raises the question of whether networks, or at least some, will become hierarchical bureaucracies.

If one maintains the definitional provision that networks involve parts of organizations and that most administration is shared among partners, even of staff, then networks such as MPOs do evolve into administrative functioning yet remain nonhierarchical in important decision-making. On this point they offer the smaller prospect that they will become bureaucracies despite some aspects of bureaucratization, particularly when their general policy-making is nonhierarchical. This is not to conclude that at some point a network cannot be "converted" to a bureaucratic agency—for example, an office of rural programs in a state that supersedes an RDC or a "transportation administration" that has the final say on a transportation improvement plan. In this sense, where networks may go next is not clear.

Finally, if networks do at some point evolve into bureaucracies, two issues may exacerbate current problems of decision-making by networks. Will networks' bureaucratic structures further remove a step in deciding on potential actions—that is, the involvement of public stakeholders in network decision and courses of action? To some, networks already do not foster stakeholder cooperation, particularly with "tension between the horizontal accountability processes of these interactive governance mechanisms and the vertical accountability procedures involved in classical representative democracy" (Klijn 2008, 519). The second issue relates to implementation. Most network agreements, plans, and decisions are operationally controlled by the participating agencies. Will emergent bureaucracies handle most of the operations, or will they remain shared among participating agencies?

Key Learning Points

Involvement in networks and acts of networking accelerate the interactive component of IGM. This activity involves recognizing and dealing with the complexities of many involved agencies, actors, and programs, since problems or the scope of agencies rarely fall neatly into the silos and compartments of different organizations involved in the public sector. The silos and organizations remain, but they increasingly interface by networking for less complex or intermittent issues and by formal networks when they are interacting continuously across.

Managing in networks entails extending boundary-spanning management and external relations. In networks it involves not only silos and hierarchies but also interactive knowledge development, problem identification, and mutual solutions. In IGM it means working within many legal considerations, political forces, and agency missions. Somehow these forces must be dealt with when approaching interactive problems.

Interoperability in network management becomes essential when the programs, policies, or services of one network-involved organization are affected by another. At these points reciprocal, as opposed to sequential, operation is required. Interoperability means identifying mutual problems, establishing goals and standards, and clearly defining roles to meet problem needs.

Key Practice Points

To network is to meet the challenge of understanding and operating within new frameworks: managing externally and nonhierarchically, dealing with additional mixes of politics and administration, promoting and operating across organizations, collaborating in knowledge-based management, and handling continuous interdisciplinary communities. In addition, these new and demanding skill sets related to crossing boundaries and program rules and standards involve accepting buy-in from multiple stakeholders, allocating and reallocating multi-organizational resources, and handling management, performance, and accountability in network structures and decisions

(Ritchie 2013, 3–4). These IGM network concerns must be "moved in" along-side traditional public administration concerns.

Networks and networking activity operate alongside practices of bureaucratic or hierarchical organizations. Bureaucracies nevertheless continue to play important roles as networks proliferate. As functions have been added, the traditional hierarchies of the bureaucracy have changed. Johan Olsen (2006) concludes that bureaucracy is indeed still with us, embedded in democratic-constitutive principles and procedural rationality while coexisting with market and network forms, though it faces "different challenges, command[s] different resources and [is] embedded in different political and administrative traditions" (18). Bureaucracy, in a sense, needs to come to grips with exponential externalization; it must adapt to increased operation between those markets and networks that it now confronts on a regular basis. Bureaucracies are faced with the challenges of becoming conductive.

Managerial work, with the rise of networking and networks, places added expectations on managers. With the network process being both internal and external, key resources are often found outside one's organizational domain. Along with routines of connecting organizations, the missions and normal strategies may be, and often are, incompatible. To network or to become part of a formalized network then, one must call on new managerial knowledge. Its application, even in early stages of development, requires high levels of interaction and mutual problem identification and problem-solving.

Conclusion

Managing in the era of the network has ratcheted up IGM's interactive component. As Timothy Conlan and Paul Posner conclude, "Policy challenges and the resources needed to address them are not the preserve of a single level of government.... Accordingly, the programmatic and fiscal fortunes of all levels of government have become more intertwined and interdependent than ever before" (2008, 2). This is true not only with fiscal aid programs but also with regulation, particularly management-based regulation, which is involved at multiple stages of the process (Coglianese and Lazer 2003). Consequently, IGM has embarked on a new era in which more and more—public and nonpublic—programming appear to be linked in some way. The network concept in IGM is moving alongside that of hierarchical interfaces.

The network challenge encompasses understanding and operating within new and program frameworks: new skills are required related to crossing boundaries (Ritchie 2013, 3–4). These skills must be "moved in" to accommodate IGM alongside more traditional public administration concerns. If intergovernmental actors in earlier times thought their job was difficult, they should see what their contemporaries are now facing while wrestling with networking and its dynamics.

The field of public administration, particularly IGM, must therefore pay considerably more attention to the changing external or conductive role of the public manager. For the administrator in the conductive agency, it means more than reading the rules and regulations, listening at hearings, engaging in information exchanges, dealing with politically charged advocates and adversaries, or reading project reports. It involves working together to create knowledge-based public dialogue and to reach mutually arrived-at solutions to problems of mutual concern. Calibration of external information, concerns, and needs is now part of a regularized connectivity through interactive, joint problem-resolution processes. In today's form of IGM, conductive public agencies work primarily with NGO administrators on calibration, knowledge, strategy, and implementation—all collaborative processes.

CONCLUSION

The Past and Future of Intergovernmental Management

This conclusion not only ties the four IGM strands together but also identifies future areas of concern. It opens with an overview of the four approaches to understanding IGM from the four perspectives of the public management process. The interactive roles of governments and nongovernment actors are then examined from the perspective of NGOs and public bureaucracies. Reflecting an important subtheme of this volume, while they may have changed, government has not hollowed out; instead, it is transforming. The next steps in IGM follow: facing complexity, meeting the challenge of interoperability, handling digital issues, assessing the role of open-source technology, determining its public value, engaging the democratic political domain that remains in IGM, identifying the potential global impacts on IGM, and governing in other multilevel systems. The conclusion calls for extended IGM study, no matter how challenging, as its dynamic complexity continues.

Management arrangements in intergovernmental arenas are continually emerging as complex problems, and their solutions' challenges are seemingly intractable while officials try to make them operable. Neighborhood Centers in Houston, Texas, is a nonprofit that grew out of the settlement house movement. It approaches development from a people-based, bottom-up perspective. Over the past twenty-five years, Neighborhood Centers has committed hundreds of hours to getting input through one-on-one interview-like discussions and holding community meetings, to sorting out priorities, to identifying the community's natural leaders, and then to seeking external funding. It has been successful in tapping a total of thirty-seven federal, state, and local programs; grants; and contracts, particularly from the US Departments of Education, Agriculture, Labor, Health and Human Services, and Housing and Urban Development.

Neighborhood Centers offers programs at more than seventy sites, serving more than 560,000 people. One of its specialties is integrating recent immigrants to the community. Its career programs have helped 110,000 people secure jobs, and in collaborating with local community colleges, it has trained 5,600 persons in welding and pipefitting. It helps stay-at-home mothers start and operate home-based businesses, has a tax preparation help service, and operates fourteen pre-kindergarten and charter schools. Finally, its community mission involves preparing local leaders to operate within the political system, particularly with civics instruction, and to help immigrants learn how to engage in community self-improvement (Neighborhood Centers 2016).

In other situations, rather than the Neighborhood Centers' how-to "localizing" experience, IGM seems to be a "federalizing" one. The evolution of IGM since Hurricane Katrina in 2005, for instance, has shifted power upward to the federal government. The Stafford Disaster Relief and Emergency Assistance Act of 1988 authorizes the use of federal money to respond to hurricanes and other natural disasters. With the sheer number of disasters increasing, so are expenditures of federal dollars along with the federal role in local affairs. Part of the problem, argues Donald Kettl (2015, 16), is that an increasing share of the funding is federal, and it has risen from 26 percent in 1989–2004 to a post-Katrina share of 69 percent. Federal restrictions now also dictate where rebuilding might occur (e.g., above flood levels). In 2016 the Federal Emergency Management Agency proposed issuing rules that would require states to address climate change before they could become eligible for disaster relief. It is symptomatic of the shift upward to federal involvement and influence. Kettl concludes that, with the governmental collapse in New Orleans a decade ago and political embarrassments due to FEMA's problems with Katrina, "there will never be another Katrina, at least in political terms. If a disaster threatens public order, the federal government will hit fast and hard" (17). Disaster management has pushed the federal government deeply into what had long been primarily local affairs.

Indeed, while IGR is designed to respect and accommodate subnational government, the federal government has become directly involved in effecting state and local programs. During the George W. Bush years, Congress and the administration required states to assume part of the financing for Medicare prescription drug benefits, imposed rules for failing schools under the No Child Left Behind law, and mandated that states make cost-bearing security improvements to driver's licenses under the Real ID law. In addition, preemption of state actions on banking regulation, greenhouse gas emissions, and drug labels were added. Under Barack Obama's administration, funds for urban development, Medicaid, and education were channeled through the states but not without substantial state program guidance for school improvements and for transportation projects. Policy intrusion also incurred on immigration and civil rights (Vock 2016). The Patient Protection and Affordable Care Act has had the effect of threatening small, rural hospitals, as they face difficulties in meeting electronic records requirements and the threat to remove the Medicare 101 percent reimbursement of reasonable costs for small hospitals. Moreover, in the states that do not participate in Medicaid expansion coverage, the federal and state threat to hospital closings is great (Quinn 2016, 52). These are the more visible examples of the continuing federal, state, and local IGM interactions.

In recent years the Obama administration took a more collaborative approach with the states and to some degree with local governments. Given that numerous federal initiatives require state involvement at the administrative level, sensitivity and accommodation to state concerns as national policy depend on state participation. As Jessica Bulman-Pozen and Gillian Metzger (2016, 309) observe,

> Federal-state collaboration is critical to realizing Administration ends. National policy is increasingly determined by presidentially instigated executive branch action, but it is executive action taken in conjunction with the states. The resultant national policy is responsive to state demands, often accommodating the state policy preferences from across the political spectrum. Against a background of polarized national politics and a gridlocked Congress, the state role in shaping federal regulation and federal programs is thus particularly significant. It raises the possibility that states are simultaneously enabling and checking federal executive branch initiatives, it means that federal policy may be nonuniform and differentiated by state.

Such federal-state interactions occurred over waivers, grant adjustments, the incorporation of state law into federal regulations, and nonenforcement of federal concerns in policy spaces shared with the states. This collaborative approach even reached to the local level, for example, during direct negotiations over transportation grants and urban development and in some cases with school districts over No Child Left Behind waivers (Bulman-Pozen and Metzger 2016, 319–20). With clear IGM nods to law and politics, federal interdependence, and networks among executive officials, "federalism has become decidedly presidential" (311). It also has important consequences for intergovernmental operations (Conlan and Posner 2016).

These contemporary bottom-up and top-down movements demonstrate the continuing viability and complex interaction of law and politics, jurisdictional and organizational interdependency, multisector partnerships, and networking and networks. They appear to be at the core of what goes into managing across boundaries. This volume has reflected on these complexities and pointed to some approaches of managing across boundaries. While IGM normally begins within its constant connections, its horizontal and vertical orientations make it different from hierarchical management. It is not new; various forms of cross-jurisdictional transactions have been part of government policies and programs for some time. Now they involve many aspects of interaction, only some of which are visible. They await continuing development of practice into theory and theory into practice. Given the multi-pronged legal, political, and managerial challenges, IGM will continue to evolve for the foreseeable future.

A Journey through Four Phases

Basic events, programs, and practices for identifying the growing complexity in multiple dimensions of IGM have constituted the bulk of this work (chapters 2–9). As government has moved into governing, with its multiple actors dealing with programs that cross boundaries, new actors are exercising coordination and control across boundaries. They are engaging in emergent forms of managing, culminating in linkages across governments at different levels and with NGOs. R. A. W. Rhodes (1996, 653) once concluded that as a result of these forces, "government is searching for a new operating code." These changes involve government and its interlocutors in what are now regarded as systems of governance.

In a federal system like that of the United States, governance implies many working actions and transactions across governments and participants outside of government. This has been the case for some time, but these actions have grown increasingly dense and intense as the myriad of players and actions have become increasingly mutually contingent. From an operational standpoint, the four approaches to intergovernmental management are summarized and analyzed on nine bases in figure C.1.

In IGM the dominant paradigm has included but moved from the building of integral states (in the US federal government), or separate jurisdictions that minimally related to one another and eventually included not only divided but mixed jurisdictional competencies. IGR later saw the more involved NGOs partner with governments in operations that function in many ways in public service markets. The resultant complexity has led to more intensive collaborative activities, a sort of meta-governance that occurs both inside and outside the boundaries of government and nongovernmental organizations.

To the degree that there was traditional management in IGR, the earliest intergovernmental directions were predominantly top down—that is, federal to state and state to local. When this activity initially accelerated, new actors—for example, governments seeking procurement from suppliers and contractors—became the first nongovernmental agents for those governments as principals. As this type of activity grew, new tools—contracts, loans, vouchers—entered what later began to be known as IGM and, in turn, led to both top-down and bottom-up intergovernmental activity that ultimately generated building horizontal systems of different programs in the same jurisdictions.

IGM has always been laced with politics. From partisan and electoral concerns to protect and promote growing aid programs and government

FIGURE C.1. Four Intergovernmental Relations Approaches

	Law and politics	Interdependency	Government partners	Networked IGR
Dominant paradigm	Building of integral states	Divided, then mixed jurisdictional competencies	NGO partners, nonprofit, for-profit, market orientation	Interactive meta-governing and collaboration
Directional focus	Top-down (state-local) regulation; concurrent (federal-state)	Downward flow of programs, finances; emergence of horizontal nongovernment agents	Downward through accelerated tools (contracts, loans, vouchers); horizontal interactivity	Top-down, bottom-up; building of horizontal systems
Politics, policy emphasis	Expanded franchise, industrial and union politics, political party channels	New programs in employment conditions, social welfare, environment; governments lobbying governments by PIGs	NGO lobbying and politics' administrator to administrator partners in politics	Globalization, local civic engagement, collaborative efforts, neighborhood politics, devolved decision-making
Normative, legislative enablement	Divided responsibility	Program growth; overlapping functions and responsibilities	Hollowing state, contracting out, competitive tendering, de-marketing public and NGO responsibilities	Slow or nonrecognition of intergovernmental (IG) networks, some legal authorization with minor authority
Judicial concern	Appropriate power, duties of a given level	Federal and state government intervention in the structure and operations of subnational governments under IG programs	Rights and duties of the public sector in controlling NGOs	Unclear; limits on rule-making and continued protection of individual rights

(continues)

FIGURE C.1. Four Intergovernmental Relations Approaches (Continued)

	Law and politics	Interdependency	Government partners	Networked IGR
Bureaucratic organization	Hierarchy, origin of regulations, minimal conditions, grants, administration of federal-state programs	Interacting over program control, jurisdictional flexibility; subnational government direct services, shared costs	Agents, stewards, direct services externalized; agencies relational but not hollowed out	Conductive agencies, working both inside and outside
Administrative tasks	Casual oversight, compilers of basic data, post audits	Administration of grants, loans, audits, reviews, and regulatory compliance based on standard reporting	Executing the government portion of contracts or other means, data gathering, audits	Actors in networks, part of joint learning, and problem-solving strategies
Major IGM transactions	Minor subventions, program reports	Grants, regulation government-government contacts, joint IG agreements, service exchanges, etc.	Performance contracting, benchmarking, customer orientation, off-budget public companies, competitive bidding, and other business management approaches	Joint learning and problem-solving, knowledge management, joint understandings and agreements
IGM style	Passive reviewing, maintaining legal integrity, enforcing legal charges, passive and mostly cooperative federalism	Information seeking; bargaining, negotiation; compliance, discretion; spend others' money first	From contractor control to evolving partnerships	Operational connectivity, units' capacities to work in relation to others

association lobbying at the policy enactment stage, it moved somewhat later to administration, in a phase that blended in political interjurisdictional concerns, and extended to citizen involvement through grassroots politics. Although rarely recognized, politics in IGM involves not only the big picture but also political shifts at the transaction level—for example, over negotiating grants and contracts, as well as regulations, standards, and practices of interaction. Meanwhile, intergovernmental lobbying has become a major political activity. The Center for Responsive Politics reported that in 2015 state and local governments and their affiliated associations spent $70.5 million in federal lobbying, and higher education institutions spent another $76.9 million, ranking these groups' spending with that of major industries (Maciag 2016).

The actions of IGM have always been rooted in a legal enactment base. Responsibility was divided at the earliest stages to program growth and overlapping functions; then at some point operations moved out of government to NGOs, which became increasingly responsible for service delivery. Ultimately this led to the gradual understanding that the potential for some form of working together, or collaborative management, was in order.

Meanwhile, judicial involvement in IGM went from an original concern for the proper constitutional role of each level in federal programs to increased multilevel involvement regarding the appropriate operational concerns of subnational governments. Later it addressed NGOs' concerns for public versus nonpublic responsibilities, yet there are unclear limits on the roles and rights of citizens and clients. Thus, the concern went beyond intergovernmental actions of governments to those of NGO delivery agencies and their clients.

Government bureaucracy evolved and became more "external" in focus under IGM transformation. Hierarchical and administrative roles changed as transactional interactions across governments and agencies increased and NGO executants were recognized as both agents and stewards of public programs that worked conductively or interactively between government and NGOs. Administrative tasks cumulatively evolved as well, moving from less formal oversight review and fiscal post audits to more standardized grant reporting and auditing, and to government–NGO contract management. Ultimately interactive organizations began working horizontally and vertically in joint learning and problem-solving activities. In sum, more regular and more relational interactive processes emerged and became standardized parts of administrative behavior.

The most notable transactions consequently moved from program reports to complex and involved agreements and services exchanges, and they were followed by even more detailed contract-related and results-oriented concerns. Business imprinted on the public sector to some degree as new public management approaches, which led IGM's now multiple participants to undertake network-based knowledge management and other multi-organizational designs and operations. In other words, new public management approaches also became a part of IGM.

Finally, IGM styles similarly evolved. They went from passive "cooperative federalism" that entities might control to active bargaining and game-playing with emergent operating partnerships. With such increased planning and operational connectivity, the working, planning, and regular interactions are now part of management. Indeed, IGM increasingly became part of the network phenomena not as an exclusive but as an emerged approach.

Inasmuch as none of the thirty-six cell entries in figure C.1 appear particularly outmoded, IGM in full force still includes all of the elements that have developed over time. They might not be active all the time perhaps, but the approaches are clearly available and often used. Networks are prevalent, but their actions clearly have not replaced grant reports and audits or contracts or active reviews. While agencies evolve, their modified hierarchies assume new externalized and conductive functions. Indeed, IGM has incorporated all of these forces as it developed: law and politics, interdependent connections, government partners, and networking and networks. The role of government in this type of governance has changed but in no way is hollow. Indeed, the government all along the federal to state to local line remains as the "lead agency" in many respects in this evolved IGM.

Are Contracts, Networks, and Other Connections Displacing Government Agencies?

Government remains at the core of the IGM scheme, as its "middle name" suggests. The position of US government bureaucracies vis-à-vis externalized programming and networks has been a matter of discussion for some time. Kettl (2009, 31) observes that a growing reliance on interactive organizations and distributed networks instead of traditional hierarchies raises three important problems and challenges "for the boundaries of public programs, for the complexity of how these programs work, and for the puzzles for making the programs accountable to citizens and elected officials alike." Again, figure C.1 makes these issues poignantly clear. The primary concern in this volume is centrally with the first, or boundary, issue—that is, whether such protraction of intergovernmental programs have eroded government and its powers. As alluded to earlier, some have suggested that the "disarticulation" of the state through contracting and network activity has in some ways hollowed out public agencies in the same way that corporations have been (Milward, Provan, and Else 1993; Rhodes 1997; Johnston and Romzek 2010). Others claim that worldwide the core of the contemporary nation-state itself has weakened because of the impact of simultaneous globalization and decentralization on subnational actors (Keating 1999). Still others

BOX C.1

- IGM in the United States is a product of federal development with an interactive focus on law and politics, an interdependency among units and NGOs, an evolving partnership between government and NGO partners, and a system of connected networking and networks.
- Government administrative agencies remain as viable entities in the games of inter-level government and politics as interaction and interdependency accelerate over time. The authority of government does not end with IGM or any of its external manifestations.
- IGM is increasingly seen as involving complex adaptive systems, recognizing the importance of interoperability, digitization, employment of open-source technology, and value-adding assessment.
- The next steps in IGM will inevitably focus on increased abilities to assess more accurately the true social value of collaborative management, networked communication, and the performance of formal networks.

fear that connective devices such as contracts and networking mean a loss of accountability (Bozeman 1987; Frederickson 1999), and they link this fate to governments no longer being the central steering actors in the policy process as networks replace hierarchies (Klijn 1997; Castells 1996; Kickert, Klijn, and Koppenjan 1997). With regard to IGM, clearly this issue deserves further and more careful examination.

A more cautious conclusion might be that networks and forms of externalization constitute an important departure in IGM but have more modest overall effects on government agencies than expected by those that envision the "end of hierarchy." For example, regarding fourteen networks that are heavily engaged in IGM, the author's research on this question indicated that the participants—both public and NGO—do not agree that government has lost its vitality. They pointed out that the public bureaucratic agencies in the network have the last word and that networks cannot "muscle out" core public agencies or their functions (Agranoff 2007c, 219):

As is the case in the intergovernmental arena, each public agency is a bounded jurisdiction; it maintains day-to-day operational control over any potential network moves that involve its programs. Managers can normally choose to become involved in a network and/or they can choose another collaborative route, such as a contract or a dyadic working agreement. Line managers do not ordinarily seek to control any public agency in the network but their own. While the turf-protecting ability of line managers should never be discounted, they seek marginal adjustments in the network to foster solutions for difficult problems. Program specialists, the most active in the PMNs (public management networks), want technological knowledge and interdependency awareness rather than control of others' programs.

In sum, these public administrators, who work directly in both networks and hierarchies, regard the state as changing more at its margins and not necessarily at its core. It may be that the ability to control management by networks is overemphasized. For example, ultimately one cannot easily displace law or political influence.

It is also notable that public agency representatives are not necessarily passive actors in contracting or in network participation. Julia Wondolleck and Steven Yaffee (2000, 230) make clear from their research on natural resource collaboration projects that public agencies cannot devolve their legal authority to a collaborative group, such as a network or contractor, and that government participants in networks must be actively involved and not merely be passive reviewers. Their role remains at the core:

> At the same time, government agencies and institutions have a unique role and responsibility in these processes. While they should be capitalizing on opportunities to collaborate, they must recognize that they—and only they—are the final decision makers. Some argue that the role of agency participants in collaborative processes is solely as a facilitator of other participants' interactions. However, based on our review of successful collaborative processes, it is clear that where a group succeeded and was held in high regard by the broader community, the agency did not step back into a purely facilitative role. Rather, it provided essential leadership that guided the group while simultaneously representing its own interests within the process. It ensured that the sideboards provided by existing law and regulation were in place and understood, and that those individuals present recognized that implementation of decisions could occur only through established administrative processes, including procedures for public review and comment. It took on the responsibility of ensuring the accountability of the process while still promoting collaborative interaction among multiple participants. (244)

This important passage suggests that inasmuch as the public agency representatives played these roles in projects, along with participating in solving difficult multi-order problems, they led the various parties to success and accountability. Indeed, their work did not erode the core functions of the government agency.

The question of external agents' and networks' encroachment on the boundaries of government agencies therefore needs to be approached carefully. Writing in the *Oxford Handbook of American Bureaucracy*, Michael

McGuire and Robert Agranoff (2010, 373) argue for five lines of caution. First, as mentioned, while networks and the nongovernmental organizations that work with public agencies do influence policy and have a role in management, those organizations and agencies that compose these networks work *with* governments as the latter continue to maintain some important powers and controls that guide public action. Second, while an interactive interdependency has emerged within networks crossing many boundaries, the public agency and NGO connections seem to overlay the hierarchy rather than act as replacements for government action (Agranoff 2007a; Agranoff and McGuire 2003; McGuire and Silvia 2008; Salamon 1995). Third, one review of various federal and state statutes indicates that none were drafted to "authorize agencies to collaborate in networks with others" (Bingham 2008, 258). Thus, the agencies retain their authority under law. Next, as demonstrated, networks are not the exclusive mode of collaborative government-nongovernmental relations. The more standard tools of government—for example, grants, loans, regulatory programs, insurance guarantees, and cooperative agreements—tie governments together and public agencies to NGOs without using goal-directed networks (Salamon 2002). Finally, not all government agency administrators are totally or to a high degree in the business of working in networks. With the exception of certain boundary spanners who spend all their time in cross-agency work, many administrators report that they spend as little as 15–20 percent of their total work time in various types of collaborative activity (Agranoff and McGuire 2003).

As a result, lateral work with NGOs in such forms as contracts and networks have *not* eclipsed or displaced the power or centrality of government agencies. The empirical evidence from prior research on bureaucracy in general, and on networks in particular, is too mixed to support such a contention. The reality is that neither networks (or the for-profit and nonprofit partners within them) nor government agencies dominate most partnerships. Thus, despite the very broad range of network activity in the United States, the "ability [of nongovernmental actors] to influence the public agency domain is real but quite limited in scope. . . . [A]ccommodations are made, decisions are influenced, strategies are altered, resources are directed, intensive groups exert undue influence, and public responsibility is indirectly shared" (Agranoff 2007c, 219). Government remains as a focal and pivotal actor in IGM.

Next Steps in IGM

Facing Complexity

One obvious next step is to begin to regard these seemingly overwhelming network era IGM challenges as complex adaptive systems (see chapter 9 of this volume). Christopher Koliba, Jack Meek, and Asim Zia (2012) observe that governance networks are *complex* systems that are capable of emergent qualities and the ability to adapt to changing conditions and to self-organize. Complex system parts interact with sufficient intricacy that they cannot be predicted by standard linear equations; so many variables are at work in the system that their overall behavior can only be understood as an emergent consequence of the holistic sum of all the behaviors embedded within. Koliba and associates conclude that it is possible to "harness complexity" by having researchers and modelers work with practitioners to develop a situational awareness of the governance complexity around them, combining systems thinking, filtering information, and applying descriptive patterning to network adaptation (Koliba, Meek, and Zia 2012).

The dynamics of complex adaptive systems represent the self-organizing mechanisms through which complicated systems develop, adapt their internal structures, and cope with their environment (Teisman 2008). Complex adaptive systems have been applied to leadership theory, focusing on the learning, innovative, and flexible capacities within bureaucracies and in interorganizational systems (Uhl-Bien and Marion 2009). Applied to IGM and networks, this approach concentrates on capacity development, nonlinearity, and the continual process of spontaneous emergence (Koliba, Meek, and Zia 2012, 184). This approach could well be our next best route to understanding networks in IGM. As the technology of information systems grows and adapts to the interactive need of network participants, "software-based" network platforms that integrate the various partnerships, or that include only the data that is collectively and interactively needed from such agency, could be the next steps in the formation of IGM network platforms. These devices could also accelerate the successful use of interoperability.

Meeting the Challenge of Interoperability

Interoperable management, as identified in chapter 9, involves the concerted actions that different agencies take while working on the same issues or programs. There is a need for more studies of IGM processes that achieve real interoperability, which in turn will more deeply define collaborative management. Similar to that of supply-chain management in manufacturing, the process needs to be broken down into various cross-agency operational steps.

Interoperability must be understood as among the most intense forms of collaborative management, usually accomplished by network or networked actions. In IGM it refers to public programming, where a series of governmental, nonprofit, and for-profit agencies are expected or are attempting to work together, and their policies and procedures need to work interactively toward similar or common aims that combine policy and administration. Agencies obviously need to be integrated at an operating level. In this sense interoperability signifies some level of interactive working policy and management that challenges organizations in most forms of IGM.

Interoperable management thus refers to regularized programming involving two or more entities for which operating policies and processes have been interactively articulated and are executed at least to a considerable degree by multiple organizations. The US Government Accountability Office has defined this process not as an end itself but as a means to achieve the ability to respond when coordinated reciprocal actions are required. Interoperable management is based on communicated and agreed-on goals, planning, operational information, role differentiation, and an operating system that supports communication (Jenkins 2004b). With contemporary challenges, interoperability could well move to the operating center of IGM understanding.

In the future artificial intelligence will enhance the potential of interoperability. This rapid technology enables machines to perform tasks that were ordinarily done by humans. In the case of interoperability, its potential lies in a technique called deep learning, which allows systems to learn and improve by processing numerous examples rather than having the solutions being explicitly programmed. This approach is already being used to power Internet search engines, block spam emails, suggest email replies, translate web pages, recognize voice commands, and so on. Deep learning employs large amounts of computing power and training data to supercharge artificial neural networks and to establish biologically inspired brain networks. Then neurons are weighted with an activation function. Training in a neural network involves adjusting the neurons' weights so that a given input produces a desired output.

Expanded Internet use has made billions of reports, documents, and studies available that then provide artificial intelligence raw data. Such deep learning systems can thus be applied to interoperable needs in IGM networking. Its interactive processes apply to seemingly unique situations in the work of those public and NGO agencies addressing such problems as disaster responses, emergency management, human services integration, and similar network applications (*Economist* 2016a, 5).

Going Digital

The increasing visibility of citizen engagement, as in the Houston Neighborhood Centers program, has highlighted the importance of electronic contacts, which can then refocus attention to public agency contact. Donald Tapscott (2009, 257) predicts "tremendous potential for government to create new forms of value by focusing on what it does best by creating partnerships for other activities . . . [using] a Web-based platform . . . and other Web 2.0 technologies." He goes on to suggest that in dealing with contractors, governments can use a host of digital approaches that are similar to how businesses handle their suppliers and customers. Of course, government already does so. For example, it often employs information services contractors to establish digital communications, reporting, record-keeping, assessment, accounting, and other functions that involve the government agency and a contractor.

Digital or information and communications technology has also provided important support for intergovernmental networks. Agranoff and Mete Yildiz (2007, 333–34) found seven ways that digital technology can be employed in IGM:

1. Producing and posting information via web pages, emails, and teleconferencing, encouraging contact for activists and non-activists
2. Easing coordination and overcoming the limits of dyadic and triadic communication through "one-to-many" media: email, teleconferencing, website presence, electronic document transfer, and interactive chatrooms
3. Initiating interaction among administrators and specialists by electronically arranging meetings, distributing advance materials, organizing exercises and simulations, and otherwise sharing technical, legal, and financial information
4. Assisting taskgroups, workgroups, seminars, and conferences to arrange results and findings into usable information and knowledge
5. Using electronic decision-making software—for example, web-based geographic information systems, groupware, and interoperable solutions—to "broker" feasible processes and decisions
6. Pooling information and databases from partner agencies and organizations in a problem-oriented format across users to enhance the network knowledge base
7. Building management information systems' and software packages' decision-making models using data from several network partners for projects such as intelligent transportation demand models, client service flows, stream bank remediation planning, and so on

In this fast-developing digital world, additional assessments and artificial intelligence would no doubt add to this list compiled a decade ago. The time has arrived when governments use enhanced data sources for a variety of purposes, ranging from street pothole identification to prudent use of state and federal funds. For example, big data such as Boston's CityScore initiative is used to improve planning and citizen services and to engage citizens in the local processes, particularly regarding service distribution. The databases lead to extended analysis and learning by enhancing cross-departmental connections, getting staff out of their silos, and improving regulation enforcement. Then this urban data is brokered into intergovernmental advocacy and interaction support. Conversely, enhanced data-based knowledge, either programmed or developed through artificial intelligence, can also work against a jurisdiction's intergovernmental case or weaken its conclusions in pursuing additional funds, authorizing experimental programs, or seeking asymmetrical program avenues not in standards or rules. Nevertheless, as one digital government report concludes, "Municipal governments should become the guardians of the local data ecosystem, creating a framework that encourages others to share data. . ." (*Economist* 2016b, 12). Plainly the Internet and related information technologies—for example, smart phones and cloud computing—make it inexpensive and easy to communicate, collect, store, and analyze larger and larger quantities of information.

The overall conclusion is clear: IGM in the externalized and network eras makes it essential to understand and gauge the digital impact on management across governments and organizations, particularly as they amass and analyze increasing amounts of data.

Adopting Open-Source Technology

Some have noted the increased use of connective interactive management with system dynamics and call for capturing network theory-building with computer simulation modeling while using such techniques as system dynamics, agent-based modeling, social network analysis, and qualitative comparative analysis. New data-mining programs are allowing large volumes of verbal and numerical data to be analyzed for patterns (Koliba 2014). Undoubtedly they will not only enhance IGM performance but also extend knowledge in several different arenas. Other emergent techniques include augmentative mapping applied alone or coupled with public participative or collaborative GIS programming (Dragićević and Balram 2004). They also offer new sets of insights into the ways in which network members cluster around spatially related problems as well as the cleavages between network members (Mahmood et al. 2012).

More may yet be possible. In an interesting volume on networked science, or online interaction, Michael Nielson (2012) suggests that continued interaction can expand collaborative volume in some areas of inquiry, achieving what he calls conversational critical mass. This can be accomplished by modularizing collaboration, or splitting up tasks into smaller subtasks that can be attacked independently. It would also facilitate interoperability. Further, by encouraging small contributions, reducing barriers to entry, and broadening the range of expertise in solving IGM problems, a rich and well-structured information commons can emerge, building work incrementally as well as collaboratively in IGM.

Regarding IGM networks, open-source information has the potential to add to the deliberative power of interacting parties. By directing attention from information that participants already know to the information they need to approach problems, this technology serves the important function of "collective insight" (Nielson 2012, 66). To the extent that networks operate in open cultures of sharing, "where as much information is moved out of people's heads . . . and onto the network" (183), the search for meaning may well undergird network processes.

Determining Its Public Value

Do all the approaches and techniques in IGM make a difference? Put another way, how well are the involved processes and techniques employed for working across boundaries? The big question is whether IGM and networked management do make some difference. In a pathbreaking work on interagency collaboration, Eugene Bardach (1998) once invoked Mark Moore's (1995) idea that the work of managers in the public sphere is aimed at enhancing public value—that is, increasing efficiency, effectiveness, or fairness—or perhaps responding to a new political aspiration. Bardach (1998) asks, if public value is the aim, whether any two or more social entities that work together create a measure of public value that organizations working alone do not. "My hypothesis is that substantial public value is being lost to insufficient collaboration in the public sector" (11). As IGM approaches sharpen, this question has become even more important in the ensuing years, for "public value thinking and action includes the capacity to analyze and understand interconnections, interdependencies, and interactions between complex issues and across multiple boundaries" (Benington and Moore 2011, 15).

Agranoff and McGuire (2001, 318–21) once applied Bardach's collaborative management issue to networks as one of their "big questions" in this type of research. It was suggested that collaboration and networks were required to meet the increasing complexity and diversity in an information age where power is dispersed and not centralized, and where the demand for unifying tasks is increasing (Kooiman 2003; Lipnack and Stamps 1994). Moreover, in IGM the public sector is increasingly asked to take on the most difficult multisource problems, ones that require joint steering of multi-faceted courses of action, where collaborative and networked program structures may be among the best choices available (Provan and Milward 1991, 1995; Agranoff 1991; Keast, Brown, and Mandell 2007). When wide agreement is necessary and action needs to be jointly steered, network-derived actions or other collaborative approaches may be the most consistent with IGM action.

Crossing boundaries provides advantages because it may be better suited for IGM than the hierarchical structures of bureaucratic organizations that can mass-produce standardized services but also be too inflexible to address fast-developing and changing problems. In this respect, John Benington (2011, 40) concludes, "Networks have greater potential than either hierarchies or markets to function as complex adaptive systems, with capabilities for coordination between many different actors and organizations, and the organizational flexibility to respond to continuous change." Benington also maintains that public value extends beyond market and economic considerations to include social and cultural value building, social capital, social cohesion, social relationships, social meaning and cultural identity, individual and community well-being, and political value. The challenge will be even more daunting in the future, as young people are hostile to communicating through organized efforts but seek and employ digital media through more individualized expressions (Wells 2015, 6). IGM can thus add to the public realm by stimulating and supporting democratic dialogue, active public participation, and civic engagement (45).

More research on how and why IGM patterns, collaborative ventures, transactions, and networks emerge will help expand the value-based understanding of various program approaches and results. The complex and difficult issue of how good IGM approaches are may someday be part of these analytics. One possible way to start, for example, is to test the assumptions of when networks should not be formed (e.g., problems are simple and can be solved dyadically or triadically) and when they should be formed (e.g., solutions point to multiple resources and agencies) to see if proposed advantages empirically hold true (see Vandeventer and Mandell 2007). This approach would test the flexible adaptation to the complexity dimensions at the core of this volume. If public networks are occupying some niches once held by bureaucracies, it is important to build a theory that explains key aspects of their efficacy. Such testing calls for applying forms of evaluation and assessment that extend well beyond the small number of studies currently preferred and toward meta-analyses of cases, particularly those that cross sectoral and industry boundaries (Isett et al. 2011; Berry et al. 2004).

Engaging the Public Domains

At the risk of opening up what could be another volume on the politics of IGM, suffice it to conclude with a reminder that its inherent processes of receiving input, interacting, negotiating, and bargaining are combined with political forces. In many ways IGM is or can be extensions of deliberative democracy. In a very profound analysis of dialogic accounting—that is, civil society approaches that foster critical reflection and debate—Judy Brown and Jesse Dillard (2015b, 257) suggest that accounting in the public sector must go beyond the monologic, or traditional, approach to recognize the plural nature of contemporary democracies, to engage in more conflicting and consensual perspectives, to recognize the value-laden and political nature of all perspectives, to be more sensitive to the complex power dynamics in interactive relations, and to offer promising avenues for pursuing transformative social change. Among the dialogic perspectives they offer are recognizing diverse ideological perspectives and open and contestable aspects of expertise, fostering effective participation and sensitivity to power relationships, and acknowledging the transformative potential of pluralistic dialogue.

In this respect, "smart governance systems need to be construed as smart *democratic* governance systems" (Koliba, Meek, and Zia 2012, 302). Collaborative management and networks need to bear a significant anchorage in a democratic context in order to be legitimate in the eyes of democratic "accountees." "Publicness becomes a normative value that may be applied to the complicated arrangements found in governance networks" (303). The same could be said for virtually all forms and approaches in IGM, which normally operates through these political and other normative filters.

Identifying the Impact of Globalization

Informal and formal values, norms, procedures, and institutions that help actors in the public sphere identify, understand, and address transboundary problems to varying degrees impact IGM (Weiss 2013, 2). In the era of the world networks, horizontal and vertical connectedness to some degree exists "above" or outside of the nation-state, below the state, and through the state. Horizontal networks link counterpart officials across borders, while vertical networks involve relationships between national and supranational officials to which authority has been delegated. "Hierarchy and control lose out to community, collaboration and self-organization" (Slaughter 2009, 97). Therefore, the global networks are not directed and controlled as much as they are managed and orchestrated. Power in such global networks flows from the ability to make the maximum number of valuable connections based on the knowledge and skills to harness that power and achieve common purpose (100). These increased supranational influences represent new configurations of power, yet in the same way that domestic networks do not replace government but are to some degree "rearticulated" and "reterritorialized" emerging connections in relation to global forces; for example, global city-regions and other territorialized matrices have emerged while state-organized territorial power remains (Brenner 1998, 3). Both cities and regions are relevant.

Among the more relevant impacts of global forces on the theory and practice of IGM are (1) the influence of cross-national organizations, such as the International City and Country Management Association, in connecting local governments; (2) the within-country trends that originate and spread, for example, the US-developed municipal home-rule movement; (3) the substantive cross-national influences such as the International Convention on the Rights of Persons with Disabilities; (4) the changes from other governments' experiences, such as big data's impact on professionals who have been influenced by international trends and standards, particularly in environmental management; and (5) the governing influences that are raised by international trends but implemented within subnational governments—for example, citizen involvement in planning horizontal networks that support the elderly in their homes. For any type of subnational government, it is a matter of using knowledge, experience, and action to find some equilibrium between central policy-making and administration and what B. Guy Peters (2015) identifies as "metagovernance," or control over devolved local delegation and coadministration. Such meta-governing forces are now part of global influences, including those of IGM, because of the "inescapable reality that no one can go it alone" when it comes to the challenges of globalization (Lindenberg and Dobel 1999, 22).

Global networks, according to Manuel Castells (2012, 221–28), represent common features that characterize cross-national movements. First, they are multimodal, decentered, maximizing opportunities for participating. Second, whereas they may begin communications connections on Internet social movements, they tend to occupy defined spaces—for example, urban space—making the Internet their core vehicle. Third, they generate their own form of "timeless time," eschewing clock time in anticipation of constant change. Fourth, they are called to action from the space of flows that easily create community. Fifth, these networked movements are virtual, inasmuch as the demonstration effects of several movements spring up in many places. Sixth, the deliberations that occur, if any, take place in the "space of autonomy," particularly when dealing with leaderless movements. Seventh, such horizontal, multimodal networks create elements of togetherness as a source of empowerment. Eighth, they are self-reflective networks, not necessarily in "assemblies," but through multiple Internet fora, such as blogs and interactive discussions. Finally, their demands are normally citizen based and oriented to deliberation-based consensus. Whereas Castells's global criteria were first defined for social protest movements, they also appear to apply quite well to global impacts on local governance. He concludes, "The digital social networks based on the internet and wireless platforms are decisive tools for organizing" (229; see also Wells 2015).

As applied to subnationalism—that is, the actions of regional, provincial, and similar second-order governments and localities like cities, counties, and city regions—networking is today considered to be primarily bottom-up activity that adds to national-level efforts in legal and economic policy. As Allen Scott (2002, 6) observes, "The local *can* be an important arena of social reconstruction in its own right, as being a conduit through which diverse national policies are mediated. The *local* is all the more important given the psychic and political distance of the central state from many of the constituencies that make up modern global city regions, as compared with the immediacy and relevance of the local community." In this regard, Scott's observation regarding global and local impacts includes not only economic interests but also, as suggested by Castells, the impact of social movements, civic organizations, and increased emphasis on democratic participation and representation. The future course of globalization's impact remains open, as Scott concludes. Moreover, "political debates . . . will be waged in the coming decades over its principal direction of change" (7).

Transnational governance networks are normally characterized by non-binding "soft" rules—such as standards and guidelines, benchmarking, and monitoring—in contrast to the legally based rules that are more characteristic of Westphalian (tiered) government that emphasize socialization, accultural-ization, and normative pressures, along with more open access to member-ship and resources. Transference is not unilateral or hierarchical but ongoing and multidirectional and involves overlapping forces of policy and practice, largely engendered by multi-spaced social action (Kennett 2010).

Governing in Other Multilevel Systems: Administrative Local-National Linkages

The deepening complexity in contemporary governing systems—interna-tional to local—has led to greater visibility of the role of all subnational gov-ernments and connected NGO service delivery agencies. The chain of agents from higher-level governments, including cross-organizational operations, down through intermediate, regional, and state governments now includes various types of government and externalized service operations. As with IGM in the United States, this emerged "governance" is cross national. It "is being shaped and reshaped in constellations of public and private actors that include (nation) states, international and regional organizations, professional associations, expert groups, civil society groups and business corporations" (Kennet 2010, 31). Thus, new political structures and policy spaces have multiplied as new IGM networks are leading to innovative layers of gover-nance, organizational strategies, and new public technologies. These actions are based in rules or institutions, or what Paul Steinberg (2015, 11) calls "the machinery that makes coordinated social activity possible" and "the big levers that will ultimately decide whether we can reconcile the pursuit of prosperity with thoughtful stewardship" (12).

As is the case in the United States, this complexity generates multiple ties, which are sometimes referred to, particularly in the European con-text, as multilevel governance. Like IGM it focuses particular attention on the operational level—that is, on regional and local entities, governments, and NGOs involved in infrastructure, services, and retailed operations appli-cations for citizens where they live. The implementation level—normally, local administration—is no longer some backwater relegated as unimport-ant. Exchange of practice experiences have focused on the administrative dimensions as analyses, and varied actors have become involved in program networks dealing with the day-to-day challenges of understanding and sifting through issues of law and political power into networked working systems involving multiple parties. As B. Denters and L. E. Rose (2005) observe, such analytics call for a broad shift from government to models of governance based on increased inter-level interactions, mutual agreements, service contracting, partnerships, and networking, along with new or refined public management approaches similar to those raised throughout this volume.

The administrative implications of multilevel governance everywhere thus need to be explored and placed on the governing research agenda. The multilevel governance work of Lisbet Hooghe and Gary Marks (2003, 2009) usefully incorporates levels of government that articulate power over territory (type I) and functions that share services and responsibilities (type II). Most important, this model introduces the key concepts that impact subnational governments in their communities, particularly at the administrative level, along with their relative degree of dependency on other governments and their degree of autonomy, thought of as units functioning independently of other governments. Subsequently, Hooghe and Marks (2013, 197) have found that both distance and population changes affect how self-rule and shared rule shape political and policy tensions between centralization and decentralization, balancing efficiency versus dialogue between government and citizens. Even more is at stake than multilevel arrangements, shared services, and citizen dialogue. The complexity of institutional arrangements and interactive practices is constrained by their embeddedness in particular settings, making the establishment of frameworks for comparison problematic (Stoker 2006). Indeed, "clear and stable divisions of functions between levels is no longer possible. More horizontal coordination, *ad hoc* functional flexibility and programmatic interinstitutional cooperation is [*sic*] required" (Thoenig 2006, 282).

These relationships are not only complex but subject to rapid change. For example, a multi-country study of local and regional governments and their national governments in Europe depicts a shift over time from self-contained local entities as agents for their central states or general governments to subsequent models of local "choice" that give local authorities greater freedom to develop their own approaches in national frameworks without detailed regulation from a higher authority (Loughlin, Hendriks, and Lidström 2011, 5). From a comparative perspective, it is important to examine governmental systems and program delivery approaches dynamically, or from broader intergovernmental perspectives. In particular, multilevel administration means focusing on the newest managerial challenges that have emerged and have the effect of protracting governance between administrators through the practices of managing intergovernmental relations. Although similar to

IGM, it is not as distinct from earlier periods of "separated" tiers and entities, with consequently more or less divided functions. It is an emergent comparative challenge.

Conclusion

The evolution of management in intergovernmental relations—IGR—now has more than eight decades of experience to review. In looking at the fifty years since Congress formed the US Advisory Commission on Intergovernmental Relations in 1959 (and closed in 1996), Carl Stenberg (2011) points out that reformers have sought ways of sorting out responsibilities among intergovernmental actors. Further, he traces the interest in studying how the federal system operates to a few hundred academic specialists and public interest associations that specialized in patterns and trends in programs, and later it blurred as intergovernmental management studies by academics and by practitioners who grew interested in collaborative management and networks that span boundaries first between levels of government and later to NGOs.

Apparently recent IGM has considerably expanded because those who practice it have become extensively broader and more creative in their scope of actions. Even though one may not readily identify as being involved in IGM today, persons dealing with the tough problems—for example, those issues in Medicaid-based I/DD programs—are unknowingly on the front lines of IGM. Public administrators in this policy area are trying to meet complexity and build locally based systems that involve the intake of clients, assessment, treatment planning, referral, and service and direct care in communities that include medical hospitals and mental disability institutions, small- or medium-size residential facilities, community clinics, day treatment programs, rehabilitation workshops, schools, family supports, and many other life-sustaining and developmental services and agents.

These expectations place heavy burdens on both program connections and service network building. It has been maintained that the major transactional mode of government sector and NGO contact is now through purchase-of-service contracting that ties delivery agents to public sector sponsoring and governance. These government-NGO connections have proliferated under interdependent programs of financing, residential, treatment, and other service alternatives outside of publicly operated institutions. These programs, of course, are authorized and based on the general constitutional and legal powers of federal and state governments. The integral state in the United States uses its distributive powers to authorize and fund mental disability programs available for the entire country. Thus, in I/DD, as in many other "domestic" policy arenas, IGM in all its emergent complexity requires operational development across lines, from law and politics to networks, to meet contemporary challenges.

As IGM approaches the new points of emphasis among the phases, more and more people are involved with public programs. To operate intergovernmentally today, normally one must bridge across networks, NGO executants, shared competences, and constitutional and legal "moats" to function. Then politics are mixed in as the complex of public agencies and NGOs attempt to work interactively. Each concern—law and politics, interdependency, partnership, networking—remains real today. Practitioners have discovered and are acting on these premises. Hopefully this volume will prompt academia to catch up. Whereas only a few study IGM, they are challenged to come to grips with the many who practice it.

REFERENCES

Abels, Michael. 2012. "Managing through Collaborative Networks: A Twenty-First Century Mandate for Local Governments." *State and Local Government Review* 44 (Supplement 1): 295–435.

Administrative Conference of the United States, Office of the Chairman. 1990. *Drafting Federal Grant Statutes: Studies in Administrative Law and Procedure, 90-1.* Washington, DC: US Government Printing Office.

Agranoff, Robert. 1986. *Intergovernmental Management: Perspectives from Problem Solving in Six Metropolitan Areas.* Albany: State University of New York Press.

———. 1991. "Human Services Integration: Past and Present Challenges in Public Administration." *Public Administration Review* 51 (November/December): 426–36.

———. 1992. "Intergovernmental Policy-Making." Paper presented at Conference on Transitions in Public Administration, Örebro University, Grythyttan, Sweden.

———. 1996. "Federal Evolution in Spain." *International Political Science Review* 17 (4): 385–401.

———. 2001. "Managing within the Matrix: Do Collaborative Intergovernmental Relations Exist?" *Publius: The Journal of Federalism* 31 (Spring): 31–56.

———. 2007a. "Intergovernmental Policy Management: Cooperative Practices in Federal Systems." In *The Dynamics of Federalism in National and Supranational Political Systems*, edited by Michael A. Pagano and Robert Leonardi, 248–84. Basingstoke: Palgrave Macmillan.

———. 2007b. "Local Governments in Spain's Multilevel Arrangements." In *Spheres of Governance: Comparative Studies of Cities in Multilevel Governance Systems*, edited by Harvey Lazar and Christian Leuprecht, 23–70. Montreal: McGill-Queen's University Press.

———. 2007c. *Managing within Networks: Adding Value to Public Organizations.* Washington, DC: Georgetown University Press.

———. 2008. "Conductive Public Organizations in Networks." In *Civic Engagement in a Networked Society*, edited by Kaifeng Yang and Erik Bergrud, 85–108. Charlotte, NC: Information Age Publishing.

———. 2010a. *Local Governments and Their Intergovernmental Networks in Federalizing Spain.* Montreal: McGill-Queen's University Press.

———. 2010b. "Towards an Emergent Theory of IGR Governance at the Dawn of the Network Era." In *Governance and Intergovernmental Relations in the European Union and the United States*, edited by Edoardo Ongaro, Andrew Massey, Marc Holzer, and Ellen Wayenberg, 51–86. Cheltenham: Edward Elgar.

———. 2012. *Collaborating to Manage: A Primer for the Public Sector.* Washington, DC: Georgetown University Press.

———. 2013. "The Transformation of Public Sector Intellectual/Developmental Disabilities Programming." *Public Administration Review* 73 (Special Issue): 127–38.

———. 2014. "Relations between Local and National Governments." In *The Oxford Handbook of State and Local Relations*, edited by Donald Haider-Markel, 27–70. Oxford: Oxford University Press.

Agranoff, Robert, and Valerie A. Lindsay. 1983. "Intergovernmental Management: Perspectives from Human Services Problem-Solving at the Local Level." *Public Administration Review* 43 (May/June): 227–37.

Agranoff, Robert, Jennifer Mandel, Michael McGuire, and Craig Richards. 1992. *First Year Evaluation of the Pioneer Search Communities Program*. Bloomington, IN: School of Public and Environmental Affairs.

Agranoff, Robert, and Michael McGuire. 1998. "Multi-Network Management: Collaboration and the Hollow State in Local Economic Policy." *Journal of Public Administration Research and Theory* 8 (1): 67–91.

———. 1999. "Managing in Network Settings." *Policy Studies in Review* 16 (1): 18–41.

———. 2001. "American Federalism and the Search for Models of Management." *Public Administration Review* 61 (6): 671–81.

———. 2003. *Collaborative Public Management: New Strategies for Local Governments*. Washington, DC: Georgetown University Press.

———. 2005. "The Olmstead Decision, the ADA and Federal-State Relations." Paper presented at Annual Meeting of American Political Science Association, Washington, DC, September 1–4.

Agranoff, Robert, and Alex N. Pattakos. 1979. *Dimensions of Services Integration*. Rockville, MD: Project SHARE.

Agranoff, Robert, and Beryl A. Radin. 2015. "Deil Wright's Overlapping Model of Intergovernmental Relations: The Basis for Contemporary Intergovernmental Relations." *Publius: The Journal of Federalism* 45 (1): 139–59.

Agranoff, Robert, and Mete Yildiz. 2007. "Decision-Making in Public Management Networks." In *Handbook of Decision-Making*, edited by Göktuğ Morcöl, 319–46. Boca Raton: Taylor and Francis.

Alam, Quamrul, Md Humayun Kabir, and Vivek Chaudhri. 2014. "Managing Infrastructure Projects in Australia: A Shift from a Contractor to a Collaborative Public Management Strategy." *Administration and Society* 46 (4): 422–44.

Allocation of Powers Project. 2010. *The Allocation of Powers in Politically Decentralized Countries: A Comparative Study*. Barcelona: Pompeu Fabra University, Observatory of Institutions.

Alter, Catherine, and Jerald Hage. 1993. *Organizations Working Together*. Newbury Park, CA: Sage.

Anderson, William. 1955. *The Nation and the States, Rivals or Partners?* Minneapolis: University of Minnesota Press.

———. 1960. *Intergovernmental Relations in Review*. Minneapolis: University of Minnesota Press.

Ansell, Chris, and Alison Gash. 2008. "Collaborative Governance in Theory and Practice." *Journal of Public Administration Research and Theory* 18 (4): 543–72.

Anton, Thomas. 1984. "Intergovernmental Changes in the United States: An Assessment of the Literature." In *Public Sector Performance*, edited by Trudi Miller, 691–720. Baltimore: Johns Hopkins University Press.

Argullol Murgadas, Enric, dir. 2004. *Federalismo y Autonomía*. Barcelona: Ariel.

Ashford, Douglas E. 1988. "Decentralizing Welfare States: Social Policies and Inter-governmental Politics." In *The Dynamics of Institutional Change: Local Governmental Reorganization in Western Democracies*, edited by Bruno Dente and Francesco Kjellberg, 19–43. London: Sage.

Associated Press. 2009. "FSSA Largest State Agency." November 14, 2.

———. 2011. "Funding for Charter Schools." January 25.

———. 2017. "North Carolina Bathroom Bill Reset Gets Applause, Jeers." April 3.

Bächtiger, André, and Anina Hitz. 2007. "The Matrix Extended: Federal-Municipal Relations in Switzerland." In *Spheres of Governance: Comparative Studies of Cities in Multilevel Governance Systems*, edited by Harvey Lazar and Christian Leuprecht, 71–96. Montreal: McGill-Queen's University Press.

Bailey, Brian E. 2000. "Federalism: An Antidote to Congress's Separation of Powers Anxiety and Executive Order 13,083." *Indiana Law Journal* 75: 333–51.

Balogh, Brian. 2009. *A Government Out of Sight: The Mystery of National Authority in Nineteenth-Century America*. New York: Cambridge University Press.

Bardach, Eugene. 1977. *The Implementation Game: What Happens after a Bill Becomes a Law*. Cambridge, MA: Massachusetts Institute of Technology (MIT) Press.

———. 1998. *Getting Agencies to Work Together*. Washington, DC: Brookings Institution Press.

Barrett, Katherine, and Richard Greene. 2010. "Cutting Medicaid Costs." *Governing Daily*, December 1. www.governing.com/authors/Katherine-Barrett-and-RichardGreene.html.

Barron, David J. 2001–2. "A Localist Critique of the New Federalism." *Duke Law Journal* 51: 377–433.

Beam, David R., and Timothy Conlan. 2002. "Grants." In *The Tools of Government*, edited by Lester M. Salamon, 340–80. New York: Oxford University Press.

Beer, Samuel H. 1973. "The Modernization of American Federalism." *Publius: The Journal of Federalism* 3 (Fall): 49–96.

———. 1978. "Federation, Nationalism and Democracy in America." *American Political Science Review* 72 (1): 9–21.

———. 1993. *To Make a Nation: The Rediscovery of American Federalism*. Cambridge, MA: Belknap Press.

Behn, Robert D., and Peter A. Kant. 1999. "Strategies for Avoiding the Pitfalls of Performance Contracting." *Public Productivity and Management Review* 22 (4): 470–89.

Bendix, Reinhard. 1978. *Kings or People: Power and the Mandate to Rule*. Berkeley: University of California Press.

Benington, John. 2011. "From Private Choice to Public Value?" In *Public Value: Theory and Practice,* edited by J. Benington and M. H. Moore, 39–52. Basingstoke: Palgrave MacMillan.

Benington, John, and M. H. Moore. 2011. "Public Value in Complex and Changing Times." In *Public Value: Theory and Practice,* edited by John Benington and M. H. Moore, 3–38. Basingstoke: Palgrave Macmillan.

Benjamin, Stuart Minor, and Ernest A. Young. 2008. "Tennis with the Net Down: Administrative Federalism without Congress." *Duke Law Journal* 57: 2111–55.

Benson, George S. 1942. *The New Centralization*. New York: Rinehart.

Berkowitz, Edward D. 1987. *Disabled Policy: America's Programs for the Handicapped*. Cambridge: Cambridge University Press.

Berman, David R. 2003. *Local Government and the States.* Armonk, NY: M. E. Sharpe.

Bernstein, Susan R. 1991. *Managing Contracted Services in the Nonprofit Agency.* Philadelphia: Temple University Press.

Berry, F. S., R. S. Brower, S. Ok Choi, W. X. Goa, H. Jang, M. Kwon, and J. Word. 2004. "Three Traditions of Network Research: What the Public Management Research Agenda Can Learn from Other Research Communities." *Public Administration Review* 64 (5): 539–52.

Bingham, Lisa B. 2008. "Legal Frameworks for Collaboration in Governance and Public Management." In *Big Ideas in Collaborative Management*, edited by Lisa B. Bingham and Rosemary O'Leary, 247–69. Armonk, NY: M. E. Sharpe.

Blackwell, Jeffrey. 2015. "Cincinnati Police Chief: Body Cameras Should Be Required Equipment: Interview with Jeffrey Blackwell." By Gwen Ifill. *PBS NewsHour.* July 15. http://www.pbs.org/newshour/bb/cincinnati-police-chief-body-cameras-required-equipment/.

Bloomington Herald Times. 2014. "Governors—PREH Compliance Has Barriers." May 25.

Bogason, Peter, and Theo A. J. Toonen. 1998. "Networks in Public Administration." *Public Administration* 76 (Summer): 205–27.

Booher, David E. 2005. "A Call to Scholars from the Collaborative Democracy Network." *National Civic Review* 94 (3): 64–67.

———. 2008. "Civic Engagement as Collaborative Complex Adaptive Networks." In *Civic Engagement in a Network Society*, edited by Kaifeng Yang and Erik Bergrud, 111–48. Charlotte, NC: Information Age Publishing.

Bourgon, Jocelyne. 2009. "New Directions in Public Administration: Serving beyond the Predictable." *Public Policy and Administration* 24 (3): 309–30.

Boviard, Tony. 2004. "Public-Private Partnerships: From Contested Concepts to Prevalent Practice." *International Review of Administrative Sciences* 70 (2): 199–215.

Bowman, Ann O. M., and Richard C. Kearney. 2014. "Transforming State-Local Relations." Paper prepared for Deil Wright Symposium, Washington, DC, March 14–18.

Bozeman, Barry. 1987. *All Organizations Are Public.* San Francisco: Jossey-Bass.

———. 2007. *Public Values and Public Interest.* Washington, DC: Georgetown University Press.

Braddock, David, Richard E. Hemp, and Mary C. Rizzolo. 2004. "State of the States in Developmental Disabilities: 2004." *Mental Retardation* 42 (5): 356–70.

———. 2008. *The State of the States in Developmental Disabilities.* 7th ed. Washington, DC: American Association on Intellectual and Development Disabilities.

Bradley, Valerie J. 2009. Personal correspondence, April 22.

Bradley, Valerie J., and Charles Moseley. 2007. "National Care Indicators: Ten Years of Collaborative Performance Measurement." *Intellectual and Development Disabilities* 45 (5): 354–58.

Braun, Dietmar. 2006. "Between Market-Preserving Federalism and Intergovernmental Coordination: The Place of Australia." *Swiss Political Science Review* 12 (2): 1–36.

Brenner, Neil. 1998. "Global Cities, Global States: Global City Formation and State Territorial Restructuring in Contemporary Europe." *Review of International Political Economy* 5 (1): 1–37.

Brewer, Garry D., and Peter de Leon. 1983. *The Foundations of Policy Analysis.* Homewood, IL: Dorsey Press.

Briffault, Richard. 1994. "What about the 'Ism'? Normal and Formal Concerns in Contemporary Federalism." *Vanderbilt Law Review* 47: 1303–53.

Brinkley, Alan. 1995. *The End of Reform: New Deal Liberalism in Recession and War.* New York: Vintage Books.

Brodkin, Evelyn Z. 2013. "Street-Level Organizations and the Welfare State." In *Work and the Welfare State: Street-Level Organizations and Workfare Politics.* Edited by Evelyn Z. Brodkin and Gregory Marston. Washington, DC: Georgetown University Press.

Brody, Ralph. 1982. *Problem Solving: Concepts and Methods for Community Organizations.* New York: Human Sciences Press.

Brooks, JoAnn M., Deb Bodeau, and Jane Fedorowicz. 2013. "Network Management in Emergency Response: Articulation Practices of State Level Managers—Interweaving Up, Down, and Sideways." *Administration and Society* 45 (8): 911–48.

Brown, David L., and Nina L. Glasgow. 1991. "Capacity Building and Rural Government Adaptation to Population Change." In *Rural Policies for the 1990s.* Edited by Cornelia B. Flora and James A. Christenson. Boulder, CO: Westview Press.

Brown, Douglas M. 2007. "Federal-Municipal Relations in Australia." In *Spheres of Governance: Comparative Studies of Cities in Multilevel Governance Systems,* edited by Harvey Lazar and Christian Leuprecht, 97–124. Montreal: McGill-Queen's University Press.

Brown, Judy, and Jesse Dillard. 2015a. "Dialogic Accountings for Stakeholders: On Opening Up and Closing Down Participatory Governance." *Journal of Management Studies* 52 (7): 961–85.

———. 2015b. "Opening Accounting to Critical Scrutiny: Towards Dialogic Accounting for Policy Analysis and Democracy." *Journal of Comparative Policy Analysis* 17 (3): 247–68.

Brown, L. David. 1983. *Managing Conflict at Organizational Interfaces.* Reading, MA: Addison-Wesley.

Brown, Trevor L., and Matthew Potoski. 2004. "Managing the Public Service Market." *Public Administration Review* 64 (6): 656–68.

Brown, Trevor L., Matthew Potoski, and David Van Slyke. 2008a. *The Challenge of Contracting for Large Complex Projects: A Case Study of the Coast Guard's Deepwater Program.* Washington, DC: IBM Center for the Business of Government.

———. 2008b. "Simple and Complex Contracting." *PA Times,* July 2008, 5.

———. 2009. "The Dynamics of Complex Contracting." Paper presented at Tenth National Public Management Research Conference, Columbus, OH, October 1–3.

———. 2016. "Managing Complex Contracts: A Theoretical Approach." *Journal of Public Administration Research and Theory* 26 (2): 294–308.

Brudney, Jeffrey L., Sergio Fernandez, Jay Eungha, and Deil S. Wright. 2005. "Exploring and Explaining Contracting Out: Patterns among the American States." *Journal of Public Administration Research and Theory* 15 (3): 393–419.

Bryce, James. 1941 (1895). *The American Commonwealth.* Vol. 2. 3rd ed. New York: Macmillan.

Bryner, Gary. 1987. *Bureaucratic Discretion: Law and Policy in Federal Regulatory Agencies.* New York: Pergamon Press.

Bryson, John M. 1988. *Strategic Planning for Public and Nonprofit Organizations.* San Francisco: Jossey-Bass.

Bryson, John M., and Barbara C. Crosby. 1992. *Leadership for the Common Good*. San Francisco: Jossey-Bass.

———. 2008. "Failing into Cross-Sector Collaboration Successfully." In *Big Ideas in Collaborative Public Management*, edited by Lisa Bingham and Rosemary O'Leary, 55–78. Armonk, NY: M. E. Sharpe.

Bryson, John M., Barbara C. Crosby, Melissa M. Stone, and Emily O. Saunoi-Sandgren. 2009. *Designing and Managing Cross-Sector Collaboration: A Case Study in Reducing Traffic Congestion*. Washington, DC: IBM Center for the Business of Government.

Bulman-Pozen, Jessica, and Heather Gerken. 2009. "Uncooperative Federalism." *Yale Law Journal* 118 (7): 1256–310.

Bulman-Pozen, Jessica, and Gillian E. Metzger. 2016. "The President and the States: Patterns of Contestation and Collaboration under Obama." *Publius: The Journal of Federalism* 46 (3): 308–36.

Bulpitt, Jim. 1983. *Territory and Power in the United Kingdom*. Manchester: Manchester University Press.

Burbank, Jane, and Frederick Cooper. 2010. *Empires in World History: Powers and the Politics of Difference*. Princeton, NJ: Princeton University Press.

Burke, Brendan F. 2014. "Understanding Intergovernmental Relations, Twenty-Five Years Hence." *State and Local Government Review* 46 (1): 63–76.

Burman, Alan V. 2008. "Inherently Governmental Functions: At a Tipping Point?" *The Public Manager*, Spring: 37–41.

Callanan, Mark. 2003. "Local Government and the European Union." In *Local Government in Ireland: Inside Out*, edited by Mark Callanan and Justin Keogan, 404–28. Dublin: Institute of Public Administration.

Cammisa, Anne Marie. 1995. *Governments as Interest Groups: Intergovernmental Lobbying and the Federal System*. Westport, CT: Praeger.

Campbell, Andrew, and Michael Gould. 1999. *The Collaborative Enterprise*. Reading, MA: Perseus Books.

Carley, Sanya, Sean Nicholson-Crotty, and Eric J. Fisher. 2014. "Capacity, Guidance, and the Implementation of the American Recovery and Reinvestment Act." *Public Administration Review* 75 (1): 113–25.

Carpenter, Daniel. 2001. *The Forging of Bureaucratic Autonomy: Reputations, Networks, and Policy Innovation in Executive Agencies, 1862–1928*. Princeton, NJ: Princeton University Press.

———. 2005. "The Evolution of the National Bureaucracy in the United States." In *The Executive Branch*, edited by Joel D. Aberbach and Mark A. Peterson, 41–70. New York: Oxford University Press.

Castellani, Paul J. 2005. *From Snake Pits to Cash Cows: Politics and Public Institutions in New York*. Albany, NY: State University of New York Press.

Castells, Manuel. 1996. *The Rise of the Network Society*. Oxford: Blackwell.

———. 2012. *Networks of Outrage and Hope: Social Movements in the Internet Age*. Cambridge: Polity Press.

Chen, Bin. 2008. "Assessing Interorganizational Networks for Public Service Delivery." *Public Performance and Management Review* 31 (3): 348–63.

Chernow, Ron. 2004. *Alexander Hamilton*. New York: Penguin Press.

Chubb, John E. 1985. "The Political Economy of Federalism." *American Political Science Review* 79 (4): 994–1015.

Cigler, Beverly A. 1995. "Not Just Another Special Interest: Intergovernmental Representation." In *Interest Group Politics*. 4th ed., edited by Allan J. Cigler and Burdett A. Loomis, 131–53. Washington, DC: Congressional Quarterly Press.

Clark, Jane Perry. 1938. *The Rise of the New Federalism*. New York: Columbia University Press.

Clayton, Ross, and Dan M. Haverty. 2005. "Modernizing Homeland Defense and Security." *Journal of Homeland Security and Emergency Management* 2 (1): 1–11.

Clegg, Stewart R. 1990. *Modern Organizations: Organization Studies in the Postmodern World*. London: Sage.

Closa, Carlos, and Paul M. Heywood. 2004. *Spain and the European Union*. New York: Palgrave Macmillan.

Coglianese, Cary, and David Lazer. 2003. "Management-Based Regulation: Prescribing Private Management to Achieve Public Goals." *Law and Society Review* 37 (4): 691–730.

Cohen, Steven, and William Eimicke. 2008. *The Responsible Contract Manager: Protecting the Public Interest in an Outsourced World*. Washington, DC: Georgetown University Press.

Conlan, Timothy J. 1988. *New Federalism: Intergovernmental Reform from Nixon to Reagan*. Washington, DC: Brookings Institution Press.

———. 1998. *From New Federalism to Devolution: Twenty-Five Years of Intergovernmental Reform*. Washington, DC: Brookings Institution Press.

———. 2008. "Between a Rock and a Hard Place: The Evolution of American Federalism." In *Intergovernmental Management for the 21st Century*, edited by Timothy J. Conlan and Paul L. Posner, 26–41. Washington, DC: Brookings Institution Press.

Conlan, Timothy J., and Paul L. Posner. 2008. *Intergovernmental Management for the 21st Century*. Washington, DC: Brookings Institution.

———. 2016. "American Federalism in an Era of Partisan Polarization: The Intergovernmental Paradox of Obama's 'New Nationalism.'" *Publius: The Journal of Federalism* 46 (3): 281–307.

Conlan, Timothy J., Paul L. Posner, and David R. Beam. 2014. *Pathways of Power: The Dynamics of National Policymaking*. Washington, DC: Georgetown University Press.

Cooper, Terry L., Thomas A. Bryer, and Jack W. Meek. 2006. "Citizen-Centered Collaborative Public Management." *Public Administration Review* 66 (6): 76–88.

Corwin, Edward S. 1913. *National Supremacy*. New York: Henry Holt.

———. 1934. *The Twilight of the Supreme Court*. New Haven, CT: Yale University Press.

Cover, Robert M. 1982–83. "Federalism and Administrative Structure." *Yale Law Journal* 92: 1342–43.

Cross, Rob, Andrew Parker, Laurence Prusak, and Stephen P. Borgatti. 2003. "Knowing What We Know: Supporting Knowledge Creation and Sharing in Social Networks." In *Networks in the Knowledge Economy*, edited by Rob Cross, Andrew Parker, and Lisa Sasson, 208–34. New York: Oxford University Press.

Davenport, Thomas H. 2005. *Thinking for a Living: How to Get a Better Performance and Results from Knowledge Workers*. Boston: Harvard Business School Press.

Davenport, Thomas H., and Larry Prusak. 2000. *Working Knowledge: How Organizations Manage What They Know*. Boston: Harvard Business School Press.

Davis, Dwight F. 1990. "Do You Want a Performance Audit or a Program Evaluation?" *Public Administration Review* 50: 35–41.

Davis, Randall, Amanda Girth, and Edmund Stazyk. 2013. "Contract Performance in Federal Agencies: Assessing the Impact of Incentives on Contract Services." Paper prepared for American Political Science Association Annual Meeting, Chicago, August 29–September 1.

Davis, Randall S., and Edmund C. Stazyk. 2016. "Examining the Links between Senior Managers Engagement in Networked Environments and Goal and Role Ambiguities." *Journal of Public Administration Research and Theory* 26 (3): 433–47.

DeHoog, Ruth Hoogland, and Lester M. Salamon. 2002. "Purchase-of-Service Contracting." In *The Tools of Government*, edited by Lester M. Salamon, 319–39. New York: Oxford University Press.

deLeon, Peter, and Linda deLeon. 2002. "What Ever Happened to Policy Implementation? An Alternative Approach." *Journal of Public Administration Research and Theory* 12 (4): 467–92.

DeNardis, Laura. 2014. *The Global War for Internet Governance*. New Haven, CT: Yale University Press.

Denters, B., and L. E. Rose. 2005. "Towards Local Governance?" In *Comparing Local Governance*, edited by B. Denters and L. Rose, 46–62. Basingstoke: Palgrave Macmillan.

Derthick, Martha. 1970. *The Influence of Federal Grants: Public Assistance in Massachusetts*. Cambridge, MA: Harvard University Press.

Dietze, Gottfried. 1999. *The Federalist: A Classic on Federalism and Free Government*. Baltimore: Johns Hopkins University Press.

Dilger, Robert Jay. 2009. *Federal Grants-In-Aid: A Historical Perspective on Contemporary Issues*. Washington, DC: Congressional Research Service.

Dinan, John. 2013. "Implementing Health Care Reform: The Sources and Extent of State and Federal Government Leverage in Bargaining over the Affordable Care Act." Paper prepared for American Political Science Association Annual Meeting, Chicago, August 29–September 1.

Doonan, Michael. 2013. *American Federalism in Practice: The Formulation and Implementation of Contemporary Health Policy*. Washington, DC: Brookings Institution Press.

Dormady, Noah C. 2012. "The Political Economy of Collaborative Organization." *Administration and Society* 45 (6): 748–72.

Dragićević, S., and S. Balram. 2004. "A Web GIS Collaborative Framework to Structure and Manage Distributed Planning Processes." *Journal of Geographical Systems* 6 (2): 133–53.

Drucker, Peter F. 1995. *Managing in a Time of Great Change*. New York: Truman Talley Books.

Durant, Robert F. 2011. "Global Crises, American Public Administration, and the New Interventionism Revisited." *Administration and Society* 43 (3): 267–300.

Durisch, Lawrence L. 1941. "Local Government and the T.V.A. Program." *Public Administration Review* 1 (4): 326–34.

Economist. 2015. "Business High School." July 18, 26.

———. 2016a. "Artificial Intelligence: The Return of the Machinery Question." June 25 Special Report, 1–16. http://www.economist.com/news/special-report/21700761 -after-many-false-starts-artificial-intelligence-has-taken-will-it-cause-mass.

———. 2016b. "Special Report on Technology and Politics," March 26. http://www .economist.com/news/special-report/21695198-ever-easier-communications -and-ever-growing-data-mountains-are-transforming-politics.

Edner, Sheldon, and Bruce D. McDowell. 2002. "Surface-Transportation Funding in a New Century." *Publius: The Journal of Federalism* 32 (1): 7–24.

Eisinger, Peter K. 1988. *The Rise of the Entrepreneurial State.* Madison: University of Wisconsin Press.

Elazar, Daniel J. 1961. *Illinois Local Government.* Urbana: University of Illinois Press.

———. 1962. *The American Partnership: Intergovernmental Cooperation in the Nineteenth-Century United States.* Chicago: University of Chicago Press.

———. 1967. "Urban Problems and the Federal Government: A Historical Inquiry." *Political Science Quarterly* 82 (December): 511–23.

———. 1984. *American Federalism: A View from the States.* 3rd ed. New York: Harper and Row.

———. 1987. *Exploring Federalism.* Tuscaloosa: University of Alabama Press.

———. 1994. *The American Mosaic: The Impact of Space, Time, and Culture on American Politics.* Boulder, CO: Westview Press.

———. 1996. "From Statism to Federalism: A Paradigm Shift." *International Political Science Review* 17 (4): 417–30.

Elmore, Richard F. 1985. "Forward and Backward Mapping: Reversible Logic in the Analysis of Public Policy." In *Policy Implementation in Federal and Unitary Systems,* edited by Kenneth Hanf and Theo A. J. Toonen, 33–70. Dordrecht: Martnus Nijhoff.

Eoyang, Carson K., and Peter D. Spencer. 1996. "Designing Effective Programs." In *Handbook of Public Administration.* 2nd ed., edited by James L. Perry, 232–49. San Francisco: Jossey-Bass.

Eskridge, William N., Jr., and Lauren E. Baer. 2008. "The Continuum of Deference: Supreme Court Treatment of Statutory Interpretations from *Chevron* to *Hamdan.*" *Georgetown Law Review* 96: 1083–226.

Esteve, Marc, George Boyne, Vicenta Sierra, and Tamyko Ysa. 2013. "Organizational Collaboration in the Public Sector: Do Chief Executives Make a Difference?" *Journal of Public Administration Research and Theory* 23 (4): 927–52.

Farmer, Liz. 2016. "Purchase Power." *Governing the States and Localities* 29 (6): 46–53.

Ferguson, Ernest B. 2004. *Freedom Rising: Washington in the Civil War.* New York: Vintage Books.

Fernandez, Sergio. 2007. "What Works Best When Contracting for Services? An Analysis of Contracting Performance at the Local Level in the U.S." *Public Administration* 88 (4): 1119–41.

———. 2009. "Understanding Contracting Performance: An Empirical Analysis." *Administration and Society* 41 (1): 67–100.

Ferris, James, and Elizabeth Graddy. 1986. "Contracting Out: In What? With Whom?" *Public Administration Review* 46 (July/August): 332–44.

Finegold, Kenneth. 1982. "From Agrarianism to Adjustment: The Political Origins of New Deal Agricultural Policy." *Politics and Society* 11 (1): 1–27.

Finsterbusch, Kurt, Cecelia Formichella, Meredith S. Ramsay, and Daniel Kuennen. 1990. "How Rural Counties Can Generate Jobs." *Sociological Practice* 8: 176–82.

Flanagan, Richard M. 1999. "Roosevelt, Mayors and the New Deal Regime: The Origins of Intergovernmental Lobbying and Administration." *Polity* 31 (Spring): 415–50.

Fleming, Casey J., Emily B. McCartha, and Toddi A. Steelman. 2015. "Conflict and Collaboration in Wildlife Management: The Role of Mission Alignment." *Public Administration Review* 75 (3): 445–54.

Flora, Cornelia Butler, and Jan L. Flora. 1990. "Developing Entrepreneurial Rural Communities." *Sociological Practice* 8: 197–207.

Flora, Peter, and Arnold Heidenheimer. 1981. *The Development of Welfare States in Europe and America.* New Brunswick, NJ: Transaction Books.

Foner, Eric. 1988. *Reconstruction: America's Unfinished Revolution, 1863–1877.* New York: HarperCollins.

Forester, John. 1999. *The Deliberative Practitioner: Encouraging Participatory Planning Processes.* Cambridge, MA: MIT Press.

———. 2009. *Dealing with Differences: Dramas of Mediating Public Disputes.* New York: Oxford University Press.

Foster, Kathryn A. 1997. *The Political Economy of Special-Purpose Governments.* Washington, DC: Georgetown University Press.

Fox-Grage, Wendy, Donna Folkemer, and Jordan Lewis. 2003. *The State's Response to the Olmstead Decision: How Are States Complying?* Washington, DC: National Conference of State Legislatures.

Frederickson, H. George. 1997. *The Spirit of Public Administration.* San Francisco, CA: Jossey-Bass.

———. 1999. "The Repositioning of American Public Administration." *PS: Political Science and Politics* 32 (4): 701–71.

Frederickson, H. George, and Edmund C. Stazyk. 2010. "Myths, Markets, and the 'Visible Hand' of American Bureaucracy." In *The Oxford Handbook of American Bureaucracy,* edited by Robert F. Durant, 349–71. New York: Oxford University Press.

Freeman, Jody. 1997. "Collaborative Governance in the Administrative State." *UCLA Law Review* 45: 1–72.

———. 2003. "Extending Public Law Norms through Privatization." *Harvard Law Review* 116 (5): 1285–352.

Freeman, Jody, and Jim Rossi. 2012. "Agency Coordination in Shared Regulation." *Harvard Law Review* 125 (5): 1–80.

Frumkin, Peter, and Alice Andre-Clark. 2000. "When Missions, Markets and Politics Collide: Values and Strategy in the Nonprofit Human Services." *Nonprofit and Voluntary Sector Quarterly* 29 (1): 141–63.

Fry, Earl H. 1990. "State and Local Governments in the International Arena." *Annals* 509 (May): 118–27.

Fung, Archon. 2006. "Varieties of Participation in Complex Governance." *Public Administration Review* 66 (S1): 66–75.

Gage, Robert W. 1984. "Federal Regional Councils: Networking Organizations for Policy Management in the Intergovernmental System." *Public Administration Review* 44 (2): 134–45.

Gagnon, Alain-G., and Charles Gibbs. 1999. "The Normative Basis of Asymmetrical Federalism." In *Accommodating Diversity: Asymmetry in Federal States*, edited by Robert Agranoff, 73–93. Baden-Baden, Germany: Nomos.

Galbraith, Jay. 1977. *Organization Design*. Reading, MA: Addison-Wesley.

Galle, Brian. 2008. "Federal Grants, State Decisions." *Boston University Law Review* 88: 875–935.

Galle, Brian, and Mark Seidenfeld. 2008. "Administrative Law's Federalism: Preemption, Delegation, and Agencies at the Edge of Federal Power." *Duke Law Journal* 57 (7): 1933–2022.

Gallego, Raquel, Ricard Gomà, and Joan Subirats. 2003. "Las Políticas Sociales de la Unión Europea." In *Estado de Bienestar y Comunidades Autónomas*, edited by Raquel Gallego, Ricard Gomà, and Joan Subirats, 15–45. Madrid: Technos.

Gaus, John M., and Leon O. Wolcott. 1940. *Public Administration and the United States Department of Agriculture*. Chicago: Public Administration Service.

Gazley, Beth. 2008a. "Beyond the Contract: The Scope and Nature of Informal Government-Nonprofit Partnerships." *Public Administration Review* 68 (1): 141–54.

———. 2008b. "Intersector Collaboration and the Motivation to Collaborate: Toward Integrated Theory." In *Big Ideas in Collaborative Public Management*, edited by Lisa Bingham and Rosemary O'Leary, 963–84. Armonk, NY: M. E. Sharpe.

———. 2010. "Why *Not* Partner with Local Government? Nonprofit Managerial Perceptions of Collaborative Disadvantage." *Nonprofit and Voluntary Sector Quarterly* 39 (1): 51–76.

Gerken, Heather K. 2012. "A New Progressive Federalism." *Democracy Journal* 20, no. (24): 37–48.

Gerstle, Gary. 2015. *Liberty and Coercion: The Paradox of American Government*. Princeton, NJ: Princeton University Press.

Gettings, Robert M. 2003. "Building a Comprehensive Quality Management Program: Organizing Principles and Privacy Operating Components." In *Quality Enhancement in Development Disabilities*, edited by Valerie J. Bradley and Madeleine H. Kimmich, 221–34. Baltimore: Paul H. Brookes.

———. 2011. *Forging a Federal-State Partnership: A History of Federal Developmental Disabilities Policy*. Washington, DC: American Association on Intellectual and Development Disabilities.

Gill, Corrington. 1945. "Federal-State-City Cooperation in Congested Production Areas." *Public Administration Review* 5 (1): 28–33.

Girth, Amanda M. 2012. "Government Contracts and 'Managing the Market': Exploring the Costs of Strategic Management Responses to Contract Vendor Competition." *Administration and Society* 44 (1): 3–29.

———. 2014. "A Closer Look at Contract Accountability: Exploring the Determinants of Sanctions for Unsatisfactory Contract Performance." *Journal of Public Administration Research and Theory* 24 (2): 317–48.

Gofen, Anat. 2014. "Mind the Gap: Dimensions and Influence of Street Level Divergence." *Journal of Public Administration Research and Theory* 24 (2): 473–93.

Goldsmith, Stephen, and William D. Eggers. 2004. *Governing by Network*. Washington, DC: Brookings Institution Press.

Goodnow, Frank J. 1900. *Politics and Administration*. New York: Macmillan.

Gortner, Harold F., Julianne Mahler, and Jeanne Bell Nicholson. 1987. *Organization Theory: A Public Perspective*. Chicago: Dorsey Press.

Graves, W. Brooke. 1964. *American Intergovernmental Relations*. New York: Scribner's.

Gray, Barbara. 1989. *Collaborating: Finding Common Ground for Multiparty Problems*. San Francisco: Jossey-Bass.

Greater Beloit Economic Development Corporation. 2014. "About GBEDC." Greaterbeloitworks.com.

Greve, Michael S. 2001. "Laboratories of Democracy: Anatomy of a Metaphor." *AEI Quarterly* 6 (12889): 1–8.

Griffith, Ernest S., and Charles R. Adrian. 1983. *A History of American City Government: The Formation of Traditions, 1775–1870*. Washington, DC: University Press of America.

Grodzins, Morton. 1966. *The American System: A New View of Government in the United States*. Edited by Daniel J. Elazar. New Brunswick, NJ: Transaction Books.

Gunningham, Neil. 2009. "Environmental Law, Regulation and Governance: Shifting Architectures." *Journal of Environmental Law* 21 (2): 179–212.

Gunther, John. 1990. *Federal-City Relations in the United States*. Newark: University of Delaware Press.

Haas, Peter M. 1990. *Saving the Mediterranean: The Politics of International Environmental Cooperation*. New York: Columbia University Press.

———. 1992. "Introduction: Epistemic Communities and International Policy Coordination." *International Organization* 46 (1): 1–35.

Haider, Donald. 1974. *When Governments Come to Washington*. New York: Free Press.

Hale, Kathleen. 2001. *How Information Matters: Networks and Public Policy Innovations*. Washington, DC: Georgetown University Press.

Hall, Jeremy L., and Edward T. Jennings, Jr. 2012. "Administrators' Perspectives on Successful Interstate Collaboration." *State and Local Government Review* 44 (2): 127–36.

Hanf, Kenneth. 1978. Introduction. In *Interorganizational Policy Making: Limits to Coordination and Central Control*, edited by Kenneth Hanf and Fritz W. Scharpf, 1–15. London: Sage.

Hayes, Catherine, Linda Joyce, and Elizabeth Couchoud. 2003. "Federal Policy and Practice in Transition: A Look Ahead at the ICF/MR Program." In *Quality Enhancement in Development Disabilities*, edited by Valerie J. Bradley and Madeleine H. Kimmich, 199–220. Baltimore: Paul H. Brookes.

Heclo, Hugh. 1989. "The Emerging Regime." In *Remaking American Politics*, edited by Richard A. Harris and Sidney M. Milkis, 52–71. Boulder, CO: Westview Press.

Heidler, David, and Jeanne Heidler. 2003. *Old Hickory's War: Andrew Jackson and Quest for Empire*. Baton Rouge: Louisiana State University Press.

Henderson, Alexander C., and Daniel E. Bromberg. 2015. "Performance Information Used in Local Government: Monitoring Relationships with Emergency Medical Services Agencies." *Public Performance and Management Review* 39 (1): 58–82.

Henry, Nicholas. 2011. "Federal Contracting: Government's Dependency on Private Contractors." In *The State of Public Administration*, edited by Donald C. Menzel and Harvey L. White, 221–37. Armonk, NY: M. E. Sharpe.

Herranz, Jr., Joaquín. 2008. "The Multisectoral Trilemma of Network Management." *Journal of Public Administration Research and Theory* 18 (1): 1–32.

———. 2010. "Network Performance and Coordination: A Theoretical Review and Framework." *Public Performance and Management Review* 33 (3): 311–41.

Herring, E. Pendleton. 1934. "Social Forces and the Reorganization of the Federal Bureaucracy." *Southwestern Social Science Quarterly* 15 (3): 185–200.

Hills, Roderick M., Jr. 1998. "The Political Economy of Comparative Federalism: Why State Autonomy Makes Sense and 'Dual Sovereignty' Doesn't." *Michigan Law Review* 76: 1692–767.

———. 2005. "Is Federalism Good for Localism? The Localist Case for Federal Regimes." *Journal of Law and Politics* 21: 182–221.

Hjern, B. 1982. "Implementation Research: The Link Gone Missing." *Journal of Public Policy* 2 (3): 301–8.

Holbeche, Linda. 2005. *The High Performance Organization*. Amsterdam: Elsevier.

Honadle, Beth Walter. 1981. "A Capacity-Building Framework: A Search for Concept and Purpose." *Public Administration Review* 41 (5): 575–80.

Hood, Christopher. 1991. "A Public Management for All Seasons?" *Public Administration* 69 (1): 3–19.

Hood, Christopher, and Ruth Dixon. 2015. *A Government That Worked Better and Cost Less? Evaluating Three Decades of Reform and Change in UK Central Government*. Oxford: Oxford University Press.

Hooghe, Liesbet, and Gary Marks. 2003. "Unraveling the Central State, but How? Types of Multi-level Governance." *American Political Science Review* 97 (2): 233–43.

———. 2009. "Does Efficiency Shape the Territorial Structure of Government?" *Annual Review of Political Science* 12: 225–41.

———. 2013. "Beyond Federalism: Estimating and Explaining the Territorial Structure of Government." *Publius* 43 (2): 179–204.

Howitt, Arnold M. 1984. *Managing Federalism: Studies in Intergovernmental Relations*. Washington, DC: Congressional Quarterly Press.

Human Services Research Institute (HSRI). 2005. "Status Report: Litigation Concerning Home and Community Services for People with Disabilities." Tualatin, OR: HSRI.

Hummel, Ralph P., and Camilla Stivers. 2010. "Postmodernism, Bureaucracy and Democracy." In *The Oxford Handbook of American Bureaucracy*, edited by Robert F. Durant, 324–45. New York: Oxford University Press.

Hyneman, Charles S. 1950. *Bureaucracy in a Democracy*. New York: Harper and Brothers.

Imperial, Mark. 2004. *Collaboration and Performance Management in Network Settings: Lessons from Three Watershed Governance Efforts*. Washington, DC: IBM Center for the Business of Government.

Indiana Association of Rehabilitation Facilities (INARF). 2005. "Maintaining 317 as the Indiana *Olmstead* Response." Indianapolis: INARF.

———. 2009. "Person-Centered Planning." E-mail to Interested Parties, August 6.

Ingram, Helen. 1977. "Policy Implementation through Bargaining: The Case of Federal Grants-in-Aid." *Public Policy* 25 (4): 499–526.

Isett, K. R., I. A. Mergel, K. LeRoux, K. Mischer, and K. Rethemeyer. 2011. "Networks in Public Administration Scholarship." *Journal of Public Administration Research and Theory* 21 (1): 167–73.

Janowitz, Morris. 1974. *Social Control of the Welfare State.* New York: Elsevier.

Jenkins, William O. 2004a. Statement. "Emergency Preparedness: Federal Funds for First Responders." GAO-04-788T. Washington, DC: US Government Accountability Office.

———. 2004b. "Homeland Security: Federal Leadership and Intergovernmental Cooperation Required to Achieve First Responder Interoperable Communications." Testimony. GAO-04-740 (04-963T). Washington, DC: US Government Printing Office.

———. 2006. "Collaboration over Adaptation: The Case for Interoperable Communications in Homeland Security." *Public Administration Review* 66 (3): 319–22.

Jensen, Jennifer M., and Jenna Kelkres Emery. 2011. "The First State Lobbyists: State Offices in Washington during World War II." *Journal of Policy History* 23 (2): 117–49.

Jensen, Merrill. 1950. *The New Nation: A History of the United States during the Confederation, 1781–1789.* New York: Random House.

John, DeWitt. 1991. "When Does a State Need a Rural Policy?" Unpublished paper, Aspen Institute, Washington, DC.

John, Richard R. 1996. "In Retrospect: Leonard D. White and the Invention of Administrative History." *Reviews in American History* 24 (2): 344–60.

———. 1997. "Governmental Institutions as Agents of Change: Rethinking American Political Development in the Early Republic, 1787–1835." *Studies in American Political Development* 11 (Fall): 347–80.

Johnson, Kimberley. 2010. "The 'First New Federalism' and the Development of the Administrative State, 1883–1924." In *The Oxford Handbook of American Bureaucracy,* edited by Robert F. Durant, 52–76. New York: Oxford University Press.

Johnston, Jocelyn M., and Amanda Girth. 2012. "Government Contracts and 'Managing the Market': Exploring the Costs of Strategic Management Responses to Weak Vendor Competition." *Administration and Society* 44 (1): 3–29.

Johnston, Jocelyn M., and Barbara Romzek. 2010. "The Promises, Performance, and Pitfalls of Government Contracting." In *The Oxford Handbook of American Bureaucracy,* edited by Robert F. Durant, 396–420. New York: Oxford University Press.

Joondeph, Bradley W. 2011. "Federalism and Health Care Reform: Understanding the States' Challenges to the Patient Protection and Affordable Care Act." *Publius: The Journal of Federalism* 41 (3) (Summer): 447–70.

Kallis, Giorgos, Michael Kiparsky, and Richard Norgaard. 2010. "Collaborative Governance and Adaptive Management: Lessons from California's CALFED Water Program." *Environmental Science and Policy* 12 (6): 631–43.

Kamieniecki, Sheldon, Robert O'Brien, and Michael Clarke. 1985. "Intergovernmental Cooperation in Environmental Policy-Making." Paper presented at Annual Meeting of the American Political Science Association, New Orleans, August 21–September 1.

Kapucu, Naim, and Qian Hu. 2016. "Understanding Multiplexity of Collaborative Emergency Management Networks." *American Review of Public Administration* 46 (4): 399–417.

Katz, Michael B. 1986. *In the Shadow of the Poorhouse: A Social History of the United States*. New York: Basic Books.

Kaufmann, Franz-Xaver. 1986. "The Relationship between Guidance, Control, and Evaluation." In *Guidance, Control, and Evaluation in the Public Sector*, edited by F.-X. Kaufmann, G. Majone, and V. Ostrom, 211–28. Berlin: Walter de Gruyter.

Keast, Robyn L., Kerry Brown, and Myrna P. Mandell. 2007. "Getting the Right Mix: Unpacking Integration Meanings and Strategies." *International Public Management Journal* 6 (3): 363–71.

Keating, Michael. 1999. "Regions and International Affairs: Motives, Opportunities and Strategies." *Regional and Federal Studies* 9 (1): 1–16.

Keiser, Lael R., and Susan M. Miller. 2013. *Collaboration between Government and Outreach Organizations*. Washington, DC: IBM Center for the Business of Government.

Keleman, R. Daniel. 2004. *The Rules of Federalism*. Cambridge, MA: Harvard University Press.

Kennett, Patricia. 2010. "Global Perspectives on Governance." In *The New Public Governance*, edited by Stephen Osborne, 19–35. London: Routledge.

Kerwin, Cornelius M. 1999. *Rulemaking: How Government Agencies Write Law and Make Policy*. 2nd ed. Washington, DC: Congressional Quarterly Press.

Kesler, Charles R. 1999. Introduction. In *The Federalist Papers*, edited by Clinton Rossiter, vii–xxxv. New York: Penguin.

Kettl, Donald F. 1981. "The Fourth Face of Federalism." *Public Administration Review* 41 (3): 366–71.

———. 1987. *The Regulation of American Federalism*. Baltimore: Johns Hopkins University Press.

———. 2009. *The Next Government of the United States*. New York: Norton.

———. 2015. "Katrina's Lasting Legacy: The Storm Has Redistributed Power—in Washington's Direction." *Governing* 28 (11): 16–17.

Key, V. O., Jr. 1937. *The Administration of Federal Grants to States*. Chicago: Public Administration Service.

Kickert, Walter J. M. Erik-Hans Klijn, and Joop F. M. Koppenjan. 1997. "Managing Networks in the Public Sector." In *Managing Complex Networks*, edited by Walter J. M. Kickert, Erik-Hans Klijn, and Joop F. M. Koppenjan, 166–91. London: Sage.

Kickert, Walter J. M., and Joop F. M. Koppenjan. 1997. "Public Management and Network Management: An Overview." In *Managing Complex Networks*, edited by Walter J. M. Kickert, Erik-Hans Klijn, and Joop F. M. Koppenjan, 3–37. London: Sage.

Kilduff, Martin, and Wenpin Tsai. 2003. *Social Networks and Organizations*. Los Angeles: Sage.

King, Preston. 1982. *Federalism and Federation*. Baltimore: Johns Hopkins University Press.

Kingdon, John W. 1995. *Agendas, Alternatives, and Public Policies*. 2nd ed. New York: Longman.

Klijn, Erik-Hans. 1996. "Analyzing and Managing Policy Process in Complex Networks." *Administration and Society* 28 (1): 90–119.

———.1997. "Policy Networks: An Overview." In *Managing Complex Networks*, edited by Walter J. M. Kickert, Erik-Hans Klijn, and Joop F. M. Koppenjan, 38–62. London: Sage.

———. 2008. "Governance and Governance Networks in Europe." *Public Management Review* 10 (4): 505–25.

Klijn, Erik-Hans, and Joop F. M. Koppenjan. 2000. "Politicians and Interactive Decision-Making: Institutional Spoilsports or Playmakers." *Public Administration* 78 (2): 365–87.

Kluger, Richard. 2007. *Seizing Destiny: How America Grew from Sea to Shining Sea.* New York: Knopf.

Koliba, Christopher. 2014. "Governance Network Performance." In *Network Theory in the Public Sector,* edited by Robyn Keast, Myrna Mandell, and Robert Agranoff, 84–102. New York: Routledge.

Koliba, Christopher, Erica Campbell, and Asim Zia. 2011. "Performance Management Systems of Congestion Management Networks: Evidence from Four Cases." *Public Performance and Management Review* 34 (June): 520–48.

Koliba, Christopher, Jack Meek, and Asim Zia. 2012. *Governance Networks: Public Administration Policy in the Midst of Complexity.* New York: Taylor and Francis.

Kolpakov, Aleksey. 2014. "Structural Development of Public Management Networks Over Time: Where Process Meets Structure." PhD diss., School of Public and Environmental Affairs, Indiana University.

Kolpakov, Aleksey, Robert Agranoff, and Michael McGuire. 2016. "Understanding Interoperability in Collaborative Network Management: The Case of Metro High School." *Journal of Health Science* 4 (10): 318–32.

Kooiman, Jan. 2003. *Governing as Governance.* London: Sage.

Koontz, Tomas M., Toddi A. Steelman, JoAnn Carmin, Katrina Smith Korfmacher, Cassandra Moseley, and Craig W. Thomas. 2004. *Collaborative Environmental Management: What Roles for Government?* Washington, DC: Resources for the Future.

Koppenjan, Joop F. M., and Erik-Hans Klijn. 2004. *Managing Uncertainties in Networks.* London: Routledge.

Kramer, Larry D. 1994. "Understanding Federalism." *Vanderbilt Law Review* 47: 1485–561.

———. 2000. "Putting the Politics back into the Political Safeguards of Federalism." *Columbia Law Review* 100: 215–93.

Kramer, Ralph M. 1981. *Voluntary Agencies in the Welfare State.* Berkeley: University of California Press.

Krane, Dale. 2002. "The State of American Federalism, 2001–2002: Resilience in Response to Crisis." *Publius: The Journal of Federalism* 32 (1): 1–28.

———. 2003. "Home Rule." *Encyclopedia of Public Administration and Public Policy.* New York: Marcel Dekker.

Krane, Dale, and Deil S. Wright. 1998. "Intergovernmental Relations." In *International Encyclopedia of Public Policy and Administration,* edited by Jay M. Schafritz, 1163–64. Boulder, CO: Westview.

Krane, Dale, Platon Rigos, and Melvin Hill Jr. 2001. *Home Rule in America.* Washington, DC: Congressional Quarterly Press.

Kraus, Neil. 2013. *Majoritarian Cities: Policy Making and Inequality in Urban Politics.* Ann Arbor: University of Michigan Press.

Krueger, Skip, and Ethan M. Bernick. 2010. "State Rules and Local Governance Choices." *Publius: The Journal of Federalism* 40 (4): 697–718.

Krueger, Skip, Robert W. Walker, and Ethan Bernick. 2011. "The Intergovernmental Context of Alternative Service Delivery Choices." *Publius: The Journal of Federalism* 41 (4): 686–708.

LaGanga, Maria L., and Maeve Reston. 2014. "Oregon Poised to Dump State Health Exchange Website, Go with Federal One." *Bloomington Herald-Times*, April 25, E9.

Larson, Martin A. 1984. *Jefferson: Magnificent Populist*. Greenwich, CT: Devin-Adair.

Lawther, Wendell. 2002. *Contracting for the 21st Century*. Washington, DC: IBM Center for the Business of Government.

Lawton, Alan, and Frédérique Six. 2011. "New Public Management: Lessons from Abroad." In *The State of Public Administration: Issues, Challenges, and Opportunities*, edited by Donald C. Menzel and Harvey L. White, 409–23. Armonk, NY: M. E. Sharpe.

Leach, Richard H. 1970. *American Federalism*. New York: Norton.

Leach, William D., Christopher M. Weible, Scott R. Vince, Saba N. Siddiki, and John Calanni. 2014. "Fostering Learning through Collaboration: Knowledge Acquisition and Belief Change in Marine Aquaculture Partnerships." *Journal of Public Administration Research and Theory* 24 (3): 591–622.

Lee, Mordecai. 2011. "History of U.S. Public Administration in the Progressive Era." *Journal of Management History* 17 (1): 88–101.

Leech, Beth L., Frank Baumgartner, Timothy La Pira, and Nicholas A. Semanko. 2005. "Drawing Lobbyists to Washington: Government Activity and the Demand for Advocacy." *Political Research Quarterly* 58 (1): 19–30.

Leibfried, Stephan, and Paul Pierson, eds. 1995. *European Social Policy: Between Fragmentation and Integration*. Washington, DC: Brookings Institution Press.

Leuchtenburg, William E. 1963. *Franklin D. Roosevelt and the New Deal: 1932–1940*. New York: Harper and Row.

Levy, John M. 1990. *Economic Development Programs for Cities, Counties and Towns*. 2nd ed. New York: Praeger.

Levy, S. 1993. *Artificial Life: A Report from the Frontier Where Computers Meet Biology*. New York: Random House.

Liebschutz, Sarah F. 1991. *Bargaining under Federalism: Contemporary New York*. Albany: State University of New York Press.

Light, Paul C. 2008. *A Government Ill Executed: The Decline of the Federal Service and How to Reverse It*. Cambridge, MA: Harvard University Press.

Lilienthal, David. 1939. "The T.V.A.: An Experiment in the 'Grass Roots' Administration of Federal Programs." Address to Southern Political Science Association, Knoxville, TN. Quoted in Dwight Waldo. 1948. *The Administrative State*. New York: Ronald.

Lin, Alice. 2007. "Implementation of Local Management Entities in North Carolina." Report to the State of North Carolina Division of Mental Health, Developmental Disabilities, and Substance Abuse Services, Department of Human Services, August.

Lindenberg, Marc, and J. Patrick Dobel. 1999. "The Challenges of Globalization for Northern International Relief and Development NGOs." *Nonprofit and Voluntary Sector Quarterly* 28 (4): 4–24.

Lindquist, Evert. 2009. "Waiting for the Next Wave: Trajectories, Narratives and Conveying the State of Public Sector Reform." *Policy Quarterly* 5 (1): 44–52.

Lipnack, J., and J. Stamps. 1994. *The Age of the Network*. New York: John Wiley and Sons.

Lipsky, Michael. 1980. *Street-Level Bureaucracy: Dilemmas of the Individual in Public Services*. New York: Russell Sage Foundation.

Livingston, William S. 1952. "A Note on the Nature of Federalism." *Political Science Quarterly* 67 (1): 81–95.

Lorenz, Patsy Hashey. 1982. "The Politics of Fund Raising through Grantsmanship in Human Services." *Public Administration Review* 42 (3): 244–51.

Loughlin, John. 2000. "Regional Autonomy and State Paradigm Shifts in Western Europe." *Regional and Federal Studies* 10 (2): 10–34.

———. 2007. "Reconfiguring the State: Trends in Territorial Governance in European States." *Regional and Federal Studies* 17 (4): 385–404.

Loughlin, John, Frank Hendriks, and Anders Lidström. 2011. Introduction. In *The Oxford Handbook of Local and Regional Democracy in Europe*, edited by John Loughlin, Frank Hendriks, and Anders Lidström, 1–23. Oxford: Oxford University Press.

Lovell, Catherine H. 1979. "Coordinating Federal Grants from Below." *Public Administration Review* 39 (5): 432–39.

Lutz, Donald S. 1988. *The Origins of American Constitutionalism*. Baton Rouge: Louisiana State University Press.

Maciag, Mike. 2016. "Gov2Gov: The Lobbying that Falls under the Radar." *Governing* 29 (10): 56–57.

Mahmood, M.N., M. Horita, Robyn Keast, and K. Brown. 2012. "Using Argumentative Mapping and Qualitative Probabilistic Network in Resettlement Planning Process." In *Proceedings of the 2012 International Conference on Construction and Real Estate Management*, October 1–2, Kansas City, MO, 97–103. Beijing: China Architecture and Building Press.

Mahoney, Joseph T., Anita M. McGahan, and Christos N. Pitelis. 2009. "The Interdependence of Private and Public Interests." *Organization Science* 201 (6): 1034–52.

Malatesta, Deanna, and Julia L. Carboni. 2014. "The Public-Private Distinction: Insights for Public Administration from the State Action Doctrine." *Public Administration Review* 75 (1): 63–74.

Mandell, Myrna P. 2001. "The Impact of Network Structures on Community—Building Efforts: The Los Angeles Round Table for Children Community Studies." In *Getting Results through Collaborative Networks and Network Structures for Public Policy and Management*, edited by Myrna P. Mandell, 129–49. Westport, CT: Quorum Books.

Mandell, Myrna P., and Toddi A. Steelman. 2003. "Understanding What Can Be Accomplished through Interorganizational Innovations: The Importance of Typologies, Content and Management Strategies." *Public Management Review* 5 (2): 197–224.

Manning, Seaton W. 1962. "The Tragedy of the Ten-Million-Acre Bill." *Social Service Review* 36 (March): 44–50.

Margerum, Richard D. 2011. *Beyond Consensus: Improving Collaborative Planning and Management*. Cambridge, MA: MIT Press.

Martin, Roscoe C. 1963a. *The Cities and the Federal System*. New York: Atherton Press.

———. 1963b. *Metropolis in Transition*. Washington, DC: US Housing and Home Finance Agency, Government Printing Office.

Marvel, Mary K., and Howard P. Marvel. 2007. "Outsourcing Oversight: A Comparison of Monitoring for In-House and Contracted Services." *Public Administration Review* 67 (4): 521–30.

Mashaw, Jerry L. 2005. "Securing a 'Dense Complexity': Accountability and the Project of Administrative Law." *Issues of Legal Scholarship* 6–7: 1–38.

———. 2006. "Recovering American Administrative Law: Federalist Foundations, 1787–1801." *Yale Law Journal* 115 (6): 1256–344.

———. 2012. *Creating the Administrative Constitution: The Lost One Hundred Years of American Administrative Law.* New Haven, CT: Yale University Press.

Mashaw, Jerry L., and Dylan S. Calsyn. 1996. "Block Grants, Entitlements, and Federalism: A Conceptual Map of Contested Terrain." *Yale Law Journal and Policy Review* 14: 297–324.

Massey, Jane, and Jeffrey D. Straussman. 1985. "Another Look at the Mandate Issue." *Public Administration Review* 45 (2): 292–300.

Mathew, George, and Rakesh Hooja. 2009. "Republic of India." In *Local Governments and Metropolitan Regions in Federal Systems*, edited by Nico Steytler, 167–200. Montreal: McGill-Queens University Press.

Matland, Richard E. 1995. "Synthesizing the Implementation Literature: The Ambiguity Conflict Model of Policy Implementation." *Journal of Public Administration Research and Theory* 5 (2): 145–74.

May, Peter J. 2002. "Social Regulation." In *The Tools of Government*, edited by Lester M. Salamon, 156–85. New York: Oxford University Press.

Mazmanian, Daniel A., and Paul A. Sabatier. 1983. *Implementation and Public Policy.* Glenville, IL: Scott Foresman.

McDowell, Bruce D. 1996. "Intergovernmental Accountability: The Potential for Outcome-Oriented Performance Management to Improve Intergovernmental Delivery of Public Works Programs: Report to Vice President Al Gore." Washington, DC: US Advisory Commission on Intergovernmental Relations.

———. 1997. "Advisory Commission on Intergovernmental Relations in 1996: The End of an Era." *Publius: The Journal of Federalism* 27 (2): 111–28.

McGuire, Michael. 1999. "The 'More Means More' Assumption: Contingency in Local Economic Development Research." *Economic Development Quarterly* 13 (2): 157–71.

———. 2002. "Managing Networks: Propositions on What Managers Do and Why They Do It." *Public Administration Review* 62 (5): 599–609.

———. 2009. "The New Professionalism and Collaborative Activity in Local Emergency Management." In *The Collaborative Public Manager*, edited by Rosemary O'Leary and Lisa B. Bingham, 71–94. Washington, DC: Georgetown University Press.

McGuire, Michael, and Robert Agranoff. 2010. "Networking in the Shadow of Bureaucracy." In *Oxford Handbook of American Bureaucracy*, edited by Robert F. Durant, 372–95. New York: Oxford University Press.

———. 2014. "Network-Management Behaviors: Closing the Theoretical Gap." In *Network Theory in the Public Sector: Building New Theoretical Frameworks*, edited by Robyn Keast, Myrna Mandell, and Robert Agranoff, 137–56. New York: Routledge.

McGuire, Michael, and Chris Silvia. 2008. "Does Leadership in Networks Matter?" Paper presented at Annual Meeting of the American Political Science Association, Boston, August 29–September 1.

Mead, Timothy D. 1981. "Identifying Management Capacity among Local Governments." *Urban Affairs Papers* 3: 1–12.

Meier, Kenneth J., and E. Thomas Garman. 1995. *Regulation and Consumer Protection*. Houston: Dame Publications.

Meier, Kenneth J., and Laurence J. O'Toole. 2003. "Public Management and Educational Performance: The Impact of Managerial Networking." *Public Administration Review* 63 (6): 689–99.

Menzel, Donald. 1990. "Collecting, Conveying, and Convincing: The Three C's of Local Government Interest Groups." *Public Administration Review* 50 (3): 401–5.

Metzenbaum, Shelley M. 2008. "From Oversight to Insight: Federal Agencies as Learning Leaders in the Information Age." In *Intergovernmental Management in the 21st Century*, edited by Timothy J. Conlan and Paul L. Posner, 209–42. Washington, DC: Brookings Institution Press.

Metzger, Gillian E. 2008. "Administrative Law as the New Federalism." *Duke Law Journal* 57: 2073–109.

Micklethwait, John, and Adrian Wooldridge. 2014. *The Fourth Revolution: The Global Race to Reinvent the State*. New York: Penguin.

Milward, H. Brinton, Keith G. Provan, and Barbara A. Else. 1993. "What Does the Hollow State Look Like?" In *Public Management: The State of the Art*, edited by Barry Bozeman, 309–22. San Francisco: Jossey-Bass.

Minow, Martha. 2003. "Public and Private Partnerships: Accounting for the New Religion." *Harvard Law Review* 116: 1229–70.

———. 2004–5. "Outsourcing Power: How Privatizing Military Efforts Challenges Accountability, Professionalism, and Democracy." *Boston College Law Review* 46: 989–1026.

Mintzberg, Henry. 2013. *Simply Managing: What Managers Do—and Can Do Better*. San Francisco: Berret-Koehler.

Montjoy, Robert S., and Laurence J. O'Toole, Jr. 1979. "Toward a Theory of Policy Implementation: An Organizational Perspective." *Public Administration Review* 39 (5): 465–76.

Moore, Mark. 1995. *Creating Public Value: Strategic Management in Government*. Cambridge, MA: Harvard University Press.

Morgan, David R., Michael Hirlinger, and Robert E. England. 1988. "The Decision to Contract Out City Services: A Further Explanation." *Western Political Quarterly* 41 (2): 363–72.

Moseley, Cassandra. 2010. *Strategies for Supporting Frontline Collaboration: Lessons from Stewardship Contracting*. Washington, DC: IBM Center for the Business of Government.

Mosher, Frederick C. 1980. "The Changing Responsibilities of the Federal Government." *Public Administration Review* 60 (4): 540–49.

Mossberger, Karen. 2000. *The Politics of Ideas and the Spread of Enterprise Zones*. Washington, DC: Georgetown University Press.

Moynahan, Donald P. 2008. *The Dynamics of Performance Management: Constructing Information and Reform*. Washington, DC: Georgetown University Press.

Moynahan, Donald P., and Joe Soss. 2014. "Policy Feedback and the Politics of Administration." *Public Administration Review* 74 (3): 320–32.

Nakamura, Robert J., and Frank Smallwood. 1980. *The Politics of Policy Implementation*. New York: St. Martin's Press.

Neighborhood Centers. 2016. "Our Impact, 2015–2016." www.neighborhood-centers .org/annual-report.

Newell, Sue, Maxine Robertson, Harry Scarbrough, and Jacky Swan. 2002. *Managing Knowledge Work*. Houndsmills, UK: Palgrave.

Nicholson-Crotty, Sean. 2004. "The Politics and Administration of Privatization: Contracting Out for Corrections Management in the United States." *Policy Studies Journal* 32 (1): 41–57.

Nielson, Michael. 2012. *Reinventing Discovery: The New Era of Networked Service*. Princeton, NJ: Princeton University Press.

Noh, Shihyun, and Dale Krane. 2014. "Partisan Polarization, Administrative Capacity, and State Discretion in the Affordable Care Act." Paper prepared for Deil S. Wright Symposium, American Society for Public Administration Conference, Washington, DC, March 14.

Nownes, Anthony J. 2014. "Local and State Interest Group Associations." In *The Oxford Handbook of State and Local Government*, edited by Donald P. Haider-Markel, 137–63. Oxford: Oxford University Press.

O'Leary, Rosemary. 1996. "Managing Contracts and Grants." In *Handbook of Public Administration*. 2nd ed., edited by James L. Perry, 263–76. San Francisco: Jossey-Bass.

Olsen, Johan P. 2006. "Maybe It Is Time to Rediscover Bureaucracy." *Journal of Public Administration Research and Theory* 16 (1): 1–24.

———. 2008. "The Ups and Downs of Bureaucratic Organization." *Annual Review of Political Science* 11: 13–37.

Onuf, Peter S. 1997. *Statehood and Union: A History of the Northwest Ordinance*. Bloomington: Indiana University Press.

Oomsels, Peter, and Geert Bouckaert. 2014. "Studying Interorganizational Trust in Public Administration: A Conceptual and Analytical Framework for 'Administrational Trust.'" *Public Performance and Management Review* 37 (4): 577–604.

Organization for Economic Cooperation and Development (OECD). 1998. *Public Sector Management Reform and Economic and Social Development*. Paris: OECD.

Osborne, David, and Ted Gaebler. 1992. *Reinventing Government*. Reading, MA: Addison-Wesley.

Ostrom, Vincent. 1985. "Multiorganizational Arrangements in the Governance of Unitary and Federal Political Systems." In *Policy Implementation in Federal and Unitary Systems*, edited by Kenneth Hanf and Theo A. J. Toonen, 1–16. Dordrecht, Netherlands: Martinus Nijhoff.

———. 1987. *The Political Theory of a Compound Republic*. 2nd ed. Lincoln: University of Nebraska Press.

O'Toole, Laurence J., Jr. 1996a. "Hollowing the Infrastructure: Revolving Loan Programs and Network Dynamics in the American States." *Journal of Public Administration Research Theory* 6 (2): 225–42.

———. 1996b. "Implementing Public Programs." In *Handbook of Public Administration*. 2nd ed., edited by James L. Perry, 250–62. San Francisco: Jossey-Bass.

———. 1997. "Treating Networks Seriously: Practical and Research-Based Agendas in Public Administration." *Public Administration Review* 57 (1): 45–52.

———. 2000. "Research on Policy Implementation: Assessment and Practices." *Journal of Public Administration Research and Theory* 10 (2): 268–88.

———. 2015. "Networks and Networking: The Public Administration Agenda." *Public Administration Review* 75 (3): 361–71.

O'Toole, Laurence J., and Kenneth J. Meier. 1999. "Modeling the Impact of Public Management: Implications of Structural Context." *Journal of Public Administration Research and Theory* 9 (4): 505–26.

———. 2004. "Desperately Seeking Selznick: Cooperation and the Dark Side of Public Management Networks." *Public Administration Review* 64 (6): 681–93.

Page, Stephen. 2008. "Managing for Results across Agencies: Building Collaborative Capacity in the Human Services." In *Big Ideas in Collaborative Public Management*, edited by Lisa Bingham and Rosemary O'Leary, 138–61. Armonk, NY: M. E. Sharpe.

Patterson, James T. 1969. *The New Deal and the States: Federalism in Transition.* Princeton, NJ: Princeton University Press.

———. 1981. *America's Struggle against Poverty, 1900–1980.* Cambridge, MA: Harvard University Press.

Perlman, Bruce J. 2013. "The Ins and Outs of Outsourcing." *State and Local Government Review* 67 (4): 521–30.

Perrin, Edward B. 1974. "The Cooperative Health Statistics System." *Health Services Reports* 89 (1): 13–15.

Pessen, Edward. 1969. *Jacksonian America: Society, Personality and Politics.* Homewood, IL: Dorsey Press.

Peters, B. Guy. 2015. *Pursuing Horizontal Management: The Politics of Public Sector Coordination.* Lawrence: University Press of Kansas.

Peterson, John E. 2011. "Trickle-Down Cuts." *Governing* 24 (4): 46.

Peterson, John, and Laurence J. O'Toole, Jr. 2001. "Federal Governance in the United States and the European Union: A Policy Network Perspective." In *The Federal Vision: Legitimacy and Levels of Governance in the United States and European Union*, edited by Kalypso Nicolaidis and Robert Howse, 300–34. New York: Oxford University Press.

Peterson, Paul E., Barry G. Rabe, and Kenneth K. Wong. 1986. *When Federalism Works.* Washington, DC: Brookings Institution Press.

Pierson, Paul. 1996. "The New Politics of the Welfare State." *World Politics* 48 (2): 143–79.

Pollitt, Christopher, and Geert Bouckaert. 2004. *Public Management Reform: A Comparative Analysis.* 2nd ed. Oxford: Oxford University Press.

Posner, Paul L. 1998. *The Politics of Unfunded Mandates.* Washington, DC: Georgetown University Press.

———. 2002. "Accountability Challenges of Third Party Government." In *The Tools of Government: A Guide to the New Governance*, edited by Lester M. Salamon, 523–51. New York: Oxford University Press.

———. 2008. "Mandates: The Politics of Coercive Federalism." In *Intergovernmental Management in the 21st Century*, edited by Timothy J. Conlan and Paul L. Posner, 286–309. Washington, DC: Brookings Institution Press.

Posner, Paul L., Timothy J. Conlan, and Priscilla Regan. 2013. "The Politics of Accountability: The American Recovery and Reinvestment Act of 2009 ARRA." Paper prepared for 2013 American Political Science Association Conference, Chicago, August 29–September 1.

Pressman, Jeffrey. 1975. *Federal Programs and City Politics: The Dynamics of the Aid Process in Oakland.* Berkeley: University of California Press.

Pressman, Jeffrey L., and Aaron Wildavsky. 1973. *Implementation.* Berkeley: University of California Press.

Price, B. E., and Norma M. Riccucci. 2005. "Exploring the Determinants of Decisions to Privatize State Prisons." *The American Review of Public Administration* 35 (3): 223–35.

Provan, Keith G., and Patrick Kenis. 2007. "Modes of Network Governance: Structure, Management and Effectiveness." *Journal of Public Administration Research and Theory* 18 (2): 229–52.

Provan, Keith G., and H. Brinton Milward. 1991. "Institutional Level Norms and Organizational Involvement in a Service Implementation Network." *Journal of Public Administration Research and Theory* 1 (4): 391–417.

———. 1995. "A Preliminary Theory of Interorganizational Network Effectiveness: A Comparative Study of Four Community Mental Health Systems." *Administrative Science Quarterly* 40 (1): 1–33.

Prueller, Isabella. 2006. "Trends in Local Government in Europe." *Public Management Review* 8 (1): 7–30.

Pulver, Glen C. 1986. *Community Economic Development Strategies.* Madison: University of Wisconsin Extension.

Quinn, Mattie. 2016. "Critical Condition: Rural Hospitals Need Federal, State and Regional Help to Keep Their Doors Open." *Governing* 29 (10): 49–55.

Raab, Jörg, and Patrick Kenis. 2009. "Heading toward a Society of Networks: Empirical Developments and Theoretical Challenges." *Journal of Management Inquiry* 18 (3): 198–210.

Raadschelders, Jos C. 2000. "Administrative History of the United States: Development of the State of the Art." *Administration and Society* 32 (5): 499–528.

Radin, Beryl A. 2006. *Challenging the Performance Movement.* Washington, DC: Georgetown University Press.

———. 2008. "Performance Management and Intergovernmental Relations." In *Intergovernmental Management in the 21st Century*, edited by Timothy J. Conlan and Paul L. Posner, 243–62. Washington, DC: Brookings Institution Press.

———. 2012. *Federal Management Reforms in a World of Contradictions.* Washington, DC: Georgetown University Press.

Radin, Beryl A., Robert Agranoff, C. Gregory Buntz, Ann O'M. Bowman, Barbara Romzek, and Robert Wilson. 1996. *New Governance for Rural America: Creating Intergovernmental Partnerships.* Lawrence: University of Kansas Press.

Ramos, Juan A., and Ruth Cicuéndez. 2005. "La Dimensión Institucional de las Relaciones Autonómico-Locales en un Contexto de Gobierno Multinivel." Ponencia presentada al Congreso de Ciencias Políticas Española, Madrid.

Reagan, Michael D. 1987. *Regulation: The Politics of Policy.* Boston: Little, Brown.

Reed, Douglas S. 2014. *Building the Federal Schoolhouse: Localism and the American Federal State*. Oxford: Oxford University Press.

Regan, Priscilla, and Torin Monahan. 2014. "Fusion Center Accountability and Intergovernmental Information Sharing." *Publius: The Journal of Federalism* 44 (3): 478–98.

Reich, Robert B. 1991. *The Work of Nations*. New York: Knopf.

Rhodes, R. A. W. 1996. "The New Governance: Governing without Government." *Political Studies* 44 (3): 652–67.

———. 1997. *Understanding Governance: Policy Networks, Governance, Reflexivity and Accountability*. Buckingham, UK: Open University Press.

———. 2003. "Putting People Back in Networks." In *Governing Networks*, edited by Ari Salminen, 9–23. Amsterdam: IOS Press.

Richardson, Jesse J., Jr. 2011. "Dillon's Rule Is from Mars, Home Rule Is from Venus: Local Government Autonomy and the Rules of Statutory Construction." *Publius: The Journal of Federalism* 41 (4): 662–85.

Rieger, Elmar. 1995. "Protective Shelter or Straight Jacket: An Institutional Analysis of the Common Agricultural Policy of the European Union." In *European Social Policy: Between Fragmentation and Integration*, edited by Stephan Leibfriend and Paul Pierson, 194–230. Washington, DC: Brookings Institution Press.

Riker, William H. 1964. *Federalism: Origin, Operation, Significance*. Boston: Little, Brown.

Ring, Peter Smith, and Andrew H. Van de Ven. 1994. "Developmental Processes of Cooperative Interorganizational Relationships." *Academy of Management Review* 19 (1): 90–118.

Ritchie, Nolan R. 2013. "The Challenges of Working across Levels of Government and Sectors When Externalizing State Departments of Transportation." Washington, DC: American Society for Public Administration Founders' Fellows Program.

Rittel, Horst W. J., and Melvin M. Webber. 1973. "Dilemmas in a General Theory of Planning." *Policy Sciences* 4 (2): 155–69.

Robertson, David Bryan. 1993. "The Return to History and the New Institutionalism in American Political Science." *Social Science History* 17 (1): 1–36.

Rocco, Philip. 2013. "Forging a Complex Republic: Policy Conflict and Statutory Mandates for Intergovernmental Collaboration in the United States, 1947–2008." Paper prepared for American Political Science Association Conference, Chicago, August 29–September 1.

Romzek, Barbara S., and Jocelyn M. Johnston. 2002. "Effective Contract Implementation and Management." *Journal of Public Administration Research and Theory* 12 (3): 423–53.

———. 2005. "State Social Services Contracting: Exploring Determinants of Effective Contract Accountability." *Public Administration Review* 65 (4): 436–45.

Rose, Richard. 1984. *Understanding Big Government*. London: Sage.

Rosen, Jeffrey. 2016. "States' Rights for the Left." *New York Times*, December 4.

Rosenbaum, Sara, Alexandra Stewart, and Joel Teitelbaum. 2002. *Defining "Reasonable Pace" in the Post-Olmstead Environment*. Washington, DC: Center for Health Services Research and Policy, George Washington University.

Rosenbaum, Sara, and Joel Teitelbaum. 2004. Olmstead *at Five: Assessing the Impact.* Washington, DC: Kaiser Commission on Medicaid and the Uninsured.

Rosenthal, Steven R. 1984. "New Directions in Evaluating Intergovernmental Programs." *Public Administration Review* 44: 469–76.

Ross, Bernard, and Myron Levine. 2006. *Urban Politics: Power in Metropolitan America.* 7th ed. Belmont, CA: Thomson Wadsworth.

Ross, Doug, and Robert E. Friedman. 1991. "The Emerging Third Wave: New Economic Development Strategies." *Entrepreneurial Economy Review* 9 (Autumn): 3–10.

Rossiter, Clinton, ed. 1991. *The Federalist Papers.* New York: Penguin. Based on the original McLean edition of 1788.

Rowland, Allison. 2007. "The Interaction of Municipal and Federal Governments in Mexico: Trends, Issues and Problems." In *Spheres of Governance: Comparative Studies of Cities in Multilevel Governance Systems,* edited by Harvey Lazar and Christian Leuprecht, 201–28. Montreal: McGill-Queen's University Press.

Rubin, Herbert. 1986. "Local Economic Development Organizations and the Activities of Small Cities in Encouraging Economic Growth." *Policy Studies Journal* 14 (3): 363–88.

Ryu, Sangyub. 2014. "Networking Partner Selection and Its Impact on the Perennial Success of Collaboration." *Public Performance and Management Review* 37 (4): 632–57.

Sabatier, Paul A., and Hank Jenkins-Smith. 1993. *Policy Change and Learning: An Advocacy Coalition Approach.* Boulder, CO: Westview Press.

Saint-Onge, Hubert, and Charles Armstrong. 2004. *The Conductive Organization.* Amsterdam: Elsevier.

Salamon, Lester M. 1981. "Rethinking Public Management: Third-Party Government and the Changing Forms of Government Action." *Public Policy* 29 (3): 255–75.

———. 1995. *Partners in Public Service.* Baltimore: Johns Hopkins University Press.

———. 1999. "Government-Nonprofit Relations in International Perspective." In *Nonprofits and Government: Collaboration and Conflict,* edited by Elizabeth T. Boris and C. Eugene Stever, 41–62. Washington, DC: Urban Institute Press.

———. 2002. *The Tools of Government.* New York: Oxford University Press.

Savas, E. S. 2000. *Privatization and Public-Private Partnerships.* New York: Chatham House.

Saz-Carranza, Angel, Susanna Salvador Iborra, and Adrià Albareda. 2016. "The Power Dynamics of Mandated Network Administrative Organizations." *Public Administration Review* 76 (3): 438–62.

Scharpf, Fritz W. 1988. "The Joint-Decision Trap: Lessons from German Federalism and European Integration." *Public Administration* 66 (3): 239–78.

Scheiber, Harry N. 1966. "The Condition of American Federalism: A Historian's View." Washington, DC: Committee on Government Operations, US Senate, October 15. Reprinted in Laurence J. O'Toole, Jr., ed. 1993. *American Intergovernmental Relations.* 2nd ed. Washington, DC: Congressional Quarterly Press.

Schick, Allen. 1975. "The Intergovernmental Thicket: The Questions Are Better Than the Answers." *Public Administration Review* 35 (Special Issue): 717–22.

Schorr, Lisbeth B. 1988. *Within Our Reach.* New York: Anchor Press.

Schrage, Michael. 1995. *No More Teams: Mastering the Dynamics of Creative Collaboration*. New York: Doubleday.

Schram, Sanford F., Joe Soss, Linda Houser, and Richard C. Fording. 2010. "The Third Level of US Welfare Reforms: Governmentality under Neoliberal Paternalism." *Citizenship Studies* 14 (6): 739–54.

Scott, Allen J. 2002. Introduction. *Global City-Regions*, edited by Allen J. Scott, 1–8. Oxford: Oxford University Press.

Scott, James C. 2006. "High Modernist Social Engineering: The Case of the Tennessee Valley Authority." In *Experiencing the State*, edited by Lloyd I. Rudolph and John Kurt Jacobsen, 121–40. New Delhi: Oxford University Press.

Senge, Peter M. 1990. *The Fifth Discipline: The Art and Practice of the Learning Organization*. New York: Doubleday.

Shafroth, Frank. 2013. "The Secret Tax Explosion: Special Districts Are Growing Like Weeds—and Raising Tax Burdens as They Proliferate." *Governing*, September: 66.

Shefter, Martin. 1978. "Party, Bureaucracy and Political Change in the United States." In *Political Parties: Development and Decay*, edited by Louis Maisel and Joseph Cooper, 211–65. Beverly Hills: Sage.

Sherman, Howard, and Ron Schultz. 1998. *Open Boundaries: Creating Business Innovation through Complexity*. Reading, MA: Perseus Books.

Shlaes, Amity. 2007. *The Forgotten Man: A New History of the Great Depression*. New York: Harper.

Siciliano, Michael D. 2017. "Professional Networks and Street-Level Performance: How Public School Teachers' Advice Networks Influence Student Performance." *American Review of Public Administration* 47 (1): 79–101.

Silvia, Chris. 2011. "Collaborative Governance Concepts for Successful Network Leadership." *State and Local Government Review* 43 (1): 66–71.

Silvia, Chris, and Michael McGuire. 2010. "Leading Public Sector Networks: An Empirical Examination of Integral Leadership Behaviors." *Leadership Quarterly* 21 (1): 264–77.

Simon, Herbert A. 1981. *The Sciences of the Artificial*. 2nd ed. Cambridge, MA: MIT Press.

Skelcher, Chris. 2004. "The New Governance of Communities." In *British Local Government into the 21st Century*, edited by Gerry Stoker and David Wilson, 25–42. Basingstoke: Palgrave Macmillan.

Skocpol, Theda. 1995. *Social Policy in the United States*. Princeton, NJ: Princeton University Press.

Skowronek, Stephen. 1982. *Building a New American State: The Expansion of National Administrative Capacities, 1877–1920*. Cambridge: Cambridge University Press.

Slaughter, Anne-Marie. 2009. "America's Edge: Power in the Networked Century." *Foreign Affairs* 88 (1): 94–110.

Smith, Steven R. 1999. "Government Financing of Nonprofit Activity." In *Nonprofits and Government: Collaboration and Conflict*, edited by Elizabeth T. Boris and C. Eugene Steuerle, 177–210. Washington, DC: Urban Institute Press.

Smith, Steven R., and Helen Ingram. 2002. "Policy Tools and Democracy." In *The Tools of Government*, edited by Lester M. Salamon, 565–84. New York: Oxford University Press.

Smith, Steven R., and Michael Lipsky. 1993. *Nonprofits for Hire: The Welfare State in the Age of Contracting.* Cambridge, MA: Harvard University Press.

Snape, Stephanie. 2004. "Liberated or Lost Souls: Is There a Role for Non-Executive Councilors?" In *British Local Government into the 21st Century*, edited by Gerry Stoker and David Wilson, 62–80. Basingstoke: Palgrave.

Social Security Administration. 2007. "Annual Performance Plan for Fiscal Year 2008." Washington, DC: Social Security Administration. www.ssa.gov/budget/hist /FY2008/FY08APP.pdf.

Solé-Vilanova, Joaquim. 1990. "Regional and Local Government Finance in Spain: Is Fiscal Responsibility the Missing Element?" In *Decentralization, Local Government, and Markets*, edited by Robert J. Bennett, 331–54. Oxford: Clarendon.

Solo, Paula, and George Pressberg. 1998. "Beyond Theory: Civil Society in Action." In *Community Works: The Revival of Civil Society in America*, edited by E. J. Dionne, Jr., 81–87. Washington, DC: Brookings Institution Press.

Sørenson, Eva, and Jacob Torfing, eds. 2007. *Theories of Democratic Network Governance.* Basingstoke: Palgrave Macmillan.

Soss, Joe, Richard Fording, and Sanford Schram. 2011. "The Organization of Discipline: From Performance Management to Perversity and Punishment." *Journal of Public Administration Research and Theory* 21 (Supplement 2): 203–32.

Sousa, Gerald. 2013. "Mass in B Minor, BWV 232." Program notes prepared for April performance, Bloomington, Indiana.

Staloff, Darren. 2005. *Hamilton, Adams, Jefferson: The Politics of Enlightenment and the American Founding.* New York: Hill and Wang.

Stanton, Thomas H. 2002. "Loans and Loan Guarantees." In *The Tools of Government*, edited by Lester M. Salamon, 381–409. New York: Oxford University Press.

Starr, Paul. 1982. *The Transformation of American Medicine.* New York: Basic Books.

Steelman, Toddi A. 2010. *Implementing Innovation: Fostering Enduring Change in Environmental and Natural Resource Governance.* Washington, DC: Georgetown University Press.

Steinberg, Paul F. 2015. *Who Rules the Earth? How Social Rules Shape Our Planet and Our Lives.* Oxford: Oxford University Press.

Stenberg, Carl W. 1992. "The Deregulation Decade: Debate, Delusion, Dilemma." Paper presented at Conference on Transitions in Public Administration, Örebro University, Grythyttan, Sweden.

———. 2011. "An ACIR Perspective on Intergovernmental Institutional Development." *Public Administration Review* 71 (2): 169–76.

Stenberg, Carl W., and Ricardo S. Morse. 2014. "Leveraging Change: The States' Role." Paper prepared for Deil S. Wright Symposium, Washington, DC, March 14.

Stepan, Alfred. 1999. "Federalism and Democracy: Beyond the U.S. Model." *Journal of Democracy* 10 (4): 19–34.

Stephens, G. Ross, and Nelson Wikstrom. 2007. *American Intergovernmental Relations.* New York: Oxford University Press.

Steuerle, C. Eugene, and Eric C. Twombly. 2002. "Vouchers." In *The Tools of Government*, edited by Lester M. Salamon, 445–65. New York: Oxford University Press.

Stewart, Alexandra, Marisa Cox, Joel Teitelbaum, and Sara Rosenbaum. 2003. *Beyond Olmstead and toward Community Integration: Measuring Progress and Change*. Washington, DC: George Washington University Medical Center.

Stewart, Alexandra, Joel Teitelbaum, and Sara Rosenbaum. 2002. "Implementing Community Integration: A Review of State *Olmstead* Plans." Report prepared for Medicaid Managed Care Program, George Washington University Medical Center, Washington, DC.

Stewart, William H. 1984. *Concepts of Federalism*. Lanham, MD: University Press of America.

Steytler, Nico. 2007. "National, Provincial and Local Relations: An Uncomfortable Menage à Trois (in South Africa)." In *Spheres of Governance: Comparative Studies of Cities in Multilevel Governance Systems*, edited by Harvey Lazar and Christian Leuprecht, 229–56. Montreal: McGill-Queen's University Press.

———. 2009. "Comparative Conclusions." In *Local Government and Metropolitan Regions in Federal Systems*, edited by Nico Steytler, 393–436. Montreal: McGill-Queen's University Press.

Stoker, Gerry. 2006. "Comparative Local Governance." In *The Oxford Handbook of Political Institutions*, edited by R. A. W. Rhodes, S. Binder, and B. Rockman, 226–55. Oxford: Oxford University Press.

Strauss, Anselm. 1988. "The Articulation of Project Work: An Organizational Process." *Sociological Quarterly* 29 (2): 163–78.

Study Committee on Policy Management Assistance. 1975. "Improving Policy Management in the Federal System." *Public Administration Review* 35 (Special Issue).

Sundquist, James L., and David W. Davis. 1969. *Making Federalism Work: A Study of Program Coordination at the Community Level*. Washington, DC: Brookings Institution Press.

Tapscott, Don. 2009. *Grown Up Digital: How the Net Generation Is Changing Your World*. New York: McGraw-Hill.

Tapscott, Don, and Anthony D. Williams. 2010. *Macrowikinomics: Rebooting Business and the World*. New York: Portfolio Premium.

Tarr, G. Alan. 2000. *Understanding State Constitutions*. Princeton, NJ: Princeton University Press.

Teaford, Jon C. 2002. *The Rise of the States: Evolution of American State Government*. Baltimore: Johns Hopkins University Press.

Teisman, Geert R. 2008. "Complexity and Management of Improvement Programmes." *Public Management Review* 10 (3): 341–59.

Terman, Jessica N., and Richard Feiock. 2014. "Improving Outcomes in Fiscal Federalism: Local Political Leadership and Administrative Capacity." *Journal of Public Administration Research and Theory*, June 12.

Thoenig, T. 2006. "Territorial Institutions." In *The Oxford Handbook of Political Institutions*, edited by R. A. W. Rhodes, S. Binder, and B. Rockman, 256–88. Oxford: Oxford University Press.

Thomas, Craig W. 2003. *Bureaucratic Landscapes: Interagency Cooperation and the Preservation of Biodiversity*. Cambridge, MA: MIT Press.

Thompson, Frank J. 2012. *Medicaid Politics: Federalism, Policy Durability and Health Reform*. Washington, DC: Georgetown University Press.

———. 2013. "The Rise of Executive Federalism: Implications for Picket Fence and IGM." *The American Review of Public Administration* 43 (1): 3–25.

Thompson, James D. 1967. *Organizations in Action*. New York: McGraw-Hill.

Tocqueville, Alexis de. 1988. *Democracy in America*. Edited by J. P. Mayer. New York: HarperCollins.

Trubek, David M., and Louise G. Trubek. 2007. "New Governance & Legal Regulation: Complimentarity, Rivalry, and Transformation." *Columbia Journal of European Law* 13 (Summer): 539–64.

Turner, Mark, and David Hulme. 1997. *Governance, Administration and Development*. West Hartford, CT: Kumarian Press.

Uhl-Bien, Mary, and Russ Marion. 2009. "Complexity Leadership in Bureaucratic Forms of Organizing: A Meso Model." *Leadership Quarterly* 20 (4): 631–50.

US Advisory Commission on Intergovernmental Relations. 1962. *Alternative Approaches to Governmental Reorganization in Metropolitan Areas*. Washington, DC: US Government Printing Office, June. http://www.library.unt.edu/gpo/acir/Reports/policy/a-11.pdf.

———. 1984. *Regulatory Federalism: Policy, Process, Impact and Reform*. Washington, DC: US Government Printing Office. http://www.library.unt.edu/gpo/acir/Reports/brief/B-7.pdf.

US Department of Health and Human Services. 2011. Centers for Medicare and Medicaid Services. "Medicaid Program; Home and Community-Based Services (HCBS) Waivers." *Federal Register* 76 (73): 21311.

US Department of Homeland Security. 2005. *A Comprehensive and Sustained Management Approach Needed to Achieve Management Integration*. GAO-05-139. Washington, DC: Government Printing Office.

———. 2016. "State and Major Urban Area Fusion Centers." http://www.dhs.gov/state-and-major-urban-area-fusion-centers.

US Government Accountability Office (GAO). 2010. "Opportunities to Reduce Potential Duplication of Government Programs." Washington, DC: GAO.

Van de Ven, Andrew H., and Gordon Walker. 1984. "The Dynamics of Interorganizational Coordination." *Administrative Science Quarterly* 29 (4): 598–621.

Vandeventer, Paul, and Myrna Mandell. 2007. *Networks That Work*. Los Angeles: Community Partners.

Van Slyke, David. M. 2003. "The Mythology of Privatization in Contracting for Social Services." *Public Administration Review* 63 (3): 296–315.

———. 2007. "Agents or Stewards: Using Theory to Understand the Government-Nonprofit Social Service Contracting Relationship." *Journal of Public Administration Research and Theory* 17 (2): 157–87.

Vieg, John A. 1941. "Working Relationships in Governmental Agricultural Programs." *Public Administration Review* 1 (2): 141–48.

Visser, Jaap de. 2009. "Republic of South Africa." In *Local Government and Metropolitan Regions in Federal Systems*, edited by Nico Steytler, 267–97. Montreal: McGill-Queen's University Press.

Vock, Daniel C. 2016. "At Odds: State Governments Haven't Been Willing Political Partners." *Governing* 29 (9): 24–31.

Wade, Cheryl L. 1999. "For-Profit Corporations That Perform Public Functions: Politics, Profit, and Poverty." *Rutgers Law Review* 51 (Winter): 323–68.

Waldo, Dwight. 1948. *The Administrative State.* New York: Ronald.

———. 2007. *The Administrative State: A Study of the Political Theory of American Public Administration.* New Brunswick, NJ: Transaction Books. First published 1948 by Ronald Press.

Walker, David B. 2000. *Rebirth of Federalism: Slouching toward Washington.* Chatham, NJ: Chatham House.

Walzer, Michael. 1998. "The Ideal of Civil Society: The Path to Social Reconstruction." In *Community Works: The Revival of Civil Society in America,* edited by E. J. Dionne, Jr., 123–43. Washington, DC: Brookings Institution Press.

Walzer, Norman, and John Gruidl. 1991. "Local Economic Development: Perceptions and Actions of Small City Officials in Illinois." In *Rural Community and Economic Development,* edited by Norman Walzer, 43–60. New York: Praeger.

Wang, Weniyie. 2016. "Exploring the Determinants of Network Effectiveness: The Case of Neighborhood Governance Networks in Beijing." *Journal of Public Administration Research and Theory* 26 (2): 375–88.

Warner, Mildred, and Amir Hefetz. 2004. "Pragmatism over Politics: Alternative Service Delivery in Local Government, 1952–2002." In *Municipal Year Book 2004,* 8–16. Washington, DC: International City/County Management Association (ICMA).

———. 2009. "Cooperative Competition: Alternative Service Delivery, 2002–2007." In *Municipal Year Book 2009,* 117–31. Washington, DC: ICMA.

Waterman, Richard W., and Kenneth J. Meier. 1998. "Principal Agent Models: An Expansion." *Journal of Public Administration Research and Theory* 8 (2): 173–202.

Watts, Ronald. 1999a. *Comparing Federal Systems in the 1990s.* 2nd ed. Kingston, Ontario: Institute of Intergovernmental Relations.

———. 1999b. *The Spending Power in Federal Systems: A Comparative Study.* Kingston, Ontario: Institute of Intergovernmental Relations.

Weber, Edward, and Anne Khademian. 2008. "Managing Collaborative Processes: Common Practices Uncommon Circumstances." *Administration and Society* 40 (5): 431–64.

Wechsler, Herbert. 1954. "The Political Safeguards of Federalism." *Columbia Law Review* 54: 543–59.

Wedel, Kenneth R. 1983. "Purchase of Services Contracting in Human Services." In *Human Services on a Limited Budget,* edited by Robert Agranoff, 185–94. Washington, DC: International City Management Association.

Wehner, Joachim. 2003. "The Institutional Politics of Revenue Sharing in South Africa." *Regional and Federal Studies* 13 (Spring): 1–30.

Weidner, Edward W. 1944. "State Supervision of Local Government in Minnesota." *Public Administration Review* 4 (3): 226–33.

Weiner, Myron E. 1990. *Human Services Management.* 2nd ed. Belmont, MA: Wadsworth.

Weiser, Philip J. 2001a. "Federal Common Law, Cooperative Federalism, and the Enforcement of the Telecom Act." *New York University Law Review* 76 (6): 1692–767.

———. 2001b. "Towards a Constitutional Architecture for Cooperative Federalism." *North Carolina Law Review* 79 (3): 663–720.

Weiss, Thomas. 2013. *Global Governance: Why? What? Whither?* Cambridge: Polity Press.

Wells, Chris. 2015. *The Civic Organization and the Digital Citizen: Communicating Engagement in a Networked Age.* New York: Oxford University Press.

Wenger, Etienne. 2000. "Communities of Practice: The Key to Knowledge Strategy." In *Knowledge and Communities*, edited by Eric L. Lesser, Michael A. Fontaine, and Jason A. Slusher, 3–20. Boston: Butterworth-Heinemann.

White, Leonard D. 1939. *Introduction to the Study of Public Administration.* New York: Macmillan.

———. 1948. *The Federalists: A Study in Administrative History, 1789–1801.* New York: Free Press.

———. 1951. *The Jeffersonians: A Study in Administrative History, 1801–1829.* New York: Macmillan.

———. 1954. *The Jacksonians: A Study in Administrative History, 1829–1861.* New York: Macmillan.

———. 1958. *The Republican Era, 1869–1901: A Study in Administrative History.* New York: Macmillan.

Williams, Walter W. 1980. *Government by Agency: Lessons from the Social Program Grants-in-Aid Experience.* New York: Academic Press.

———. 1981. *Government by Agency: Administering Grants-in-Aid Programs.* New York: Academic Press.

Williamson, Oliver E. 1984. *The Economics of Capitalism: Firms, Markets, Relational Contracting.* New York: Free Press.

Wills, Gary. 1982. "Introduction: The Fight for New York." In *The Federalist Papers by Alexander Hamilton, James Madison, and John Jay*, edited by Gary Wills, 3–11. New York: Bantam Books. Based on the text established by Jacob Cooke, *The Federalist*, Wesleyan University, 1961.

Wilson, James Q. 1975. "The Rise of the Bureaucratic State." *The Public Interest* 41 (Fall).

Wilson, Woodrow. 1887. "The Study of Administration." *Political Science Quarterly* 2 (June): 197–222. Reprinted, 55 (December 1941): 481–506.

Wise, Charles R. 2006. "Organizing for Homeland Security after Katrina: Is Adaptive Management What's Missing?" *Public Administration Review* 66 (3): 302–18.

Wise, Charles R., and Rania Nader. 2002. "Organizing the Federal System for Homeland Security: Problems, Issues, Dilemmas." *Public Administration Review* 62 (September): 54–65.

Wogan, J. B. 2014. "Losing Their Voice: Government Associations Have Lost Some of Their Influence in Washington." *Governing: The States and Localities* 27 (June): 52–55.

Wolfensberger, Wolf. 1972. *Normalization: The Principle of Normalization in Human Services.* Toronto: National Institute on Mental Retardation.

Wondolleck, Julia M., and Steven L. Yaffee. 2000. *Making Collaboration Work*. Washington, DC: Island Press.

Wright, Deil S. 1988. *Understanding Intergovernmental Relations*. 3rd ed. Pacific Grove, CA: Brooks/Cole.

———. 2003. "Federalism and Intergovernmental Relations: Traumas, Tensions and Trends." *Spectrum: The Journal of State Government*, Summer: 10–13.

Wright, Deil S., and Dale Krane. 1998. "Intergovernmental Management (IGM)." In *International Encyclopedia of Public Policy and Administration*. Edited by Jay M. Shafritz. New York: Henry Holt.

Wright, Deil S., Carl W. Stenberg, and Chung-Lae Cho. 2010. "The Changing Landscape of Intergovernmental Relations and Multi-level Governance in the United States." In *Governance and Intergovernmental Relations in the European Union and the United States*, edited by Edoardo Onogarno, Matthew Massey, Marc Holzer, and Ellen Wayenberg, 108–58. Cheltenham: Edward Elgar.

———. 2011. "Historic Relevance Confronting Contemporary Obsolescence? Federalism, Intergovernmental Relations, and Intergovernmental Management." In *The State of Public Administration: Issues, Challenges, and Opportunities*, edited by Donald Menzel and Harvey White, 297–315. Armonk, NY: M. E. Sharpe.

Wright, Vincent. 1994. *Privatization in Western Europe: Pressures, Problems, and Paradoxes*. London: Pinter.

Young, Dennis R. 1999. "Complimentary, Supplementary, or Adversarial? A Theoretical and Historical Examination of Nonprofit-Government Relations in the United States." In *Nonprofits and Government: Collaboration and Conflict*, edited by Elizabeth T. Boris and C. Eugene Steuerle, 31–67. Washington, DC: The Urban Institute.

Young, Ernest A. 2001. "Two Cheers for Process Federalism." *Villanova Law Review* 46: 1349–95.

Young, Robert. 2009. "Canada." In *Local Government and Metropolitan Regions in Federal Systems*, edited by Nico Steytler, 106–35. Montreal: McGill-Queen's University Press.

Yusuf, Juita-Elena (Wie), and Lenahan O'Connell. 2014. "Outsourcing Expert Services by State Transportation Departments: A Look at Effects on Cost, Quality, and Changing Employment Levels." *American Review of Public Administration* 44 (4): 477–92.

Zimmerman, Joseph F. 1992. *Contemporary American Federalism: The Growth of National Power*. New York: Praeger.

———. 1995. *State-Local Relations: A Partnership Approach*. 2nd ed. New York: Praeger.

INDEX

Boxes and figures are indicated by b *and* f *following the page number.*

ABOUT THE AUTHOR

Dr. Robert Agranoff is a professor emeritus at Indiana University–Blooming-ton's School of Public and Environmental Affairs. He joined the university in 1980 and continues to be active in research, teaching, and professional ser-vice. He specializes in intergovernmental relations and management, public administration, economic and community development, and federalism.

Agranoff's books and scholarship have garnered national recognition and honors. *Collaborative Public Management*, coauthored with Michael McGuire, won the American Political Science Association's prestigious Mar-tha Derthick Book Award and the National Academy of Public Administra-tion's Louis Brownlow Book Award. He is also the author of *Collaborating to Manage: A Primer for the Public Sector* and *Managing within Networks: Add-ing Value to Public Organizations*, which was winner of both the Best Book Award from the Public and Nonprofit Division of the Academy of Manage-ment and the 2008 Best Book Award given by the Section on Public Adminis-tration Research of the American Society for Public Administration.

He has applied his award-winning scholarship on the subject to contri-butions internationally, with project involvement in South Africa, Australia, Ukraine, and Spain. Since 1990 Agranoff has been affiliated on a regular basis with the Government and Public Administration Program of the Instituto Universitario Fundación José Ortega y Gasset in Madrid, Spain.